ABUSIR XII

MINOR TOMBS IN THE ROYAL NECROPOLIS I

(THE MASTABAS OF NEBTYEMNEFERES AND NAKHTSARE,
PYRAMID COMPLEX LEPSIUS no. 24
AND TOMB COMPLEX LEPSIUS no. 25)

Excavations of the Czech Institute of Egyptology

ABUSIR XII

MINOR TOMBS IN THE ROYAL NECROPOLIS I

(THE MASTABAS OF NEBTYEMNEFERES AND NAKHTSARE,
PYRAMID COMPLEX LEPSIUS no. 24
AND TOMB COMPLEX LEPSIUS no. 25)

Jaromír Krejčí, Vivienne G. Callender, Miroslav Verner

with contributions by Viktor Černý, Martina Kujanová, Eugen Strouhal
and Hana Vymazalová

**Czech Institute of Egyptology,
Faculty of Arts, Charles University in Prague
Prague 2008**

Reviewers:
Břetislav Vachala, Vassil Dobrev

Photographs:
Archive of the Czech Institute of Egyptology, Jan Brodský (JB), Viktor Černý (VČ),
Jaromír Krejčí (JK), Martina Kujanová (MK), A. M. Sarry *et al.* (AMS),
Eugen Strouhal (ES), Kamil Voděra (KV), Milan Zemina (MZ)

Illustrations:
Jaromír Krejčí, Jolana Malátková, Lucie Vařeková, Hana Vymazalová,
Luděk Wellner

This book was published from the financial means allocated for the research project
of Ministry of Education, Grant No. MSM-0021620826.

ISBN 978-80-7308-181-2

Contents

6. Anthropological material 235

Appendix
Stone Vessels from the Cemetery of Members of the Royal Families of Abusir (*Vivienne Gae Callender*) 257

Bibliography

Abbreviations and Journals

ÄAT	Ägypten und Alten Testament, Wiesbaden
ACER	Australian Centre for Egyptology Report, Sydney
ÄF	Ägyptologische Forschungen, Glückstadt–Hamburg–New York, Wiesbaden
ÄgAbh.	Ägyptologische Abhandlungen, Wiesbaden
Ä&L	Ägypten und Levante, Vienna
AmerAnt	American Antiquity, Washington DC
Amer. J. Phys. Anthropol.	American Journal of Physical Anthropology, Philadelphia
AV	Archäologische Veröffentlichungen, Mainz am Rhein
ArOr	Archiv orientální, Prague
Ars Orientalis	Ars Orientalis, Washington
ASAE	Annales du service des antiquités de l'Égypte, Cairo
ASAW	Abhandlungen der Sächsischen Akademie der Wissenschaften zu Leipzig, Berlin
BACE	Bulletin of the Australian Center for Egyptology, Sydney
BAR	British Archaeological Reports, Oxford
Beiträge Bf.	Beiträge zur ägyptischen Bauforschung und Altertumskunde, Zürich, Wiesbaden
BiEtud	Bibliothéque des études, Cairo
Bull. soc. anthrop.	Bulletin de la Société d'Anthropologie, Paris
CAA	Corpus Antiquitatum Aegyptiacarum Lose-Blatt-Katalog Ägyptischer Altertümer, Mainz am Rhein
CASAE	Cahiers. Supplément aux Annales du Service des Antiquité de l'Égypte, Cairo
CCE	Cahiers de la Céramique égyptienne, Cairo
DAWW	Denkschrift der Kaiserlichen Akademie der Wissenschaften in Vienna, Philosophisch-historische Klasse, Vienna; see also: *DÖAW*
DE	Discussions in Egyptology, Oxford
DÖAW	Denkschriften der Österreichischen Akademie der Wissenschaften, Philosophisch-historische Klasse, Vienna
EA	Egyptian Archaeology, London
FIFAO	Fouilles de l'Institut français d'archéologie orientale, Cairo
GM	Göttinger Miszellen, Göttingen
GOF	Göttinger Orientforschungen, Wiesbaden
HÄB	Hildesheimer ägyptologische Beiträge, Hildesheim
IBAES	Internet Beiträge zur Ägyptologie und Sudanarchäologie, Berlin
Internationale Archäologie	Internationale Archäologie, Espelkamp
JEA	Journal of Egyptian Archaeology, London
J. Forensic Sci.	Journal of Forensic Science
J. Hum. Evol.	Journal of Human Evolution, New York
JNES	Journal of Near Eastern Studies, Chicago
LÄ	Lexikon der Ägyptologie. Begründet von Wolfgang Helck und Eberhard Otto. Herausgegeben von Wolfgang Helck und Wolfhardt Westendorf. I–VII, Wiesbaden–Hamburg 1975–1992

MÄS	Münchener ägyptologische Studien, Munich–Berlin
MÄU	Münchener ägyptologische Untersuchungen, Frankfurt am Main
MDAIK	Mitteilungen des Deutschen Archäologischen Instituts, Abteilung Kairo, Berlin, Wiesbaden, Mainz am Rhein
MonAeg.	Monumenta Aegyptiaca, Bruxelles
NAWG	Nachrichten von der Akademie der Wissenschaften zu Göttingen, phil.-hist. Klasse, Göttingen
OBO	Orbis biblicus et orientalis, Fribourg–Göttingen
Or	Orientalia, Nova Series, Roma
OrMonsp.	Orientalia Monspeliensia, Montpellier
PASA	Publications of The Archaeological Society of Alexandria, Alexandria
PES	Pražské egyptologické studie, Prague
RdE	Revue d'Égyptologie, Cairo, Paris
RevArch	Revue archéologique, Paris
SAGA	Studien zur Archaologie und Geschichte Altägyptens, Heidelberg
SAK	Studien zur altägyptischen Kultur, Hamburg
SAOC	Studies in Ancient Oriental Civilisations, Chicago
SASAE	Supplément aux Annales du service des antiquités de l'Égypte, Cairo
SDAIK	Sonderschrifte des Deutschen archäologischen Institut, Abt. Kairo, Mainz am Rhein
Technology and Culture	Technology and Culture, Baltimore
SSEA Studies	The Society for the Study of Egyptian Antiquities Studies, Mississauga
WVDOG	Wissenschaftliche Veröffentlichungen der Deutschen Orient-Geselschaft, Leipzig
WZKM	Wiener Zeitschrift für die Kunde des Morgenlandes, Vienna
ZÄS	Zeitschrift für Ägyptische Sprache und Altertumskunde, Leipzig, Berlin

Monographs and miscellanea bands

Abusir and Saqqara 2000 – M. Bárta, J. Krejčí (eds.), *Abusir and Saqqara in the Year 2000. Archiv Orientální Supplementa IX*, Prague 2001

Abusir and Saqqara 2001 – F. Coppens (ed.), *Abusir and Saqqara in the Year 2001. Proceedings of the Symposium (Prague, September 25th–27th, 2001)*, ArOr 70/3, 2002

Abusir and Saqqara 2005 – M. Bárta, F. Coppens, J. Krejčí (eds.), *Abusir and Saqqara in the Year 2005*, Prague 2008

Ägyptische Tempel – R. Gundlach, M. Rochholz (eds.), *Ägyptische Tempel – Struktur, Funktion und Programm (Akten der Ägyptologischen Tempeltagungen in Gosen 1990 und in Mainz 1992)*, HÄB 37, 1994

Altenmüller, *Mehu* – H. Altenmüller, *Die Wanddarstellungen im Grab des Mehu in Saqqara*, AV 42, 1998

Arnold, *Building* – Di. Arnold, *The Building in Egypt. Pharaonic Stone Masonry*, New York 1991

Arnold, *Baulexikon* – Di. Arnold, *Lexikon der ägyptischen Baukunst*, Zürich 1994

Arnold, *Architecture* – Di. Arnold, *The Encyclopedia of Ancient Egyptian Architecture*, Cairo 2003

Arnold, *Control Notes* – F. Arnold, *The Control Notes and Team Marks (The Metropolitan Museum of Art Egyptian Expedition*, vol. 23), New York 1990

Arnold, Bourriau, *Ancient Egyptian Pottery* – Do. Arnold, J. Bourriau, *An Introduction to Ancient Egyptian Pottery*, SDAIK 17, 1993

L'art de l'Ancien Empire égyptien – Ch. Ziegler (ed.), *L'art de l'Ancien Empire égyptien, Actes du colloque organisé au Musée du Louvre par la Service culturel les 3 et 4 avril 1998*, Paris 1999

L'art égyptienne – Do. Arnold, K. Grzymski, Ch. Ziegler (eds.), *L'art égyptien au temps des pyramides*, Paris 1999

Aston, *Stone Vessels* – B. G. Aston, *Ancient Egyptian Stone Vessels, Materials and Forms*, SAGA 5, 1994

Badawy, *Egyptian Architecture* – A. Badawy, *History of Egyptian Architecture I, From the Earliest Times to the End of Old Kingdom*, Giza 1954

Baer, *Rank and Title* – K. Baer, *Rank and Title in the Old Kingdom*, Chicago 1960

Barta, *Opferliste* – W. Barta, *Die altägyptische Opferliste von Frühzeit bis zur griechisch-römischen Epoche*, MÄS 3, 1963

Bárta, *Qar* – M. Bárta, *Abusir XIII. The Tomb Complex of the Vizier Qar, His Sons Qar Junior and Senedjemib, and Iykai*, in press

Baud, *Famille royal* – M. Baud, *Famille royale et pouvoir sous l'Ancien Empire égyptien*, BiEtud 126, 1999

Borchardt, *Re-Heiligtum* I – L. Borchardt, *Das Reᶜ-Heiligtum des Königs Ne-woser-reᶜ (Rathures). Herausg. von F. H. F. von Bissing. Band I, Der Bau*, Berlin 1905

Borchardt, *Neuserre* – L. Borchardt, *Das Grabdenkmal des Königs Ne-user-reᶜ*, WVDOG 7, 1907

Borchardt, *Neferirkare* – L. Borchardt, *Das Grabdenkmal des Königs Nefer-ir-keȝ-reᶜ*, WVDOG 11, 1909

Borchardt, *Sahure* I – L. Borchardt, *Das Grabdenkmal des Königs Saȝḥu-reᶜ, Band I – Bau*, WVDOG 14, 1910

Borchardt, *Sahure* II – L. Borchardt, *Das Grabdenkmal des Königs Saȝḥu-reᶜ, Band II – Die Wandbilder*, WVDOG 26, 1913

Borchardt, *Denkmäller* I – L. Borchardt, *Denkmäler des Alten Reiches (ausser den Statuen) im Museum zu Kairo Nr. 1295–1808*, Berlin, Cairo 1937

Bourriau, *Pharaohs and Mortals* – J. Bourriau (with a contribution by Stephen Quirke), *Pharaohs and Mortals, Egyptian Art in the Middle Kingdom*, Cambridge 1989

Buikstra, Ubelaker, *Standards for Data Collection* – J. E. Buikstra, D. H. Ubelaker *Standards for Data Collection from Human Skeletal Remains, Research Series 44*, Fayetteville 1994

Callender, *Eye of Horus* – G. Callender, *The Eye of Horus; A History of Ancient Egypt*, Melbourne, 1993

Carter, Mace, *Tutankhamen* III – H. Carter, A. Mace, *The Tomb of Tutankhamen*, vol. III, London 1933

CEAEM[2] – S. Clark, R. Engelbach, *Ancient Egyptian Masonry. The Building Craft*, Oxford 1930; 2nd edition: *Ancient Egyptian Construction and Architecture*, New York 1992

Cherpion, *Mastabas* – N. Cherpion, *Mastabas et hypogées d'Ancien Empire. Le probleme de la datation*, Bruxelles 1989

Critères de datation – N. Grimal (ed.), *Les critères de datation stylistiques à l'Ancien Empire*, BiEtud 120, 1998

Description de l'Egypte – Ch. C. Gillispie, M. Dewachter, *Monuments of Egypt: the Napoleonic edition. The Complete Archaeological Plates from La description de l'Egypte*, Princeton 1987

Dreyer, *Elephantine* VIII – G. Dreyer, *Elephantine VIII. Der Tempel der Satet. Die Funde des Frühzeit und des Alten Reiches*, AV 39, 1986

Duel, *Mereruka* – P. Duell, *The Mastaba of Mereruka* I–II, Chicago 1938

Dunham, Simpson, *Mersyankh* – D. Dunham, W. K. Simpson, *Giza Mastabas*, vol. I. *The Mastaba of Queen Mersyankh III. G 7530–7540*, Boston 1974

Egyptian Art in the Age of the Pyramids – Do. Arnold (ed.), *Egyptian Art in the Age of the Pyramids*, New York 1999

Egyptian Museum Collections – M. Eldamaty, M. Trad (eds.), *Egyptian Museum Collections around the World*, Cairo 2002

Egyptology at the Dawn of the 21 century – Z. Hawass, L. P. Brock (eds.), *Egyptology at the Dawn of the 21 century. Proceedings of the Eighth International Congress of Egyptologists, Cairo 2000*, Cairo 2002

Emery, *Funerary Repast* – W. B. Emery, *A Funerary Repast in an Egyptian Tomb of the Archaic Period*, Leiden 1962

Fs Sawi – K. Daoud, S. Abd el-Fatah (eds.), *The World of Ancient Egypt. Essays in Honor of Ahmed Abd el-Qader el-Sawi*, SASAE 35, 2006

Garstang, *Mahasna and Bêt Khallâf* – J. Garstang, *Mahasna and Bêt Khallâf*, London 1903

Garstang, *Reqaqnah* – J. Garstang, *Report of Excavations at Reqaqnah, 1901–2: Tombs of the Third Egyptian Dynasty at Raqâqnah and Bêt Khallâf*, Westminster 1904

Hall, *Royal Scarabs* – H. R. Hall, *Catalogue of Egyptian Scarabs, etc., in British Museum, Volume I, Royal Scarabs*, London 1913

Harpur, *Decoration* – Y. Harpur, *Decoration in Egyptian Tombs of the Old Kingdom, Studies in orientation and scene content*, London 1987

Harpur, Scremin, *Kagemni* – Y. Harpur, P. Scremin, *Egypt in Miniature, Vol. I, The Chapel of Kagemni, Scene Details, Oxford Expedition to Egypt*, Reading 2006

Hassan, *Gîza* – S. Hassan, *Excavations at Gîza*, vols. I–X, Oxford, Cairo 1929–1960

Hölz, *Ägyptische Opfertafeln und Kultbecken* – R. Hölz, *Ägyptische Opfertafeln und Kultbecken. Eine Form-und Funktionsanalyse für das Alte, Mittlere und Neue Reich*, HÄB 45, 2002

Homm. Leclant – C. Berger, G. Clerc, N. Grimal (eds.), *Hommages à Jean Leclant. I–IV*, BdE 106/1, 1994

Homm. Lauer – C. Berger, B. Mathieu (eds.), *Études sur l'Ancienne Empire et la nécropole de Saqqâra dédiées à Jean-Philippe Lauer*, OrMonsp. IX, 1997

Hornung, Staehelin, *Skarabäen Basel* – E. Hornung, E. Staehelin, *Skarabäen und andere Siegelamulette aus Basler Sammlungen, Ägyptische Denkmäler in der Schweiz, Band 1*, Basel 1976

Ikram, *Choice Cuts* – S. Ikram, *Choice Cuts: Meat Production in Ancient Egypt, Orientalia Lovaniensia Analecta 69*, Leuven 1995

Jacquet-Gordon, *Domaines funéraires* – H. K. Jacquet-Gordon, *Les noms des domaines funéraires sous l'ancien empire égyptien*, BdE 34, Cairo 1962

Jánosi, *Pyramidenanlagen* – P. Jánosi, *Die Pyramidenanlagen der Königinnen. Untersuchungen zu einem Grabtyp des Alten un Mittleren Reiches*, DÖAW 13 (1996)

Jánosi, *Giza* – P. Jánosi, *Giza in der 4. Dynastie, Band I: Die Mastabas der Kernfriedhöfe und die Felsgräber*, DÖAW 30, 2005

Jánosi, *Gräberwelt* – P. Jánosi, *Die Gräberwelt der Pyramidenzeit*, Mainz 2006

Jones, *Titles* – D. Jones, *An Index of Ancient Egyptian Titles, Epithets and Phrases of the Old Kingdom*, BAR 866, 2000

Junker, *Gîza* – H. Junker, *Bericht über die von der Akademie der Wissenschaften in Vienna auf gemeinsame Kosten mit Dr. Wilhelm Pelizaeus unternommenen Grabungen auf dem Friedhof des Alten Reiches bei den Pyramiden von Gîza. I–XII, DAWW 69–75, 1929–1953*

Kamal, *Tables d'Offrandes* – A. Bey Kamal, *Tables d'Offrandes, CG 23001–23256*, 2 vols, Cairo 1906–1909

Kanawati, Hassan, *Nedjetempet* – N. Kanawati, A. Hassan, *The Tombs of Nedjet-empet, Ka-aper and Others, The Teti Cemetery at Saqqara I*, ACER 8, 1996

Khouli, *Egyptian Stone Vessels* – A. El-Khouli, *Egyptian Stone Vessels Predynastic Period to Dynasty III*, vol. 1, Mainz am Rhein 1978

Krejčí, *Ptahshepses* – J. Krejčí, *Abusir XI, The Architecture of the Mastaba of Ptahshepses*, Prague 2009

Labrousse, Lauer, *Ouserkaf* – A. Labrousse, J.-Ph. Lauer, *Les complexes funéraires d'Ouserkaf et de Néferhétepès*, BdE 130, 2000

Lacau, Lauer, *Pyr. à degrés IV* –P. Lacau, J.-Ph.Lauer, *La Pyramide à Degrés IV, Inscriptions Gravées sur les Vases*, Cairo 1959

Lacau, Lauer, *Pyr. à degrés V* – P. Lacau, J.-Ph.Lauer, *La Pyramide à Degrés V, Inscriptions à l'Encre sur les Vases*, Cairo 1965

Lauer, *Pyr. à degrés I* – J.-Ph. Lauer, *La Pyramide à degrés I*, Cairo 1936

Lauer, *Hist. mon.* I – J.-Ph. Lauer, *Histoire monumentale des pyramides d'Egypte, Vol. 1, Les Pyramides à degrés (IIIe Dynastie)*, Cairo 1962

LD – K. R. Lepsius, *Denkmäler aus Aegypten und Aethiopien*, Berlin 1849–1859

LD, Text I – K. R. Lepsius, *Denkmäler aus Aegypten und Aethiopien. Text*, Eduard Naville (ed.), Lepzig 1897

Lehner, *Complete Pyramids* – M. Lehner, *The Complete Pyramids*, Cairo 1997

Lilyquist, *Egyptian Stone Vessels* – C. Lilyquist, *Egyptian Stone Vessels. Khian through Tuthmoses IV*, New York 1995

Lucas, *Materials* – A. Lucas, *Ancient Egyptian Materials and Industries* (4th Edition), revised by J. R. Harris, London 1962

Mariette, *Mastabas* – A. Mariette, *Les mastaba de l'ancienne empire. Fragment du dernier ouvrage de A. Mariette, publié d'après le manuscrit de l'auteur par G. Maspero. Livraison 1–8*, Paris 1882–1885

Manuelian, *Slab Stelae* – P. Der Manuelian, *Slab Stelae of the Giza Necropolis*, New Haven and Philadelphia 2003

Martin, Saller, *Lehrbuch der Anthropologie* – R. Martin, K. Saller, *Lehrbuch der Anthropologie in Systematischer Darstellung*, Stuttgart 1979

Martin, *Stelae* – G. T. Martin, *Stelae from Egypt and Nubia in the Fitzwilliam Museum, Cambridge, c. 3000 B.C.–A.D. 1150*, Cambridge 2005

Martin-Pardey, *CAA Hildesheim 6* – E. Martin-Pardey, *Pelizaeus-Museum Hildesheim. Lieferung 6: Grabbeigaben, Nachträge und Ergänzungen, CAA* 1991

McKern, Stewart, *Skeletal Age Changes* – T. W. McKern, T. D. Stewart *Skeletal Age Changes in Young American Male, Analysed from the Standpoint of Identification*, Natick 1957

Minault-Gout, Deleuze, *Balat II* – A. Minault-Gout, P. Deleuze, *Balat II, Le Mastaba d'Ima-Pepi, FIFAO* 33, 1992

de Morgan, *Carte de la nécropole memphite* – J. de Morgan, *Carte de la nécropole memphite. Dahschour, Sakkarah, Abou-Sir*, Cairo 1897

Mostaffa, *Opfertafeln* – M. M. F. Mostafa, *Untersuchungen zu Opfertafeln im Alten Reich, HÄB* 17, 1982

Moussa, Altermüller, *Nefer and Ka-hay* – A. M. Moussa, H. Altermüller, *The Tomb of Nefer and Ka-hay, AV* 5, 1971

MRA – V. Maragioglio, C. Rinaldi, *L'architettura delle piramidi menfite* II–VII, Rapallo–Torino 1963–1977

Mummies and Magic – S. D'Auria, P. Lacovara, C. Roehrig (eds.), *Mummies and Magic*, Boston, 1990

Nester, Heizer, *Making Stone Vases* – T. R. Nester, R. F. Heizer, *Making Stone Vases: Ethnoarchaeological Studies at an Alabaster Workshop in Upper Egypt*, Malibu 1981

OKAA – M. Bárta (ed.), *Old Kingdom Art and Archaeology*, Prague 2004

Olivier, *Pratique anthropologique* – G. Olivier, *Pratique anthropologique*, Paris 1960

Paice, *Pottery of Daily Life* – P. Paice, *The Pottery of Daily Life in Ancient Egypt, SSEA* Studies No. 5, Mississauga 1997

Patočková, *Fragmenty soch* – B. Patočková, *Fragmenty soch z Ptahšepsesovy mastaby v Abúsíru* (Fragments of the statues from the Mastaba of Ptahshepses in Abusir), Unpublished M.A. Thesis, Charles University in Prague 1994

Perring, *Pyramids* – J. S. Perring, *The Pyramids of Gizeh* III, London 1842

Perring, Vyse, *Appendix* – J. S. Perring, H. Vyse, *Appendix to Operations Carried on at the Pyramids of Gizeh in 1837*, London 1842

Petrie, *Abydos* – W. M. F. Petrie, *Abydos* I–II, London 1902–1903

Petrie, *Tools and Weapons* – W. M. F. Petrie, *Tools and Weapons*, London 1917

Petrie, *Stone and Metal Vases* – W. M. F. Petrie, *Stone and Metal Vases*, British School of Archaeology in Egypt Vol. VII, London 1937

PM – B. Porter, R. L. B. Moss, *Topographical Bibliography of Ancient Egyptian Hieroglyphic Texts, Reliefs and Paintings*, 7 vols, Oxford 1927–52, *PM²* since 1960 revised and augmented by J. Málek

Posener-Kriéger, de Cenival, *Abu Sir Papyri* – P. Posener-Kriéger, J. L. de Cenival, *Hieratic Papyri in the British Museum. Fifth Series. The Abu Sir Papyri*, London 1968

Posener-Kriéger, *Les papyrus d'Abousir* – P. Posener-Kriéger, *Les archives du temple funéraire de Néferirkareᶜ-Kakai (Les papyrus d'Abousir), Traduction et commentaire I–II, BdE* 65, 1976

Posener-Kriéger, Verner, Vymazalová, *Papyrus Archive – Abusir X. The Pyramid Complex of Raneferef. The Papyrus Archive*, Prague 2007

Proceedings of the Seventh Congress – C. J. Eyre (ed.), *Proceedings of the Seventh International Congress of Egyptologists, Cambridge, 3–9 September 1995, OLA* 82, 1996

Quibell, *Yuaa and Thuiu* – M. J. Quibell, *C.G.C. Tomb of Yuaa and Thuia*, Cairo 1908

Ranke, *PN* – H. Ranke, *Die ägyptischen Personennamen* I–II, Glückstadt 1935; Glückstadt – Hamburg – New York 1949–1952

Regner, *Skarabäen und Skaraboide* – Ch. Regner, *Skarabäen un Skaraboide, Bonner Sammlung von Aegyptiaca, Band 1*, Wiesbaden 1995

Reisner, *Mycerinus* – G. A. Reisner, *Mycerinus. The Temples of the Third Pyramid at Giza*, Cambridge, Mass. 1931

Reisner, *Naga-ed-Dêr* III – G. A. Reisner, *A Provincial Cemetery of the Pyramid Age, Naga-ed-Dêr* Part III, University of California Publications Egyptian Archaeology Vol. VI, Oxford 1932

Reisner, *Tomb Development* – G. A. Reisner, *The Development of the Egyptian Tomb to the Accession of Cheops*, Cambridge, Mass. 1936

Reisner, *Gîza Necropolis I* – G. A. Reisner, *A History of the Gîza Necropolis, Volume I*, Oxford 1942

Reisner, Smith, *Giza Necropolis II* – G. A. Reisner, W. S. Smith, *A History of the Gîza Necropolis, Volume II, The Tomb of Hetep-heres*, Cambridge 1955

Ricke, *SH Userkaf* – H. Ricke, H., *Das Sonnenheiligtum des Königs Userkaf* I–II, *Beiträge Bf* 7–8, 1965–1969

Roth, *Egyptian Phyles* – A. M. Roth, *Egyptian Phyles in the Old Kingdom, SAOC* 48, Chicago 1991

Schinz et al., *Lehrbuch der Röntgendiagnostik* – H. R. Schinz, W. E. Baensch, W. E. Friedl and E. Uehlinger, *Lehrbuch der Röntgendiagnostik*, Stuttgart 1952

Schmitz, *Königssohn* – B. Schmitz, *Untersuchungen zum Titel S3-NJŚWT, „Königssohn"*, Bonn 1976

Science in Egyptology – A. R. David (ed.), *Science in Egyptology. Proceedings of the Science in Egyptology Symposia*, Manchester 1986

Seipel, *Ägypten, Götter, Gräber* – W. Seipel, *Ägypten, Götter, Gräber und die Kunst 4000 Jahre Jenseitsglabe, Katalogbuch zur Ausstellung im Schlossmuseum Linz*, Linz 1989

Simpson, *Qar and Idu* – W. K. Simpson, *The Mastabas of Qar and Idu. G 7101 and 7102. Giza Mastabas 2*, Boston 1976

Soukiassian, *Balat* III – G. Soukiassian, M. Wuttmann, L. Pantalacci, *Balat* III. *Les ateliers de potiers d'Ayn-Asil. Fin de l'Ancien Empire, Première Période Intermédiaire, FIFAO* 34, 1990

Spencer, *Brick Architecture* – A. J. Spencer, *Brick Architecture in Ancient Egypt*, Warminster 1979

Stadelmann, *Pyramiden* – R. Stadelmann, *Die ägyptischen Pyramiden – vom Ziegelbau zum Weltwunder*, Mainz 1991

Strouhal, Bareš, *Secondary Cemetery* – E. Strouhal, L. Bareš, *Secondary Cemetery in Mastaba of Ptahshepses at Abusir*, Prague 1993

Structure and Significance – P. Jánosi (ed.), *Structure and Significance. Thougths on ancient Egyptian architecture, DÖAW* 33, 2005

Studies Simpson – P. der Manuelian (ed.), *Studies in Honor of William Kelly Simpson*, Boston 1996

Times, Signs and Pyramids – V. G. Callender, L. Bareš, M. Bárta, J. Janák. J. Krejčí, (eds.), *Times, Signs and Pyramids*, in press

Valloggia, *Balat* IV – M. Valloggia, *Balat* IV. *Le monument funéraire d'Ima-Pepy/Ima-Meryre, FIFAO* 38, 1998

Verner, *Reliefs* – M. Verner, *Abusir I, The Mastaba of Ptahshepses. Reliefs I/1*, Prague 1986

Verner, *Baugraffiti* – M. Verner, *Abusir II, Baugraffiti der Ptahschepses Mastaba*, Prague 1992

Verner, *Khentkaus* – M. Verner, *Abusir III, The Pyramid Complex of Khentkaus*, Prague 1995

Verner, *Pyramids* – M. Verner, *Pyramids. The Mystery, Culture, and Science of Egypt's Great Monuments*, New York 2001

Verner, Callender, *Djedkare's Cemetery* – M. Verner, V. G. Callender, *Abusir VI. Djedkare's Family Cemetery*, Prague 2002

Verner, *Realm of Osiris* – M. Verner, *Abusir. Realm of Osiris*, Cairo 2003

Verner *et al., Raneferef* – M. Verner *et al., Abusir IX, The Pyramid Complex of Raneferef, The Archaeology*, Prague 2006

Warren, *Minoan Stone Vases* – P. Warren, *Minoan Stone Vases*, Cambridge 1969

Wb – A. Erman, H. Grapow (eds.), *Wörterbuch ägyptische Sprache*, I–VI, Berlin–Leipzig 1926–1961

Wiese, *Stempelsiegel-Amulette* – A. B. Wiese, *Die Anfänge der ägyptischen Stempelsiegel-Amulette, OBO* 12 , 1996

Winterhalter, Brodbeck, *Antikenmuseum Basel* – S. Winterhalter, A. Brodbeck, *Antikenmuseum Basel und Sammlung Ludwig. Die Ägyptischen Abteilung*, Mainz am Rhein 2001

1. Introduction

This monograph presents a report on the results of the archaeological excavations of the Czech Institute of Egyptology undertaken from 1987 until 2004 and held in the area of the minor tombs belonging to the members of the royal family clustered around the pyramid tombs of the Fifth Dynasty kings in Abusir. These results comprise the Mastabas of Nebtyemneferes and Nakhtsare as well as the Pyramid Complex Lepsius no. 24 and the Tomb Complex Lepsius no. 25* – all of which are located in the southern part of the Abusir Royal Necropolis. As most of these tombs certainly belonged to the members of the royal family of the Old Kingdom, this collection of data represents a contribution to our knowledge of the funerary practices and beliefs of the Egyptian élite living during the Fifth Dynasty, as well as providing some additional information for the data base of the royal family tree of the Abusir kings. In addition, material obtained in this area has been important as a source of factual evidence for the building techniques of the Old Kingdom masons and architects, as well as adding to our understanding of ancient Egyptian architecture during the time of the Fifth Dynasty.

Reis **Tallal el-Kereti.**

Related to the architecture is the corpus of *Baugraffiti* documented on the core masonry of the tombs as well as among the loose blocks; these marks have been particularly important in regard to the pyramid known as Lepsius no. 24. On the other hand, due to the attacks of tomb robbers and stone robbers, the deleterious state of preservation regarding these monuments has presented serious difficulties for these investigations and these depredations have made it a challenge even to identify the owners of the individual tombs. The damage has been so severe that even identifying some of these persons has, in some cases, been beyond us. These issues have in part also defined many of the questions connected to these monuments and their badly damaged contents.

---

*In this monograph, the graphical appearance of Lepsius' names for three tomb complexes – Lepsius no. **XXIV**, Lepsius no. **XXV** and also Lepsius no. **XXIII** has been rendered as Lepsius no. **24**, Lepsius no. **25** and Lepsius no. **23**. These changes have been made mainly due to the simplification of reading, as well as the homogeneity of the denominations of the monuments in the entire monograph.

The second chapter is devoted to the excavation and description of the Mastaba of Nebtyemneferes, a rather enigmatic identity – probably a princess – who was buried among the tombs of the members of the royal family in the southern part of the Abusir Pyramid Necropolis. The tomb includes common features of Abusir tombs of the second half of the Fifth Dynasty.

The third chapter deals with research into the Mastaba of Nakhtsare, located to the south of Raneferef's mortuary temple; it is the northernmost tomb in a row of tombs located on the southern border of the royal necropolis. The important position of this badly destroyed tomb is also indicated by its rich burial equipment, as well as by the several masons' marks found on the masonry of the mastaba.

The fourth chapter is devoted to the pyramid complex of an unknown queen in a tomb known as Lepsius no. 24. Because a large number of masons' marks was present on this pyramid's walls, and, in addition, because of the bad state of preservation of this monument, we have been able to study in an unique way the methods used by the ancient architects and builders in the construction of royal monuments in the middle of the Fifth Dynasty.

A further chapter is dedicated to a most exceptional tomb complex – the monument known to us now as Lepsius no. 25. This monument represents a double tomb with complex substructures. Unfortunately, it is in a desolate state of preservation, so much so that many details of its intriguing architecture as well as the burial equipment, *etc.*, have been lost to us forever. A unique find from this tomb complex was the discovery of fragments of a papyri (the text has been prepared by Hana Vymazalová).

The sixth chapter is devoted to the anthropological material discovered during the archaeological excavations of these monuments (the text has been prepared by Martina Kujanová, Eugen Strouhal and Viktor Černý). The majority of this material is represented by remains coming from the Late Period cemeteries, which once covered this area. In addition to this fairly large group, there is one very significant study featuring the fragments of a female mummy which might have belonged to the owner of the Pyramid Complex Lepsius no. 24.

The study included in an appendix (prepared by V. G. Callender) deals with the stone vessels found in the monuments discussed in this monograph. This material supplements the stone vessel corpus from the neighbouring tomb complex of King Raneferef, as well from other places in this area of the Memphite Necropolis.

The collection of pottery vessels and sherds found during the archaeological excavations of the minor tombs in the southern part of the Abusir Royal Necropolis shall be discussed in its entirety in the next volume of monographs on the Abusir Pyramid Necropolis; in the present monograph, only significant examples of pottery have been featured in the catalogues concerning the individual tombs.

Reis **Ahmed el-Kereti.**

During the work, which is a result of the research project MSM-0021620826, the authors of the present monograph have not only been able to use the plan, the archaeological records as well as the architectural and photographic documentation held in the archives of the Czech Institute of Egyptology, but they have also had the opportunity of studying the architecture of the monuments as well as the finds coming from them. The authors are most grateful to the Government of the Czech Republic who funded this work. Moreover, the archaeological works in Abusir would not be possible without our close co-operation with the administration of the Supreme Council of Antiquities of Egypt, as well as with the Inspectorates of the SCA in Saqqara and in Abusir. We appreciate very much the partnership with our colleagues and friends from the SCA. Without the expertise of overseers of workers, the *reiseen* Tallal el-Kereti, Ahmed el-Kereti, Mittal el-Kereti and Khaled el-Kereti, our esteemed colleagues and friends, the work in Abusir would have had little chance of success.

I would like, in the name of co-authors of this monograph, to offer our sincere thanks to all of our colleagues who helped in the preparation of this monograph. It could never have been finished without the industry and patience of Ladislav Bareš (for the translation of the find cards from Czech into English; this rendering was very important for the work of Vivienne G. Callender), Hana Benešovská (for her translation of the find cards and valuable discussions on the part of the corpus of material discovered in all the tombs), Vladimír Brůna (for the geodetical survey and co-operation on the preparation of the plan of the Tomb Complex Lepsius no. 25), Marek Dospěl (for his help with the work in the photographical archives of the Institute), Jolana Malátková (for her preparation of many of the illustrations, editing the manuscript and creating the monograph's layout), Dušan Magdolen (for his dedicated help during the archaeological excavations and numerous discussions regarding problems connected with the monograph), Miroslav Ottmar (for the scanning of photographs, plans and maps), Marta Štrachová (for the scanning of the photographs, plans and maps), Lucie Vařeková (for her preparation of illustrations regarding the archaeological finds), Hana Vymazalová (for her additional preparation of the illustrations for the chapter on stone vessels and for her translation of the find cards from Czech into English), Luděk Wellner (for preparations regarding the majority of the plans for the publication), Lenka Suková (for correction of chapters 5.1.–5.3. and 5.4.1.–5.4.3.) and other colleagues from the Czech Institute of Egyptology, Faculty of Arts at the Charles University in Prague. Dr. Vivienne Gae Callender is not only one of the authors of the book, but she has also corrected the English of the great majority of the texts published in this book.

Jaromír Krejčí
Prague, Autumn 2007

2. The Mastaba of Nebtyemneferes

Prior to the excavation of this tomb, approximately thirty metres to the east of the pyramid Lepsius no. 24, lay a low mound of a roughly rectangular, north–south oriented shape. In the middle of the mound, covered with sherds of rough pottery (beer jugs, bread moulds and models of offering vessels) from the Fifth Dynasty and fragments of local greyish limestone, were two shallow depressions (*fig. 2.1*). Thus

Fig. 2.1 Overall view of the area of the Mastaba of Nebtyemneferes before the archaeological excavations in 1987. In the background the Tomb Complex Lepsius no. 25.
Photo JB

already, the survey of the site indicated that the debris was very likely to contain the remains of a mastaba, dating very probably from the late Fifth Dynasty. The exploration of the monument began in the mid February 1987 and lasted through to the end of the month.

Fig. 2.2 View of the remains of the tomb's masonry around the offering room. The Mastaba of Nebtyemneferes.
Photo JB

2.1. The superstructure

The remains of the mastaba's superstructure lay relatively very close to the surface of the desert, under a ca 10–20 cm thick layer of sand. The mastaba had a rectangular (15.90 × 11.50 m) plan oriented in a north–south direction. It had been badly destroyed, as the initial excavation revealed: the height of the extant masonry fluctuated between 30 (eastern outer wall) – 120 cm (western outer wall) (*fig. 2.2*).

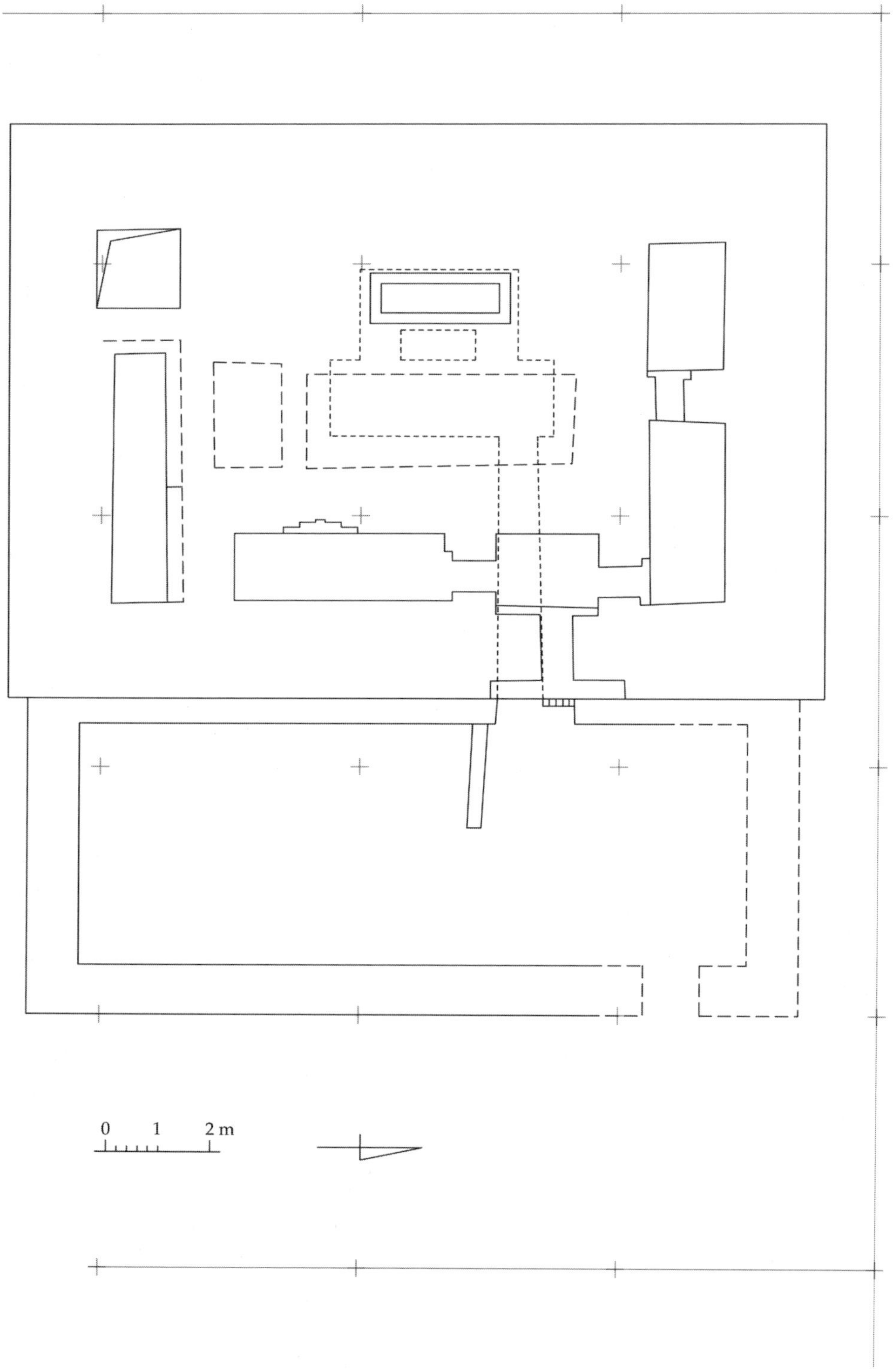

Fig. 2.3 Overall plan of the Mastaba of Nebtyemneferes.

0 1 2 m

The superstructure of the mastaba comprised five rooms – a vestibule flanked on the south by an offering room and on the north by two storerooms, and a serdab on the southern side of the offering room (*fig. 2.3*).

The masonry of the superstructure was formed by the mudbrick core, cased with small ashlars of greyish limestone joined by means of whitish plaster. Both the outer and the inner walls were only roughly dressed and, except for the false door in the western wall of the offering room (see the text below), were left undecorated.

Judging by the find of a large, ca 180 cm long ceiling slab of limestone in the northern part of the offering room, the rooms in the superstructure were originally very probably roofed by flat slabs of grey limestone rather than barrel vaults of mudbrick. The same flat limestone slabs were also used for roofing the rooms in the substructure (see the text below). The flooring was not the same in all the rooms: in some rooms (offering room, vestibule), it was formed by a pavement made of flat pieces of limestone, in some other, less important rooms (storerooms, serdab), it was made of beaten clay mixed with small limestone chips (see also *fig. 2.2*).

Fig. 2.4 The entrance to the substructure of the Mastaba of Nebtyemneferes, superimposed by the entrance to the vestibule and other parts of the superstructure.
Photo JB

2.1.1. Entrance

The entrance to the mastaba lies in the eastern outer wall and closer to the north-eastern corner of the monument (approximately at one third of the wall's length). The entrance is formed by a shallow, only 15 cm deep and 2.60 m broad niche (*fig. 2.4*), and a 60 cm wide passage giving access to a small vestibule.

2.1.2. Vestibule

The vestibule has a rectangular (2 × 1.6 m), north–south oriented plan. A passage opening in the southern wall of the vestibule gives access to the offering room, whereas another passage leading from the vestibule to the north gives access to two small storerooms. Both the vestibule and the passages were buried under a layer of decomposed mudbrick masonry, coming from the side walls of the building, and fragments of limestone. In the vestibule, no artefacts were found except for small sherds of the aforesaid late Fifth Dynasty pottery.

2.1.3. Offering room

The adjacent vestibule had been buried up to the crown of its walls by a thick layer of decomposed mudbrick masonry in which the aforecited ceiling block had been found. This same heavy deposit was also found in the northern part of the north–south oriented offering room (4 × 1.4 m). The character of the fill in

Fig. 2.5 Lower part of
the false door found
in situ in the offering
room of the Mastaba of
Nebtyemneferes.
Photo JB

the offering room did not basically differ from that in the vestibule. The southern part of the room was filled mostly by grey sand (made up of sand and decayed mudbrick). In the southern half of the western wall of the room were revealed the remains of the bottom part of a false door (see *figs. 2.2, 2.5*). In front of the false door lay a fragment of the left door jamb on which, luckily, the name of the tomb owner, Nebtyemneferes, survived (see *chapter 2.4.*). In the lowest part of the false door remained in position two symmetrically arranged representations of the seated tomb owner wearing a long, tightly fitting robe and holding a lotus flower.

2.1.4. Storerooms

The northern part of the superstructure filled two small, slightly irregular, east–west oriented rooms arranged one after another. The western storeroom (2 × 1.45 m) was smaller than the eastern one (3.6–3.7 × 1.45 m). The storerooms represented no exception as far as the debris is concerned: they, too, were buried under a layer of decomposed mudbrick masonry mixed with potsherds and fragments of limestone. As was the case in the preceding rooms, so it also was the case with the storerooms, that the limestone casing of the walls had been removed (very probably, this had occurred in antiquity) by stone robbers.

Fig. 2.6 Late or Graeco-
Roman secondary burial
in the area of the false
shaft. The Mastaba of
Nebtyemneferes.
Photo JB

Fig. 2.7 View of the pillar between the antechamber and the burial chamber in the substructure of the Mastaba of Nebtyemneferes.
Photo JB

In the western storeroom (2 × 1.45 m) were found on the floor, under the layer of decomposed mudbrick masonry and sand, only a few items which survived from the original contents of the room. There was a clay model of a libation basin, fragments of small cups of gabro and diorite, a fragment of a model of an alabaster bowl, a flint blade (see *chapter 2.4.*).

2.1.5. Serdab
The serdab was a long, narrow, slightly irregular room (5.1 × 0.9–1 m) which filled the south–east corner of the mastaba. The room was built of mudbrick and its walls were not cased with limestone as in other rooms in the superstructure. In the debris filling the serdab and consisting of the decomposed mudbrick masonry were found the remains of a nearly completely destroyed secondary burial dating probably from the Late to the Graeco-Roman Period (exc. no. 8/M/87, see *chapter 6.2.3.4.*).

2.2. Substructure
The substructure was accessible by means of a sloping corridor beginning directly under the entrance to the mastaba (see *fig. 2.4*). The corridor was 86 cm wide and 73 cm high and it ended in the antechamber of the burial chamber lying ca 2 m under the mastaba's ground level. The plan of the substructure can be interpreted in two ways namely, as one room with a deep niche in its western wall, a part of which supports the ceiling of the room, or, it may be seen as two rooms: an antechamber and a burial chamber, separated by means of a masonry pillar (*fig. 2.7*).

Fig. 2.8 Remains of the protecting barrel vault made of mudbricks above the ceiling of the antechamber and burial chamber in the Mastaba of Nebtyemneferes. Photo JB

2.2.1. Antechamber

The antechamber was a relatively well preserved; it was a high room (ca 160 cm) of a rectangular, north–south oriented plan (ca 4.6 × 1.5 m). Its walls were cased by summarily dressed ashlars of grey limestone. The ceiling, formed by flat slabs of inferior quality limestone, was protected by a relieving barrel vault of mudbrick (*fig. 2.8*), above and around which was a layer of potsherds (beer jugs, miniature vessels) mixed with sand. In the western wall of the antechamber, at each end of the burial chamber, were two openings, each eighty centimetres wide, giving access to the sarcophagus.

The ceiling of the antechamber had been broken through by robbers on both the northern and the southern end of the room (*fig. 2.9*). It was via these two holes that clean blown sand had penetrated inside antechamber and soon filled the entire room.

On the eastern wall of the antechamber, below the ceiling and close to the descending corridor, were found the remains of a cursive inscription (*fig. 2.10*) in

Fig. 2.10 Remains of a cursive inscription found in the antechamber of the Mastaba of Nebtyemneferes. Photo JB

black paint. Unfortunately, the inscription is, except for few signs, unreadable since it was additionally erased. It probably consisted of one horizontal line (beginning with the date ?) and four columns of text.

2.2.2. Burial chamber

The burial chamber was constructed in the same way as the antechamber. However, in contrast to the antechamber, it was somewhat shorter (see *fig. 2.3*). Also this chamber was attacked by robbers from above, near the northern end of the ceiling. Through the robbers' hole had after the robbery penetrated drift sand which flooded major part of the sarcophagus.

The whole burial chamber was filled by a summarily dressed, box shaped sarcophagus (chest: 270 × 100 × 94 cm, lid: 270 × 95 × 30 cm) of limestone. The slightly curved lid of the sarcophagus had been pushed aside by the robbers. From the looted burial, only the remains, including a few fragments of bones and the rags of the mummy wrappings, survived. The anthropological examination showed that the mummy belonged to a gracile lady who died in her thirties.[1]

In the burial chamber only two artefacts were found: a fragment of a wooden statue (see *chapter 4.2.*) and a few sherds of a jug, found around the south-east corner

---

[1] Personal communication of the anthropologist E. Strouhal. See also *chapter 6.2.3.2.*

of the sarcophagus and dating probably from the late Roman Period. The jug might have belonged to the robbers.

2.2.3. False shaft

In the south-west corner of the mastaba's superstructure were unearthed the remains a shaft (1.6 × 1.65 m and ca 1.5 m deep) built of mudbrick and secondarily filled with the decomposed masonry of the upper parts of the shaft. This shaft apparently represents a false shaft detected as in Abusir as in other Old Kingdom tombs on the Memphite Necropolis.[2] The shaft was additionally reused for the burial of an about one year old child in a small, box shaped coffin (102 × 48 × 27 cm) made of wood and covered with a pink stucco and whitewashed (exc. no. 13/M/87; see *fig. 2.6* and *chapter 6.2.2.3.*). The coffin lay at the eastern wall of the shaft. The body faced east with its head oriented to the north. The right hand of the child was laid alongside the body, whereas the left one was placed on the breast. The coffin was decomposed and so was the body, too. Judging by the age of the child, the nicely worked coffin and the position of the burial in the subsidiary shaft in the south-west corner of Nebtyemneferes's mastaba, it can not be excluded that it was the child of the tomb owner herself.

Under the coffin was found fragment of the damaged horn with a small piece of the skull of a young bull. The horns were used as feeding cups for children whose mothers were not able to suckle them. Is it possible that this could have been a symbolic feeding horn? Neither the burial nor the shaft contained any other artefacts.

2.3. Open courtyard

In front of the whole eastern façade of the mastaba was built an open courtyard, five metres wide, surrounded by a low, one metre thick mudbrick wall. The courtyard, the floor of which was made of beaten clay, had a rectangular plan and was entered from the north through an opening near the north-west corner of the mastaba. In the courtyard, near the entrance to the mastaba, were found two artefacts, a fragment of relief and a fragment of statue (see *chapter 2.4.*), which very probably came from the mastaba.

2.4. Finds

Fragment of a false door – left outer jamb
1/M/87
Limestone
88 × 33 × 23 cm
Fifth Dynasty
Offering chamber, quarried out from a niche in the western wall, found lying on the floor ca 1 m to the east from the niche and ca 0.5 m above the floor in the layer of the yellow sand and debris.

Fragment of the lower part of a left outer jamb of a false door with a representation of the tomb owner's figure (*Nbtj-m-nfr.ś*) and her two daughters (*figs. 2.11–2.12*). The name of the tomb owner has been engraved above the figure of Nebtyemneferes and her daughters. The surface of the jamb in the area of the upper part of the woman's torso is corroded. Nebtyemneferes is depicted standing with the right hand hanging along her torso and her left hand bent below her left breast. Nebtyemneferes is dressed in the tight robe with shoulder traps. She wears bracelets on the wrists and also circlets. To the right, one of two of her daughters is depicted in much smaller scale. The daughter is also dressed in a tight robe with shoulder traps. She wears a broad

[2] Cf. T. Rzeuska, The Necropolis at West Saqqara: The Late Old Kingdom Shafts with no Burial Chamber. Were they False, Dummy, Unfinished or Intentional?, in: *Abusir and Saqqara 2001*, 402; Verner, Callender, *Djedkare's Cemetery*, 115–116.

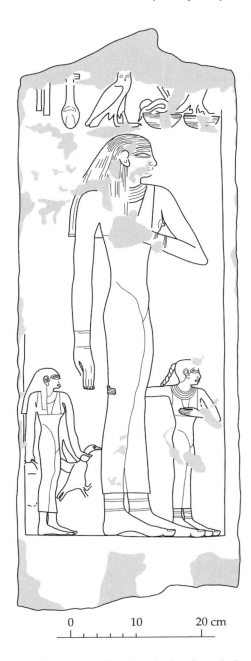

0   10   20 cm

Fig. 2.11 Left jamb of Nebtyemneferes' false door.
Photo JB

Fig. 2.12 Left jamb of Nebtyemneferes' false door.

necklace and holds – by her right hand – Nebtyemneferes' right leg from behind. As is the case with her mother, the daughter's left hand is bent below her breast. The daughter wears a children's plait in her hair. The other daughter of Nebtyemneferes is depicted to the left of her mother. Also this daughter is depicted standing, dressed in a tight robe with shoulder traps. In contrast to her sister, she is holding a duck and, in her right hand, what appears to be a bag or a vessel with a handle made of rope. She is wearing a long wig. Below the scene, three bands of colour survived – red (3 cm broad), yellow (3 cm broad), black (5 cm broad). The figure in the centre is 62 cm high, the to the left 25 cm and the figure to the right 27 cm high.

On the surface of the relief, there are tiny remains of the red and blue colour. On the rear side of the block there were remains of pink mortar used for inserting of the block into the false door.

Lower part of the false door
1/M/87a
Limestone
W: 1.0 m, max. H: 0.39 m
Found *in situ* in the western wall of the offering room, in its southern part.

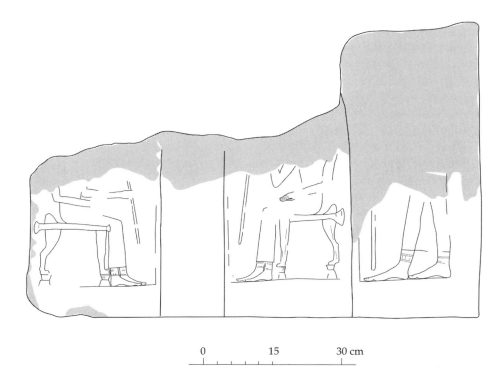

**Fig. 2.13 Lower part of
Nebtyemneferes' false door.**

0   15   30 cm

Lower part of a false door. The outer left jamb of the false door is missing (apparently it is represented by a false door jamb 1/M/87). Only lowermost parts of the female figures are preserved (see *figs. 2.5* and *2.13*). In the right outer jamb, a female figure is depicted. The lady is dressed in the long, tight robe. On contrary to the supposed left outer jamb (exc. no. 1/M/87), the lady is depicted as having in one of her hands a kind of a stick, which lower part is preserved on the false door. In the middle of the false door, there are on the both jambs another two female figures. Both of them (only partially preserved) are sitting on a chair. The chairs on both inner jambs had legs made in the form of a lion's paw. Both female figures are depicted dressed in the long robe. All three women depicted on this piece wear circlets around their ankles.

Fragment of the false door (?)
7/M/87
Limestone
H: 28 cm, W: 24 cm
Fifth Dynasty
The fragment was found in the same situation as a left jamb of the false door 1/M/87.

A fragment of the false door (?) with remains of two hieroglyphic signs (*imȝḫw*) in its lower left part. Remnants of a sign are detectable in the neigbouring register. The signs have been made in a slightly raised relief (*figs. 2.14–2.15*).

Fragment of a relief
14/M/87
Limestone
8 × 7 cm
Fifth Dynasty
Found to the east of the mastaba doorway, in the mudbrick destruction layer. A fragment of a relief with part of a representation of a man (*figs. 2.16–2.17*): part of a head with an eye, emphasized eyebrow and the lower part of a wig (it is not possible to discern whether it was a curled wig) and a right-hand shoulder with the upper part of his right hand. Traces of red survived on the body and black paint

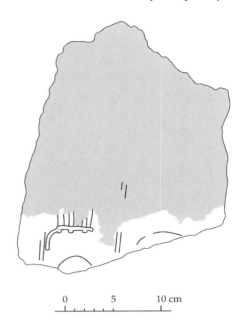

Fig. 2.14 Fragment of Nebtyemneferes' false door (?). Photo JB

Fig. 2.15 Fragment of Nebtyemneferes' false door (?).

Fig. 2.16 Fragment of a relief with a part of a representation of a man. Photo JB

Fig. 2.17 Fragment of a relief with a part of a representation of a man.

on the wig. Unfortunately, it is not possible to ascertain from which scene type the fragment comes.

Due to the place of the fragment's discovery (outside the mastaba), it is not certain that the fragment could have come from the tomb itself. It might have been brought from another tomb, perhaps from the neighbouring pyramid complex of Khentkaus II.[3] On the other hand, we cannot fully exclude the idea that this fragment was originally part of the relief decoration of Nebtyemneferes' tomb. If so, the tomb would be extraordinary in comparison with the other minor tombs in the royal necropolis discussed in this monograph (together with recently excavated tomb of Werkaure) as their excavations did not uncover any relief fragment.

Fragment of a statue
3/M/87
Wood
L: 26 cm, W: 4 cm, thickness: 0.5 cm
Fifth Dynasty
Found in the clean sand filling the space between the sarcophagus and the eastern wall of the burial chamber, ca 0.2 m above the floor.

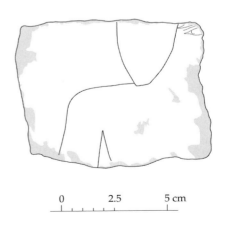

---

[3] Verner, *Khentkaus*, 63–78.

Fragment of the left hand of a statue (the forearm, back of the hand, and thumb – *fig. 2.18*). The surface of the fragments is smoothly polished and the details have been carefully done. The fragment, bearing no traces of the polychromy, comes from the left forearm (from the hand survived only the thumb) of a standing female statue – very probably the statue of the tomb owner.[4]

Fragment of a statue
17/M/87
Travertine
L: 8 cm, H: 4.4 cm, W: 2.1 cm
Fifth Dynasty
Found on the floor of the courtyard in front of entrance to the mastaba, ca 3 m to the east from it.

A fragment of an ankle of a left foot, polished surface (*fig. 2.19*).

Model of a basin
4/M/87
Clay
L: 7.5 cm, H: 4.5 cm, W: 5.2 cm
Found in the storeroom in the south-western corner of the mastaba, on the floor in the south-eastern corner of the room, below the layer of the mudbrick destruction and limestone detritus.

The model (*figs. 2.20–2.21*) is made of fine clay, its outer wall polished and whitewashed. There is a break fracturing the model into two parts. Along the fractures, the model is partly damaged. Due to the damage, a part of the basin is missing.

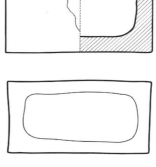

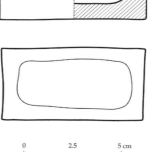

Fragment of a bowl
5/M/87
Gabbro
L: 7.5 cm, max. H: 3.2. cm, W of the rim: 0.7 cm
Fifth Dynasty

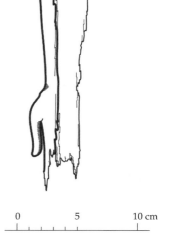

Fig. 2.18 Fragment of a wooden statue.

Fig. 2.19 Fragment of a travertine statue 17/M/87.

Fig. 2.20 Clay model of a basin.
Photo JB

Fig. 2.21 Clay model of a basin.

---

[4] In relation to the form of the statue's hand, it is more probable that it was a part of a female statue rather than that of a man: the hand was hanging freely alongside the body; the fingers were not clenched into a fist, and the hand does not hold any object (staff, *etc.*). Among examples which can be considered as analogies to our example from Nebtyemneferes' mastaba we can enumerate catalogue numbers published by J. Harvey in her *Wooden Statues*: A7, A 30–32; B1. For other finds of wooden statues in the area of the southern part of the Abusir Pyramid Necropolis see: Verner, Callender, *Djedkare's Cemetery*, 74–76 and Benešovská, in Verner *et al.*, *Raneferef*, 405–425. For general issues concerning the dating of wooden statues, see: J. Harvey, Old Kingdom Wooden Statues: Stylistic Dating Criteria, in: *L'art de l'Ancien Empire égyptien*, 355–379.

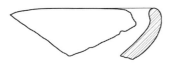

Fig. 2.22 Fragment of a gabbro bowl.

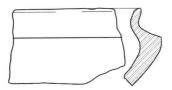

Fig. 2.23 Fragment of a diorite bowl.

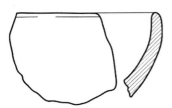

Fig. 2.24 Fragment of a travertine miniature bowl.

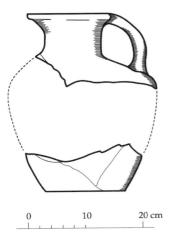

0   10   20 cm

Fig. 2.25 Jug-like pottery vessel.

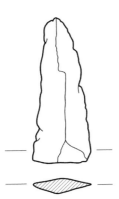

Fig. 2.26 Flint blade.

Found in the storeroom in the north-western corner of the mastaba, on the floor in the centre of the room, below the mudbrick destruction and limestone detritus.

A fragment of a bowl with a slightly shrinking back rim and a well polished surface (*fig. 2.22*).

A fragment of a bowl
9/M/87
Diorite
max. L: 6 cm, max. H: 4 cm, W of the rim: 0.4 cm (max. W of the bowl's wall 1.2 cm)
Fifth Dynasty
Found on the surface of the terrain, during the survey in the area of the south-western corner of the mastaba.

A fragment of a carinated bowl with re-curved rim (*fig. 2.23*). Surface of the bowl has been polished.

A fragment of a bowl
10/M/87
Travertine
L: 2 cm, H: 2.4 cm, W of the bowl's rim: 0.25 cm (max. W of the bowl's wall is 0.4 cm)
Fifth Dynasty
Found on the surface of the terrain, during the survey in the area of the south-western corner of the mastaba.

A miniature bowl with a rounded bottom (*fig. 2.24*). Surface of the bowl has been polished.

Jug
11/M/87
Red burned pottery
frg. 1: diam. of mouth: 7.5–12.5 cm, H: 9 cm
frg. 2: diam. of the bottom: 14 cm, H: 8 cm
Old Kingdom ?, Late Period ?
Found in the burial chamber, around south-eastern corner of the sarcophagus in the sandy layer on the floor of the chamber. In the proximity, several fragments of fabric were found.

Fragments of a jug-like pottery vessel, the mouth of the vessel is outwards opened, the spout is only slightly indicated (*fig. 2.25*). Bottom of the jug was flat. The surface of the vessel was coarsened.

Blade
6/M/87 (*fig. 2.26*)
Flint
L: 4.7, max. W: 1.8 cm, max. thickness: 0.5 cm
Fifth Dynasty
Found in the storeroom in the north-western corner of the mastaba, in the centre of the room, on the floor, below the layer of the mudbrick destruction and limestone detritus.

Blades
15/M/87a, b (*fig. 2.27*)
Flint
a) L: 5.8 cm, W: 3 cm, max. thickness: 0.55 cm
b) L: 6.3 cm, W: 1 cm, max. thickness: 0.3 cm
Fifth Dynasty

Found ca 2 m to the east and 2 m to the south from the entrance to the mastaba, in the layer of the mudbrick destruction.

On contrary to the neighbouring monuments, especially to the mortuary complex of King Raneferef[5], but also Khentkaus' II[6] the number of flint blades is low. Only three blades were found during the archaeological excavations of the Mastaba of Nebtyemneferes. In one case, we recognize blade endscraper (15/M/87a) with trapezoid section. Other two examples, 6/M/87 and 15/M/87b, represents the most frequent flint blade form in Abusir Pyramid Necropolis with pointed striking edge (and in the case of 6/M/2008 with lateral retouches). Due to the place where the flint blades were found, it is not possible to say whether they were a part of the burial equipment of the tomb owner, or whether they were used during the cultic practice in the aboveground part of the mastaba.

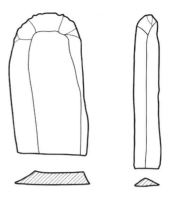

Fig. 2.27 Flint blades 15/M/87a–b.

2.5. Conclusions

Despite the fact that we know her name, unfortunately, the archaeological excavations of her mastaba did not bring a direct answer concerning the social rank of Nebtyemneferes. Investigations into the epigraphic and mainly archaeological material obtained from the tomb have enabled us to estimate the date and the social rank of the tomb owner. Ironically, Nebtyemneferes' mastaba is the only tomb among other minor tombs discussed in this volume attributable to a identifiable person. In other cases, even in regard to the mastaba "Q" attributed to Prince Nakhtsare the association of the monuments to known persons is not fully certain.

The name of Nebtyemneferes – *Nbty-m-nfr.ś* ('Her beauty is from the Nebty') itself seems to be linguistically important. Even though the name is not attested in other instances in the epigraphical material coming from the Old Kingdom, it is one of a handful of names[7] including the *nbty* element. The element *nbty* – referring for Two Ladies, but more probably directly for the king himself[8] – is an element which can almost exclusively link Nebtyemneferes to the royal family, following the opinion of H. G. Fischer it is a strong indication of such a link. This conclusion can be also made through another possible reading of the supposed tombowner. Following the rules of the ancient Egyptian grammar and having in mind that in this case the element nebty was written first because of honorific transposition (the name's allusion to the divine being(s) – Wadjet with Nekhbet or the king), *Nebty* can be read in several ways. The woman's name can be read as: *M-nfr.ś-nbty*.[9] In her article on the unusual names of the royal ladies living during the Fifth Dynasty, Vivienne Callender reads the same name as *Nfr.ś-m-nbty* – "Her beauty is from the Nebty".[10] Nevertheless, we can also translate the name as follows: "Her beauty is of the Nebty", or even: "Her beauty is Nebty". This reading is no doubt connected with the two tutelary goddesses of Upper and Lower Egypt, the king's crown and the king himself as well.[11] It should be also underlined here that the name *Nbty-m-nfr.ś* / *M-nfr.ś-nbty* / *Nfr.ś-m-nbty* is not attested in Ranke's *Personennamen*. Are there any other clues that might strengthen this connection to the royal family?

One important clue seems to be the location of the tomb. The mastaba is located amid of the tombs and pyramid complexes certainly owned by members of the royal family; especially significant might have been its tomb-owner's connection with the owner of the pyramid Lepsius no. 24 because of its close

---

[5] J. A. Svoboda, in: Verner *et al.*, *Raneferef*, 502–510.

[6] *Op. cit.*, 509.

[7] Ranke, *PN*, 423, 22–23.

[8] *Cf.* H. G. Fischer, *NBTY in Old-Kingdom titles and names*, *JEA* 60, 1970, 98.

[9] Cf. Ranke, *PN*, 143.

[10] V. G. Callender, Curious Names of 5th Dynasty Royal Women (in preparation).

[11] H. G. Fischer, *Egyptian Women of the Old Kingdom and of the Heracleopolitan Period*, New York 1989, 18–19.

proximity, however, the same can be said with in connection with Werkaure's mastaba (Lepsius' pyramid no. 23).[12] Beside these elements, the tomb includes some features which are also attested in these tombs – but it must also be admitted that some of these features can appear in some of the non-royal tombs of the period, *i.e.*, of the mid-Fifth Dynasty: the groundplan of the burial apartment accessible through the descending corridor as well as the layout of the mastaba's superstructure with the central vestibule.

It is interesting that the architecture of the Mastaba of Nebtyemneferes includes features of both main groups of tombs in the central cemeteries in Abusir. We note, first of all that the plan of Nebtyemneferes' tomb resembles the ground plans of several other tombs in Abusir pyramid cemetery in its central part, especially those of Djadjaemankh[13] and of the first building stage (the Initial Mastaba) of the Mastaba of Ptahshepses.[14] This tomb is in the Cemetery of Nobles and is located to the east from the Niuserre's pyramid, where it lies on the southern edge of the royal necropolis. A high degree of similarity can also be found in the case of the tombs in Djedkare's family cemetery[15] labelled by M. Verner as Type-I tombs:[16] *i.e.* Hedjetnebu's, Khekeretnebty's (in this latter case, we refer to the original appearance of the tomb) and Neserkauhor's mastabas in addition to the anonymous tomb L. In all these instances, the entrance to each tomb – located in its eastern façade – was followed by a vestibule. This space gave access to other rooms located to the north (a magazine or in the case of Nebtyemneferes' tomb two magazines) and south (with serdab and offering chapel). Moreover, the substructure of the Mastaba of Nebtyemneferes, with its massive central pillar, resembles the subterranean part of the tomb of Ptahshepses Junior II,[17] as well as the layout of burial chambers in the Mastabas of Princesses[18] and of Userkafankh.[19]

Nebtyemneferes' burial apartment was accessible by means of a descending corridor. Both the layout of the burial chamber and way in which the access to it was designed lay in strict contrast to the examples of the tombs from Djedkare's Family Cemetery: their burial chambers consisted of simple north–south oriented rooms accessible by means of vertical shafts.[20]

In contrast to the situation with the layout of the main burial chamber, Nebtyemneferes' tomb resembles the Type-I tombs of Djedkare's Family Cemetery in that it has a false shaft in south-western part of the mastaba. This feature, which was also included in the tomb of Ptahshepses Junior II located in front of the entrance to the Mastaba of the Vizier Ptahshepses at Abusir[21] has also been documented in other archaeological sites in the Memphite Necropolis. These false shafts very probably served as storage for what remained after process of mummification of tomb owner's corpse and/or of the funerary banquet.[22] Nevertheless, following the opinion of M. Bárta, the false shafts may have been proposed to deceive the tomb robbers in their plan to plunder the burial chamber.[23]

---

[12] Results of the excavation of this tomb shall be included in the next volume of the present monograph.

[13] Borchardt, *Neuserre*, Bl. 22.

[14] Jánosi, in: *Abusir and Saqqara 2000*, 456, Abb.5; Krejčí, *Ptahshepses*, 37–38.

[15] Jánosi, „Im Schatten der Pyramiden" Die Mastabas in Abusir. Einige Beobachtungen zum Grabbau der 5. Dynastie, in: *Abusir and Saqqara 2000*, 451; Verner, Callender, *Djedkare's Cemetery*, 113.

[16] Verner, Callender, *Djedkare's Cemetery*, 109–117.

[17] Bárta, *Ä&L* 10, 2000, 56, 62, fig. 2.

[18] Borchardt, *Neuserre*, Blatt 25.

[19] *Op. cit.*, Blatt 22.

[20] *Cf.* Verner, Callender, *Djedkare's Cemetery, passim*.

[21] Bárta, *Ä&L* 10, 2001, 55, fig. 2.

[22] *Cf.* T. Rzeuska, The Necropolis at West Saqqara: The Late Old Kingdom Shafts with no Burial Chamber. Were they False, Dummy, Unfinished or Intentional?, in: *Abusir and Saqqara 2001*, 402; Verner, Callender, *Djedkare's Cemetery*, 115–116: authors of this monograph called the false shafts "subsidiary shafts".

[23] Bárta, *Ä&L* 10, 2000, 61.

Having in our mind the horizontal stratigraphy of the site, it seems that the tomb was very probably built *after* the erection of the Tomb Complex Lepsius no. 25 and Pyramid Complex Lepsius no. 24, and *before* the construction of the tomb in the cemetery of members of Djedkare's family: older monuments lie closer to the nucleus of the pyramid necropolis than the tomb of Nebtyemneferes. As was already indicated above, this conclusion follows from the examination of the ground plan and architectural features used in the mastaba. Whereas the ground plan of Nebtyemneferes' mastaba is similar to that of the tombs belonging to the members of Djedkare's family, its substructure is equivalent (with the entrance corridor and a massive central pillar in the burial chamber) to the older tombs built in the Abusir necropolis. We can, therefore, give a relative date to Nebtyemneferes' tomb: to the concluding part of Niuserre's reign, or even to the lesser-known period of Menkauhor.

3. The Mastaba of Nakhtsare

3.1. History of exploration of the Mastaba of Nakhtsare

A mastaba tomb, marked in our archaeological map of Abusir as "Q", lies in the close vicinity of the Pyramid Complex of Raneferef,[1] east of the enclosure wall of the latter and south of the slaughterhouse adjoined to the king's mortuary temple. The distance of the mastaba's enclosure wall from the enclosure wall of Raneferef's complex is 2.20 m and from the slaughterhouse only 0.50 m (*fig. 3.1*). At the same time, the mastaba lies at the northern edge of a row of four tombs running in the north–south direction and representing the southernmost part of the Abusir pyramid plateau.

Fig. 3.1 Archaeological plan of the Mastaba of Nakhtsare.

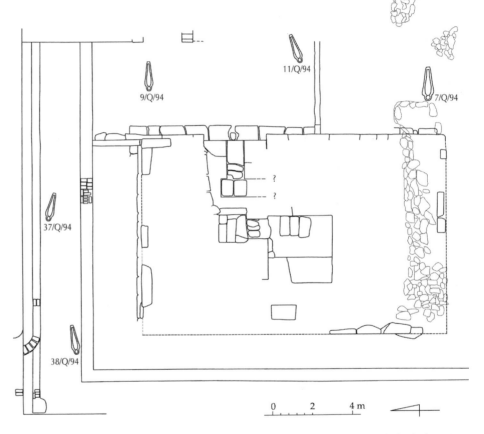

Prior to excavation, the area with the aforesaid row of tombs[2], belonging hypothetically to members of Raneferef's family or to his courtiers, was neither examined in a more detailed way nor surveyed by geophysical means. The tomb of Nakhtsare was explored during the autumn 1994, during the same season as work took place on the Pyramid Complex Lepsius no. 24.[3]

---

[1] See M. Verner *et al.*, *Raneferef*.

[2] We can see the mounds of this group of mastabas as in the map of Lepsius, de Morgan and Maragioglio and Rinaldi. However, any of these authors did not aim any attention to these tombs.

[3] In the field work took part M. Verner, J. Krejčí, L. Bareš, B. Patočková, N. Math (Vienna University) and M. Zemina. The SCA was represented by the inspectors Ezzat el-Gindi and Ramadan Hashim, headmen of the workmen were *reis* Mohamed Tallal el-Kereti and Ahmad el-Kereti; see also the report by M. Verner, Excavations at Abusir. Seasons of 1994/95 and 1995/96, *ZÄS* 124, 1997, 89–90.

3.2. Description of the mastaba

3.2.1. Situation prior to the excavation

Before exploration began, the monument appeared to be only one meter high. On the surface, it was a north–south oriented mound of grey sand mixed with limestone rubble. The mound was ca 28 m long and ca 23 m broad and in its middle was a shallow depression filled with wind blown sand. The height of the mound rose to about 1 to 1.5 m above the terrain of the desert. On the rest of the surface lay scattered several fragments of limestone, red granite and basalt. Compared to other parts of the Abusir pyramid plateau, the surface of the mound displayed very few potsherds. Importantly from the stratigraphic point of view, the aforesaid rubble was superimposed on a layer of drift sand lying at the level of the extant crown of the southern wall of the slaughterhouse.

3.2.2. Unearthing the mastaba

The extant top of the mastaba's superstructure lay under this layer of wind blown sand, the thickness of which fluctuated from 0.70 to 2.70 m (*fig. 3.2 a–b*). The highest point of the extant masonry lay 1.82 m above the floor level of the entrance to the mastaba. Some parts of the superstructure were quarried away down to the level of the foundation of the walls.

The unearthing of the mastaba commenced from its north-east corner. In this area, there occurred besides the relatively numerous fragments of red granite and quartzite also a few fragments of travertine. The layers of rubble here lay on the layers of drift sand. This fact indicates that the mastaba had been devastated in several stages separated by long spaces of time.

The precise dating for this first looting of the tomb is rather difficult to judge, but it may date from the First Intermediate Period, as is the case with the Abusir pyramids.[4] Destruction of the tomb, however, very probably begun not before the New Kingdom as we can see in the neighbouring mortuary temple of Raneferef. The earliest destruction wave seems to be represented by a deep crater, the bottom

Fig. 3.2a The area of the Mastaba of Nakhtsare at the beginning of the archaeological excavation. Photo JK

of which lay in above the original burial chamber. A thick layer of drift sand in the crater showed that the looted tomb had been left open for quite a long period of time. A sherd of a Late Period jar found in the vertical shaft giving access to the burial chamber may provide the date for the second major wave of the tomb's devastation: this would correspond with the quarrying of stone in the nearby tomb

---

[4] *Cf.* Bareš, in: *Abusir and Saqqara 2000*, and Di. Arnold, Zur Zerstörungsgeschichte der Pyramiden, *MDAIK* 47, 1991, 21–27.

complexes, Lepsius no. 24 and 25. This is likely to have occurred during the Late Period, before the time when the secondary cemeteries started to arise in this area of the Abusir Necropolis.[5]

The third period of activity in the area of the mastaba was linked with a layer of grey sand mixed with fragments of limestone, ca 2.70 m above the floor level of the entrance to the tomb. The layer rested above the eastern part of the mastaba and the open courtyard in front of the latter's eastern façade. Apparently, in this place the limestone blocks from not only the mastaba but also from the adjacent tomb complexes, Lepsius no. 24 and 25, were cut into smaller pieces by stone robbers. The precise dating of this layer is not quite apparent. Judging indirectly by the chronology of the surrounding tombs and pyramid complexes, it could have occurred at any time from the late Roman to the early Christian periods.

Stratigraphically very important was the narrow space between the northern wall of the mastaba and the southern wall of the slaughterhouse of Raneferef's pyramid complex. The bottom part of the fill of this space formed an ashy-clay layer of detritus, with frequent occurrences of beer jars, bread moulds and stands. The layer also contained sherds of Meidum pottery,[6] fragments of clay sealings, flint blades, animal bones, *etc*. Obviously, the aforesaid objects largely represented the detritus from Raneferef's mortuary temple and the slaughterhouse. On the bottom rested a thick layer, about one metre deep, of wind blown sand and on this alone was superimposed a layer of rubble pertaining to the destruction of the mastaba. The stratigraphy of the space between the mastaba and the slaughterhouse thus corroborates the conclusion that, between the construction of the mastaba and its destruction, quite a long period of time had elapsed.

In spite of the extensive devastation of the mastaba, in the fill of the remains of its masonry were found many artefacts coming from the original burial

Fig. 3.2b The area of the Mastaba of Nakhtsare during the archaeological excavation.
Photo MZ

---

[5] Due to the repeated attacks of tomb robbers and stone robbers in the area of Nakhtsare's tomb, we can not to date this destruction more precisely. M. Verner is of a different opinion – he supposes that the main destruction of the royal monuments in the southern part of the Abusir Pyramid Necropolis fell victim to the construction of Saite-Persian shaft tombs located to the south-west from the pyramid necropolis – see Verner *et al.*, *Raneferef*, 111–112. The south-west direction of the layers of rubble from the smashed masonry blocks seems to support this conclusion, too.

[6] As it has been already mentioned, pottery finds shall be discussed in the second volume of this monograph.

equipment. Most of the artefacts were found in the bottom levels of the burial shaft as well as around its preserved mouth in the rubble covering the northern part of the monument (see *fig. 3.3*). The distribution of artefacts inside the space of the mastaba thus indicates that an important part of the burial equipment had been removed from the burial chamber via the shaft and this took place only during the devastation of the monument. However, the arrangement of the artefacts seems to suggest that there had been an earlier wave of robbery that took place in the burial chamber: this robbery supposedly focused on the most precious artefacts and must have preceded the devastation of the mastaba. We can show it through the location of items belonging to the burial equipment (in the passage between the burial chamber and the shaft, bottom of the shaft and in area around the preserved mouth of the shaft). Their distribution documents that the tomb robbers used still complete internal space of the mastaba. Importantly, both in the burial chamber and in other parts of the mastaba, no physical remains of the tomb owner were found. We can only surmise that the robbers, in search of precious artefacts put directly on the body, took the latter out of the burial chamber and "examined" it in the daylight.

In the upper levels of the shaft filling and on the northern and southern side of the mastaba were found several secondary burials (see below in this chapter and also *chapter 6.*). The fact that these burials found in the shaft were damaged and not in a correct anatomical position further corroborates the previously mentioned multiple devastation of the mastaba.

Fig. 3.3 A model offering (28/Q/94) as found in the area of the burial chamber.
Photo JK

Fig. 3.4 An overall view of the mastaba.
Photo JK

3.2.3. Superstructure
3.2.3.1. The masonry

The mastaba has an oblong, north–south oriented plan that is 15.10 m long and 10.10 m wide (ca 30 × 20 cubits). The casing of the mastaba formed large (up to 2.50 × 1.00 × 0.90 m) blocks of fine white limestone, the face of which was carefully smoothed (*fig. 3.4*). The blocks were joined by means of a pink lime mortar. As is the case of the adjacent Pyramid Complex Lepsius no. 24, for example, the core masonry of this tomb was built of small chunks of local grey limestone only superficially joined together (with a very low usage, if any, of muddy mortar) and with free spaces between the stone even filled with sand.[7] The foundation of the mastaba casing, as shown in the parts devastated by the stone robbers, consisted of a thick layer of large flat white limestone blocks (ca 0.50 m) embedded in a layer of grey sand mixed with fragments of mudbricks and potsherds ca 1–1.20 m thick. The limestone foundation platform overlapped the mastaba's superstructure by ca 0.35 m. The sandy foundation layer also supported the core masonry of the mastaba (*figs. 3.5* and *3.6*).

The ground level of the mastaba corresponded with the upper surface of the limestone foundation blocks and, at the same time, the floor level in the entrance to the tomb. The face of the eastern side of the mastaba was inclined at an angle of 80° 30´– 82°, that of the southern wall of 81° 30´.

3.2.3.2. Offering chapel and its entrance

The entrance to the mastaba lies approximately in one third of the length of the eastern façade, ca 4.50 m south of the north-east corner of the tomb. The entrance was formed by a niche (3.08 × 0.25–0.28 m) and a 0.79 m wide passage which

Fig. 3.5 A view of the section through the core masonry and foundation layer of the mastaba (the burial shaft in the foreground and the vertical shaft on the right). Photo JK

Fig. 3.6 A view of the section through the core masonry and foundation layer of the mastaba (to the west from the area of the burial chamber). Photo JK

---

[7] See p. 91.

**Fig. 3.7 The area of
destroyed offering chapel.**
Photo JK

survived to a length of only 1.07 m. Originally, the passage might have been up
to 2 m long – as shown by the traces in the extant pavement. Unfortunately, only a
small piece of the pavement in the northern part of the chapel survived (*fig. 3.7*). The
fragments of the masonry of the room indicate that it was an L-shaped type of the
chapel with its false door in the southern part of the western wall.[8] This supposition
also seems to correspond with the position of the burial chamber, because the burial
chamber was nearly always located behind or in the vicinity of the false door. The
extant fragments of the chapel enable us to estimate that it was ca 5.50 m long and
1 m wide.

It is important to mention that as it is the case with Lepsius no. 24 and no. 25, no
relief decoration was not detected on the surviving parts of the chapel's walls.[9]

3.2.3.3. Substructure
3.2.3.3.1. Vertical descending shaft

The shaft to the burial chamber lay in the northern part of the mastaba, ca 3.85
m from the eastern and 4.10 m from the northern face of the tomb. The walls of the
shaft, largely devastated by stone robbers, were built of grey limestone ashlars (*fig.*

---

[8] Reisner, *Giza Necropolis* I, 8.
[9] Such situation existed, *e.g.*, in the case of Khekeretnebty's tomb in Djedkare's Family
Cemetery, see Verner, Callender, *Djedkare's Cemetery*, 77–84, figs. F1–F7, pls. XIX Ff1–Ff2, XX
Ff3–Ff4.

Fig. 3.9 A fragment of a bovine skull found in the bottom levels of the burial shaft.
Photo JK

Fig. 3.8 The partially destroyed burial shaft from the south.
Photo JK

3.8). The bottom of the shaft lay 3.50 m below the ground level of the mastaba. On one of the blocks in the bottom part of the western wall of the shaft was revealed a cursive inscription in red paint reading *s3 nśwt Nḫt-s3-R^c* (see the discussion on p. 65). In the lower portion of the shaft were revealed some artefacts left here by the robbers and a fragment of a bovine skull, that had been put upon a 0.40 m thick layer of fine limestone rubble, which may refer to a rite during the burial ceremony (*fig. 3.9*).[10]

The entrance to the burial chamber opened out from the bottom of the southern wall of the shaft.[11] The entrance, ca 1 m wide and 1 m deep, was blocked by a

Fig. 3.10 Burial shaft and the passage connecting it with the burial chamber (view from the east).
Photo MZ

---

[10] See the similar situation in the Mastaba of Princess Khekeretnebty – Verner, Callender, *Djedkare's Cemetery*, 19, Bf3. On contrary to Nakhtsare's tomb, the offering of a gazelle was put in the princess' shaft.

[11] *Cf.*, for example situation in Khekeretnebty's burial shaft – *loc. cit.*

Fig. 3.11 Burial shaft and the
passage connecting it with
the burial chamber (view
from the north).
Photo MZ

(largely damaged) wall built of limestone fragments and clay mortar (*figs. 3.10–
3.11*). However, due to the disturbance of the masonry in the shaft and the entrance
doorway to the burial chamber, the ceiling of the doorway did not survive. We
can only assume that it was constructed to a height of ca 1 m (this reading would
correspond with the width of the doorway). We can classify the shaft as Reisner's
Type 1b.[12]

3.2.3.3.2. Burial chamber

As will be obvious from the previous description, the burial chamber lay
south of the shaft. The entrance from the vertical shaft was located at the eastern
end of the chamber's northern wall. This chamber, too, was largely damaged
by stone robbers. Though only small parts of the chamber's masonry survived
(a part of the western wall formed by a large limestone block see *figs. 3.1* and
3.12), it seems that the north–south oriented chamber was originally 3.15 m long
and 2.10 m wide. Unfortunately, the height of the chamber is uncertain. The
masonry survived only up to a height of 1.25 m. Paved by flat limestone blocks,
the floor of the burial chamber lay 2.71 m below the pavement of the chapel.
We suppose that the side walls of the burial chamber were also lined – with
large, finely worked and smoothed blocks of white limestone. Unfortunately,
due to the large scale disturbance of the area of the burial chamber and the very

---

[12] Reisner, *Giza Necropolis* I, 87–88, 92.

**Fig. 3.12 A large limestone
block forming a part of the
western wall
of the burial chamber.**
Photo MZ

dangerous situation in its western half, it was not possible to excavate fully
the area of the chamber. If there were any sarcophagus fragments, these were
not unearthed because of the dangerous conditions in the tomb. No fragment
of any sarcophagus was found during the excavation (it is probable that the
sarcophagus, however, was one of the main targets for the stone robbers in the
area of the mastaba). We suppose that it would have been placed in the western
part of the chamber.

3.2.3.4. Open courtyard

Along nearly the entire eastern wall of the mastaba extended an open courtyard
(9.50 × 2.25 m) surrounded by an enclosure wall of mudbrick. Additionally, two
more mudbrick walls were built onto the mastaba. One wall, on the northern side
of the tomb, was built on a layer of roughly worked blocks of limestone and its
purpose was to contain the detritus and sand accumulated between the mastaba
and the slaughterhouse. Another mudbrick wall built in the southern part of the
courtyard had the same purpose – to prevent falling of rubbish and sand piling up
in the southern part of the courtyard.

The 1.90 m broad entrance to the courtyard lay opposite to the north-east corner
of the mastaba. Its position was probably due to a need to facilitate an easier
communication with the surrounding tombs and pyramid complexes namely, but
also with the temples of Raneferef and Khentkaus II.[13]

The floor of the courtyard was made of beaten clay and had been repeatedly
coated with a thin layer of mud. On the floor, along the foundation of the mastaba,
ran a 5.0–6.5 cm wide white stripe (in the north, the line was 1.07 m long, in the
south it was 2.45 m; it seems that the lines were originally longer, in the time of the

---

[13] We can suggest that to the east of the Mastaba of Nakhtsare, there was a passage delimited
on its eastern side by the tomb complexes Lepsius no. 25 and 24 on the east side and by
(supposed) continuation of the eastern wall of the courtyard of the mastaba. If the situation
in case of other three tombs laying to the south of Nakhtsare's mastaba is same, then we
can suppose that supposed passage gave access also to these tombs, also through entrances
located in the east walls of their open courtyards.

archaeological excavations their larger parts have already fainted) terminated by two short (12 and 13 cm long) white lines perpendicular to the face of the mastaba (*fig. 3.13*). These short lines were not matching with the edges of the entrance to the mastaba chapel. In front of the entrance (0.79 m), the lines marked an area which was broader (1.31 m) than the wideness of the entrance. The precise meaning of these white stripes and lines is not readily explicable. We can only hypothesize that

Fig. 3.13 The north-western part of the mastaba's courtyard with the entrance to the mastaba and white stripes on the floor.
Photo MZ

they were important during the rituals running in the courtyard; *e.g.*, they might have been used as a kind of markers during rituals (processions, *etc.*).

The open court was buried under a thick, in some places up to 2.75 m high layer of drift sand. On this sand rested a layer of limestone rubble, attesting that the limestone blocks had once been cut up here by the stone robbers. No potsherds, ash or any other sort of detritus were found on the floor of the court, which seems to indicate that the court must have been regularly cleaned. This feature may underline the meaning of the courtyard as a place in which some funerary cult ceremonies had regularly occurred. In contrast to the courtyard in front of Khekeretnebty's tomb, no additional installation which might have been used during rituals was erected in front of the Mastaba of Nakhtsare.[14]

3.2.3.5. Enclosure wall

As previously mentioned, the enclosure wall was built of mudbrick and it lay 2.30 m far from the northern and 1.80 m from the western face of the mastaba (see *figs. 3.1* and *3.14–3.15*). Since the area south and east of the mastaba was not excavated, the precise positions of the southern and eastern wings of the enclosure wall remain unknown.

---

[14] See note 9.

Fig. 3.14 Overall view of the
mastaba with its enclosure
wall as well as other
mudbrick masonry.
Photo JK

Fig. 3.16 Dismantled
original rounded corner of
the protection wall along
the outer walls of the Ritual
Slaughterhouse.
Photo JK

>Fig. 3.17 View of the area
between the enclosure of
the Mastaba of Nakhtsare
and the outer wall of the
Ritual Slaughterhouse.
Photo JK

Due to the architectural development of Raneferef's mortuary complex[15] the shape of the protection wall along the outer walls had been radically changed at the time when the masonry of the *Ḥwt-nmt* and the Early Temple were connected.[16] The originally rounded south-west corner of this wall was dismantled and only about 5–10 cm high remains of the original masonry of the wall which once connected the reconstructed southern outer wall of the Ritual Slaughterhouse and the eastern wing of the court around Raneferef's Unfinished Pyramid (*figs. 3.16–3.17*) remained *in situ*.

[15] Verner, in: Verner, *et al.*, *Raneferef*, 100–112.
[16] Krejčí, in: Verner *et al.*, *Raneferef*, 125–126, Verner, *op. cit.*, 88, 105–106.

Mudbrick	Size	Material	Bonding[17]
Enclosure wall of the mastaba	0.29 × 0.13 × 0.08 m	Brown-greyish clay mixed with fine limestone rubble	A2(1)
Protection wall around the slaughterhouse (southern wing)	0.36 × 0.14–0.20 × 0.08–0.09 m	Brown-greyish clay mixed with sand	A1(1)
Wall between the north-east corner of the mastaba and the enclosure wall	0.26 × 0.123 × 0.08 m	Brown-greyish clay mixed with fine limestone rubble	Irregular, a layer of small limestone blocks has been used
Southern wing of the wall of the courtyard	0.26 × 0.12 × 0.06 m	Brown-greyish clay mixed with fine limestone rubble	A1(1)
Walls of the entrance to the courtyard	0.39 × 0.135 × 0.08 m	Brown-greyish clay mixed with sands	A2

Table 3.1 shows the fact that the enclosure walls of the mastaba and of the open courtyard were not built in the same period. We can suppose that the enclosure wall around the mastaba was built first.[18] An interesting fact is that mudbricks used for the construction of the eastern wall of the mastaba's courtyard are rather different from those used in the enclosure wall. It thus encourages us to suppose that they were built in different moments of time.[19] There is no clue as to which of these two masonries was older. Two walls reducing the extent of the courtyard were built apparently after some period of its use. The wall between the north-east corner of the mastaba and the enclosure wall was built on a layer of small limestone and roughly worked blocks which levelled up the base of the wall. This base layer corresponded to the height of the waste layer originating during the cultic use of the mastaba and its courtyard. Even though the formats of bricks used for the construction of these two walls are not same, we cannot to fully eliminate the premise that the walls were built in the same period.

Tab. 3.1
Mudbrick masonry from the area of Nakhtsare's mastaba.

3.3. Secondary burials in the area of Nakhtsare's mastaba

As was already mentioned, the burial of the tomb owner was not found: apparently, it had been destroyed (it is pointless to date a disarticulated burial 12/Q/94 which had been found in the burial shaft of the Old Kingdom tomb, following the find of an ostracon dated to the Fifth Dynasty) in antiquity. Nevertheless, several secondary burials datable to the Late and Graeco-Roman Period were unearthed in the area of the mastaba and around it (see *fig. 3.1* and *chapter 6*). It is apparent that the secondary burials from area "Q" formed one of the secondary cemeteries which started to originate in the Late Period. This cemetery lasted in the southern part of the Abusir Pyramid Necropolis[20] till the end of the Roman Period.

Disarticulated human remains **4/Q/94** were found in the layer of blown sand. The remains were originally placed in the now almost totally destroyed wooden coffin. The coffin, made of massive planks, was oriented along a general east–west axis, with the head of the coffin being in the west. It is apparent that the coffin had an anthropoid form. Parts of the coffin and the corpse of the deceased were found scattered over an area of 3.20 × 0.40 m, but only small bones and small fragments of bandages impregnated with resin were preserved. The coffin was painted (remains of a blue colour were detected). The remains of the coffin cover revealed that it had

---

[17] For the list of the individual mudbrick bondings, see Spencer, *Brick Architecture*, Pls. no. 1–20 (*Corpus of brick bonds*).

[18] It is possible that structural change of the Ritual Slaughterhouse's protection wall precede the construction of the enclosure wall of Nakhtsare's mastaba.

[19] Unfortunately, it was not possible, due to the complex dangerous archaeological situation to study thoroughly join between the enclosure wall of the mastaba and the eastern wall of the mastaba's open courtyard.

[20] Strouhal, Bareš, *Secondary Cemetery*.

once been 10 cm high, and the trough of the coffin had been 15 cm high and 34–40 cm broad.

The secondary burial **9/Q/94** was found in the layer of yellow blown sand in the area of south-eastern corner of the mastaba, on the level of the preserved crown of the enclosure wall around Raneferef's Unfinished Pyramid. As is the case of 4/Q/94, the burial is badly damaged. These human remains had also been laid within a wooden coffin. No burial equipment was found during the unearthing of the burial. This anthropoid coffin was oriented along the east–west (head) axis. The corpse had been laid down in an extended position, with hands resting on thighs. The coffin was 1.52 m long and maximally 0.48 m broad. The burial pit (traces of which were not discernible during the archaeological excavations) was along its southern side, lined with smaller fragments of local limestone. Nonetheless, the head part of the coffin was devastated. Similar limestone fragments were also found below the coffin. However, it is not clear whether they were laid down in this position intentionally or whether these limestone fragments were part of an older destruction.

The heavily damaged secondary burial **10/Q/94** was found in the layer of yellow blown sand, above the eastern wing of the enclosure wall of the mastaba, ca 0.4 m above the preserved north-eastern corner of the mastaba. Only a few remains of the wooden coffin were found. The burial was oriented along the eastern–western axis with the head of the deceased in the west. The corpse was laid out in an extended position, with hands crossed on the chest (the right hand above the left hand). In the close vicinity of the burial an arybalos (11/Q/94 – for the dating of the vessel, see below) was found. We can only suppose that it was a part of the original equipment of this secondary burial. It is thus possible to estimate a date for the burial of 10/Q/94 to the late Roman Period.

Another heavily damaged secondary burial **12/Q/94** was found in the layer of larger limestone blocks and grey sand filling the burial shaft and 0.80 m below the preserved crown of the eastern wall of the shaft. Bones of the deceased were found in disarticulated positions. Among the bones, there were small fragments of a wooden coffin (its original form and its orientation was not possible to reconstruct). It is apparent that the burial was not found in its original position. In the same level, the ostracon 3/Q/1994 dated to the Old Kingdom (see below) was found. Unfortunately, to use this ostracon for the more precise dating of 12/Q/94 is not possible.

The better preserved secondary burial **37/Q/94** (see *figs. 3.18–3.19*) was found to the east from the north-east corner of the mastaba, 1.30 m from the eastern enclosure

Fig. 3.18 Secondary burial 37/Q/94 from the north.
Photo JK

Fig. 3.19 Remains of face part of the cartonnage above the corpse of the secondary burial 37/Q/94.
Photo JK

wall of the courtyard, 9.70 m to the south from the southern outer wall of the Ritual Slaughterhouse and 0.70 m below the preserved crown of this wall. The deceased was lying in an outstretched position, with hand crossed on the chest (right hand above the left hand); its head was to the west, the toes pointing east (with a slight deflection to the south-east). The corpse was wrapped in bandages and was decorated with a colourful cartonnage headpiece. The face of the cartonnage was painted with rose colour for the flesh and partly gilded. The wig had additions in gilding and blue. The cartonnage also included a *mnḫ*-collar with golden ornamentation. There were also tiny remains of the cartonnage in the area of the soles of the feet, which were decorated with blue and golden stripes. Needless to say, the cartonnage as well as the wooden coffin (covered by a layer of stucco) were in a very bad state of preservation. This secondary burial can be dated to the Late or Ptolemaic Period.

Fig. 3.20 Secondary burial 38/Q/94 – upper part of the body before removing of tiny remains of the cartonnage.
Photo JK

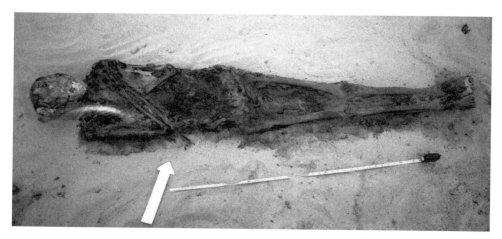

Fig. 3.21 Secondary burial 38/Q/94 – the corpse after removing of remains of the cartonnage.
Photo JK

Another well preserved secondary burial **38/Q/94** (*figs. 3.20–3.21*) was found in the layer of blown yellow sand to the north from the north-west corner of the mastaba, 0.60 m from the northern wall of the mastaba eastern enclosure wall of the courtyard, 1.15 m to the south from the southern outer wall of the Ritual Slaughterhouse and 0.70 m below the preserved crown of this wall. The deceased was lying in an extended position, with hand crossed on the chest (right hand above the left hand); the orientation of the secondary burial is the same as in the case of 37/Q/94, with a slight deviation to the south-west. The corpse was wrapped in bandages and was embellished by cartonnage which was similar to that laid on the secondary burial 37/Q/94. It also incorporated the *mnḫ*-collar with golden adornment. The face of the cartonnage was gilded and the wig had a blue colour. In contrast to 38/Q/94, remains of a face masque made of a thick wooden plank with reddish face and blue wig were unearthed. Only some remains of the wooden coffin were discovered. 38/Q/94 can be dated to the Late or Ptolemaic Period and it is apparent that this burial, together with 37/Q/94, originates from the same period. Nevertheless, mainly due to the similar orientation of the burials, we can suppose that also 4/Q/94, 9/Q/94 and 10/Q/94 belong to the same chronological phase of the secondary cemetery in this part of the Abusir Pyramid Necropolis.

3.4. Finds
3.4.1. Stone vessels

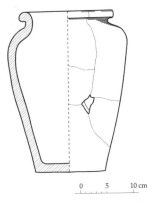

0   5   10 cm

Fig. 3.22 Canopic jar 5/Q/94.

Canopic jar (*fig. 3.22*)
5/Q/94
White limestone
Fifth Dynasty
H: 30 cm, diam. of the mouth: 7 cm, diam. of the bottom: 6.5 cm
Found scattered in several fragments (altogether in 22 fragments) in the debris layer of grey sand and limestone splinters, below the surface of the mound, in its western part.

Limestone canopic jar broken into many fragments. The mouth of the vessel is rolled, the bottom was flat. The surface of the vessel is covered by signs of its working and polishing.

Fragments of a canopic jar
29/Q/94
White limestone
Fifth Dynasty
Found in the north-eastern corner of the burial chamber, in a layer of yellow sand and limestone debris above the pavement of the burial chamber (*i.e.* in the same situation as 24/Q/94; see *chapter 3.4.8.*).

Fragments (altogether 22 fragments) of a canopic jar made of polished, quality limestone. The rim of its mouth is flat from above, but from the side it is slightly protruding. The bottom of the vessel is flat. Unfortunately, it was not possible to glue the fragments together.

Fig. 3.23 Lid of a canopic jar (30/Q/94).
Photo MZ

Lid of a canopic jar (and a fragment of another?) (*fig. 3.23*)
30/Q/94
White limestone
a) diam.: 16.7 cm, H: 3 cm
b) 4.5 × 3.8 cm
Fifth Dynasty
Found in the north-eastern corner of the burial chamber, in the layer of yellow sand and limestone debris above the pavement of the burial chamber (*i.e.* in the same situation as 24/Q/94).

The upper surface of the polished lid is convex, the lower side is provided by a protrusion which enables the lid to fit into the mouth of a canopic jar. The protrusion is 1.1 cm high.

Unfortunately, only one canopic jar was possible to reconstruct with all its features. Nevertheless, the broken examples of the canopic jars show that this set was one of the finer examples of such jars from the Fourth and Fifth Dynasties. It also seems that the canopic jars were not uniformly the same. The use of white limestone for making the canopic jars for Prince Nakhtsare contrasts with the canopic jars buried together with the queen in the pyramid Lepsius no. 24 which were made of travertine. In this way, we can see the difference in the social position of Nakhtsare and the owner of the pyramid Lepsius no. 24. An analogical set of canopic jars was found in the tomb of Khekeretnebty.[21] However, these examples are much more robust, especially in the lower part of the vessels, in comparison with canopic jar exc. no. 5/Q/1994. The thickness of this vessel's walls and of the bottom is smaller than examples from the Mastaba of Khekeretnebty. See also find of the canopic jar fragments in the Tomb Complex Lepsius no. 25 (p. 185) as well as *Appendix 1*.

Fig. 3.24 Offering tray 19/Q/94.
Photo MZ

An offering tray (*fig. 3.24*)
19/Q/94
Travertine
diam.: 15.2 cm, H: 1.1 cm
Fifth Dynasty
Found in the shaft in the layer of grey sand, at a depth of 2.10 m below the western wall of the burial vertical shaft, about 1.20 m from the north-west corner of the shaft.

A well polished board of a model offering tray, the upper side being flat, the lower side curved. On the upper side, there are tiny remnants of an offering (in a form of an oval with diameter of 9.5 cm); on the lower side are the remnants of a join from a stand (presumably also made of travertine) with a diameter of 3 cm.

Tray
Limestone
49 b/Q/94
Fifth Dynasty
L: 8.4 cm, max. W: 4 cm, H: 1.17 cm
Found in the same situation as 49 a/Q/94.

A model of a tray of oval shape, with a handle on one side; the surfaces has been polished.

Fig. 3.25 Bowl 36/Q/94.
Photo MZ

Bowl (*fig. 3.25*)
36/Q/94
White limestone
L: 10 cm, W: 7.5 cm, H: 5.4 cm
First Millennium BC
Found in a space of the southern wall of the burial chamber, in the level of the pulled out pavement, in the layer of grey sand and small limestone fragments.

Only roughly worked, shallow, tear-shaped bowl, with non-polished surface with numerous traces of work with a metal, most probably iron, instrument. Apparently, this bowl is not a part of the original burial equipment which is shown by its unfinished state as well as the traces of the iron instrument. This fact would enable to date the bowl more rather to the First Millennium BC than to the older periods. We can suppose that material for this bowl was obtained from an item of the original burial equipment or from a block used in the construction of the burial chamber – a block of the pavement, chamber's casing, or even from the (supposed) sarcophagus.

Fig. 3.26 Model of a beer jar 17/Q/94.
Photo MZ

Model of a beer jar with the stopper (*figs. 3.26* and *fig. 3.28b, pl. I*)
17/Q/94
Travertine
H: 8.7 cm, diam. of the mouth: 3.5 cm, max. diam.: 4.7 cm
Fifth Dynasty
Found in the vertical burial shaft in the layer of grey sand close to the north wall, at a depth of 1.80 m below the crown of the western wall of the shaft.

---

[21] Verner, Callender, *Djedkare's Cemetery*, 31–32.

A model of a beer jar with a stopper made of pinkish travertine; the interior of the jar is indicated by only 0.5 cm deep drilling. The rim and the bottom of the vessel are partly damaged.

Fig. 3.27 Model vessel 18/Q/94. Photo MZ

Model of a vessel (*fig. 3.27*)
18/Q/94
Basalt
H: 9.2 cm, diam. of the rim: 5.5 cm, diam. of the vessel's interior: 5 cm
Fifth Dynasty
Found in the vertical burial shaft in the layer of grey sand close to the north wall, at a depth of 2 m below the crown of the western wall of the shaft, 1 m to south from the north-west corner of the shaft.

A well polished model vessel with a broad rim. The drilling of the interior of the vessel (bowl) is not on the axis of the vessel. The surface of the vessel is slightly damaged on the lower side of the mouth rim. There are remnants of ochre on the upper side of the mouth rim and remnants of red colour on the surface of the bottom of the vessel.

Fig. 3.28a Model vases 18 and 33/Q/94. Photo MZ

Model of a vessel (*fig. 3.28a–b, see also pl. I*)
33/Q/94 A
Travertine
H: 9 cm, diam. of the rim: 5.2 cm, diam. of the mouth: 1.4 cm, diam. of the bottom: 2.1 cm
Fifth Dynasty
Found in the layer of the grey sand and small fragments of limestone fragments, in the south part of the passage between the vertical shaft and the burial chamber, close to the east wall and to the wall built in the passage.

A well polished model vessel with a broad rim, almost exaggerating the width of the lower part of the model. There are easily visible marks of drilling on the interior of the vessels located precisely in the axis of the vessel.

Fig. 3.29 Six of eight model bowls 26/Q/94. Photo MZ

Models of bowls (*fig. 3.29*)
26a–h/Q/94
Travertine

a) W: 6.0 cm, H: 1.7 cm
b) W: 6.1 cm, H: 2.1 cm
c) W: 5.7 cm, H: 1.5 cm
d) W: 5.9 cm, H: 1.4 cm
e) W: 5.7 cm, H: 2.2 cm
f) W: 5.3 cm, H: 2.5 cm
g) W: 5.6 cm, H: 1.9 (?) cm
h) W: 4.1 cm, H: 2 cm
Fifth Dynasty
The bowls were found in the north-east corner of the burial chamber, in the layer of yellow sand and limestone debris above the pavement of the burial chamber: 26a–b/Q/94 found in the layer of the grey sand mixed with the limestone fragments, close to the east wall of the passage between the vertical shaft and the burial chamber, 1.40 m to the south from the north wall of the shaft; 26c–e/Q/94 found in the same level, but for 0.5 m to the south from

the previous find, 26f/Q/94 found in the same level, but in the centre of the burial chamber.

Models of shallow bowls made of polished travertine with some marks of drilling. The fact that the ratio of their width and height fluctuates indicates the lower quality of the workmanship, used for making of these model vessels. It is in contrast with high quality of the model offerings. Is it possible to explain this fact with supposition that this part of the burial was made in hurry in a different workshop?

Model of a bowl
20/Q/94
Travertine
Diam.: 6.3 cm, H: 1.7 cm
Fifth Dynasty
Found in the layer of grey sand mixed with limestone fragments, close to the east wall of the passage between the vertical shaft and the burial chamber, 1.40 m south of the north wall of the shaft.

A model of a shallow bowl made of polished travertine with some marks of drilling.

Fragment of a bowl
6/Q/94
Limestone
Diam.: 20 cm, W: 18 cm, H: 8 cm
Fifth Dynasty
Found in the debris layer of grey sand and limestone splinters, below the surface of the mastaba's mound at the beginning of the archaeological excavations, in the western part of the mound (does it show the direction in which the tomb-robbers were transporting the stolen artefacts?). In the same situation the canopic jar 5/Q/94 was also found.

It is a half-finished bowl with a rim, and a 2 cm deep interior.

Fragments of a bowl
31/Q/94a–c
Travertine
5.4 × 5 cm, 2.3 × 1.5 cm, 5.5 × 4.7 cm
Fifth Dynasty
The fragment 31a/Q/94 was found in the layer of sand and limestone debris above the extracted pavement of the burial chamber, close to the western wall of the chamber, the pieces exc. no. 31b–c/Q/94 were found in the same level, but in the south-east corner of the burial chamber.

Fragments of a low, polished travertine bowl.

Fragment of a vessel
Limestone
49a/Q/94
Fifth Dynasty
Upper diam.: 6.4 cm, diam. of the bottom: 3.2 cm, H: 5.9 cm
Found in the muddy rubbish layer (0–40 cm above the ground) between the northern wing of the outer wall of the mastaba and the low enclosure wall of Raneferef's Ritual Slaughterhouse.

A lower part of a vessel.

Fig. 3.30 Aryballos.
Photo MZ

Aryballos (*figs. 3.30 and 3.28b, pl. I*)
11/Q/94
Travertine
H: 5.4 cm, diam. of the bottom: 4.4 cm, diam. of the mouth: 4.2 cm
Late Roman Period[22]
Found in the layer of yellow blown sand, above the eastern wing of the mudbrick enclosure wall, 0.4 m above the preserved crown of the masonry in the north-eastern corner of the mastaba. This aryballos was found very close to the secondary burial 10/Q/94 which is dated to the Ptolemaic Period (for the anthropological investigation of the human remains of this burial, see pp. 234–235).

A well polished aryballos vessel, with flat bottom and straight, flat mouth. The traces on the interior walls of the vessels clearly shows that it was made by means of drilling. This item clearly shows another strata of usage of the area of the Mastaba of Nakhtsare. During the Graeco-Roman period the area of the mastaba became an area for secondary burying. We can suppose that this aryballos was originally given as the burial equipment to one of the graves deposited in simple pits dug out into the blown sand layers covering the decayed mastaba.

3.4.2. Models of offerings

>>**Fig. 3.31a Model of a goose or a duck 3/Q/94.**
Photo MZ

Fig. 3.31b Model of a goose or a duck 3/Q/94.

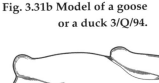

Model of an offering (goose or duck) (*figs. 3.31a–b*)
3/Q/94
Travertine
a) L: 24 cm, W: 13 cm, H: 16 cm
b) L: 7 cm, W: 4.5 cm, H: 1.5 cm
c) L: 14 cm, W: 10.5 cm, H: 3 cm
Fifth Dynasty

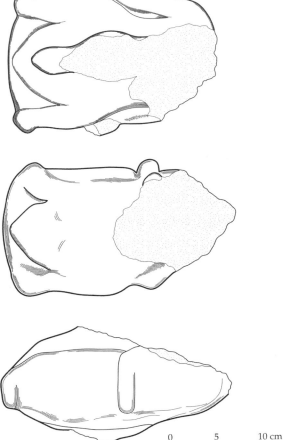

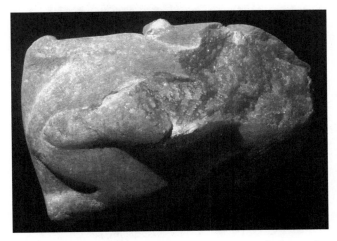

The fragment 3a/Q/94 was found 1 m below the surface of the mound, in a layer of the grey sand mixed with the limestone splinters, in the western part of the mound. 3b–c/Q/94 were found in the same layer as 3a/Q/94, but ca 3 m to the south of it.

A partially damaged and fragmentarily preserved model of a plucked goose/duck made of travertine. The lower parts of the bird's limbs are amputated; the head is lying on the back of the bird. The main damages were made in the area of the head and of its lower side. It was possible to assemble this main piece with other two representing in the case of fragment b an upper part of the bird's head and in

0   5   10 cm

---

[22] Aston, *Stone Vessels*, 90.

the case of fragment c a part of the parson's nose. There are no traces of polychromy on the surface of the fragments.

As it is also the case with 16/Q/94, 21/Q/94 and 27/Q/94 there is a possibility to identify the birds as ducks. The bill of the plucked birds are quite broad and this fact enables us to compare them with the duck vessels coming from the burial equipments of the Old Kingdom kings.

Model of an offering (goose or duck) (*figs. 3.32–33*)
16/Q/94
Travertine
L: 26 cm, W: 15 cm, H: 14.5 cm
Fifth Dynasty
Found close to the eastern wall of the vertical burial shaft, in the layer of grey sand and limestone debris and detritus.

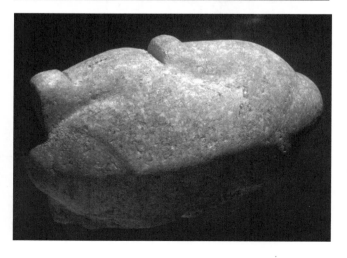
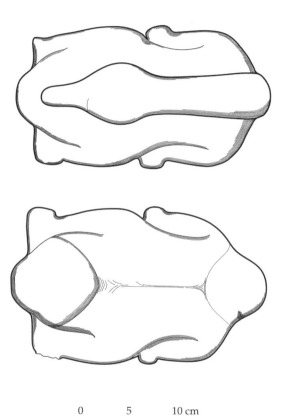

Fig. 3.32 Model of a goose or a duck 16/Q/94.
Photo MZ

Fig. 3.33. Model of a goose or a duck 16/Q/94.

A model of a plucked goose or duck made of travertine. The lower parts of the bird's limbs are amputated; the head is lying on the back of the bird. The surface of the model is polished and tiny remains of polychromy on it have been reported.

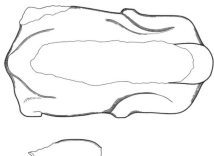

Fig. 3.34. Model of a goose or a duck 21/Q/94. Photo MZ

Fig. 3.35 Model of a goose or a duck 21/Q/94.

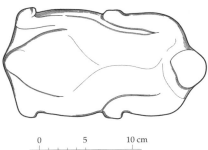

Model of an offering (goose or duck) (*figs. 3.34–35*)
21/Q/94
Travertine
L: 22.5 cm, W: 13.5 cm, H: 11 cm
Fifth Dynasty

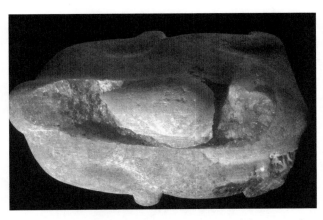

A model was found close to the north-west corner of the mastaba, in the layer of grey sand and limestone debris, about 0.5 m below the crown of the preserved masonry of the northern face of the mastaba.

The model of a plucked goose or duck with the lower parts of the bird's limbs amputated. The head is lying on the back of the bird. The surface of the model is polished. The model is partly damaged: the head of the bird was broken off, but it was also found and joined to the main part of the model. The larger part of the bird's neck is missing. No traces of polychromy found.

Fig. 3.36. Model of a goose or a duck 27/Q/94. Photo MZ

Fig. 3.37 Model of a goose or a duck 27/Q/94.

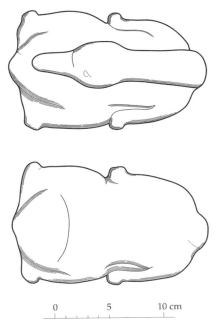

Model of an offering (goose or duck) (*figs. 3.36–37*)
27/Q/94
Travertine
L: 18 cm, W: 12 cm, H: 9 cm
Fifth Dynasty
The item was found in the north-west corner of the burial chamber, in the level of the torn out pavement, in the layer of grey sand and small limestone fragments.

A model of a plucked goose or duck made of travertine. The lower parts of the bird's limbs are visualised as amputated and their remaining sections are protruding from the surface of the model; the head is lying on the back of the bird. On the lower part a parson's nose is indicated by a slight protrusion.

Model of an offering (a rump or gigot of meat) *(figs. 3.38–39)*
22/Q/94
Travertine
L: 27 cm, W: 18 cm, H: 11 cm
Fifth Dynasty
This model was found close to the north-west corner of the mastaba, in the layer of grey sand and limestone debris, about 0.5 m below the crown of the preserved masonry of the northern face of the mastaba.

Fig. 3.38 Model of an offering (a rump or gigot of meat) 22/Q/94. Photo MZ

Fig. 3.39 Model of an offering (a rump or gigot of meat) 22/Q/94.

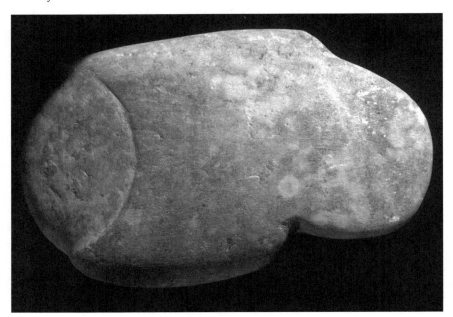

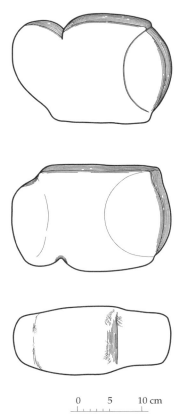

The model of a rump or gigot. On the upper side of the model of an irregular shape, an oval line probably marking the border between the bone and the flesh can be seen. The line was incised into the surface of the model. On the model's lower side a slight protrusion was made in the surface of the model; it corresponds with the trace of the line on the upper side of the model. The surface of the model has been polished, no remnants of polychromy have been discerned.

Model of an offering (bread?, egg?) *(figs. 3.40–41)*
23/Q/94
Travertine
L: 11.8 cm, W: 8 cm, H: 5 cm
Fifth Dynasty

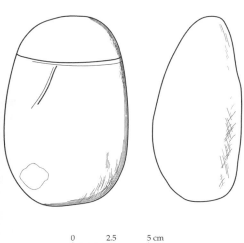

Fig. 3.40 Model of an offering (bread?, egg?) 23/Q/94. Photo MZ

Fig. 3.41 Model of an offering (bread?, egg?) 23/Q/94.

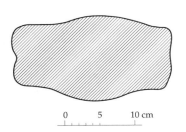

Fig. 3.42 A model of an offering (a leg of meat) 28/Q/94.

The item was found in the north-east corner of the burial chamber, in the layer of yellow sand and limestone debris, about 0.7 m below the crown of the preserved masonry of the passage between the vertical burial shaft and the burial chamber.

A model of an oval offering, presumably that of a loaf of bread or an egg. The surface of the model has been polished.

A model of an offering (a leg of meat) (see *figs. 3.3* and *3.42*)
28/Q/94
Travertine
L: 24.5 cm, W: 12 cm, H: 12.5 cm
Fifth Dynasty
Found in the north-east corner of the burial chamber, in the layer of yellow sand and limestone debris, above the pavement of the burial chamber, together with 24/Q/94 (see *chapter 3.4.8.*).

A model of a leg of meat. The object has a generally triangular shape, with both oval, protruding ends. Both of them are divided by their slight protrusion. From the lateral view, one can see that both protruded ends were from one side modelled so that they should resemble the jointed parts of a femur. The middle part would then resemble a piece of flesh in the middle of the bone.

Model of the offering (*ḫpš*-offering?) (*figs. 3.43–44*)
32/Q/94
Travertine
L: 27 cm, W: 16.5 cm, H: 10 cm
Fifth Dynasty
A model was found in the north-west corner of the burial chamber, at a

level 0.10 m below the level of the pulled out pavement, in the layer of grey sand and small limestone fragments.

Fig. 3.43 Model of the offering (*ḫpš*-offering?) 32/Q/94.
Photo MZ

The model of a *ḫpš*-offering (?) with a polished surface; on the lower side, a slight protrusion running along the longer axis of the object is distinctly visible. The object is damaged on its both ends and some parts are missing.

Fig. 3.44 Model of the offering (*ḫpš*-offering?) 32/Q/94.

Fragment of a model of an offering
35/Q/94
Travertine
L: 6.7 cm, W: 7.5 cm, H: 4.7 cm
Fifth Dynasty
Found in space of the southern wall of the burial chamber, at the level of the pulled out pavement, in the layer of grey sand and small limestone fragments.

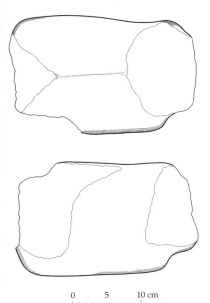

A model of an offering (some kind of bread?) in an oval form with a polished surface. Presumably, a half of the model is missing now; the fracture of the stone is ancient, so that the model was damaged a long period ago its unearthing.

In contrast to the burial equipment found in the Pyramid Lepsius no. 24, the examples from the Mastaba of Nakhtsare are not food containers; however, they portray themselves as copies of the genuine article. Models of offerings and offerings themselves played, as a matter of course, an important role in the burial cult, as we know from the beginning of the Old Kingdom. The offerings themselves might have been substituted by models and this is the case of the burial equipment found in the Mastaba of Nakhtsare. It is probable that the number and types of offerings were standardized and canonized. They included the most important food groups: meat, poultry and bread.[23] All three groups are also attested in the material from the Nakhtsare mastaba. In Abusir, the best preserved set of the offering containers has been unearthed in the burial chamber of Kar Junior in Abusir-South.[24]

3.4.3. Varia

Models of instruments (*figs. 3.45–46*, see also *pl. I*)
25a–e/Q/94
Copper
a) L: 12.3 cm, max. W: 2.4 cm, H: 0.2 cm
b) L: 12.9 cm, W: 1.4–2.4 cm, H: 0.2 cm
c) L: 11.9 cm, max. W: 1.1 cm, H: 0.4–0.5 cm
d) L: 9.9 cm, W: 0.8 cm, H: 0.4 cm
e) L: 9.5 cm, W: 1.3–1.8 cm, H: 0.2 cm
Fifth Dynasty
Models exc. nos. 25a–b/Q/94 were found in the north-east corner of the burial chamber, in a layer of yellow sand and limestone debris above the pavement of the burial chamber (*i.e.* in the same situation as 24/Q/94). 25c–d/Q/94 were found in the northern part of the burial chamber in the space of the torn out pavement of the chamber, in the layer of sand and small fragments of limestone.

a) A model of an adze: the edge is rounded, the other is even.
b) The object is partially damaged, one end is missing. Originally it was the same type of model as the previous object – *i.e.* an adze.
c) A model of a chisel with an even edge and a pointed end.
d) A model of a chisel with an even edge and a narrowing end (but not pointed).
e) A model of an adze, with an even edge (in contrast to the object 25a/Q/1994).

The fact that the copper model instruments were part of the burial equipment is proof of higher social status of the tomb owner. We come across adzes also in the burial equipment of the owner of the Tomb Complex Lepsius no. 25. Models of adzes were part of the burial equipment of the richer tomb owners from the Old Kingdom.[25] Chisels are among the most frequent parts of deposits of copper model implements given as burial equipment for the use of the tomb owners during the life in the netherworld.

Knife (*figs. 3.47–48*)
8/Q/94
Flint
L: 8.5 m, max. W: 2 cm
Fifth Dynasty
A knife with a double incurvation, on the edges a fine retouching; the point of the knife is missing. The knife was joined to the (wooden?) handle by means of a kind of tenon.

---

[23] S. Ikram, Portions of an Old Kingdom offering list reified, in: *OKAA*, 167–174; Hassan, *Gîza* VI.2, 365–375; Edel, *Hieroglyphische Inschriften*, 71 and fig. 25.; Barta, *Opferliste*, fig. 4 and 5.; Jéquier, *Tombeaux*, 66, figs. 67 and 29; Brovarski, *Senedjemib Complex*, 127–8, pls. 99–101a.
[24] See M. Bárta, in Kloth, Martin, Pardey, eds., *Fs Altenmüller*, 24–25; M. Bárta, The Sixth Dynasty Tombs in Abusir. Tomb Complex of the Vizier Qar and his Family, in: *OKAA*, 45–62; S. Ikram, Portions of an Old Kingdom offering list reified, in: *OKAA*, 167–174; Bárta *et al.*, *Qar*, in press.
[25] *Cf.* W. M. F. Petrie, *Tools and Weapons*, 30 and pl. XV, 45, 47.

Fig. 3.46 Models of instruments 25/Q/94a–b.

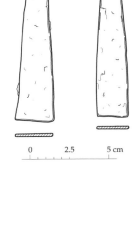

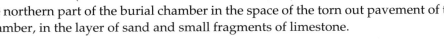

0   2.5   5 cm

Fig. 3.47 Flint knife 8/Q/94. Photo MZ

Fig. 3.48 Flint knife 8/Q/94.

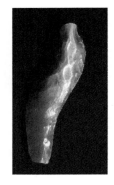

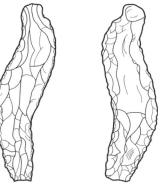

0   2.5   5 cm

Platter

47/Q/94

Red ware pottery

Fifth Dynasty

Found in the muddy rubbish layer (0–40 cm above the ground) between the northern wing of the outer wall of the mastaba and the low enclosure wall of the *Ḥwt-nmt*, about 1 m to the east from the north-east corner of the mastaba.

A fragmentary preserved large platter with ledged base. The platter is hand-built with its base pounded made of Nile C clay, with its inside and the rim red-slipped, outer walls uncoated.[26] On the inner surface a complex pattern has been made with the black ink. The centrepiece of the decoration is a head of a dog or of a lion, which is connected with a "body" *mḥn* made to look like latticework which is designed in a spiral which goes towards the centre of the tray. Because of the circumstances of discovery, we have to underline that this item came as part of the refuse from the mortuary temple of Raneferef (respectively from the Ritual Slaughterhouse).

Miniature bowl

45a/Q/94

Pottery

H: 4.5 cm, upper diam.: 7 cm, diam. of the bottom: 3.5 cm

Fifth Dynasty

Found in the layer of dark sand and fragments of pottery in the eastern part of the passage between the outer wall of the Ritual Slaughterhouse of Raneferef's mortuary temple and its low enclosure wall, in the filling above the bottom of this space.

A thin-walled, thrown on the wheel model of a bowl with straight, slanting sides opening outwards and a cut bottom. Well polished surface with a red slip.[27]

Fragments of golden foil

24/Q/94

Gold

L: 6.5 cm, W: 0.8 cm

Fifth Dynasty

Found in the north-east corner of the burial chamber, in the layer of yellow sand and limestone debris above the pavement of the burial chamber.

A crumpled fragment of golden foil, presumably originally used as the decoration. Unfortunately, it is not easy to estimate for what embellishment it was meant for, nor for which parts of the burial equipment it was used. We can hypothesize that it was – in a much smaller scale – used in the decoration of similar fragments to those gilded objects which have been found in other high-class burial chambers – such as that of Hetepheres I – where they had fallen from (or been prised off) boxes, furniture or even vessels.[28]

Fragment of polychromed decoration (*fig. 3.49*)

1/Q/94

Limestone

L: 30.5, H: 6.5 cm, depth: 9.5–13.5 cm

Fifth Dynasty

Found in the surface layer of limestone debris, to the south-west of the central pit and among other blocks of limestone.

---

[26] *Cf.* Rzeuska, *Saqqara* 2, 162–165.

[27] *Op. cit.*, Cat. no. 694.

[28] Reisner, Smith, *Giza Necropolis* II, 43–44.

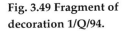

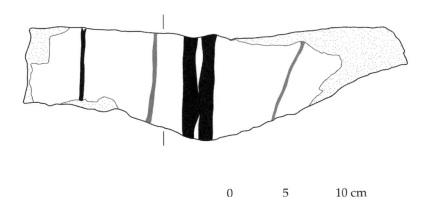

Fig. 3.49 Fragment of decoration 1/Q/94.

A part of the wall with polychromed decoration. The decoration was painted on the layer of quality stucco. The fragments of the decoration consists of several lines of black and red which enclose a space of grey, white, yellow, black and green. It is not clear if the painting was a component of a scene and, if so, which scene this was. We cannot also say whether this block originated in the Mastaba of Nakhtsare or if it was brought to the place of its find from some neighbouring monument. This block represents the only fragment of decoration found in the area of the mastaba. Also in view of this fact, the block's assignment to Nakhtsare's tomb seems to be improbable.

Inlay or tile
34/Q/94
Faience
L: 4.2 cm, W: 2.6 cm, H: 0.4 cm
Fifth Dynasty
Found in the layer of blown sand, close to the southeast corner of the mastaba, where it was lying on the foundation layer for the casing of the mastaba.

An inlay (or a tile?) made of faience of reddish core and light blue-green glaze. The upper side is flat, on the lower side there are six incised lines and a coarse black-green band.

Inkwell
49c/Q/94
White limestone
L: 5 cm, W: 3 cm, H: 1.3 cm
Fifth Dynasty
Found in the muddy rubbish layer (0–40 cm above the ground) between the northern wing of the outer wall of the mastaba and the low enclosure wall of Raneferef's Ritual Slaughterhouse. This founding situation enables us to suppose that this item was originally used in the king's mortuary complex rather than in Nakhtsare's tomb.

A fragment of an inkwell with a preserved part of a circle for the ink, enclosed by a 2 mm high rim with a diameter of 2.4 cm, inside the circle remnants of black colour.

Beads
24/Q/94
Faience
Max. L: 3.8 cm, diam.: 0.20–0.40 cm
Fifth Dynasty
Found in the north-east corner of the burial chamber, in the layer of yellow sand and limestone debris above the pavement of the burial chamber.

Sixteen pieces of long, and eleven of short cylindrical beads made of faience with blue-green glaze on their surface. The beads were pierced and strung on a fibre of some sort. Because of the fact that the beads were found in the area of the burial chamber, we can suppose that they were part of the burial equipment of the tomb owner.

Beads
46/Q/94
Faience
Max. L: 4.2 cm, max. diam.: 0.4 cm
Fifth Dynasty
Found in the bottom layer of dark sand and fragments of pottery in the eastern part of the passage between the outer wall of Raneferef's Ritual Slaughterhouse and its low, protective enclosure wall. Because of these finding circumstances we can assume that the beads might have come from the area or of the Ritual Slaughterhouse or from the king's mortuary temple itself.

Find of 35 pieces of cylindrical beads made of faience with blue-green and green glaze. The beads were pierced and strung on a fibre of some sort.[29]

Sealing (*fig. 3.50*)
15/Q/1995
Clay
Fifth Dynasty
Found in the waste layer of dark sand mixed with pottery sherds, to the north from the north-east corner of the mastaba, 0.3-0.5 m above the floor of the open courtyard to the east of the mastaba.

Fig. 3.50 Mud ceiling 15/Q/94.
Photo MZ

[29] Both finds of faience beads please *cf.* with voluminous finds of faience beads in the area of Raneferef's mortuary temple – Callender, in: Verner *et al.*, *Raneferef*, 442–449.

An almost orbicular clay sealing with upper surface flat and lower surface a little bit compressed. On the upper surface there is a horizontal imprint of a seal with the text: *ḥnty* [*š*] *pr-ʿ3*. Unfortunately the seal imprint is very eroded, therefore, it is a question whether the inscription was connected with the title *ḥntj-š* or whether the inscription has been a part of a longer title mentioning some connection with the king himself or the god Re – *ḥnty pr-ʿ3*. This eventuality seems to be substantiated by the fact that after *pr-ʿ3* the sun disk and the Horus on the standard is written. This seal imprint was found in the dump area for Raneferef's mortuary temple thus it is very probable that this seal impression belongs to the finding unit of this monument.

Cylindrical seal
43/Q/94
Limestone
L: 3.7 cm, diam.: 2.8 cm
Fifth Dynasty
Found in the layer of dark sand, fragments of the pottery in the eastern part of the passage between the enclosure wall of the mastaba and the outer wall of the Ritual Slaughterhouse of Raneferef's mortuary temple, ca 0.5 m below the crown of the enclosure wall of the mastaba.

A fragment of a cylindrical seal with uneven – though slightly smoothed – surface. The seal was pierced and once had been suspended on a string. There are bare incised lines and signs representing a ladder-like pattern accompanied by a sign resembling a hissing cobra (?) or the hieratic sign of *m*.[30]

Aramaic graffiti (*fig. 3.51*)
14/Q/94
L: 27 cm, H: 7.5
Late Period?
Found on a block to the east of the entrance to the court of the tomb, in the layer of blown sand and large fragments of limestone, 1.5 m below the present surface.

Fig. 3.51 Aramaic graffiti 14/Q/94.
Photo MZ

One line of graffiti incised into the surface of a block of local limestone, traced by black ink.

---

[30] *Cf.* Verner *et al.*, *Raneferef*, 207

3.5. Masons' marks

Gr 1/Q/1994 (*fig. 3.52a–b*, see also *pl. I*)

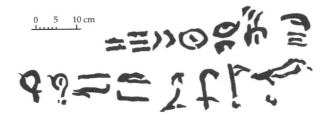

Fig. 3.52b Masons' mark Gr 1/Q/94.

Found on the block built *in situ* in the lower part of the western wall of the horizontal shaft leading to the burial chamber. The masons' mark is built in an upside down position and painted by a faint reddish colour.

3bd 3 3ḫt šw 25(26?)
(wr nṯr(y)?) s3 nśwt Nḫt-s3-Rˁ
"third month of inundation, day 25 (26?)
(working phyle *wer*, phyle *netjeri* ?) King's son Nakhtsare"

Unfortunately, this is the only available inscription found in the mastaba which includes a personal name. One of the reasons is the large scaled destruction of the mastaba's superstructure – especially, in the area of the offering chapel. Even a fragment of a false door or a part of the chapel's decoration with the tomb owner name or titles were found. Therefore we have to take into our consideration this masons' mark. The fact that the graffiti is painted on a block built in the wall of the burial shaft and not on loose block seems to help to ascribe the mastaba to King's son Nakhtsare. This name is not attested in the epigraphic material[31] (for the discussion concerning the ownership of the mastaba, see further in the *chapter 3.6.*).

Gr 2/Q/1994 (*fig. 3.53a–b*, see also *pl. II*)

Fig. 3.53b Masons' mark Gr 2/Q/94.

Found during the excavations of the western part of the mastaba on a large loose block of quality white limestone. On the masons' mark, made in faint red-pink colour, we can see two pyramids. Apparently, we can connect this mark with the numerous finds of the builder's marks unearthed in the tomb Lepsius no. 25. These signs represent a part the name of a monument written with two signs of pyramids – *Rś-mrwj* (for the discussion see *chapter 5.*). It is probable that this loose block was meant to be used in another neighbouring monument and it could be left unused and later utilized during the construction of the Mastaba of Nakhtsare.

Gr 3/Q/1994 (*figs. 3.54a–b, 3.55a–b*, see also *pl. II*)
Found during the excavations of the area of the burial shaft. The graffiti is painted on a stone ostracon on its both sides.

---

[31] Nevertheless, there was attested certain Nakhtsaes, whose name is similar to the name of prince Nakhtsare – Ranke, *PN* I, 209.

avers

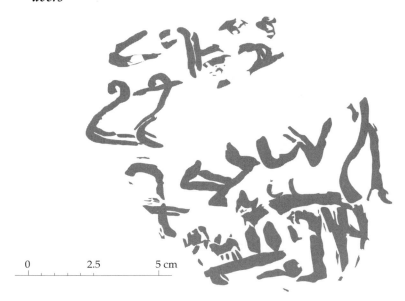

0   2.5   5 cm

**Fig. 3.54b Masons' mark
Gr 3/Q/94 (*avers*).**

...

imj-r3 bitjw Wśr-k3.f-ʿnḫ

...

"Overseer of beekeepers(?) Userkafankh."[32]

revers

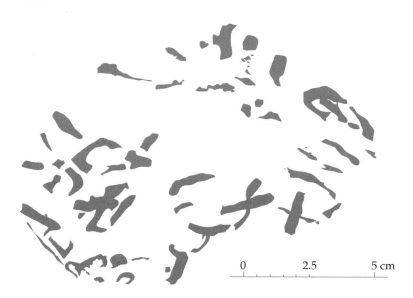

**Fig. 3.55b Masons' mark
Gr 3/Q/94 (*revers*).**

0   2.5   5 cm

3bd 3 šmw...

"3rd month of winter, ..."

Unfortunately, this ostracon is not very well readable – therefore also its interpretation is not easy if not impossible. It is an interesting fact that a name of an individual has been found in the tomb of a member of the royal family. We can only hypothesize that this Userkafankh was one of the subordinates of the tomb owner or was in another relationship to this person. He then might have been obliged to contribute to the construction of his lord's tomb. Unfortunately, the person mentioned in the inscription is not identifiable with the owner of the tomb in the Cemetery of Nobles in the central part of Abusir.[33]

---

[32] *Cf.* Jones, *Titles*, 109–110 and Hannig, *GHÄD*, 54.
[33] *Cf.* Borchardt, *Neuserre*, Blatt 22.

3.6. Conclusions

The question of the name of the tomb owner remains not fully answered. The masons' mark unearthed in the burial shaft (see *chapter 3.4.*) mentioning *s3 nśwt Nḫt-s3-Rˁ* very probably, however not fully securely, names the tomb owner, King's Son Nakhtsare ('Strong is the protection of Re'). This name has not been yet attested in the epigraphical material.[34] Even though the ascription of mastaba "Q" to the so-far unknown Royal Prince Nakhtsare is not completely secure (see *chapter 3.4.*), the location of the mastaba amidst the monuments belonging to the members of the royal family shows that the tomb owner was a member of the royal family. Ascription is also substantiated by the use of high quality white limestone for the casing of the tomb's outer walls, as well as the composition of the burial equipment found in the mastaba.

From its position in the northern end of the row of the mastabas[35] which is running to the south from Raneferef's mortuary temple (*i.e.* from the *Ḥwt-nmt*) it seems to indicate that there is a connection between Nakhtsare (and possibly the owners of other tombs in this row) and King Raneferef. This supposition is underlined by the fact that the Mastaba of Nakhtsare has been built directly along the southern wall of Raneferef's *Ḥwt-nmt*.[36] Unfortunately, this supposition can not be further substantiated from the written or archaeological material found either at the site, or in Raneferef's mortuary complex. As the tomb of Nakhtsare had been built in the northernmost place of the line of the tombs, it is probable that it was built earlier than other tombs in the line; it is also probable that the tomb owner was the most important person among the tomb owners in this row of mastabas. Does this mean that Nakhtsare was the eldest son of Raneferef?

In comparison with either tomb of Nebtyemneferes (see *chapter 2.* in this monograph), or with the tombs from the cemetery of Djedkare Isesi, the plan of the superstructure of Nakhtsare's mastaba is very simple, without any annex attached to its mass. It consisted of an L-shaped chapel,[37] accessible from the opened courtyard in front of the mastaba through a doorway. The chapel very probably included only one niche. Substructure of the Mastaba of Nakhtsare is also simple and similar to those in Djedkare's cemetery; it consisted of a vertical shaft and a burial chamber.[38] Following the form of the mounds of remaining, unexcavated tombs located to the south of Raneferef' complex, we can suppose that the layout of these tombs was the same as Nakhtsare's and that they were built in the same period. Why these tombs were built in such a simple way is an important question. We can conjecture that they were constructed in this form due to the lack of resources and especially lack of qualified craftsmen sent to work on another building projects, who should be involved in the case of the more complex layout.[39]

However, such an explanation is not satisfying. The form of Nakhtsare's offering chapel provide an important clue concerning the tomb dating. The use of the L-shaped chapels was in the Saqqara-Abusir region chronologically delayed in comparison with Giza[40] – we can thus suppose that Nakhtsare's chapel can be dated to the second half of the Fifth Dynasty.

---

[34] There is, however, the similarly constructed name of *Nḫt-s3.ś* – Ranke, *PN* 211, 11.

[35] Verner, *ZÄS*, 1995, 151–152.

[36] Verner, in Verner *et al.*, *Raneferef*, 87–99.

[37] Reisner, *Giza Necropolis* I, 185 – it seems that in the case of Nakhtsare's tomb we can suppose that Reisner's Type 3b or 3c was used.

[38] Due to the destruction of the burial chamber we can only suppose that Reisner's Type 4b was used – see Reisner, *Giza Necropolis* I, 87–91.

[39] This lack of resources might be connected with the supposition that these tombs belonged to the children of a king who died prematurely, and that their position at the royal court was low or at least questionable.

[40] In Giza necropolis, this type of chapels is connected with the Fourth Dynasty – M. Bárta, Non-royal cemeteries at Abusir-South, in: *Abusir and Saqqara 2000*, 341; *cf.* Reisner, *Giza Necropolis* I, 185, 203ff., Harpur, *Decoration*, 316, Table 5.2.

To sum up, from the position of the tomb of Nakhtsare, the most northern tomb from the small cemetery *en echelon* south of the Unfinished Pyramid of King Raneferef – who died prematurely whilst still quite young[41] – we might suppose that the tomb marked a row of relatives who were contemporaries of that king. As Raneferef was physically mature enough to beget children before his death,[42] we suspect that some of the tomb owners might also have been members of the royal family. Given the strong bonds of family ties, it is likely that Raneferef's brother, King Niuserre, then would be obliged to build and finish the tombs of Raneferef's children, among them, possibly, the tomb of Nakhtsare. As was the case for many other constructions in the Abusir Royal Necropolis, Niuserre did indeed fulfil his duties to the dead members of his family.[43] However, in many cases – and the Mastaba of Nakhtsare is one of them – it seems that he fulfilled his obligations only as duty which can also explain why the tomb was not decorated.[44] If this should indeed be the case, the Mastaba of Nakhtsare would have been built during the final part of Niuserre's reign.

---

[41] Strouhal, Němečková, in: Verner *et al.*, *Raneferef*, 517–518.

[42] E. Strouhal and A. Němečková suppose that the king died in the age of 20–23 years – *loc. cit.*

[43] J. Krejčí, The Origins and Development of the Royal Necropolis at Abusir during the Old Kingdom, in: *Abusir and Saqqara 2000*, 480.

[44] The necessary (relief) decoration of the tomb might have been included in the false door or the niche of the false door and on other walls omitted.

4. Pyramid Complex Lepsius no. 24

4.1. History of exploration of the complex

A group of small monuments in the southern outskirts of the pyramid field in Abusir never attracted much attention of archaeologists. In the first map of the Memphite Necropolis by Napoleon' surveyors these monuments were left unnoticed and near Abusir only the pyramids of Sahure, Neferirkare and Niuserre were marked in the map.[1] J. S. Perring, who surveyed the monuments of Abusir in the 1830s, was more accurate than Napoleon's scholars and indicated in his map two rectangular monuments south-east of the Unfinished Pyramid (see *fig. 4.1*).[2] Even more attention was paid to the monuments in Abusir by the Prussian expedition of C. R. Lepsius which came to Abusir in the early 1840s. Lepsius, who

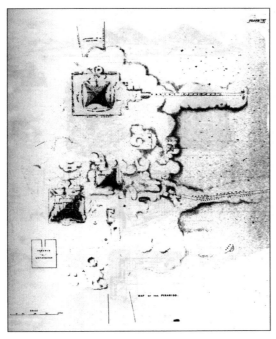 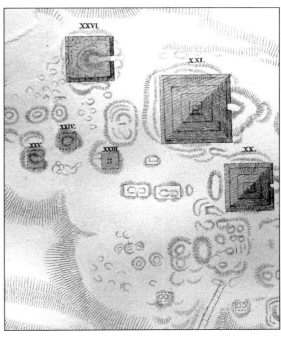

Fig. 4.1. The Abusir Pyramid Necropolis on the map of J. Perring.

Fig. 4.2. Minor tombs in the Abusir Pyramid Necropolis on the map of C. R. Lepsius.

marked in his archaeological map of the Memphite Necropolis the pyramids by Roman numerals, identified in the south-east outskirts of the Abusir pyramid field three small pyramids and attributed them the nos. XXIII, XXIV and XXV (see *fig. 4.2*).[3] Judging by his brief description of the monuments,[4] it can not be excluded that he even made in them some minor trial digging. Following Lepsius's map, J. de Morgan took in his map of the Memphite Necropolis[5] these monuments for pyramids, too. L. Borchardt,[6] who explored the major monuments in the Abusir pyramid field at the beginning of the Twentieth century, made some trial diggings in the pyramid nos. 24 and 25 and subsequently rejected their identification as the pyramids (see *fig. 4.3*). He took them for private tombs. Interestingly, for a private tomb, a twin mastaba, he also took the pyramid of Khentkaus II lying in the vicinity of the pyramid Lepsius no. 24. Last observations before the exploration of these

---

[1] *Description de l'Egypte* A, vol. V, Paris 1809, pl. 1.

[2] Perring, *Pyramids*, pl. V.

[3] *LD* I, 32.

[4] *LD* Text I, 136f.

[5] De Morgan, *Carte de la nécropole memphite*, pl. 11.

[6] Borchardt, *Sahure* I, 145 and plan B 1/2; Borchardt, *Neuserre*, 6.

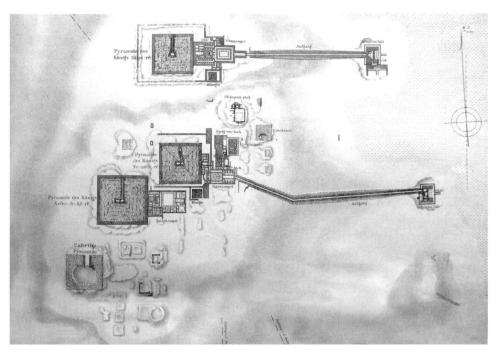

Fig. 4.3. The Abusir Pyramid Necropolis on the map of L. Borchardt.

monuments by the Czech archaeological team were made by V. Maragioglio and C. Rinaldi.[7] In contrast with Borchardt and in accordance with Lepsius, they identified the monuments as pyramids but, surprisingly, they were hesitant to date them from the same time as the large pyramids in Abusir.

The Czech archaeological team in Abusir began to examine the pyramid Lepsius no. 24 as early as 1981 and concluded the pyramid's exploration in the year 1994. With some longer intervals, the exploration of the monument was carried out in three seasons, and simultaneously with the excavation in the Pyramid Complex of Raneferef and in the tomb of Nakhtsare.[8]

In the season of 1981, about three meters broad and twenty meters long trench was excavated from the east towards the south-east corner of the pyramid in order to identify the precise position of the corner. Unfortunately, the casing of the pyramid had long ago been stripped off by stone robbers (and so was also the casing of the north-eastern corner of the pyramid as shown by later excavation) but the corner of the pyramid core's remained in position. In the trench were revealed the remains of primitive structures the walls of which were built of fragments of limestone and which, judging by fragments of painted pottery, were temporary shelters of the New Kingdom stone robbers. Interestingly, in the trench were also revealed lump soft stone bearing builders' mark in the shape of labrys (or, the cursive sign *ts*). This find had a great chronological meaning since the same marks were also found in the devastated cult pyramid in the adjacent Pyramid Complex of Khentkaus II. The marks thus indicated that the pyramid Lepsius no. 24 and the expansion of Khentkaus's pyramid complex, which included the construction of the cult pyramid,[9] dated from the same time. Only much later, during the excavation of the Tomb Complex Lepsius no. 25, the true meaning of the aforesaid mark became apparent: it was an abbreviation of the name of Hanebu, a person who might have been the owner of the eastern and larger tomb in this tomb complex, *i.e.* L 25/1 (see discussions in *chapter 5.5.8.*).

The excavation in the season of 1987 (see *fig. 4.4*) led to the unearthing of the whole southern half of the mortuary temple. From the eastern wall of the temple survived only few blocks in position which, fortunately, enabled us to identify the

---

[7] *MRA* VII, 188–190.
[8] See the preliminary reports of the respective seasons by M. Verner in: *ZÄS* 111, 1984, 77f.; *ZÄS* 115, 1988, 168–171; *ZÄS* 124, 1997, 71–76.
[9] Verner, *Khentkaus*, 51.

Fig. 4.4. View of pyramid at the beginning of the archaeological excavations.
Photo JB

N   S

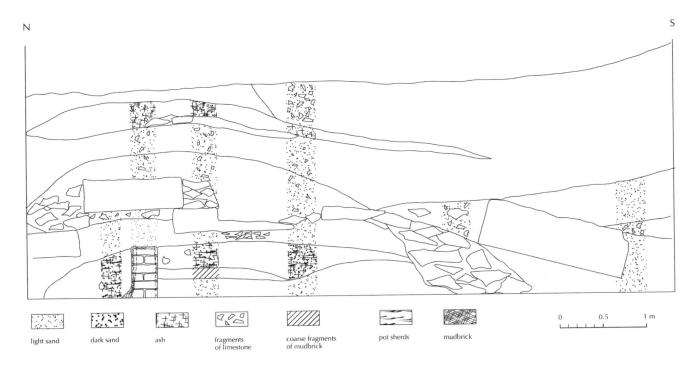

light sand	dark sand	ash	fragments of limestone	coarse fragments of mudbrick	pot sherds	mudbrick		0 0.5 1 m	

Fig. 4.5. Section through the area 1 m to the east from the eastern outer wall of the mortuary temple.

entrance to the temple. In front of the entrance were uncovered the remains of an about one meter broad path made of beaten clay and curbed on each side by a low, ca 20 cm high mudbrick wall. Beyond the walls were detritus deposits containing organic elements and ash (see *fig. 4.5*). In this detritus layer were found thin walled, red ware hemispherical cups which dated from the early Twelfth Dynasty, the period of a brief revival of the cults in the Abusir pyramid complexes.

During this season it also became obvious that the temple was nearly completely devastated and quarried away by stone robbers after whom remained in the site only several primitive shelters built of lump soft stone. The stratigraphy of the site and the pottery found here indicated that the first and major wave of devastation of the monument came as early as the New Kingdom but was followed by other waves in the Late Period and in the late Roman Period (see also *fig. 4.6*).

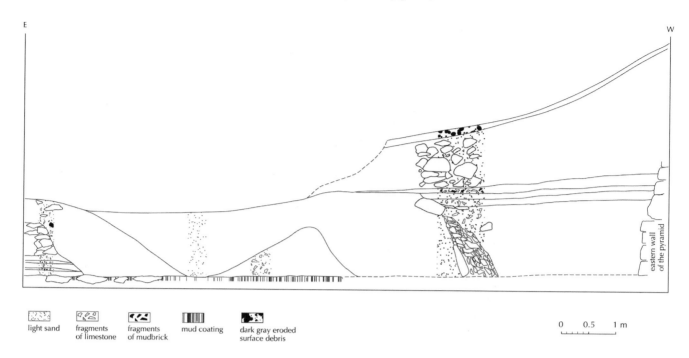

light sand   fragments of limestone   fragments of mudbrick   mud coating   dark gray eroded surface debris

0   0.5   1 m

The excavation of the northern half of the mortuary temple was completed after a longer break, in the season of 1994. Under thick layers of limestone fragments and grey sand were uncovered the remains of the northern outer wall of the temple and four storerooms adjacent to the wall from the south. In rather thin layer of clay and dark sand on the limestone floor of the storerooms (see *fig. 4.7*) were

Fig. 4.6. Section through the area of the mortuary temple.

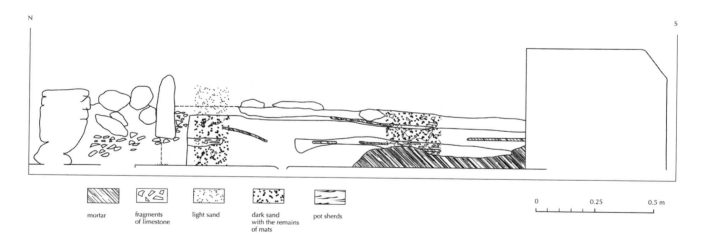

mortar   fragments of limestone   light sand   dark sand with the remains of mats   pot sherds

0   0.25   0.5 m

found fragments of Fifth Dynasty pottery and the remains of mats which indicated that the rooms might have served in the terminal period of the temple's function for housing purposes. In the central part of the temple, adjacent to the pyramid, were found the remains of the offering hall. From the north–south oriented hall survived in position two blocks of the western wall (see *fig. 4.8*), an impression of the eastern wall in the pavement and a small piece of the latter wall, including the whitewashed plaster, in position. Finally, there also survived an impression of the entrance to the hall from the south. In the debris covering the hall was found a fragment of a limestone basin, a corroded fishing hook of copper, fragments of red granite, quartzite and one dressed fragment of black granite.

Fig. 4.7. Section through the lowermost part of the filling of Room no. 3.

As in the southern (for the situation in the area of the remaining masonry of the cult pyramid see *fig. 4.9*) also in the northern half of the temple there were

Fig. 4.8. Remains of the western wall in the offering hall. Photo MZ

Fig. 4.9. Section through the area to the south of the mortuary temple with remains of the cult pyramid; *1* – block of the cult pyramid *in situ*.

unearthed primitive walls built of fragments of limestone. Undoubtedly, some of them helped the stone robbers quarrying the limestone to contain the layers of sand and rubble and to prevent in this way falling of this trash down, in the track of the stone robbers. In the north-east corner of the temple was found a hearth and a layer of sand mixed with ash. In this layer was found a red ware hemispherical cup, a copper needle and a fragment of a flint knife. An important find made in the north-west sector of the temple represented a block coming from the cult pyramid. The

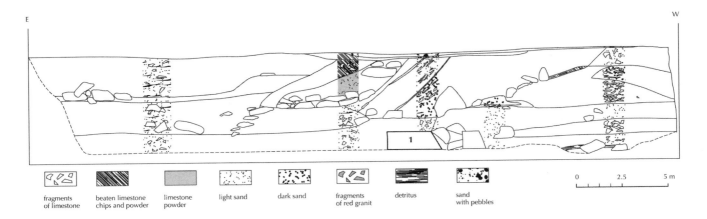

| fragments of limestone | beaten limestone chips and powder | limestone powder | light sand | dark sand | fragments of red granit | detritus | sand with pebbles |

0   2.5   5 m

block formed one half of the second uppermost layer of the cult pyramid. Outside the eastern wall of the temple were found several models of clay including a small chest and a small inscribed tablet.

After unearthing the remains of the mortuary temple, we began to explore the open crater of rubble, yellow sand and fragments of mudbricks and pottery (*bd3-moulds*) inside the pyramid. In the rubble was found a small fragment of the drum coming from a looted small tomb in the vicinity of the pyramid, a fragment of a travertine canopic jar, a corroded fishing hook of copper and some other artifacts.

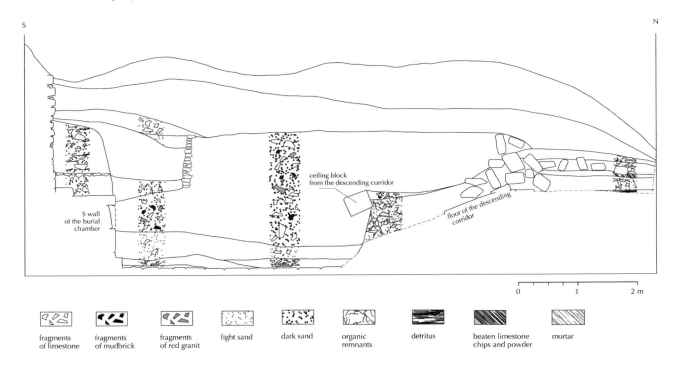

Fig. 4.10. North–south section through the descending corridor and constructional pit inside the pyramid.

The robbers penetrated into the burial chamber several times (see *figs. 4.10–4.11*). One of their attacks led from above, through a hole cut in the south-east corner of the chamber's ceiling. The access to the chamber was facilitated by means of a primitive staircase made of mudbricks and lumps of limestone. At the foot of the

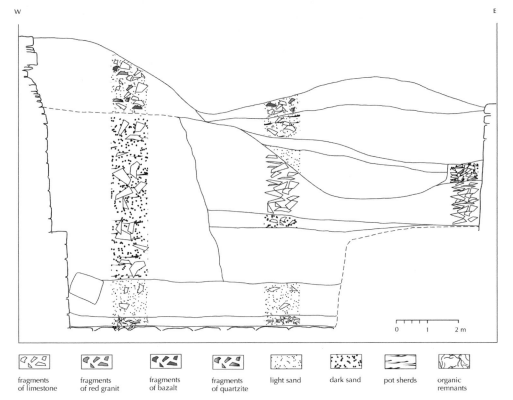

Fig. 4.11. East–west section through the descending corridor and construction pit inside the pyramid.

Fig. 4.12. Penultimate ceiling block of the corridor *in situ*.
Photo JK

staircase were found the remains of reed mats. The hole was filled with drift sand indicating that the place was left open after the robbers finished their work. Next to the hole, above the level of the ceiling of the burial chamber, was a compact layer of small limestone chips indicating that in this place the stone robbers cut in pieces the fine white limestone blocks extracted from the burial chamber. This destruction can probably be dated to the Saite-Persian Period when limestone was quarried and cut in smaller ashlars used in the construction of shaft tombs not far away from the pyramid Lepsius no. 24, in the West Abusir. A fragment of a dark blue glazed jug found in the rubble above the burial chamber dates from the last robbers' activities in the pyramid dating from the Middle Ages. From the same time date the fragments of two dark green glazed oil lamps found in the fill of the burial chamber. However, all these robbers were preceded by the robbers who also penetrated into the burial chamber from above, but in this case in the place where the descending corridor opens in the burial chamber. This was the shortest way into the pyramid's substructure, through the pyramid's wall directly to the burial chamber. In order to protect themselves from the fill of rubble above the burial chamber, the robbers left the last but one ceiling block of the corridor in position (see *fig. 4.12*).[10] This early

Fig. 4.13. Fragments of a mummified body belonging to an unknown woman (49/J/94): remains of the scull and of the torso.
Photo JK

---

[10] The same method was used by the robbers in the pyramid of Raneferef, see Verner *et al.*, *Raneferef*, 16, fig. 1.1.11.

looting of the burial chamber may date, as in other pyramids in Abusir, to the First Intermediate Period.

In the mixed fill inside the burial chamber were revealed, besides the relatively well preserved though broken remains of a female mummy 49/J/94 (see *figs. 4.13–4.14*) many artefacts coming from the burial equipment of the pyramid owner. The mummy originally lay in a large red granite sarcophagus with a slightly convex lid. The sarcophagus was broken in many pieces, some of them quite large. It is not quite certain when the sarcophagus was destroyed. It might have been in Late Roman – Early Christian Period judging by a rag of decorated cloth found in the fill of the chamber but it might have been the Middle Ages, too. A circle in red paint on one of large fragments of red granit found in the chamber indicated that it was intended to be worked as a mill stone (see *fig. 4.15*).

In fill of the chamber were also found fragments of a large whitewashed red ware plate with a raised rim, fragments of travertine models of offerings, fragments of a small wooden chest together with tiny pieces of a gold foil, fragments of canopic jars and some other artifacts. In the layer of debris resting on the floor of the chamber lay travertine models of plates, fragments of travertine canopic jars, fragments of travertine trays, pieces of mummy wrappings, fragments of the ordinary late Fifth Dynasty red ware pottery, fragments of cattle and poultry bones, *etc*. In a gap between floor blocks were found relatively well preserved copper models of different tools together with tiny pieces of a gold foil (see *fig. 4.16*).

Fig. 4.14. The lower part of mummified body belonging to an unknown woman (49/J/94).
Photo JK

Fig. 4.15 Area of the burial chamber during the archaeological excavations. On the left side, a large granite fragment intended to be worked as a mill stone.
Photo JK

Fig. 4.16 Copper models of instruments coming from the burial equipment of the owner of Lepsius no. 24 at the time of unearthing.
Photo JK

At the end of the 1994 season was briefly examined also the area around the entrance to the pyramid's substructure. On both sides of the entrance were found in position the remains of blocks from the lowest course of the casing (*fig. 4.17*). However, no remains of an entrance chapel were revealed. The area in front of the entrance to the pyramid was largely devastated and covered by a layer of limestone chips and powder indicating that in this place the casing blocks of the pyramid were cut in pieces and dressed. A fragment of a painted pottery found among the limestone chips dates the destruction activity to the New Kingdom.

Fig. 4.17 Blocks from the lower part of the pyramid's casing on the western side of the entrance.
Photo MZ

In the subsequent years, the extant masonry of the pyramid was consolidated, the damaged burial chamber was reconstructed and the scanty remains of the mortuary temple were again covered with sand.

4.2. The location of the Pyramid Complex Lepsius no. 24

The Pyramid Complex Lepsius no. 24 represents a typical example of a pyramid complex for a queen.[11] The Abusir complex consists of standard parts of a queen's pyramid complex of the Fifth and the Sixth Dynasties: a pyramid, a mortuary temple and a still new (from the time of Khentkaus II)[12] element – a cult pyramid – is located on the eastern edge of the Abusir pyramid plateau, 7.5 m to the east from the mortuary temple of Raneferef[13] and 8 m to the south-east of the pyramid complex of Khentkaus II (*fig. 4.18, pl. III*).[14] Despite all the efforts we made to find an enclosure wall of the Pyramid Complex Lepsius no. 24 (through an archaeological

---

[11] For discussion concerning the status of the owner of the small pyramid complex, Jánosi, The Queens of the Old Kingdom and Their Tombs, *BACE* 3, 1992, 51–57; see *idem, Pyramidenanlagen,* 179. We have to underline here that the supposition that the pyramid complexes were built for the queens-mothers is in the contrast with the conclusions of the osteological investigation of the mummy found in the burial chamber of the pyramid (49/J/94). This lady did not have give birth, it means that she could not be marked as a mother of a royal successor – see *chapters 4.7.* and *6.2.* of this monograph.

[12] Jánosi in: Verner, *Khentkaus,* 160–161, Fig. 3a, Pl. 50.

[13] Verner *et al., Raneferef,* xvi–xviii.

[14] Verner, *Khentkaus,* 13–15.

trench made between the area of the cult pyramid and the Tomb Complex Lepsius no. 25), we did not succeed in unearthing it.[15]

4.3. Description of the monument

4.3.1. Pyramid

The pyramid itself lies in the western part of the complex (*fig. 4.19, pl. IV*) and is preserved only in its lower part (up to the height of 7.5 m). During our works, the eastern and a part of the northern outer wall of the pyramid were cleared (*fig. 4.20*). In the trench in the axis of the northern wall, some blocks of white limestone of the casing were still found *in situ* (see *chapter 4.1.* and *fig. 4.17*). Nevertheless, the

Fig. 4.20 Northern wall of the pyramid Lepsius no. 24 after excavation.
Photo MZ

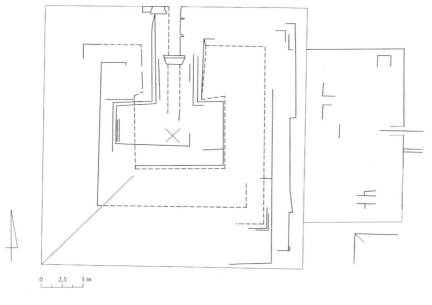

0   2.5   5 m

Fig. 4.21. Plan of the Pyramid Complex Lepsius no. 24.

pyramid was deprived of the majority of its casing, therefore, the largest dimension of the pyramid's core which is now preserved is 27.10 m. Following the situation with the north-western corner of the mortuary temple (where a part of the northern

---

[15] Nevertheless, the existence of such a wall at one time is very probable.

outer wall of the temple survived) it seems that the width of the filling masonry plus the casing of the pyramid on the both ends of the individual pyramid wall was 2 m (= 4 cubits). As a result, one side of the pyramid might have been 31.10 m long (which is almost precisely 60 cubits – 59.80 cubits, see also *fig. 4.21*). In this way, the pyramid represented quite a large monument, and indeed resembles pyramids of queens living during the Fourth Dynasty.[16] In this connection it is also important to mention that, fortunately, some blocks of the pyramid casing were found *in situ*. This enabled us to measure the angle of the pyramid walls as being 57° 30′ (see *fig. 4.19, pl. IV* and *figs. 4.53–4.54*). With this angle and proposed length of the pyramid sides, the height of the pyramid can be reconstructed as 24.72 m (47.77 cubits).

Fig. 4.22 View of the core masonry belonging to the western wall of the descending corridor. Photo JK

The core masonry of the pyramid had been constructed in at least three steps. The core masonry was, as it shall be shown later in this chapter, built by using the caisson method[17] which was a method aimed at lowering the building cost and reducing the time taken for the pyramid's construction. On contrary to the situation in the core of Raneferef's pyramid, large blocks of limestone were not used in the frame of outer walls,[18] the blocks used in L24 are smaller, measuring up to 0.50 × 0.50 × 1.00 m (see *fig. 4.22*).

In the axis of the northern wall of the pyramid, located just above the foot of the wall, there is an entrance to the descending corridor leading to the burial chamber. Unfortunately, there is no direct proof whether or not the corridor had originally been blocked. However, a weathered block of white limestone found during the archaeological excavations and perfectly fitting in the width of the corridor seems to correspond with our idea of closing the corridor's entrance (*fig.4.23*). This block would then be a plugging of the entrance. No traces of a kind of northern chapel (see

---

[16] *Cf.* the list of the queens' pyramids mentioned by Jánosi in: *Pyramidenanlagen*, 184 – Tabelle II: Maßangaben zu Kapitel II.1.
[17] Despite the fact this method is not described by M. Verner as "caisson" we can quote here his chapter on the core masonry of Raneferef's Unfinished Pyramid in: Verner *et al.*, *Raneferef*, 11, figs. 1.1.5–1.1.7.
[18] Verner, in: Verner *et al.*, *Raneferef*, 9.

also *chapter 4.1.* and *fig. 4.20*) were detected during the archaeological excavations, therefore, we do not suppose its existence.[19]

Only some parts of the corridor's masonry still remain *in situ* now. This is the case with (*figs. 4.24–4.27*) the upper part of the eastern and the western side walls and also of the upper part of the floor. Only one block of the corridor ceiling remains *in situ*

Fig. 4.23 A weathered block of white limestone found at the corridor's entrance.
Photo JK

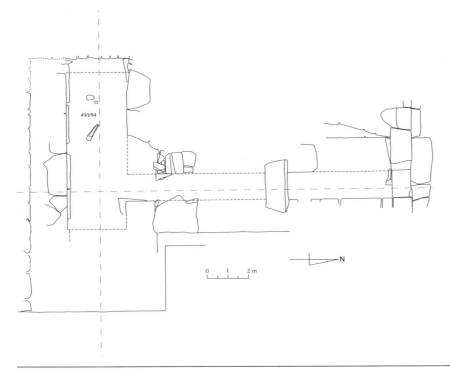

Fig. 4.24 Plan of the descending corridor and the burial chamber in the pyramid.

[19] *Cf.* Verner, in: Verner *et al.*, *Raneferef*, 14–15, figs. 1.1.3a, 1.1.9–1.1.10 and P. Jánosi, Bemerkungen zu den Nordkapellen des Alten Reiches, *SAK* 22, 1995, 145 – who does not exclude the existence of these installation already in the Fifth Dynasty; see also Posener-Kriéger, *Les papyrus d'Abousir* I, 24; II, 448f., 509.

(see *figs. 4.24, 4.25, 4.26a, 4.28* and also *fig. 4.12*). Its dimensions are 2.60 × 0.80–0.85 × 0.95 m. The corridor was at least 13.76 m long and its height was 1.26 and width 1.37 m. The slope of the corridor was quite low 20° 50′–21° 00′. Unfortunately, the lower part of the descending corridor is destroyed to a greater degree than is the case with its upper part (*fig.4.28*). This is as the case with the ceiling, as the floor and the side walls. Therefore, the reconstruction of the angle of the corridor in this part is more complicated to determine; nevertheless, we can say that the angle was

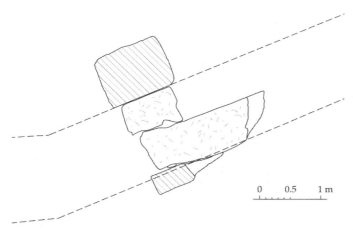

Fig. 4.25 Section through the remaining part of the masonry of the descending corridor *in situ*.

Fig. 4.26a–b Blocks of the descending corridor *in situ*.
Photo JK

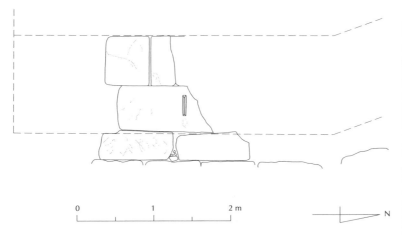

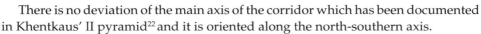

reduced towards the end of the corridor. We can reconstruct this angle in the passage as only ca 5°. Two different inclinations of the descending corridor have been documented in Raneferef's and Niuserre's pyramid[20]. We can document such design also in the case of Khentkaus' II pyramid[21]. Two vertical building lines with small triangles documented on the eastern and the western wall of the trench in which the descending corridor was constructed may mark the area in which the inclination of the descending corridor changed (see *figs. 4.104–4.105*). Unfortunately, there is no fact which would document the existence of an anteroom at the end of the corridor.

Fig. 4.27 Casing of the horizontal part of the corridor *in situ*.

Fig. 4.28 Descending corridor from the south. Photo JK

There is no deviation of the main axis of the corridor which has been documented in Khentkaus' II pyramid[22] and it is oriented along the north-southern axis.

At the end of the descending corridor, there was a simple entrance into the burial chamber. It also was largely destroyed (*fig. 4.29*). Because of this destruction it was possible (as is also the same case with the descending trench into the constructional pit) to study the mason's marks and lines in this section – see *chapter 4.6.5.–6*. The stone robbers destroyed not only the ceiling, but all the major parts of the western, northern and eastern walls of the tomb (see *fig. 4.30*). However, it was possible to quite easily reconstruct the original dimensions of the chamber: it was 7.44 m (14.3 cubits) long, its width was (eastern wall) 2.86 m (5.5 cubits) up to (western wall) 2.93 m (5.63 cubits), the flat ceiling was constructed at a level of 2.60 m (5 cubits) from the floor paving. The flat ceiling[23] was constructed with rectangular beams of limestone, however, none of them was found during the excavation of the pyramid. As a matter of course, the floor, side wall casing and the ceiling beams were all made of white limestone.

4.3.2. Mortuary temple

The mortuary temple of the Pyramid Complex Lepsius no. 24 is, unfortunately, largely destroyed (*fig. 4.31–4.32*). It was a rectangular, north–south oriented building leaning against the eastern wall of the pyramid itself (the masonry of the mortuary temple was joined with the backing stones of the pyramid's core). The masonry of the mortuary temple is also very badly destroyed, even much worse than is the case with the pyramid. Only the northern and the north-eastern part as well as the western part of the central sector of the temple are better preserved than the first-mentioned sections (*figs. 4.33–4.34*) – we can follow at least some features of

---

[20] Verner, in: Verner *et al.*, *Raneferef*, fig. 1.1.3a; *MRA* VIII, 12.

[21] Jánosi, in: Verner, *Khentkaus*, 147, fig. 67a–b, 68, 69.

[22] Verner, in: Verner, *Khentkaus*, 18, fig. 3a; Jánosi, in: *op.cit.*, 145–148, figs. 3a, 69.

[23] Flat ceilings were typical for the burial chambers of queens of the Old Kingdom – Jánosi, *Pyramidenanlagen*, 109–114.

Fig. 4.29a The construction pit and the burial chamber of the pyramid from the east. Photo JK

Fig. 4.29b Burial chamber from south-east. Photo JK
Fig. 4.30a Remaining part of the southern wall of the burial chamber.

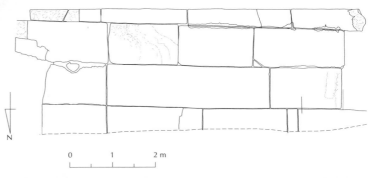

Fig. 4.30b Remaining part of the southern wall of the burial chamber. Photo JK

Fig. 4.30c Remaining part of the nothern wall of the burial chamber.

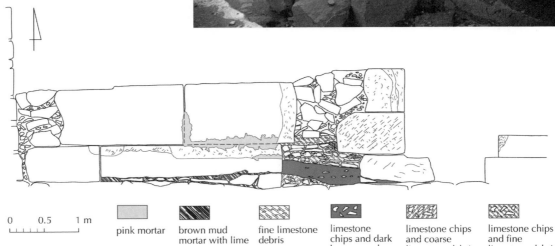

pink mortar   brown mud mortar with lime coating   fine limestone debris   limestone chips and dark brown sand   limestone chips and coarse limestone debris   limestone chips and fine limestone debris

Fig. 4.31 Mortuary temple and pyramid after archaeological excavation. Photo JK

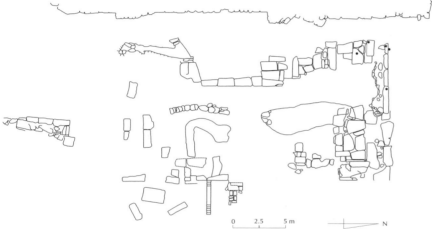

Fig. 4.32 Plan of the mortuary temple.

Fig. 4.33 Southern part of the mortuary temple and remains of the cult pyramid. Photo JK

its ground plan there. In contrast to this part, other parts of the temple are almost totally destroyed and they do not allow us to reconstruct their layout.

Despite the fact that the temple was almost totally destroyed, we can reconstruct its outer dimensions as being 11.40 × 21.10 m – the temple's longer axis was oriented

Fig. 4.34 Northern part of the mortuary temple.
Photo JK

Fig. 4.35 Corridor-like room in the eastern part of the mortuary temple.
Photo JK

in a north–south direction. The thickness of the outer wall was not the same as the dimensions in its northern wing – 1.60 m – and eastern wing – 1.56 m. It seems that there was only one entrance cut into the outer wall; however, its precise location can not be reconstructed.[24] Either it might have been located in the axis of the eastern wall of the temple, or it might have been located to the south of this axis – as could be shown by the location of remains of a corridor-like room in the southern part of the temple (see *fig. 4.32* and *4.35*). Following its preserved part, this room might have been 0.98 m broad and it was, at least in its preserved part, oriented along the east–west axis. It seems that this room was connected with the entrance to the temple and functioned as a communication with inner parts of the temple, that is, the offering room and hypothetical open courtyard. As a result, it had to be connected with the entrance to the temple by another corridor which would have had to change its direction twice (from west to south and then back to the west again, no matter where the location of its entrance might have been.

To the north of the preserved part of this corridor, there was an area where we found a part that consisted of layers of under-floor blocks of limestone. They may indicate that the eastern part of the middle sector of the temple was covered by an open (and possibly pillared) courtyard, which was a part of the architecture of the queen's temple structure in the Fifth and Sixth Dynasties.[25] Unfortunately, no part of any side wall or of the courtyard pavement was found. Therefore, we cannot

---

[24] Almost in all cases there was only one entrance to the mortuary temples of the Old Kingdom queens (*Cf.* Jánosi, *Pyramidenanlagen*, 123–144, Abb. 57–76, with an exception of GIIIc – *op. cit.*, 134–135, Abb. 66–68).
[25] See *op. cit.*, 150–153.

Fig. 4.36 Remains of the offering room.
Photo JK

reconstruct the original layout and appearance of the courtyard. In contrast to the neighbouring mortuary temple of Khentkaus II,[26] no part of a pillar was found *in situ*, or even in a fragmentary form during the excavations of the temple, we can therefore suppose that this courtyard did not have pillars. The dimensions of this supposed courtyard is almost impossible to reconstruct. If we look at the empty space in between the remaining masonry or its imprints, we can suppose that this courtyard might have represented quite a narrow space oriented along the north–south axis and it could not be broader than 4.5 m or longer than 11 m.

We can only speculate that the above mentioned corridor was connected with the courtyard by means of a doorway. There is no proof of whether this corridor was running along the southern and western part of the courtyard (in order to give access to the offering chapel, which was oriented along the north–south axis), or

Fig. 4.37 Remains of the eastern wall of the offering room.
Photo MZ

[26] Jánosi, in: Verner, *Khentkaus*, 152–154, figs. 71, 72, 75.
[27] Cf. Jánosi, in: *op. cit.*, 157–159, fig. 75, 79b.

Fig. 4.38 Remains of the masonry in the northern part of the mortuary temple. Photo JK

whether this offering room was entered from the courtyard. Only a few remains were preserved from this focal room of the temple – a part of the lowermost part of its eastern wall (*figs. 4.36–4.37*) and all of the western wall, as well as its south-western corner (see *fig. 4.8*). These two sets of remains made it possible to measure its original dimensions: 7.60 × 1.95 m. From these remains it follows that the offering room was oriented along the north–south axis and we can only hypothesize that in its western wall, a false door was located.[27] However, no part of such a false door was found.

To the north of the offering chapel, remains of masonry have enabled us to reconstruct another room, oriented along the east–west axis and measuring 1.54 × 2.60 m (see also *fig. 4.7*). The same could be said about another room located to the north of it – its dimensions were 1.54 × min. 1.13 m. Due to their destruction, the function of these two rooms once again has to be reconstructed. As the rooms were located in the space next to the offering room, we can suppose that they served as magazines. We can suppose that instruments used during the rituals were deposited in these two rooms.

The same can be mentioned in connection with spaces which were located in the north-east sector of the temple (see *figs. 4.34* and *4.38*). Only the imprints of the side walls remained on the layer of flat limestone blocks, together with tiny remains of red colouring used during the original surveying of the temple plan on the layer of these flat limestone blocks (see *figs. 4.39a–b, pl. III*). These few traces enabled us to reconstruct dimensions of these rooms. Their sizes were almost the same – 1.50 × 1.60 m and 1.45 × min. 1.60 m. There is a possibility, in fact, that these two spaces created one room connected with other rooms probably located to the west of them: they would have been connected together in a comb-like layout resembling magazine spaces below the pyramids of the Third Dynasty.[28] Unfortunately, the

[28] Lauer, *Pyr. à degrés*, pl. XV; in Sekhemkhet's pyramid – Goneim, *Sekhem-khet*, pl. XXX; *MRA* II, 21–26, Tav. 5, and in Zawiyet el-Aryan, *MRA* II, 44–45, Tav. 6. In this connection, we have to mention here the "treasuries" located to the north and north-east of the offering halls of the mortuary temples belonging to the kings – especially that of Niuserre. In this case, we can also quite simple layout of north–south oriented rooms which were not equipped with doorways (Borchardt, *Neuserre*, 18, Bl. 28). In the mortuary complexes of queens, the magazines were usually equipped with doorways – *cf.* Pyramid Complex of Khentkaus II (east-western orientation, Verner, *Khentkaus*, fig. 3a, 32-35, Jánosi, in: Verner, *Khentkaus*, 75, 162), in double-mastaba of Nebet and Chenut (north–south orientation, Munro, *Unas-Friedhof*, 31–32, Beilage 2) and in the mortuary temples of Neith and Iput II (Neith: east–western orientation, Jéquier, *Neit et Apouit*, 10, pl. XXXVI; Iput II: north–south orientation, *op. cit.*, 45, pl. II).

supposed storage function cannot be documented in the archaeological material, although the appearance of the spaces and their masonry have enabled us to predict what had been there.

During the excavations, not a single block with a relief decoration was found. Therefore, we can theorize that either the temple was not decorated, or its decoration was confined to a very small part – most likely in the area of the offering room, which is almost totally destroyed. In the area of the northern storerooms, which is the best preserved section, such decoration is not likely.

4.3.3. Cult pyramid

Cult pyramids, it seems, first became part of the pyramid complexes of queens in Abusir – as has been attested in the Khentkaus' II pyramid complex.[29] This example was followed soon afterwards by a cult pyramid in Lepsius no. 24 complex. As is the case with the mortuary temple, the cult pyramid beside the pyramid Lepsius no. 24 had been destroyed to a large degree: only a small, north-western part of the pyramid was preserved (see *figs. 4.33, 4.40* and also *4.9*). These remains represented only a few limestone blocks with well worked and polished outer walls and they belong to the lowermost part of the pyramid. The pyramid itself is preserved only up to the height of 0.32 m. The casing blocks are of rather regular shape (rectangular, with one wall inclined) and they have been set upright in their original place. The casing enclosed the core, which consisted of inferior masonry: this was a mixture of small limestone fragments and rubble, sometimes joined by means of mortar. We have also tried to find traces of other walls and corners of the pyramid; however, despite all the efforts made, we were not successful. In the area in which the mass of the cult pyramid was once standing, there were only the layers of wind blown sand and limestone chips. Therefore, it is not also possible to reconstruct the precise dimensions of this small construction. The angle of the pyramid's walls was – as it follows from the lowermost preserved part of its casing, 57° 30´.

A very striking feature of this structure is that the pyramid is not strictly oriented along the north–south axis, but is turned some 6° 20´ to the east. What the reason for this turn in the orientation was, is not known, although we might speculate that it could be based on the haste with which this construction was built, especially during the laying down of the pyramid's groundplan.

---

[29] See Jánosi, in: Verner, *Khentkaus*, 160–161 and *idem., Pyramidenanlagen*, 161–164: we can find cult pyramids in the cases of Iput's I., Neith, Iput's II. P. Jánosi (*op. cit.*, 163) shows that a cult pyramid by a pyramid of a queen developed together with the development of the mortuary temples of queens. This feature was adopted from the mortuary architecture of kings.

4.3.4. Other parts of the pyramid complex

No part of the expected pavement of the pyramid courtyard has been unearthed. Around the pyramid and the mortuary temple, there was only a layer (thick up to 0.70–1.00 m) of hard beaten clay mixed with the sand-*dakka*. We can then only speculate that the pavement was removed by the stone robbers, or, due to the above mentioned haste in which the pyramid complex was built, that the pavement was never laid down and that the clay layer was a kind of replacement for a pavement.

4.4. Pyramid Complex Lepsius no. 24 – Remarks on techniques used during its construction

As was already mentioned, pyramid Lepsius no. 24 and its mortuary temple is a very desolated monument. Nevertheless, this destruction of the complex enables us, on the other hand, to study the techniques and methods used for its construction very well. Not only is its masonry easily accessible, but also a large collection of masons' marks and lines have been studied throughout the investigation of this monument.

4.4.1. Construction of the pyramid

Burial chamber and the pit for its construction

Due to a number of circumstances,[30] it was not possible to fully excavate the foundations of the pyramid itself. However, the walls of the burial apartment were destroyed to such a great degree that it was only possible to investigate its smaller parts, especially in the area of the join of the northern wall of the burial chamber and that of the descending corridor.

It is apparent that, at first, a pit for the construction of the burial apartment was dug out in the subsoil of *tafla* for the future pyramid complex. Then, one (or two?) layers of flat blocks of local limestone were laid down on the bottom of the excavated pit.[31] On the one hand, this layer represented a sub-floor level and, on the other hand, it was inserted as a base for the construction of the lining of the side walls.

The lining of the construction pit was made up of small fragments of local limestone joined together by mud mortar.[32] As one can realise from the stone robbers' break made in the masonry of the "plinth" (see further), the side walls of the pit were formed by layers of brown sand (we cannot say whether this represents the subsoil of the monument, or, whether the sand was put down for some unknown reason, between the side walls of the hewn pit and the said lining.

After lining the side walls, the builders started to lay down the pavement of the burial chamber itself. This was made of well worked flat blocks of white limestone. The pavement blocks apparently did not reach the whole extent of the bottom of the construction pit – the "free" spaces between the edge of the pavement and the side wall of the pit (something that was hidden by the future side walls of the burial chamber) were filled by masonry of flat limestone blocks joined by mud mortar.

After the laying down of the pavement of the burial chamber, the masons began to commence the chamber's side walls. In contrast to the technique used in the case of the royal burial chambers, there was no well worked masonry built behind the casing of side walls of the burial chamber in this pyramid.[33] No masons' marks,

[30] The main reasons for the situation were due to safety and security for the workers and members of the archaeological team. The masonry of the pyramid was destroyed to such a degree that it was in danger of collapsing if any major excavations of its foundations would have been undertaken.
[31] Unfortunately, the bottom of the pit was very unstable and due to safety reasons, it was not possible to excavate further below this visible layer of flat blocks.
[32] The same situation has been documented in the case of the tomb Lepsius no. 25/2 – see p. 178–179.
[33] One of the examples of the former technique is Raneferef's burial chamber – see Verner *et al.*, *Raneferef*, 5–7, but we also find these methods in use in other pyramids of kings in Abusir – Borchardt, *Sahure*; Borchardt, *Neuserre*.

which could be connected with the surveying and measuring of the burial chamber, were found on the surface of the under-pavement blocks during our archaeological excavation[34]. The blocks of the casing of the burial chamber were large ashlars of white limestone, joined together by a quality pinkish mortar. As a matter of course,

the blocks of the casing did not have the same width, therefore, the free space between their rear sides and the lining of the construction pit had to be filled in with backing material (*fig. 4.41*). This backing masonry was made of fragments of local limestone with almost no attempt made to join the pieces. As was also the case with the construction of the steps of the pyramid's core, layers of flattened local limestone blocks were added at certain levels above the pavement of the burial chamber. This was done to give additional stability to the future walls of the burial chamber. These layers of flattened stones "closed" the filling from above and in this way improved the stability of the masonry.

> **Fig. 4.41 Backing and filling masonry between the casing of the burial chamber (northern wall) and wall of the construction pit.**
> Photo JK

> **Fig. 4.42 The plinth behind the masonry of the burial chamber and the corridor (right side of the photograph).**
> Photo JK

After reaching the desired level (2.60 m = 5 cubits) above the pavement of the burial chamber, the ceiling beams were transported and laid down in place. As was the standard way in the case of the pyramids of queens,[35] the burial chamber in L24 was covered by a flat roof. The fragments of these limestone beams were found during the excavations carried out in the actual space of the burial chamber.

At the same time as the masonry of the side walls of the burial chamber were being built (or even a little earlier), some kind of "plinth" masonry which enclosed the masonry of the burial chamber and access corridor was created as the base for the construction of the superstructure of the pyramid. The height of the "plinth" was 2.53 m above the pavement of the burial chamber (*fig. 4.42*, as well as *figs. 4.28, 4.29b*). It was created by large, quite well worked blocks of local limestone. They were joined together by grey mud mortar and the joins were even overfilled by pinkish, quality mortar (to the height of 1.7 m of the plinth and then again in the uppermost parts of the plinth).

---

[34] Such marks have been found on the under-pavement blocks in the area of the burial chamber in L25/1 – see p. 171 – and one has to suppose that a similar technique was also used in the case of the burial chamber of L24.

[35] Jánosi, *Pyramidenanlagen*, 109–116. Only one exception is represented by the pyramid of Queen Neferhetepes in Saqqara – see Labrousse, Lauer, *Ouserkaf*, fig. 346, 346, 348–349, pl. 30.

Core masonry of the superstructure

When the plinth masonry was built around the burial chamber pit, the construction of the superstructure of the pyramid began. It is apparent that it proceeded in that way because it made the construction as uncomplicated and as rapid as possible. On the plinth masonry, the masons set out the outline of the lowermost step of the pyramid core. Then the blocks of its outer walls were laid down and, at the same time, masons started filling the interior space of the step with masonry of inferior quality and by sand. This masonry was then "closed" by a layer of flat blocks of local limestone at the height of the lowermost layer of stone of the step's outer face. In the higher levels of the masonry, this methodology was repeated for several times in respect to the layers of the limestone blocks laid against the face of the step (*figs. 4.22* and *4.43*). The same method was evidently used in the case of the uppermost parts of the masonry of the first core step. The inner masonry was in this instance closed by two layers of flat limestone blocks.

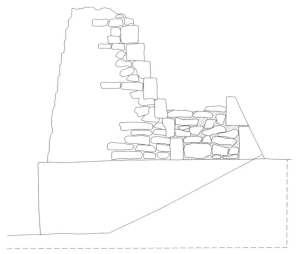

Fig. 4.43 Schematic view of masonry of the western wall of the descending corridor to the burial chamber.

Fig. 4.44a Southern wall of the building shaft with visible built up provisional entrances.

Fig. 4.44b Eastern wall of the building shaft with visible built up provisional entrances.
Photos JK

As is shown in *figs. 4.44a–b*, it is clear that, at least in the first step of the core masonry, the masons had already made provisional entrances in its masonry to allow workers to build the upper layers of the pyramid. One, a larger entrance, was created in the south-eastern corner. One can envisage that through this passage a transport ramp might have been erected, on which large blocks for the construction of the burial chamber's ceiling and also some larger blocks used in the core masonry itself were to have been transported. This provisional entrance was originally quite broad (4.75 m in the southern wall of the construction pit and 1.38 m in the eastern wall). The bottom of the passage lay on the plinth of the core masonry. The position of the entrance and also the way in which it was later built up enables us to suppose that the transportation ramp was running through this entrance passage inside the pyramid in a SE–NW direction (see *fig. 4.45*).

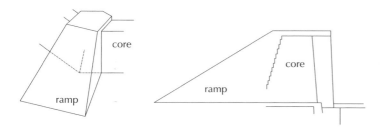

Fig. 4.45 Schema of the transportation ramp in the south-eastern corner of the pyramid.

Another temporary entrance to the construction pit of the pyramid was made in the south-western corner of the pit (see *fig. 4.44a*). As it was made in the higher levels of the first step's masonry, it is apparent that it served for the transportation of large blocks used in the construction of the first step, but also for transportation of the filling masonry brought into the construction pit. This masonry was laid down when the ceiling of the burial chamber was finished. As was also the case with the inner masonry of the pyramid core, this filling masonry consisted of smaller fragments of local limestone, smaller amount of fragments of other kinds of stone (basalt, quartzite and granite) and a larger addition of broken mudbricks and weathered pottery sherds. It is apparent that, in course of the construction of the walls of the burial chamber, of its ceiling and then the steady filling of the construction pit, the angle of the ramps running through the provisional entrances was enlarged. Moreover, the provisional entrance in the south-eastern corner of the pit was noticeably walled up in several successive stages (see *fig. 4.44*) during its use. These stages are easily visible in the masonry filling the provisional entrance – it then created part of faces of the construction pit.

After finishing of the first, lowermost step of the core and the filling in of the construction pit, a second step was commenced, built on top of the first one. The builders of the pyramid were apparently afraid that the stability of the inner, filling masonry of the first step and above all the filling masonry of the construction pit was not strong enough to support this extra weight of other stone steps. Therefore, they decided to start with the construction of the second step and, at the corners of the pyramid core, segments of the masonry which ran in a transverse direction above the filling of the construction pit (*figs. 4.46, 4.47a–b*). (In effect, this was like making a giant cross in stone from one corner of the pyramid to its opposite).[36] These segments, each about 2.5 m wide, were detected in the south-western and south-eastern corners of the pyramid core.[37] This transverse masonry consisted of five or six vertical layers of limestone fragments, carefully joined together, in order to create with one of the sides of the stone fragments a kind of a face for each vertical layer (see *fig. 4.22*).[38]

This masonry was a part of the second step of the pyramid core, which was otherwise built by means of the same technique as in the case of the lowermost step, with larger blocks of local limestone in its faces and with the inferior inner masonry used in the inner areas.

Having in mind the reconstructed height of the pyramid (see pp. 78–79), one can assume that a third step of the pyramid core had also been constructed. Its

---

[36] There are also horizontal lines on the northern outer wall of the pyramid core – two of them are accompanied by entries referring to the "outer" project zero – *mḥ 7* and *mḥ 8* above it. In this connection it is interesting to mention that the entry of *mḥ 7* matches with one of the layers of flat blocks, which is at a height of 358.5 cm above ground level. The reading of *mḥ 8* was painted on the block which was below the already-mentioned double layer of flat limestone blocks that "closed off" the inner masonry of the walls of the burial pit.

[37] See also Verner, *Pyramids*, 98–99.

[38] A much smaller section of it was documented in the northeast corner of the core.

Fig. 4.46 Segments of the transverse masonry which remains on the top of the pyramid core in its south-western and south-eastern corners.

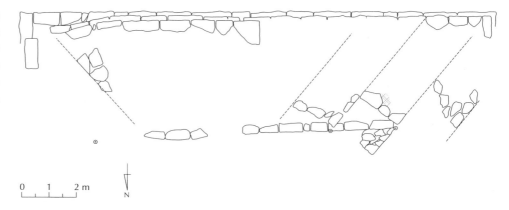

Fig. 4.47a–b Transverse masonry on the top of the south-western corner of the pyramid core.
Photos JK

construction might have been one of the reasons for the transversally laid masonry of the second step with its stabilizing function.

During these complex works, masons' marks were used in a large scale. As in the case of both side wall of the descending corridor as the walls of the building pit for the burial chamber, especially the western wall was covered by extensive net of masons' marks and lines. These marks were important for the successful completion of the works (see also *chapter 4.6.* and *figs. 4.48–4.49, pl. IV*).[39]

Corridor

The method of construction used for the descending corridor was similar to that used for the burial chamber. In this case, the masons had to at first lay down on the bottom of the trench leading to the pit for the burial chamber the layer of sub-floor pavement blocks – this was carried out using roughly worked stones. Then the pavement of the descending corridor was put down on top of it. After that, the plinth masonry and the side walls of the corridor were commenced. As was the case with the side walls of the burial chamber, the walls of the corridor were made of quality limestone blocks which were well polished after they had been set into position (see *figs. 4.25* and *4.26a–b*). The same methodology could be mentioned with regard to the ceiling blocks of the corridor. One of these blocks remained *in situ* (see *fig. 4.25*). After the ceiling of the descending corridor was set in place, the space above it was filled in, using inferior masonry. It would have been common sense practice if this filling was made at the same time as setting in place the casing of the corridor.

Casing (see also *fig. 4.17*)

After finishing the core masonry (or perhaps already during the construction of the core?) the casing of the pyramid was added. The casing part which was found *in situ* in the area of the entrance of the descending corridor was made of blocks of quality white limestone. The casing blocks were joined to the core masonry by backing stone masonry. The backing masonry was made up of smaller fragments of local limestone joined together by means of dark-brown, mud mortar. In the case of at least the eastern face of the pyramid core, the joins in the lowermost part of the backing stone masonry were filled by white calcareous mortar.

An important find represents a block coming from a layer below the pyramidion. Dimensions of the block were 150 × 74 cm in the lower face and 104 × 52 cm in its upper face and it was 43 cm high. The block made of white limestone was weathered in a large scale (*figs. 4.50–4.51*). The angle of its inclined outer walls were 59°. It is not much different from inclination as of the main pyramid and as of the cult pyramid (see above in this chapter). It thus might have been built in both constructions.[40]

Fig. 4.50 Block of the casing from a layer below the pyramidion.
Photo JK

---

[39] See also M. Verner, The Axis: an Ancient Terminus Technicus, in: *Homm. Lauer*, 433–436.
[40] *Cf.* find of a basalt pyramidion in the area of Raneferef's mortuary temple, Verner, in: Verner *et al.*, *Raneferef*, figs. 1.2.13–1.2.14; and Stadelmann, *Pyramiden*, 101, Taf. 31.

4.4.2. Construction of the mortuary temple

As is the case with the neighbouring tomb of Nakhtsare ("Q"), as well as the Tomb Complex Lepsius no. 25, the foundations of the mortuary temple were laid on top of a layer of broken mudbricks and brown sand mixed with limestone splinters and fragments of pottery. Directly onto this layer, a quite high (0.48–0.52 m) layer of blocks was laid down which created the foundation for the outer wall of the temple (its casing). The area which was enclosed by this layer of blocks was even more elevated above the terrain than the foundation layer. It was made by means of a layer of broken limestone (*raksha*). On top of this layer, a layer of flat, white, well worked limestone blocks was laid. In this way, the whole area of the future temple was brought up to one level (*fig. 4.52*). This layer of limestone blocks created the pavement of the inner rooms of the temple; in addition, it created a base for erecting the outer walls of the temple, as well as the walls of the chambers and magazines in its interior.

Fig. 4.51 Block of the casing from a layer below the pyramidion.
Photo JK

Fig. 4.52 Foundation layer for the mortuary temple.
Photo JK

Unfortunately, it is not fully clear whether the foundation and pavement layer of the mortuary temple was already laid down during the construction of the pyramid, or whether it was built later. Neither the backing stones of the pyramid nor its core masonry are directly connected with the temple, therefore one can deduce that these two parts of the pyramid complex were not constructed at the same moment in time. Nevertheless, it does not mean that these two buildings were not connected with each other. The face of the two lowermost parts of the backing stone masonry of the pyramid is not running straight, instead, it seems to create a series of some sort of protrusions or niches. The masonry is more protruded in the northern half of the pyramid's eastern wall than it is in the southern half. Is it possible to explain this effect by the masons' need to join the more solid masonry of the temple to the core of the pyramid than was the case for the southern half? In the area of the east-west axis of the pyramid, the face of the backing stones creates the first recess. This might have been connected with the offering chapel, which would have been located in just this space. Hypothetically, the need for such a layout of this masonry might have been due to the existence of a (deep) niche in the western wall of the offering chapel. Towards the south-eastern corner of the pyramid there is another recess which might have been connected to the construction of the outer southern wall of the temple.

After levelling the area of the temple, as it follows from the situation in the north-east sector of the temple, the builders started to survey and to mark the temple's ground plan onto the surface of the pavement layer (see *figs. 4.39a–b, pl. III*). At least in the area of the north-east corner of the temple, the masons' marks had the form of short straight lines made in red ink, marking the line that determined where wall faces had once been set.

Once the temple ground plan was settled and marked, the construction of the temple walls started. As a matter of fact, the outer wall of the temple has been built in a more elaborate and careful way than the masonry of the pyramid, and the builders of the temple adopted the method of construction which was used at that time. These walls were faced with casing slabs, which hid the core masonry of roughly worked stones alternating with the layers of well worked, flat limestone blocks laid in the levels matching the height of the casing blocks.[41] This "buttressing" effect would have improved the stability of the walls by "closing" the core masonry from above.

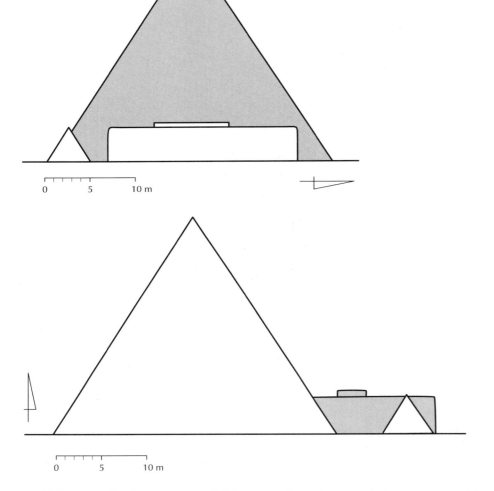

Fig. 4.53 Reconstruction of the appearance of the main pyramid and cult pyramid in addition to the mortuary temple – as seen from east.

Fig. 4.54 Reconstruction of the appearance of the main pyramid and cult pyramid in addition to the mortuary temple – as seen from south.

Unfortunately, the masonry of this temple is so destroyed that we are unable to reconstruct how the total effect of the masonry of the pyramid and of the mortuary

---

[41] For a similar method see – Arnold, *Building in Egypt*, 148–150, figs. 4.72.3 and 4.76. The same technique was documented in the case of the masonry in Niuserre's mortuary temple and in the Mastaba of Ptahshepses (see Krejčí, *Ptahshepses*, 103) in Abusir.

temple appeared in their upper levels. Common sense would dictate that the roofing terrace of the temple was directly connected to the casing of the pyramid (see *figs. 4.19, 4.53–4.54*).

During the excavation several blocks coming from the ceiling of an inner room were found. Their height varied around 0.40 m. These ceiling blocks were made from white limestone and, after being put in position, they were carefully polished. There is no clue indicating how high the ceiling was, or whether it consisted of only one layer of blocks, or whether other masonry was added. The height of the ceiling itself is not therefore possible to ascertain.

Conclusions on the Pyramid Complex Lepsius no. 24.

Thus we can see that, although this small pyramid complex has suffered badly at the hands of Time and stone robbers, sufficient traces have remained to let us attempt some sort of analysis of the outline and methods of its building structure, as well as the reconstruction of the basic features of architecture of the tomb precinct. The builders' marks on the inner walls of the burial pit, moreover, have revealed to us just how the planning of this pyramid was initially carried out. Although we have almost no evidence at all for the plan or structural shape of the mortuary temple, we can see that Pyramid Complex Lepsius no. 24 represented a typical Fifth-Dynasty pyramid complex of a queen. One detail is really striking in relation to the building techniques – that is the mediocre quality of foundations for the pyramid complex, especially those of the pyramid itself. As it has been also shown in the case of the Tomb Complex Lepsius no. 25 (see *chapter 5.3.4.*), it seems that these two complexes were built in a hurry on layers of sand. This assertion seems to be supported by non-existence of relief decoration in Lepsius no. 24 and in Lepsius no. 25 as well.

4.5. Finds

4.5.1. Limestone
4.5.1.1. Inscribed and decorated stone

Small drum with funerary formula
38/J/94
Limestone
64 × 16 × 13 cm
Late Old Kingdom
This small cylindrical drum of stone from a tomb, bearing a roughly cut funerary formula (*fig. 4.55*) was found in the debris of the pyramid, in a layer of sand and fragments of limestone in the central part of the temple, ca one metre above the floor level.

The inscription reads:
... ḥtp di 'Inpw ḫnty sḥ-nṯr kršty [m] ḥryt-nṯr smit [imntt?] (ḥb nb?) imȝḫw...
... a gift which Anubis, foremost one of the god's shrine gives that he may be buried[42] in the sacred necropolis in (?) the [Western] Desert (every festival?) the one honoured...

The text is very poorly written and has been scratched so badly that some of the signs are damaged and the end is impossible to read. The initial part has broken away where, normally, one would find the usual *ḥtp di nśwt* introduction. What remains of the text is a simplified version of the traditional offering formula, but

---

[42] *Ḳršty* in this formula has two basic meanings in Old Kingdom texts: that of "putting in the grave" (*i.e.*, burial) and in a sense of "burial rituals carried out". See Lapp, *Opferformel*, 48ff.

**Fig. 4.55 A small limestone
drum with a funerary
formula 38/J/94.**
Photo MZ

there are errors towards the end. The name of the tomb owner is now missing. The execution of the hieroglyphs shows an unpractised hand which is not uncommon in late Old Kingdom inscriptions.

Part of an offering slab

20/J/87
Limestone
12 × 12 cm
Middle Kingdom?[43]
The fragment was found in the rubble in the destroyed south-east corner of the mortuary temple.

**Fig. 4.56 Middle Kingdom
fragment of an offering
table 20/J/87.**
Photo JB

This fragment of a limestone offering table has a stylized representation in low relief of a low *ḥtp* table with offerings (*fig. 4.56*). The parallel lines form the left side of a *ḥtp* sign. The block is broken where the right side of a *Napfkuchen* should be represented. Above the table is a beaker lying next to a circular loaf of bread. A *kbḥ* vase is on the ground level beside the table.

The design of the offering table, with its grooved *ḥtp* sign and pattern of offerings is similar to Twelfth Dynasty examples,[44] but there are archaising examples from the Twenty-second and Saite Dynasties as well – though most of those examples are made of hard stone, such as granite. The simple elements in this fragment are typical of the early Twelfth Dynasty and, given the archaeological history of Abusir, it seems very likely that the tablet comes from this period.

Fragment of a rectangular stela

28/J/87
Limestone
14 × 4 cm
Middle Kingdom – late Twelfth Dynasty?
The fragment was found in the drift sand and limestone rubble outside the eastern wall of the temple.

---

[43] Judging from the remains of the relief decoration, this offering table slab should belong to the Twelfth Dynasty, for its *kbḥ* vase, beaker and round loaf are iconic elements of such tables from the time of Senusret I (Hölz, *Ägyptische Opfertafeln und Kultbecken*, 108). There is no exact parallel for this particular representation, but Ahmed Bey Kamal (*Tables d'Offrandes*) cites three limestone examples which are similar. The first, for a woman called Teti (23024, vol. 1, p. 20f.; vol. 2, Pl. XI), the second for a late Twelfth Dynasty person named Sebekdudu (23035, vol. 1, p. 28), and, thirdly, a person named Hapy, whose offering table was found at Giza (23074 vol. 1, p. 62; vol. 2, Pl. XIV). However, there are other offering tables from the Twenty-second Dynasty which are also similar to those already mentioned: (23097, vol. 1, p. 83; Pl. XX – it is a fragment of a dark granite offering plate, from Thebes, in the name of Sheshi) and the Saite period (Bakenem, 23032, vol. 1, p. 23; Pl. XIV) which are archaising models. They have almost identical workmanship details, so that, at this stage, any decision between the two eras would be questionable, but the Twelfth Dynasty seems much more appropriate for this Abusir find spot.

[44] *E.g.*, see the fine travertine example in Winterhalter, Brodbeck, *Antikenmuseum Basel*, 73, which has the simple loaf and beaker pattern on a mat with horizontal and vertical markings that the Abusir fragment has.

fig. 4.57 Fragment of a rectangular Middle Kingdom stela 28/J/87. Photo JB

Fragment of a rectangular stela with the remains of an offering scene and a fragmentary hieroglyphic inscription (*fig. 4.57*). In the scene a man is depicted raising his arm towards a low offering table with the offerings. The remnant of an inscription above the man's head reads:

...ir.n.f.

This fragment was found in the vicinity of 26/J/94, several fragments of three hemispherical cups. The cups date to the period of Senusret II or later, so it is possible that the stela belongs to this period of Middle Kingdom piety towards the person buried in the pyramid (probably a queen).

The remains of the relief are reminiscent of Twelfth Dynasty stelae, with those making the offerings being of very small proportions and the table of offerings often being disproportionately small as well. Here, the table is not only small, but very low to the ground in front of the tomb owner, whose foot is revealed on the left-hand side of the fragment. There are two stelae in the Fitzwilliam Museum in Cambridge which have a similar style of art, with minor figures in front of an offering table that is set in front of a large figure of the deceased,[45] although this very low offering table is a most unusual design motif for this period.

Fragments of an offering slab
81/J/94
Limestone, fine, white quality
Carved surfaces only: a) 7 × 8.75 cm; b) 4 × 3.4 cm
Fifth Dynasty
Found among the debris layer in the pyramid temple, near the south-east corner.

Four fragments contain parts of a pair of rectangular basins, typical of offering slabs of the Old Kingdom. From the time of Niuserre onwards, the most usual Fifth Dynasty offering slab[46] consisted of two rectangular basins lying side by side, with inscriptions written on the top and bottom (and sometimes, the central space) of the tablet (*e.g.*, the offering basin for Kahay and Meretites, *temp.* Neferirkare – Niuserre)[47]. Later on, the *ḥtp* sign with an enlarged *Napfkuchen* was introduced and this formation predominated until the end of the Old Kingdom. In the example of one of the pieces found in Abusir, a grooved channel comes from some other receptacle on the tablet and finishes at the edge of one of the basins. It does not seem likely that there had been a *ḥtp* sign on the original offering slab. Most of the offering tablets from the later Old Kingdom contain the *ḥtp* sign – it is seldom missing from these offering tablets,[48] as seems to be the case here, but the fragments are too small for one to be sure about the design. The presence of the grooved channel leading into the basin is indicative of the late Old Kingdom, where the closest parallels to the preserved elements here are found.[49]

It is not uncommon to see offering tablets within the precincts of the pyramids of queens – see the eighty offering tables recovered by the French team in the environment of two queens' complexes adjacent to Pepy I's complex, in South Saqqara.[50] The tablets found by V. Dobrev and J. Leclant are very similar to the

[45] Martin, *Stelae*, 21, 24.
[46] Mostafa, *Opfertafeln*, 103.
[47] Moussa, Altermüller, *Nefer and Ka-hay*, Pl. 42a.
[48] V. Dobrev, J. Leclant, Les Tables d'offrandes de particuliers découvertes aux complexes funéraires des Reines près de la pyramide de Pépi Iᵉʳ, in: *Critères de datation*, 145.
[49] Hölz, *Ägyptische Opfertafeln und Kultbecken*, Typ B + C, *e.g.* the variant, FMNH 105203, on p. 24. Once again, though, there is no exact parallel in the published material that was to hand.
[50] Dobrev, Leclant, in: *Critères de datation*, 143–157.

examples recorded in Borchardt,[51] whereas the Abusir example has a grooved channel leading into one of the basins. Sometimes, offering tablets were carved directly into the paving stones, as they are in the Fifth Dynasty tomb of Nyankhkhnum and Khnumhotep, or into the pavement of a queen's temple (we are unaware of this practice appearing in king's temples), frequently near doorways or the sides of the pyramid,[52] where they would be noticed by visitors to the temples.

The original Abusir tablet appears to have had only the offering basins, not the usual *ḥtp* sign – the dedication, of course is missing. These little basins after the mid-Fifth Dynasty are nearly always rectangular and are for liquids, which are occasionally entitled "water" and "beer".[53] Dobrev and Leclant[54] have suggested that, when these offering tablets are in the precincts of a royal complex, they may have had a dual purpose: to ask for offerings for the deceased, and to ask for offerings for the queen's cult as well.

Dobrev and Leclant have suggested that Pepy I marks the earliest example of the use of offering tablets in this way, but P. Munro[55] had already detected elements of a similar sort of cult for queens at the end of the Fifth Dynasty. His team had discovered in Queen Khenut's tomb the presence of numerous small recesses scooped out of the blocks around the entrance to her tomb.[56] The investigators concluded that the hollows had been once closed off by tiny false doors. They also think that these miniature items could be viewed in relation to the little offering cups found there. Munro considers that these exterior shrines avoided the necessity of the petitioner having to actually enter the tomb. This evidence from Abusir attests to the practice of a cult on behalf of the person buried in Lepsius no. 24. These pieces of offering basins, which are likely to date from the later Old Kingdom, show that attention was given to this Abusir lady – perhaps a little earlier than the time in which the tables from South Saqqara were being put down. The reason for this suggestion is the fine quality of the limestone used and the superior cutting evident for the basins. The German team have suggested that this cultic evidence may testify to the veneration of queens as goddesses.[57]

4.5.1.2. Vessels made of limestone

Unfinished model bowl
65/J/94
Limestone
Diam. at the rim: 6.3 cm, diam. at the bottom: ca 5 cm, max. H: 3.2 cm
Dating uncertain: it looks like a reworked piece, possibly from a later period.

It was found in the north-east corner of the burial chamber, in the filling of yellow sand with limestone chips, just below the place where the floor would have been and in front of the opening to the corridor.

---

[51] E.g., Borchardt, *Denkmäler* I, 17, No. 1335; 25, No. 1355; 26, No. 1357; 27, No. 1358. These all have the *ḥtp* sign forming a border along one edge of the table, the large central piece (*Napfkuchen*) almost reaching to the opposite side; two rectangular basins frame the central piece on each side.

[52] Borchardt, *Denkmäler* I, 143f., *e.g.*, in the temples of Queen Inenekinti and the Queen of the West in South Saqqara.

[53] *Loc. cit.*

[54] Borchardt, *op. cit.*, 146.

[55] C. Bieger, P. Munro, J. Brinks, Des Doppelgrab der Königinnen *Nbt* und *Ḥnwt* in Saqqara 1. Vorbericht über die Arbeiten der Gruppe Hannover im Herbst 1973, *SAK* 1, 1974, 34–54.

[56] C. Bieger, P. Munro, J. Brinks, *op. cit.*, 51. Note that it was around Queen Khenut's doorway that these little shrines were found, even as it was observed by Dobrev and Leclant that the offering tablets from the Pepy I complex were also around the doorways or the surrounds of the pyramid bases of the queens' pyramids in South Saqqara. These cultic items had therefore been placed where they would be easily seen by the passerby. Strangely, in the case of the dual mastabas of Khenut and Nebet, the more important tomb of Nebet lacked these secondary additions.

[57] C. Bieger, P. Munro, J. Brinks, *op. cit.*, 52.

This vessel is a roughly worked shallow bowl, presumably secondarily made during the destruction of the masonry of the pyramid.

Large vessel fragments (see also *fig. A.6*)
90/J/94
Limestone
Diam. of base: 26.5 cm, H of base: 2.3 cm, preserved H of walls: 11 cm, thickness of rim: 1.9 cm
New Kingdom ?
The pieces were found in the mortuary temple of Lepsius no. 24, to the south of the temple in a layer of yellow sand containing small and larger pieces of limestone. They were found at a height of 90 cm above the base of the cult pyramid and 3 m to the west of its western wall.

These remains come from a thick-walled vessel, either from a stone vat, or large beaker, shaved almost smooth on the outside, but with a noticeable unevenness on the inner surface. At least one of the possible pair of vessels appears to be an open beaker form with conical sides. It had probably been used for mixing or storing large quantities of goods.

These six fragments belong to either one, or possibly two unfinished limestone vessel(s). Inside the vessel one can see evidence of the rough shaving on the interior wall, suggesting that the vessel had been cut down from a larger item. On the outside there were also traces of remodelling from an older limestone object. These pieces may even have been remodelled from some limestone block coming from the pyramid casing.

4.5.1.3. Miscellaneous limestone objects

Gaming piece
23/J/87b
H: 2.4 cm, diam. of base: 1.7 cm
Dating uncertain. Having in mind the place of unearthing of this piece, we can suppose that it is not coming from the Old Kingdom and we can date this object with the preference to the Middle or New Kingdoms.
This item was found in front of the eastern enclosure wall of the temple, in its south-eastern sector. The gaming piece lay in the very bottom layer of yellow sand mixed with limestone chips, together with other small fragments.

Unpolished weight
47/J/94
White limestone
Upper diam.: 10.2 cm, lower diam.: 10.5 cm, H: 3.4 cm
Dating uncertain: it is roughly shaped and could be from the Old Kingdom, but equally possible, it might have been made during the New Kingdom, or later.
It was found in the layer of dark sand and fragmented local limestone pieces from the core of the masonry, near to the eastern wall of the entrance to the pyramid.

This item has a hole in the centre and it is thought to be a weight or plumb bob, used to create a straight vertical line on some building surface.

4.5.2. Diorite

Fragment of a bowl
17/J/94
Diorite
H: 3 cm; W: 4 cm; thickness: 1 cm
Fifth Dynasty

It was found in the destroyed entrance area to the temple, in the lowest layer of dark sand mixed with ash and potsherds.

This tiny fragment of the body of a diorite bowl has no rim or base reference point to indicate the size or shape of the original piece. Like most diorite vessels, it had been given a polished surface. The bowl may have been dropped by a robber on his way out of the temple, during the initial plundering of the temple.

Bowl fragment
22/J/94b
Diorite
L: 8.4 cm, W: 6.5 cm, thickness: 1 cm (top) – 2.3 cm (bottom)
Middle Kingdom
This medium-sized fragment was found in the area of the destroyed entrance to the temple, in the Middle Kingdom level mixed with pottery vessels and potsherds.

This is only a fragment of the body of a diorite bowl with an incurved rounded rim and polished surface inside and out.

These two diorite pieces (17/J/94 and 22/J/94b) do not belong to the same bowl: 22/J/94 has an average thickness of body wall measuring 1.8 cm and a gradual increase of thickness towards the base, whereas 17/J/94 has a wall thickness of 1 cm throughout its length and width. Despite their dissimilarity, it is suggested that both pieces were from vessels made in the Fourth or Fifth Dynasty.

4.5.3. Travertine[58]

4.5.3.1. Canopic jars fragments

Bottom of a canopic jar
41/J/94a
Travertine
Max. diam.: 19 cm, max. H: 7.5 cm, diam. of the base (inner measurement): 9.5 cm, diam. of base (outer measurement): 15 cm
Fifth Dynasty
Found in the upper part of a layer of white limestone rubble in the middle section of the inner area of the pyramid (ca 2 m to the south-east from the south-west corner of the passage) at ca 0.5 m above the level of the narrow courtyard surrounding the pyramid.

These two yellowish fragments of the body of a canopic jar fit together. They form parts of a shouldered jar with a cusp collar rim, marked by a line incised around the area below the rim. The exterior of the vessel is smoothed, but the outer base is only roughly worked.
See also 61/J/94.

Fragments of a canopic jar
41/J/94b
Travertine
Smaller fragment: L: 23 cm, W: 18.5 cm; larger fragment: L: 25 cm, W: 10.5 cm
Fifth Dynasty
Found in a layer of fine limestone rubble in the middle part of the burial chamber inside the pyramid (to the south of the passage), at a level ca 1 m above the foundation line marked on its western wall.

---

[58] Travertine has been previously known as "alabaster" or "calcite": for a more scientific examination of this terminology, see Aston, *Stone Vessels*, 42ff.

Two large fragments of a canopic jar; the exterior of the vessel is smoothed. It was not possible to join fragments 41/J/94b and 41/J/94a.

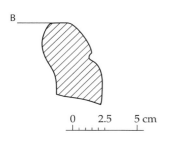

**fig. 4.58 Fragments
51/J/94a–b
of a canopic vessel.**

Neck of a canopic vessel

51/J/94a–c
Travertine
Diam.: 24 cm
Fifth Dynasty
Found in the filling of the burial chamber in a layer of grey sand, limestone rubble and bigger limestone blocks, ca 1 m above the floor of the burial chamber, ca 50 cm from the southern wall and 2.5 m from the big block coming from the western wall.

These fragments create a large part of the neck of a travertine vessel with a cusp-shaped rim. Such rims were typical of the Fourth and Fifth Dynasty stone canopic vessels. The surface is smoothed, not polished (*fig. 4.58*).

Fragments of canopic jars

61/J/94a–g
Travertine
 a) Fragment of a canopic vessel and rim: H: 21 cm, max. W: 16 cm, max. thickness: 4.7 cm
 b) Fragment of a rim: H: 6 cm, W: 15 cm, max. thickness: 4.7 cm
 c) Fragment of a rim: H: 6.5 cm, W: 8 cm, thickness: 3.4 cm
 d) Fragment of a rim: H: 11 cm, W: 10 cm, max. thickness: 3.2 cm
 e) Fragment from the body of the canopic jar: H: 9 cm, max. W: 13 cm, max. thickness: 4.5 cm (now joined to 61/J/94a)
 f) Fragment of a rim of a canopic jar: H: 18 cm, max. W: 9 cm, max. thickness: 4.6 cm
 g) Fragment of a body of a canopic jar: H: 4 cm, W: 10 cm, max. thickness: 5.5 cm
Fifth Dynasty
Found in the burial chamber, in its eastern part, in the filling of yellow sand mixed with both small and larger stone chips, near the foundation level of the chamber's pavement.

All of the fragments are made from yellowish travertine with white spots; the surface is smoothed. We also have a piece that joins fragment 92/J/94.

Fragments of canopic jars

78/J/94f, k–n
Travertine
 f) L: 18 cm, W: 9 cm, max. thickness: 4.6 cm
 k) L: 8 cm, W: 5.5 cm, thickness: 6 cm
 l) L: 9 cm, W: 4.5 cm
 m) L: 5.5 cm, W: 4 cm
 n) L: 18 cm, W: 14 cm, thickness (max.): 5.5 cm
Fifth Dynasty
These pieces were found in grey sand under the southern part of the descending corridor.

Fragment of a canopic jar

92/J/94
Travertine
L: 18.5 cm, W: 11.5 cm, max. thickness: 3.2 cm
Fifth Dynasty

Found in the filling of rubble made from small and larger limestone fragments mixed with dark sand, in the lower part of the descending corridor, near the burial chamber, where the blocks have been quarried from the western wall (ca 2 m from the north wall of the burial chamber), in a level ca 1 m above its floor.

This piece is part of the rim of a massive canopic jar made from fine crystalline travertine of ivory-white tone, with lighter banding within the stone. It has now been joined to 61/J/94.

Despite their broken state, these fragments reveal that this set of canopic jars was one of the finer examples for the Old Kingdom. Like nearly all the canopic vessels of the Fourth and Fifth Dynasties, these items were not uniformly the same as each other (for further discussion see p. 262–263). A comparison of the rim and body thicknesses (where recorded), indicate that there were at least three canopic vessels within the collection of fragments recorded above. The vessel that seems to have been the smallest records thicknesses ranging between 3.2–3.5 cm; the next is in the region of 4.5–4.7 cm; the third, between 5.5–6.0 cm. Where rim thicknesses have been recorded, a similar pattern emerges: 3.2–3.4; 4.7; 5.7 cm. On the other hand, the fragments came from four different find spots, which might indicate that four vessels had been found, but it is now impossible to be definite about this because none of the jars has been able to be completely restored, nor has it been possible to join most of the fragments to other pieces.

One of the interesting observations made in looking at comparable material in relationship to queens (for further discussion on parts of the mummified female body found in the burial chamber as well as on the pyramid owner of L24, see *chapters 4.7.* and *6.2.2.*) is that – where the canopics have been discovered and recorded – the canopic containers for Old Kingdom queen mothers are made of travertine (Hetepheres I, Khentkaus I [fragments only], Khentkaus II); the canopics found for women who were wives only were made from limestone (*e.g.* Meresankh III, Iput I – buried as a wife, not a royal mother). The remainder of queens' burial equipment in the Fourth and Fifth Dynasties has not been present in the reports on their tombs. For the Sixth Dynasty, burial customs for queens changed: pyramids came to be used for wives as well as mothers of kings, while sarcophagi tended to be either of granite or of silt stone or basalt. Much of the material regarding canopics for queens in the Sixth Dynasty has not yet been published.[59] The person oridinally intended in Lepsius no. 24 with her travertine canopics is likely to have been a queen mother, especially as she had a red granite sarcophagus, as Khentkaus I and II also seem to have had. Whether the mummy found in the pyramid was that of the person actually intended for the tomb cannot be verified. The materials may have been given to some other royal female who died unexpectedly, but of course we cannot know at this remove in time. The burial equipment and customs regarding queens seems to have altered during the Sixth Dynasty.

For detailed discussion on these canopic jars, together with comparisons made with other vessels, and relevant bibliographical material, see Appendix, p. 273–276.

4.5.3.2. Containers for food

The major portion of an offering container
43/J/94
Travertine
L: 18 cm, W: ca 12.5 cm. It is 4 cm deep at the centre and the walls of the vessel vary in thickness from 1.5 to 1.2 cm, thinning out to approximately 1 cm as they reach the bottom of the vessel.
Fifth Dynasty

---

[59] Royal wife and mother, Iput I, had roughly-made red pottery jars (five of them) for her canopic equipment. Iput died before her son, Pepy I, could come to the throne, and the king who followed Iput's husband was the enigmatic ruler, Userkare. It is thus apparent that, as well as being assigned a mastaba, not a pyramid, Iput I was buried as a royal wife. Pepy I revalorised her memorial after he came to the throne.

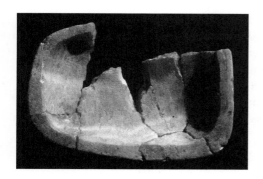

Fig. 4.59 Food container 43/J/94.
Photo MZ

This container was found in the filling of limestone rubble and yellow sand near the southern wall of the burial chamber (ca 1 m above the level of the base – near the previously mentioned builders' inscription *mḥ 3*).

These fragments belong to an offering container, rather oblong in shape, that had rounded corners and a smoothed, but not polished surface (*fig. 4.59*). The pieces have now been joined with others to make up the container, but the vessel is still incomplete. This trough-shaped container is not flat, but has some depth, with edges curving down towards a flat base.

Altogether, the remnants of about nine or ten containers for cooked food were discovered within the burial chamber of Lepsius no. 24, but all of them had been broken – often quite badly – and most of them could not be repaired.

Fragments of a food container
44/J/94a–c
Travertine
a) L: 5.5 cm, thickness: 2.9 cm, H: 3.1 cm
b) L: 6.5 cm, H: 2.8 cm, W: 4 cm
c) L: 8 cm, W: 6.5 cm
Fifth Dynasty

These were found together with fragments of a travertine model – see below – in the filling of the burial chamber, in a layer of grey sand, limestone rubble and bigger limestone blocks; ca 20 cm from the chamber's southern wall and 2.8 m from the west wall.

As is frequent with these travertine pieces, they are very irregular and the original shape of the object cannot be determined: they are broken lumps of stone. Exc. no. 44/J/94c was the corner of a food container – probably for meat or a cooked bird. Exc. no. 44/J/94a–b are fragments of an oblong container; the surface of which was smooth. There was no match with fragment no. 43/J/94.

Fragmented halves of a food container
48/J/94; 60/J/94
Travertine
L: 20 cm, W: 16 cm, H: 7 cm (dimensions after restoration)
Fifth Dynasty

Fig. 4.60a–b Food container in form of a haunch of beef 48/J/94; 60/J/94.
Photo MZ

Piece no. 48/J/94 was found in the filling of the burial chamber, in the same layer of grey sand, limestone rubble and larger limestone pieces as the previous entry, ca 1 m above floor, ca 30 cm from the southern wall and 2.75 m from the western wall of the chamber.

Another piece of this container (60/J/94) was also uncovered. It was found in the eastern part of the burial chamber, in a filling of yellow sand mixed with small and larger stone chips near the foundation level.

These two pieces were found at different levels in the burial chamber fill, but the fragments have now been joined to make a vessel in the shape of a food container suggestive of the thigh part of a haunch of beef (*fig. 4.60a–b*). The container is made from rough crystalline travertine of creamy white colour (it contains lengthy crystals) and the stone is relatively homogenous in colour and texture. The surface is smoothed; on the inner side there are four spots where the traces of the tube drill (diam.: 4.5 cm) that had been used to hollow out the interior can be seen.

Squarish dish

55/J/94a–b (one piece found with items registered as 56/J/94)
Travertine
W: 10.3 cm, L: 7.5 cm, H: 3 cm
Fifth Dynasty

Part (a) was found in the western part of the burial chamber, close to the destroyed western wall, in a layer of grey sand mixed with the limestone chips (found in the lower part of this layer), ca 0.75 m above the foundation level. Part (b) was found nearby, but with other items.

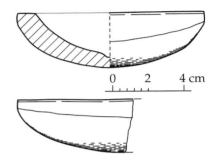

Fig. 4.61 Squarish dish 55/J/94; a section and side views.

These two fragments of a squarish basin or base of a food case that had been broken in two (now joined), fit closely together (*fig.4.61*). The interior is rounder than the exterior of the vessel, and the surface has been smoothed. The wide, flat edge to the dish suggests that it was meant to have a covering lid and, despite its small size, it was probably a food container as well. It has been suggested that some of these smaller containers may have held one of the many bread or cake offerings.[60]

Fragment of a rectangular container

56/J/94e, 58/J/94b
Travertine
W: 4.7 cm, L: 4.7 cm, H: 2.1 cm
Fifth Dynasty

Exc. no. 56/J/94e was found in the western part of the burial chamber, near its western wall, at the bottom of a layer of grey sand mixed with the limestone chips, ca 0.75 cm above the foundation level.

Exc. no. 58/J/94b was found in a layer of yellow sand with limestone chips in the northern part of the descending corridor to the burial chamber. It was close to the western wall, about 2 m above the original terrain.

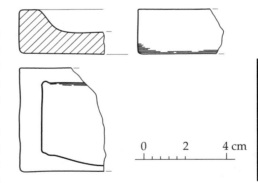

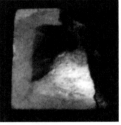

Fig 4.62b Fragment of a small tray 58/J/94b.

Fig 4.62a Fragment of a small tray 58/J/94b.
Photo MZ

58/J/94b was the bottom section of what is, apparently, one half of a rectangular container (*fig. 4.62a–b*): its walls are carefully worked and are of an even thickness, but the interior is curved, while the outer section is prismatic. 56/J/94e and 58/J/94 very possibly come from a rectangular container with semi-cylindrical interior.

Food container (*fig. 4.63*)

59/J/94d
Travertine
L: 13.3 cm, W: 6.26 cm, H: 1.5 cm
Fifth Dynasty

---

[60] Brovarski, in: *Mummies and Magic*, 94, Catalogue item no. 26.

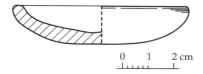

0   1   2 cm

**Fig. 4.63 Section through the
food container 59/J/94d.**

**Fig. 4.64 Fragments of a food
container 68/J/94.**
Photo MZ

Found together with model dishes and other fragments in the burial chamber, in its eastern part, in the filling of yellow sand mixed with small and bigger stone chips, about the foundation level.

This small fragment of a shallow bowl has an oval shape and a smoothed surface, but it is of indifferent workmanship. It seems to be the base of a food container. A triangular piece is missing from one side.

Fragments of the base of containers
68/J/94
Travertine
Most of the pieces were small and irregular in shape. The largest one (*fig. 4.64*) was 18 cm long and 6 cm wide. The piece at the top right in the photograph measured 15 × 7 cm, and the best preserved piece (middle left in the photograph) was 12 cm wide and 9 cm long.
Fifth Dynasty
These numerous pieces were found 20 cm under the level of the floor of the burial chamber, in a layer of grey sand and small, fragmented limestone chips, near the entrance to the descending corridor. The fragments lay 50 cm to the west of the mainly destroyed eastern wall of the burial chamber, and 80 cm from the northern wall of the burial chamber.

These fragments form part of at least two irregular shaped bases which had too many pieces missing to be restored. They are more likely to be containers for a joint of meat, rather than a fowl, since the shape that can be discerned is not symmetrical, as those of the duck-shaped containers are. The surface of the fragments is smoothed.

Fragments of containers
78/J/94d, e, g, j
Travertine
d) Fragment of a container: W: 4.8 cm, H: 5 cm, thickness of rim: 2.6 cm
e) Fragment of a container: L: 12.3 cm; W: 7.5 cm; H: 3.6 cm
g) Fragment of a larger container: L: 6.5 cm; W: 9 cm, H: 4.6 cm
j) Fragment of a larger container piece: L: 14.5 cm; max. W: 7.5 cm; H: 5.5 cm; W of rim: 1.8–2.2 cm
Fifth Dynasty
These four pieces were found with other items in the western part of the burial chamber, in a matrix of sand and limestone chips, 0–30 cm under the level of the quarried floor.

They are just four more fragments of containers for cooked food. No noticeable joins could be found with any of the previous pieces.

Food containers have quite a long history. They are present in some Archaic tombs, in a relatively small number of Old Kingdom tombs, in New Kingdom and later tombs. In the Middle Kingdom tombs it was more usual to find food – usually wrapped, as in mummification – and presented in a dish. Other food from that period was stored in stone and pottery storage jars.[61] Excavators report finding remains scattered on the floors of Middle Kingdom burial apartments, which may indicate that they were put there deliberately but, in our opinion, this unusual deposit may also be due to later disturbance by rodents. From the Middle Kingdom onwards, wooden types of containers are more common than stone vessels. Nearly all of those from the earlier periods were found empty (certainly, those found by G. Reisner contained no actual offerings)[62], but it needs to be said that few excavators from the past published the material concerning these food boxes. The large collection

---

[61] See notes on storage jars in Ikram, *Choice Cuts*, 183–187.
[62] Brovarski, in: *Mummies and Magic*, 93.

from the tomb of Inti, at South Abusir, however, not only contained meat and fowl, but the pieces of meat were found within their respective container shapes.[63] Sue D'Auria mentions that the duck cases found (apparently in the tomb of an early Eighteenth Dynasty official named Seniu), had mummified contents within their wooden cases.[64] Those cases from the tomb of Yuya and Thuya also had dried meat and fowl which had been wrapped in cloth,[65] but not mummified (as we understand the term).

All food boxes or containers have flat edges, so that the covers for the receptacles will fit snugly onto the trough. Perhaps the original intention may have been to seal these flat joins, but we are unaware of any examples known to have been properly sealed. Instead, the two halves of the container were sometimes bound together with string or bandages to keep them tightly closed. One would think that the stone vessels found in Old Kingdom tombs, such as these ones here, would have been a better storage place than the wooden boxes, for the latter might warp when the hot foods were enclosed. Then again, the rather generous use of wood in the New Kingdom period could be an indication of Egypt's overseas expansion and the subsequent trade and conquest with wood-producing regions.

4.5.3.3. Trays and table tops

Fragments from the top of an offering table[66]
46/J/94a–i, k–m; 71/J/94; 78/J/94h
Travertine
46/J/94a) H: 1.35 cm, W: 3.3 cm, L: 4.6 cm
46/J/94b) H: 1.6 cm, W: 5.3 cm, L: 9 cm
46/J/94c) H: 1.5 cm; W: 6.3 cm, L: 7.4 cm
78/J/94h) H: 1.6 cm, W: 5.5 cm, L: 10 cm,
probable original diam. of the top: ca 30 cm
Fifth Dynasty
Pieces 46/J/94a–c, d–i and k–m were found in the filling of the burial chamber in a layer of grey sand, limestone rubble and larger limestone pieces, ca 1 m above floor, ca 30 cm from the southern wall and 2.75 m from the western wall of the chamber. Another larger piece of this offering table top, 71/J/94, was also found in the burial chamber, in a layer of grey sand mixed with limestone rubble, but on contrary to pieces 46/J/94 ca 15 cm under the level of the floor of the burial chamber, 100 cm to the north from the southern wall of the burial chamber and 25 cm to the west from the level of the end of the northern wall of the burial chamber. 78/J/94h was another fragment from the top of the same offering table.

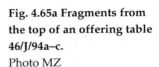

Fig. 4.65a Fragments from the top of an offering table 46/J/94a–c.
Photo MZ

Fig. 4.65b Fragments from the top of an offering table 46/J/94a–c.

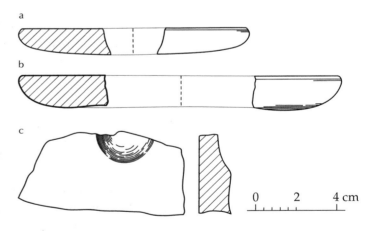

---

[63] The author is grateful to Dr. M. Bárta (whose team discovered the food containers) for permission to mention this find here. The complete report on the tomb of Inti is at present in preparation in Prague; see also M. Bárta, The Sixth Dynasty tombs in Abusir. Tomb complex of the vizier Qar and his family, in: *OKAA*, 45–62; S. Ikram, Portions of an Old Kingdom offering list reified, in: *OKAA*, 167–174; Hassan, *Gîza* VI.2, 365–375; for model offerings see also *chapter 3.4.2.* in the present monograph.
[64] S. D'Auria, in: *Mummies and Magic*, 142, Catalogue item no. 81.
[65] Quibell, *Yuaa and Thuia*, Pls. XXII–XXIII for the food containers, Nos. 51088, 51089, 51100; the wrapped joints and fowl are shown in pl. XXX and XXXI.
[66] Another table top, this time intact, was found in Prince Nakhtsare's burial (19/Q/94) at Abusir (see *chapter 3.4.1.*). Many such table tops (or entire tables) were found in Archaic graves in Abu Rawash, Sedment, Ballas and Abydos, for example (Mostafa, *Opfertafeln*, 4ff.) – for two-dimensional representations, see the slab stelae from the First Dynasty onwards in Manuelian, *Slab Stelae*.

This travertine table top was originally circular in shape, but because of the fragmentation and loss of small chips etc., the overall dimensions are hard to gauge, so the 30 cm diameter given above is approximate. The table top had been shattered into fragments, thirteen of which were recovered (see *figs. 4.65a–b*). Later, another piece that had been part of the flat table top (71/J/94) from this offering table was found – and it has now been joined to 46/J/94. It was the circular top for a typical offering table such as one finds in intact tombs,[67] presumably, there would have been a hollow for the usual small, central leg stand. The surface is smoothed.

Fragments of a small tray
78/J/94o–p
Travertine
o) 9.5 × 6.5 cm
p) 7 × 6 cm
Fifth Dynasty
Found in the burial chamber, approximately 1 m above the floor.

Two fragments of a small tray; 78/J/94o has now been joined to 78/J/94p.

4.5.3.4. Vessels

Fragment of a small bowl
40/J/94
Travertine
Diam.: 10 cm; H: 4.1 cm, thickness: 1.3 cm
Fifth Dynasty
This fragment was found at ground level, in the offering hall area of the mortuary temple.

This was the only evidence for a full-sized travertine bowl throughout the entire complex. Both sides of the shallow bowl were well polished; the rim of the bowl is flat.

Model of a shallow bowl
45/J/94; 50/J/94

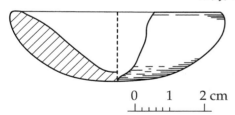

Travertine
Fifth Dynasty
Diam: 5.6 cm
The pieces were found in the filling of the burial chamber in a layer of grey sand, limestone rubble and bigger limestone blocks, ca 1 m above the floor, 20–40 cm from the southern wall and 2.7–3.0 m from the western wall.

0   1   2 cm

Fig. 4.66 Travertine model bowl 50/J/94.

The piece 45/J/94 has been now joined with 50/J/94 (*fig. 4.66*). 50/J/94 is a bowl fragment in travertine, with a diameter 6 cm. The surface of the vessel is smoothed and its walls vary in thickness, being quite thin at the centre of the base. The upper part features a rounded rim.

Two miniature bowls (see *fig. A.13*)
56/J/94b–c
Travertine
b) Diam.: 6 cm, H: 2 cm
c) Diam.: 6.4 cm, H: 2 cm
Fifth Dynasty

---

[67] E.g. Seipel, *Ägypten, Götter, Gräber* I, Cat. No. 41; Do. Arnold, in: *Egyptian Art in the Age of the Pyramids*, 492.

These were found in the western part of the burial chamber, near the remains of the western wall, at the bottom of a layer of grey sand mixed with the limestone chips, ca 0.75 cm above the foundation level for construction of the burial chamber. Altogether, the group of objects found under this number consisted of the remains of four vessels: d) a container (see above in this chapter), a) a deep cup (see below) and two bowls b) and c).

Bowl exc. no. 56/J/94c is almost preserved in its entirety, 56/J/94b is destroyed on one side. In the interior of both of them are remains of drilling (*fig. 4.67*).

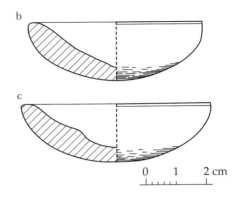

Fragments of different miniature dishes
59/J/94 a–c
Travertine
a) Diam: 6 cm, H: 1.8 cm
b) Diam: 6.2 cm, H: 1.6 cm
c) Diam: 7 cm, H: 1.6 cm
Fifth Dynasty
Found in the eastern part of the burial chamber in the matrix of yellow sand mixed with the limestone chips, in the level *mḥ nfrw*, *i.e.* of the foundation level for the subterranean part of the pyramid.

These three broken remnants are from three very low forms of dishes. Each one would have had a large, flat base and each has a different type of rim.

Miniature bowls and fragments of bowls
73/J/94a–i
Travertine
a) Diam. 6 cm, H: 2 cm
b) Diam.: 6 cm, H: 1.8 cm
c) Diam.: 5.7 cm, H: 1.75 cm
d) Diam.: 6.4 cm, H: 1.5 cm
e) Diam.: 6 cm, H: 1.6 cm
f) Diam.: 5.8 cm, H: 1.8 cm
g) Diam.: 7.1 cm, H: 1.6 cm
h) H: 1.7 cm, diam. unknown
i) H: 1.45 cm, diam. unknown
Fifth Dynasty
These bowls and fragments of bowls were found in the western part of the burial chamber (ca 2 m from the western wall), in a layer of sand and rubble, practically at floor level.

These nine small stone bowls and fragments are different in design from each other. This is particularly noticeable around the rims, where individual designs are apparent – see drawings in *fig. 4.68*. The first bowl, 73/J/94a, has a banana-shaped wall in section, its rim finishing in a thin horizontal upper edge. 73/J/94b's rim is rounded and thick, the walls tapering to a thinner base than a); 73/J/94c's walls are even in thickness, its rim being squared off to a flat plane. The incomplete walls of 73/J/94d are much thicker than any of the previous fragments, while its rim consists of two flat planes at an oblique angle to each other. 73/J/94e has walls that are thick and increase in thickness towards the bottom of the bowl. Its rim is horizontal. 73/J/94f's rim is flat. 73/J/94g's rim is also horizontal, although its walls decline in thickness towards the bottom of the bowl. 73/J/94h also has a horizontal rim, cut from outwards at an oblique angle. 72/J/94i's rim is horizontal, its walls are thicker in the middle of bowl's height.

Fig. 4.67 Two miniature bowls 56/J/94b–c.

Fig. 4.68 Miniature bowls 73/J/94a–i.

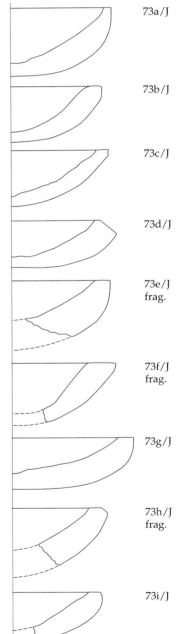

Miniature bowls (see *fig. A.13*)
78/J/94a–c, i
Travertine
a) Diam.: 6 cm, H: 2.6 cm
b) Diam.: 5.8 cm, H: 2 cm
c) Diam.: 4 cm; H: 2.8 cm
i) Diam.: 5.1 cm, H: 2 cm
Fifth Dynasty
These four bowls were found in the western part of the burial chamber, in a matrix of sand and limestone chips, 0–30 cm under the level of the quarried floor.

Beaker
56/J/94a
Travertine
Diam.: 5.7 cm, H: 2.6 cm (giving it a VI of 219)
Fifth Dynasty

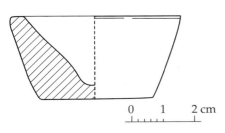

This cup was found with other objects under this number (see above) in the western part of the burial chamber, near the remains of the western wall, at the bottom of a layer of grey sand mixed with the limestone chips, ca 0.75 cm above the foundation level.

The cup has been well preserved: it has steep sides and its walls are carefully worked on the exterior and smoothed (*fig. 4.69*). The interior descends at an angle of about 45° to the base, where it is roughly worked. The top two thirds of the interior are smoothed. The vessel has a flat bottom. The size of the mouth diameter makes it unlikely that this travertine cup would be part of an Opening of the Mouth set, as it is too broad.

Fig. 4.69 Beaker 56/J/94a.

4.5.4. Pottery

Most of the pottery consisted of fragments. Only one substantial reconstruction could be made from the corpus that was found.

4.5.4.1. Old Kingdom Pottery

Storage jar[68]
75/J/94
Red ware ceramic
L: 17 cm, W: 9 cm, mouth diam.: 4 cm
Fifth – Sixth Dynasty?[69]
The vessel was found in the layer of yellow sand with limestone chips in front of the descending corridor (close to the limestone casing of the pyramid) by the north-western corner of the corridor, at a level of 0.50 m above the foot of the pyramid.

---

[68] See categories of ovoid storage jars with rounded or pointed bases in M. Bárta, The Pottery, in: Verner *et al.*, *Raneferef*, 312, 314 – Class I.CW body with Class II.DW rim.

[69] Apart from the examples given above for M. Bárta's classification scheme, see Paice, *Pottery of Daily Life*, fig. 12a. The parallels given by Paice are evidently taken from the Abydos excavations, but the jars with greatest parallels in those publications seem to be the large storage jars of the Pre- and Early Dynastic eras (*e.g.* Petrie, *Abydos* I: pl. XXVI – tomb M 12 has five examples; while Tomb M 13 on pl. XXXVII has four similar models which are large storage jars, with cusp rim and ovoid body – although not red-painted). Other examples come from Tombs 14 and 17 *etc.* Pottery from Balat (late Sixth Dynasty) has ovoid forms that are more rounded at the base and the neck rims are rolled, rather than having the cusp form – see Minault-Gout, Deleuze, *Balat* II, Inv. Nos. 1953 (p. 166), 1768 (p. 165), 1933 (p. 165). The cups rim is present on Inv. No. 1895 (p. 171), which is a vase-like stand with a broken base. All of these examples display the inner ridging typical of the Abusir vessel, but none of them was painted red.

This storage jar has a very pleasing shape, despite a slight deformity on the right-hand side. It is a shouldered jar with very low neck and everted cusp rim. The vessel has been carefully made by hand, using the coil method (as can be seen from the internal ridges of the jar). Its exterior is painted red and polished.

This was a closed jar, probably used for the storage of liquids, as its neck and mouth diameter were rather restricted[70]. It is unlikely to have been for beer since the vessel is small in size and the diameter of the mouth is much smaller than the usual beer jars.[71] The cusp rim is typical of vessels that had a skin or cloth tied over their rims: such covers were then sealed by tying string around the bottom of the rim. Pointed vessels similar to this small jar were laced into a string net and carried: the pointed base made the vessel secure in this sort of string cradle. Bottles like this frequently appear in tomb reliefs and paintings, and ofering bearers are sometimes shown carrying pointed jars in this way. Convenient examples are to be found, for example in the tombs of Kagemni[72] and Mehu[73] *(fig. 4.70)*. G. Reisner[74] has recorded a number of such bottles, but the one most like it in shape is much larger than this small vessel from Abusir.

Fragments of open vessels *(fig. 4.71)*
24/J/94a–f
Pottery
Dimensions listed separately below
Fifth Dynasty?

These fragments of pottery, whose individual details are listed separately below, were found in the drift sand outside the eastern wall of the temple. They were in the lowest layer of yellow sand mixed with fine limestone chips, lying to the east from the eastern enclosure wall of the temple.

All the fragments probably come from the original, Fifth Dynasty inventory of the temple. Such vessels, fallen out of use in the temple (probably because they were broken), were thrown out into several refuse heaps when the temple rooms were cleaned; this is why so often the fragments cannot be matched with their missing portions.

24/J/94a) A fragment of a red ware broad cup or bowl with a very thin wall, rounded bottom and a slightly projecting rim.
W: 10.5 cm, H: 4.5 cm, thickness: 0.2 cm
This profile fragment is identical to Class 3 – Small and large bowls – Type XL in Bárta's classification of the Raneferef's pottery.[75]

24/J/94b) A red ware sherd with a short spout coming from a broad, roughly made bowl. Such spouted bowls are a feature of the late Fourth and the Fifth

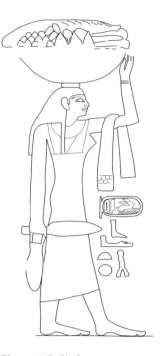

Fig. 4.70 Relief representation of a domain with a bottle in Mehu's tomb in Saqqara (after Altenmüller, *Mehu*, Taf. 27 b).

---

[70] The closest parallel to this vessel is given by P. Paice in her study of the everyday pottery used in ancient Egypt: Paice, *Pottery of Daily Life*, 23, fig. 12a. Paice remarks here that the "rounded conical base predominated for the (period post-Dynasty IV) of the Old Kingdom."

[71] On beer jars in the Fifth Dynasty, see M. Bárta, Several remarks on beer jars found at Abusir, *CCÉ* 4, 1996, 127–131, and especially 128, where he observes that the average rim opening for beer jars is between 9–10 cm.

[72] Harpur, Scremin, *Kagemni*, 312: Detail 486, the offering bearers procession on the N. Wall of Room VII; p. 478 commentary.

[73] Altenmüller, *Mehu*, Tafeln 47 b, 52. There are many examples from this tomb: see the female domains reliefs in colour in Tafeln 26 a + b, 27 a + b, where the women carry the bottles by rope handles.

[74] Reisner, Smith, *Giza Necropolis* II, fig. 82, bottom row, example from G 4733E; 14-2-115. It is practically identical with the Abusir example. Another, almost identical one, is given in a photograph from S. Hassan's *Gîza* VII (pl. II.B). This one, from an untouched burial, shows the jar in position beside the long side of the limestone sarcophagus. The untouched burial of Ankhhaf, also from Giza (Hassan, *Gîza* III, 139 and fig. 112) has another bottle similar to this one.

[75] Bárta, in: Verner *et al.*, *Raneferef*, 322.XL.O.

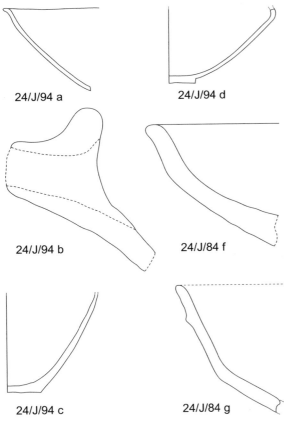

24/J/94 a

24/J/94 d

24/J/94 b

24/J/84 f

24/J/94 c

24/J/84 g

fig. 4.71 Open vessels 24/ J/94a–d, f, g.

Dynasties.[76] The profile of this one, however, suggests that this vessel was a spouted vessel with a spout that was close to its rounded base, such as an example from Ayn Asil, at Balat.[77]

W: 8.5 cm, H: 6 cm, thickness: 1 cm

24/J/94c) A red ware flat bottomed cup with a very thin (0.2 cm) wall. The rim, unfortunately, is missing. The surface of the cup is covered outside and inside by soot and it had probably been used as a lamp after its initial purpose was no longer possible.

Max. diam.: 11 cm, diam. of the base: 3.5 cm, max. H: 5.5 cm

24/J/94d) A fragment of a low, red ware broad cup with a very thin (0.2 cm) wall. The cup has a slightly incurved rim and a flat bottom. It was clearly a drinking vessel.

Max. diam. of mouth: 11.5 cm, diam. of the bottom: 4 cm, max. H: 5.5 cm

24/J/94e) A fragment of a red ware tray with a flat bottom and projecting rim. The tray had been carefully made; its walls were consistently even. The surface was covered with red slip.

12 × 11 cm, thickness: 2 cm

24/J/94f) A large fragment of an open bowl of coarse red ware, with bent sides and a rounded rim. The vessel is gently carinated 2 cm from the rim. Its walls are approximately 0.7 cm thick near the rim and increase to 1.1 cm near the base. Other vessels of similar nature are documented by G. Reisner, who calls them *bent-sided bowls*.[78]

24/J/94g) A fragment of a red ware bowl with a flaring body, which is gently carinated one third of the way up from the base. Two centimeters under the rolled rim a tiny, hemispherical plastic ledge runs around the vessel. It is another example of a bent-sided bowl, but the protruding ridge makes it a most unusual one: most decorations made under the rim are incised, not in relief, as this one is.

W: 19 cm, H: 13 cm, thickness: 0.7 cm

Beer jar
25/J/94
Red ware pottery
H: 36 cm; max. W: 20 cm
Fifth Dynasty
The beer jar was found outside the eastern wall of the temple, in a layer of drift sand and rubble. This jar has a pointed bottom and a low, slightly disfigured neck. It has an outcurved cusp rim.

When found, it was discovered filled with whitish gypsum mortar. After its initial use, it had evidently been reused as a container for mortar.

---

[76] *E.g.*, see Reisner, Smith, *Giza Necropolis* II, 83. G. Reisner dates such vessels from the end of Neferirkare's time. See also Bárta, in: Verner *et al.*, *Raneferef*, 323.XLVI.I. Nonetheless, amongst the spouted bowls from Ayn Asil (Soukiassian *et al.*, *Balat* III, pl. 26, No. 73), one of those bears a marked similarity to the Abusir fragments.
[77] Minault-Gout, Deleuze, *Balat* II, Inv. No. 2816 on p. 143.
[78] Reisner, Smith, *Giza Necropolis* II, fig. 107, *e.g.* 79, RP.17 L.

Fragments of a plate
42/J/94
Red ware pottery
Fifth Dynasty
Found in the interior of the pyramid in the north-western corner, in a space created by the quarrying of the burial chamber casing; in the midst of debris of dark sand and both small and larger stone chips, at the level of the builders' inscription on the northern wall of the pit for the burial chamber marking three cubits above the ground level of the burial chamber.

Twelve fragments (various sizes) of a plate with a raised rim. The diameter of the plate was ca 32 cm (most of the rim of the plate was present, making it possible to gauge the distance from edge to edge).

4.5.4.2. Middle Kingdom pottery

Drinking cup
3/J/94
Red ware pottery
Diam. of the mouth: 11 cm, H: 9 cm, thickness: 0.3 cm
Twelfth Dynasty
This damaged vessel was found outside the eastern wall, near the entrance to the temple, in a layer of dark grey sand mixed with ash.

This red ware hemispherical cup has a large chunk taken out of its upper region: part of the rim and body of the cup is missing. The cup is thin-walled and its red finish is typical of items frequently found in tombs belonging to royal females in the Middle Kingdom.[79] Such red painted, hemispherical cups were one of the main types found in mortuary temple debris, according to S. Allen.[80] In the light of Allen's remarks, it is very significant that these typical examples Middle Kingdom queens' equipment should be deposited here in Abusir during the Middle Kingdom revival of the Abusir mortuary cults.

Two hemispherical cups (*fig. 4.73*)
10/J/94a–b
Red ware pottery
a) Diam.: 11.8 cm, H: 8 cm, thickness: 0.3–0.5 cm
b) Diam.: 12.5 cm, H: 7 cm, thickness: 0.3–0.7 cm
Twelfth Dynasty
Found near 3/J/94, above, near the eastern wall of the temple, close to its entrance, in a layer of dark grey sand mixed with ash.

Both cups are missing part of the rim and body. They have convex exteriors that are almost upright, and each has a rolled rim curving onto the exterior. The vessels are wheel made and the fabric is sandy Nile clay. This was the most predominant form of Middle Kingdom pottery found for that period.[81] Vessel 10/J/94a appears similar to the forms made in the Twelfth Dynasty and there is a similar form from Abydos.[82] For further remarks on red ware hemispherical cups, see 3/J/94 above.

Despite the fact that these cups were found in close proximity to the former vessel, one can see that the shape of these two cups is different from 3/J/87. Their walls are also thicker than the previous shape.

---

[79] S. Allen, Queens' Ware: Royal Funerary Pottery in the Middle Kingdom, in: *Proceedings of the Seventh Congress*, 40–48.
[80] *Ibid.*, 46.
[81] *Loc. cit.*
[83] Bourriau, *Pharaohs and Mortals*, 135 and Cat. No. 135.

Two hemispherical cups (*fig. 4.73*)
13/J/94a–b
Red ware pottery
a) Diam.: 11.5 cm, H: 7.5 cm, thickness: 0.3 cm
b) Diam. 12.8 cm, H: 7.2 cm, thickness: 0.30 cm
Late Twelfth Dynasty
These two cups were found close to the preceding no. 10/J/94.

These hemispherical cups, wheel thrown and made of fine sandy Nile clay, are of finer workmanship than the previous pair: their walls are very thin. Unlike the previous vessels, these two cups were complete. See notes on red ware above.

fig. 4.72a Hemispherical cup 87/J/94.
Photo MZ

Fig. 4.72b Hemispherical cup 87/J/94.

Fragments of three hemispherical cups (*fig. 4.73*)
26/J/94
Red ware pottery
Diam.: 11 cm, H: 9.5 cm, thickness: 0.3 cm
Twelfth Dynasty
The cups were found outside the eastern wall, near the entrance to the temple, in the layer of dark sand mixed with ash.

From one cup survived part of the rim and bottom, from the remaining two only the bottom.

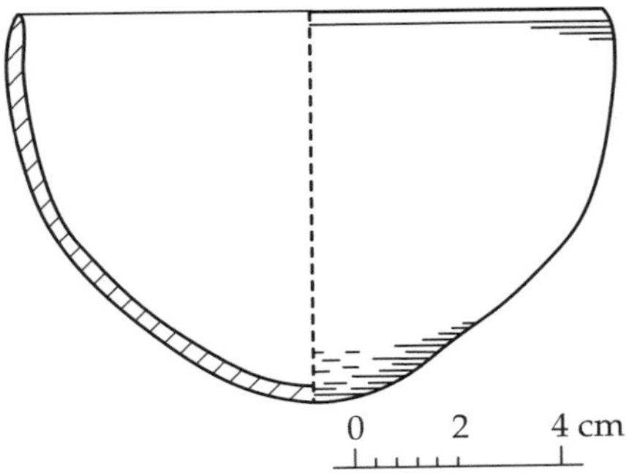

Hemispherical cup (*fig. 4.72a–b*)
87/J/94
Red ware pottery
Diam.: 12 cm, H: 8 cm, thickness: 0.30 cm
Twelfth Dynasty
This cup was found in the north-east corner of the mortuary temple, in the layer of dark sand.

0   2   4 cm

Like all of these red ware vessels, this cup had been skilfully thrown and shaped – its shape fits very comfortably into the hand – and had then been coated all over with a thick red ochre slip before being lightly polished.

This large collection of red ware Middle Kingdom hemispherical cups is of special importance to the archaeological history of Lepsius no. 24: not only does

Fig. 4.73 Distribution chart showing Middle Kingdom hemispherical cups from Abusir, in relation to their Vessel Index. ° This vessel was found in the north-eastern corner of the mortuary temple, in the layer of dark sand; *these items were found in close proximity to each other, near the temple entrance, outside the eastern wall, in a dark, sandy layer mixed with ash.

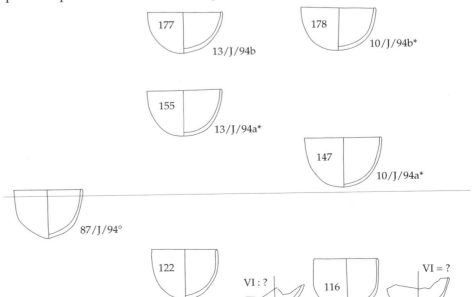

it attest to the persistence of a cult for the deceased tomb owner – which was part of the revival of interest in the cult of the entire royal cemetery during the Middle Kingdom[83] – but the presence of these particular cups, now definitely linked to the mortuary cult of queens during the Middle Kingdom (from the Eleventh to the Thirteenth Dynasties)[84], gives added weight to the circumstantial evidence that the person buried in this tomb was a royal wife.[85]

What will be noticed is that although all the cups were found in the layer of dark grey sand mixed with ash, their shapes and their vessel index reveal minor differences in their manufacture. A very similar range of shapes and vessel index sizes also exists in Do. Arnold's chart, which refers to the period of Senusret III and perhaps a little later.[86] Curiously, the chart for Abusir shows a similar distribution of vessels, falling into what may be two closely linked periods of time (*fig. 4.73*).

4.5.4.3. New Kingdom pottery

A fragment of a jar
1/J/87
Red ware, decorated with dark blue, light blue, black and red paint
6 × 5 cm, thickness: 1 cm
New Kingdom
The sherd was found in the rubble in the south-west corner of the pyramid temple.

It came from the body of a jar decorated with alternating horizontal dark blue, light blue and red bands separated from each other by black lines. The example is from the body of a jar and too small to give it further detailed classification, though its banding and colour scheme are suggestive of the lower part of a three-handled amphora of the Twentieth Dynasty.[87]

Fragments of a jar
18/J/87a–b
Red ware, light blue, black and red paint
a) 10 × 6 cm, thickness: 0.5 cm
b) 5.3 × 5 cm, thickness: 0.5 cm
New Kingdom
The sherds were found in the rubble in the south-east sector of the mortuary temple.

The fragments originated in a body of a jar. The jar had been originally decorated with alternating horizontal light blue and red bands separated from each other by black bands.

Comments on fragment no. 1/J/87 are also applicable to these two body fragments.

Jar with handles
33/J/87
Three fragments of the neck (joined together) of a jar with the remains of handles

---

[83] See L. Bareš, The destruction of the monuments at the necropolis of Abusir, in: *Abusir and Saqqara 2000*, 6.
[84] S. Allen, in: *Proceedings of the Seventh Congress*, 42.
[85] On the association of the cult pyramids with the burial of royal mothers during the Fourth and Fifth Dynasties in particular, see P. Jánosi, The Queens of the Old Kingdom and their Tombs, *BACE* 3, 1992, 51–57.
[86] Do. Arnold, Keramikbearbeitung in Dahschur 1976–1981, *MDAIK* 38, 1982, 61, Abb. 17.
[87] D. Aston, Two decorative styles of the Twentieth Dynasty, *CCÉ* 3, 1992, 74f.

Red ware ceramic of Nile silt B, creamy slip and blue and black paint
12 × 8 cm, thickness: 0.5 cm, diam. of the mouth of the jar: 9 cm
New Kingdom, mid Eighteenth Dynasty
The fragments were found outside the destroyed south-east corner of the
mortuary temple, in the layer of sand mixed with ash. Part of the layer was covered
by a large, fallen block – perhaps from the eastern side of the temple wall.

There were three separate fragments of the flaring neck of a red-brown vessel
that had been well fired and had no dark inner core: these pieces were glued
together (*fig. 4.74, pl. IV*). The fabric was Nile B clay with sharp granules of sand
and organic inclusions as well. The remains of handles can be seen on the sides.
The exterior surface had been smoothed and coated with a creamy slip. The vase
had been decorated with a light blue *sm3* sign flanked by the sign *w3s* in black paint.
The decoration appears somewhat smudged. These details, together with the colour
range and design motifs make it very likely that this vessel belongs to the period
between the reigns of Amenhotep II and Thutmose IV. In this period, designs with
horses, running bull calves, birds etc., in the middle of a wide band with bands
of colour on either side of the pictorial band, were found on a limited number of
long necked jars. The use of large hieroglyphs as the main motif in this band was a
particular feature of some of these long-necked vessels.[88]

This fragment appears to be an example of an amphora from the mid Eighteenth
Dynasty. Marl A examples are not slipped, but the Nile B examples are.[89]

Fragment of a vase
84/J/94
Light ceramic fabric and light red paint
4 × 4 cm, thickness: 1.5 cm
New Kingdom or later
Found in front of the western wall of the cult pyramid, in a layer of pure yellow
sand in which were found a few other scattered sherds.

This is the edge of a vase which has been slipped in light red over the brown, well
fired clay with a greyish core. The exterior has been smoothed and well finished.

Fig. 4.75a Painted ceramic fragments 91/J/94.
Photo MZ

Fig. 4.75b Painted ceramic fragments 91/J/94d.

Painted ceramic fragments
91/J/94a–f
Fired clay and red, light blue, black paint and an orange-red slip
The largest fragment measured 7 × 4 cm, thickness 0.5 cm
New Kingdom

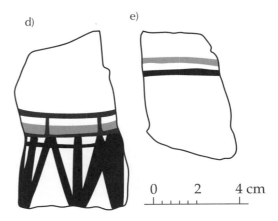

---

[88] C. Hope, Innovation in the decoration of ceramics in the mid-18th Dynasty, *CCÉ* 1, 1987,
97–122. One hieroglyphic example is Cairo SC. 12077. It has a horse on one side and an
ʿnḥ and *w3s* on the other.
[89] Hope, *CCÉ* 1, 1987, 105.

These pieces (*fig. 4.75a*) were found in a layer of dark sand with the additions of many small, non-diagnostic sherds. The sherds were found near no. 33/J/94. The find spot was located to the south from the south-west corner of the mortuary temple, and approximately 3–4 m to the west from the cult pyramid.

The group consisted of six fragments of a light brown, well-fired clay with sandy and organic inclusions. The fabric of 91/J/94a was a light red-brown with no internal core. This was the edge of a bowl. The surface, inside and out of the vessel, was coated with a yellowish slip and decorated with red and black lines. 91/J/94b was a piece of the same material with one band of red remaining. 91/J/94c was part of a plate with a slightly raised rim and a broad band with a floral motif (leaves) in a light blue colour. The pattern of light blue leaves on a red background is very striking. L. Borchardt[90] provides a very similar pattern for a circular vessel like the one given in fragment 91/J/94c.

91/J/94d was the most interesting fragment: it measured 8 × 5 cm (*fig. 4.75b*). It was part of a vase of reddish fabric that had sandy inclusions. It had been well fired and had no core. It had been coated with a dark, red-brown slip on the interior and ochre-orange slip on the outside. The exterior had a painted decoration. The pattern was that of a repeat motif of V-shapes joined in a row. A thick black line bisects the middle of each V-shape. The upper parts of the V end in a 0.1 cm black horizontal line. Another black horizontal line of the same size lies 0.5 cm below the first and it cuts across the V-shapes. Above this design unit lies a broad band of red colour, divided into a block pattern.

This distinctive design is typical of mid Eighteenth Dynasty large jar decorations. Such jars had plant or animal motifs below this V-shaped row. One example from the time of Amenhotep III is given in a catalogue from the Antikenmuseum in Basel.[91] That one has a third black horizontal line cutting across the V-shaped frieze.

In his most interesting article on tall, necked vases with this design, Colin Hope[92] surveyed the corpus known to him and found that the "attached V-shaped motif" as he called it was found on most of these large jars from the mid Eighteenth Dynasty. (Hope, too, thought that the shape was derived from the lotus petal.) The design appeared low down on the neck, while the pictorial representation occupied the widest section of the jar. All of these vases were in the region of 58 cm high, with the middle body diameter in mid-body.

Since this Abusir fragment corresponds to the colour range and a diagnostic design element of the above group, it looks as though this fragment has come from such a vase from the mid Eighteenth Dynasty.[93] The provenance of the pottery workshop is not known, but many of the examples are thought to have come from Thebes.

Little jug (*fig. 4.76a–b*)
85/J/94
Rose-coloured ceramic of marl clay
H: 18 cm, max. W: 14 cm
Late Period

The jug was found in the layer of blown sand in the area of where there was minor destruction of large blocks from the corner of the temple. The jug lay 70–90 cm below the present-day surface, approximately 2 m from the south-east corner.

Fig. 4.76a Late Period jug 85/J/94.
Photo MZ

Fig. 4.76b Late Period jug 85/J/94.

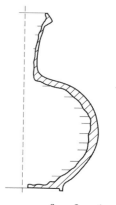

0   2   4 cm

---

[90] Borchardt, *ZÄS* 31, 1893, 9, figure taken from *LD* III.118, has a decoration – also from a circular plate – with the same floral leaves and bands.
[91] Winterhalter, Brodbeck, *Antikenmuseum Basel*, 124f., Cat. No. 84. It features a running calf (frequently illustrated in books on this period) and lotus plants on the other side. The authors mention a neck with a frieze of lotus petals. There are no other details.
[92] Hope, *CCÉ* 1, 1987, 98 and 106.
[93] Apart from C. Hope's article, see also A-M. Loyrette, M. Fekri, Un ensemble céramique du Nouvel Émpire – Vallée des reines: Tombe 18, *CCÉ* 4, 1996, 11–16. The work of these authors gives additional support to Hope's study. Of particular note is their location of a painted register from the tomb of Userhat that shows such a jar resting in its wooden cradle.

This is a small, globular, light coloured, reddish juglet with a round, flat base, a handle and a tall, narrow flaring neck. Around the mouth runs a cusp rim that is very sharply undercut where it meets the neck of the vase. The body of the vessel is more or less globular and the exterior surface has been smoothed, but this has been rather carelessly done. The handle is well joined to the body of the vessel at shoulder height, while the other end is joined to the neck below the rim.

There are many counterparts to this vessel from the excavations carried out by the French at the mastaba of Akhethotep, in Saqqara. The range of finds from that monument went from the Fifth Dynasty to the Arabic period, even as the range in the Pyramid Complex Lepsius no. 24 does. There is one pitcher represented in an illustration in the French report which, apart from the rim finish, is almost identical to this juglet found at Abusir[94], while from the same period, there is another, variant closed jar, with exactly the same unusual rim as is found on the Abusir juglet.[95]

Neck of a juglet
86/J/94
Ceramic of marl clay and ochre-like paint
H: 9 cm, W: 7 cm
Late Period
This neck fragment was found in a layer of blown sand, to the east of the eastern wall of the cult pyramid. It was lying near the south-east corner of the pyramid and 1.2 m above the level of the terrain.

The fragment consists of light, ochre-brown clay with fine sand inclusions and well-worked clay. The surface was evenly covered with a light ochre slip. Again, there is a direct parallel with the Akhethotep corpus, with this example having exactly the same neck and attachment formations.[96]

4.5.4.4. Medieval (Islamic) pottery

Lamp (see *fig. 4.77*, *pl. IV* left)
52/J/94
Coarse ware with green glaze
Middle body diam. with spout: 9 cm, H: 6 cm, diameter of base: 3.8 cm
Islamic (Mamluk) Period[97]
The lamp was found in the pyramid, in the sand and rubble at the lower end of the descending corridor. It was probably left there when later robbers came to see what spoils they could remove from the tomb.

The vessel is made of brown clay with sand inclusions and organic material; it has been well fired, with no inner core indicating burning. Most of the neck and the handle are missing, but the spout is more intact. The surface has a very even layer of dark green glaze which darkens to black. Inside the lamp were the remains of a dark organic substance. This is a small, squat vessel which originally had a long spout and flared rim. It has a recessed foot with a low, rounded ring base. On the side of the lamp, one can see traces where the handle had been attached.

---

[94] G. Lecuyet, La céramique du mastaba d'Akhethetep à Saqqara. Observation, préliminaires, *CCÉ* 6, 2000, 240 and Fig. 2.1, BE. 13; S.P. 7.

[95] Lecuyet, *CCÉ* 6, 2000, 240 and Fig. 2.1, BE. 19. G. Lecuyet observes here that most of these pitchers or juglets from Saqqara have everted openings and the handles have small joins on the shoulders and neck. The fabric is also similar to the Abusir example, having fine to medium granules of sand within the clay. The average height of the Akhethetep examples is 13.50–14 cm; MBD = 8.30 cm; neck opening = 3.10–3.50 cm; diameter of the base 3.60–5.20 cm. 85/J/94 has similar measurements, but it is a fraction larger: height = 15 cm; MBD = 11 cm.

[96] *Ibid.*, 240 and Fig. 2.1, S.P. 7.

[97] W. B. Kubiak, Mediaeval Ceramic Oil Lamps from Fustat, *Ars Orientalis* 8, 1970, 14.

From Saqqara, N. Kanawati and A. Hassan[98] report the discovery of two similar lamps with dark green glaze from the tomb of Kaaper (the find spot is not recorded). One has a flat strap handle with a thumb rest,[99] the other a rounded handle.[100] Both of them also had spouts that had been damaged, but TNE 94:101 had much more of its spout remaining. They were evidently variant models from the same period, falling into the group known as Type I, in Kubiak's typology.[101] This badly damaged example from Abusir belongs to the same type, with its ring foot and deep, dark green glaze.[102] It is useful to have the Saqqara vessels for comparison. All three finds may have come from the pottery workshop at Fustat. The horizon for such lamps is between the second half of the Twelfth, through to the Fourteenth and even Fifteenth century AD. They were prevalent in Mamluk times.

Lamp (*fig.4.78* and *fig. 4.77, pl. IV* right)
62/J/94
Ceramic with green glaze
H: 8 cm, diam. of the body: 7.3 cm
Post-Fatimid, possibly advanced Mamluk period?
The lamp was found in the debris in the descending corridor, in a layer of grey sand with large blocks of limestone.

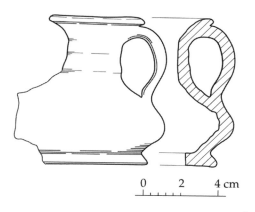

This lamp is a squat, baggy jug-like lamp, differing from the preceding no. 52/J/94, but in this example, the handle has survived. The spout where the wick burned, however, is almost entirely missing. Nonetheless, one notices how low the spout is to the well-pronounced foot. The handle connects the long, flaring neck to the body of the vessel and it has been well attached. The surface has been smoothed and glazed with a dark green glaze. No traces of a wick survive, but the interior of the vessel is sooty from burning. Even the surface has traces of burnt oil.

This lamp is more difficult to classify because it combines elements from different types in Kubiak's typology. It is closest in shape to the Post-Fatimid nozzle lamp photographed as Fig. 20 on pl. 4 of that article. Such vessels, he says,[103] do not fall into any one of the typology groups he has suggested. (Unfortunately, there is no description nor measurements given with the example he reproduced, so comparisons are hard to make.) However, the low, baggy form of this vessel and the presence of the foot suggest that it derives from Type I, even though it has a simpler handle, with no nib (or thumb rest), and this handle is attached just under the rim. The shape of the ring hole is also suggestive of a derivation from Type I.

Fig. 4.78 Islamic lamp 62/J/94.

Despite these similarities to other models, the Abusir vessel is much more crude in workmanship, suggestive of a period later than examples from Type I. The dark green glaze fits in with this Mamluk period. Dating range possible: second half of the Twelfth century – Fourteenth or Fifteenth centuries of our era. The find attests to the presence of visitors to the Abusir site in the later mediaeval period.

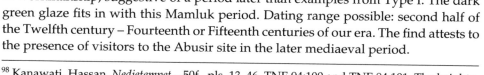

[98] Kanawati, Hassan, *Nedjetempet* – 50f., pls. 13, 46. TNE 94:100 and TNE 94:101. The heights of those lamps were 8.5 cm and 8 cm respectively; diameter of the base = 5.5 cm and 5.1 cm; diameter of rim = 4.2 cm and 4.7 cm.
[99] Kanawati, Hassan, *op. cit.*: TNE 94:101.
[100] Kanawati, Hassan, *op. cit.*: TNE 94:100.
[101] Kubiak, *Ars Orientalis* 8, 1970, 1–18; Type I is analysed on p. 13f. These two examples from Saqqara are distinctive because of their small loop handles attached to mid-body and mid-neck, and the fact that they have both an internal and external glaze, amongst other things. TNE 94:100's "fluting" (see Kanawati, Hassan, *Nedjetempet*, 50) is more likely to be accidental kiln warping than deliberate decoration, as fluting is not a feature of these lamps.
[102] See Kubiak, *Ars Orientalis* 8, 1970, 14 for details of the varieties attested to date.
[103] Kubiak, *op. cit.*, 17 mentions that the Post-Fatimid vessels have characteristics taken from "the large family of lamps with protruding nozzle and top cover and cannot be attributed to any of our types".

4.5.5. Metal Objects

Fragments of gold foil
53/J/94, 67/J/94
Gold
Fifth Dynasty
Found in the burial chamber, in the south-east corner, in the filling of sand and limestone chips, ca 0.5 m above the floor foundation.

These numerous fragments of gold foil, ranging from tiny scraps to pieces that were almost 2 cm in length, had evidently once been applied as decoration to furniture or cult objects. Similar fragments have been found in other high-class burial chambers – such as that of Hetepheres I – where they had fallen from (or been prised off) boxes, furniture or even vessels.

Model libation basin (*fig. 4.79*)
63/J/94
Copper
4.7 × 3.9 cm, thickness: 0.25 cm
Fifth Dynasty.
This small receptacle was found in the eastern part of the burial chamber (close to the destroyed eastern wall), in a layer of yellow sand which contained only a small amount of rather tiny, limestone chips. It was discovered near the level of the quarried floor.

Fig. 4.79 Model libation basin 63/J/94. Photo MZ

This copper item (somewhat distorted, presumably due to later pressure?) had originally been worked into the shape of a small tray with an oblong bottom and slightly raised corners.

These items, together with other, various, model tools of copper,[104] were found in the debris in the burial chamber. They were discovered on top of the foundation blocks which had been laid under the pavement of the chamber. Later, these paving blocks had been removed – either by tomb robbers looking for treasure, or by men seeking blocks of limestone for the stone-workers' workshop nearby. Other model tools were found in different parts of the chamber: no. 63/J/94 was near the eastern wall, no. 64/J/94 lay in the sand near the lower end of the descending corridor, no. 66/J/94 and 67/J/94 were positioned near the northern wall of the chamber, no. 69/J/94 and no. 82/J/94 lay approximately in the middle of the chamber and no. 70/J/94 in the south-west corner. It will be noticed that these find places are adjacent to and including that where the gold foil was found. It is suggested that some of this foil may have come from a coating given to the little copper basins.

Miniature libation basins are metal copies of the rectangular basins found in the offering slabs that were set into the floors or placed on low pedestals in tombs. They were to provide an offering of water for the deceased in the Afterlife – see 66/J/94b–c *etc.* below. These numerous miniature objects from Abusir, either rectangular basins (the more likely identification), or trays, of either copper or

---

[104] Prince Khnumbaf, son of Khafre, who had an untouched tomb, had in his burial chamber, to the east of the sarcophagus and close to four canopic jars of red pottery, eighty copper model implements, including a model ewer and basin, four jars, two small basins, four rectangular knives, three axe-blades (or razors, according to some archaeologists) further knives, chisels and a quantity of adze-blades. In addition, there was a full-sized practical ewer, also of copper, together with a full-sized copper basin. These last two items lay to the south of the sarcophagus (Hassan, *Gîza* VI/2, 9). We might well expect that the original set within the queen's burial chamber in the pyramid Lepsius no. 24 would have been similar. Due to repeated robbery, only a few metal items were found in this pyramid at Abusir, however.

bronze, bear close comparison to very similar basins found in the burial chamber of Queen Hetepheres I.[105]

Model libation basins (with small pieces of gold leaf)
66/J/94a
Copper/bronze and gold
The models are roughly the same size, but vary from L: 4.7–5 cm; W: 2.6–2.8 cm
Fifth Dynasty
Found in grey sand on the underfloor blocks in the northern part of the burial chamber.

Once again, these basins were discovered in relation to pieces of gold foil – see previous entry for comment.

Rectangular libation basins (with small pieces of gold leaf)
66/J/94b
Sheet copper and gold leaf
4.7 × 2.8 × 0.25 cm – all these basins are the same size
Fifth Dynasty
These seven metal model basins[106] (*fig 4.80*), were found lying in greyish sand on underfloor blocks in the northern part of the burial chamber of the pyramid. They looked as though the pieces had fallen through from the pavement above. The spot was 80 cm to the south from the northern wall of the burial chamber in its north–south axis.

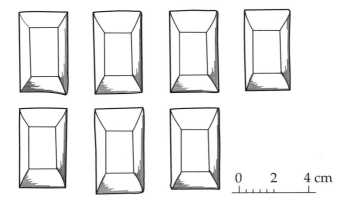

Fig. 4.80 Seven model libation basins 66/J/94b.

Libation basins are not usually found in tombs, although Khnumbaf also had two miniature basins. Once again, these ones from Abusir were discovered with gold foil pieces which may have once coated the basins.

Chisel[107]
36/J/94
Copper
L: 6.8 cm, width at tip: 0.5 cm, widest part: 0.7 cm, thickness: 0.2 cm
Fifth Dynasty
This chisel was found in the filling of debris to the south of the southern wall of the temple and to the east of the south-east corner of the main pyramid.

---

[105] Reisner, Smith, *Giza Necropolis* II, pl. 40.a, c.

[106] While it is commonly assumed that Egyptians in the Old Kingdom only had the technology to make objects from copper, the discovery of large quantities of cassiterite in the Eastern Desert, and evidence for an extensive Egyptian presence in that region has caused us to doubt the earlier assumption. See R. D. Rothe, G. Rapp, W. K. Miller, New Hieroglyphic Evidence for Pharaonic Activity in the Eastern Desert of Egypt, *JARCE* 33, 1996, 77–104, but especially103f. The authors say that they "believe cassiterite was the form in which tin was traded and used in the ancient world."

[107] For another example of a chisel like this, see Petrie, *Tools and Weapons*, pl. XV.32.

This chisel has a sharp, intact blade and a gentle bulge about 1.3 cm from the tip. It is covered evenly with verdigris.

Chisels and a spatula
66/J/94c
Copper

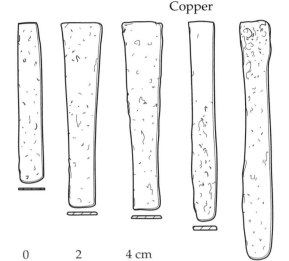

The five chisels varying in size and shape (*fig.4.81a* on *pl. V, fig. 4.81b*). Two chisels are made from a 0.2 cm thick sheet of copper and are 7.1 cm long. Two other chisels, made from a 0.05 cm thick sheet of copper, have slightly convex sides and are 7.7 and 9.2 cm long. The fifth one measures 6 × 0.9 × 0.1 cm, and the spatula measures 16 × 2 × 0.1 cm.
Fifth Dynasty
These items came from the layer of grey sand, together with other metal pieces under this number, just over 1 m from the northern wall of the burial chamber. They were found ca 15 cm under the level of the floor of the burial chamber, and had probably fallen down into the substructure during the tearing up of the paving blocks.

Fig. 4.81b Larger model chisels from the set 66/J/94c.

Fig. 4.81d Spatula from the set of models 66/J/94c.

The chisels are of different types, but all have one larger and one smaller end. The first chisel is more rectangular than the others; it is also smaller, being 6.2 cm long. It has a gentle swelling to its shaft, narrowing towards its point. The second chisel has a much broader tip that is 1.5 cm wide. It has an elegant vase-like shape, given by its concave sides. The third chisel is similar to the second, and the fourth chisel is a larger version of the first chisel. The fifth chisel has a column-like shape, with a smallish handle end, and a gentle bulge beginning 0.5 cm from its handle end.

The spatula has the shape of a leaf with a stem (*fig. 4.81c* on *pl. V, fig. 4.81d*). This tang at the end would normally have been fixed into a wooden handle.

Fine chisels
66/J/94c
Copper
L: 11.2 and 11.3 cm, W: 0.3 cm for both, thickness: 0.15 cm
Fifth Dynasty
These two items were discovered ca 15 cm under the level of the floor of the burial chamber, in a layer of grey sand, together with other metal pieces under this number, just over 1 m from the northern wall of the burial chamber (together with other chisels and the spatula mentioned above).

Fig. 4.82a Two fine chisels 66/J/96c.

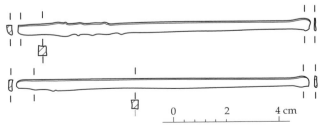

The length/width ratio of these fine chisels (*figs. 4.82a* and *4.82b* on *pl. V*) is clearly different from that of other chisels of this group of finds – these fine chisels are much narrower. Fine chisels such as these were used for engraving hieroglyphs, among other things. There were pieces of golden foil and vegetal seeds among the collection of items found – perhaps part of a burial wreath?

Chisels are frequent items when deposits of copper instruments are found, but it is again questionable what some of these chisel-like items are actually meant to represent. For those who question the identity of the implement, they are seen as being too broad and not thick enough to be a chisel. There is some substance to this objection: some of Garstang's splayed examples[108] from Bet Khallaf, for example, are more like a plasterer's spatula. However, we must not forget that these are model instruments and, like most models, may have only been approximations of actual implements.

Model razor or spatula (?)
64/J/94
Copper
L: 6.3 cm, max. W: 3.4 cm, thickness: ca 0.25 cm
Fifth Dynasty
Found in the north-east corner of the burial chamber, near the end of the descending corridor, in a layer of yellow sand, near the level with the quarried floor.

The instrument has a softly beaten surface; there are no traces of corrosion. Items like these are sometimes called razors, sometimes spatulas. They are model instruments made for the burial, so they need not have the sharp edges that razors have. However, Junker[109] has suggested that the short tangs on these instruments are designed for inserting into wooden handles. Flinders Petrie[110] referred to them as "razors", but the longer bladed ones he referred to as "flaying knives"[111]. In this case, the items are not likely to be razors, but rather some sort of spatula. They are present in some tombs from the Third to the Sixth Dynasty.

Models of razors or spatulas (?)
66/J/94a
Copper
W: 3.1–3.3 cm, L: 6.1–6.5 cm; the tangs are between 1.0–1.3 cm long
These objects are of approximately the same size, but with small variations: see *figs. 4.83a–b*
Fifth Dynasty
These seven items were registered together with another six items (exc. no. 64/J/94). Model spatulas were found in the northern part of the burial chamber, in a layer of grey sand, just below the quarried floor.

Fig. 4.83a Model razors or spatulas (66/J/94a and 64/J/94).
Photo MZ

Fig. 4.83b Model razors or spatulas (66/J/94a and 64/J/94).

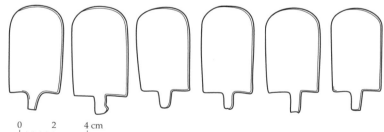

0   2   4 cm

The spatulas are of typical sizes and shape for the Old Kingdom (see, for example, the similar instruments in the burial chamber of Hetepheres I,[112] also,

---

[108] Garstang, *Mahasna and Bêt Khallâf*, from the tomb of Hen-nakht (*i.e.* King Sanakht), (K.4), 13, 18, 27, pl. XXIII.
[109] Junker, *Gîza* VII, 48.
[110] Petrie, *Tools and Weapons*, 49.
[111] Petrie, *op. cit.*, 22 and pl. XXXI.K4.
[112] Reisner, Smith, *Giza Necropolis* II, pl. 40.a, c.

the collections of copper implements from the Mastaba of Ankhhaf.[113] Examples from Balat are also recorded[114]. These Abusir examples are the same type and size as no. 64/J/94.

Model awl (borer/burin)
95/J/94
Copper
L: 11 cm, W: 0.8 cm, max. thickness: 0.5 cm
Fifth Dynasty
Found during the cleaning of the burial chamber, in a chink among the underfloor blocks, 50 cm under the level of the floor of the burial chamber.

This model of a copper awl (see notes on this identification in 69/J/94, below) is relatively well preserved: the end is pointed, for boring holes, the handle end is squared off (*fig. 4.84*). The side elevation reveals a graceful curve towards the handle end on both sides of the awl.

Models of an adze and an awl (or burin, or even cosmetic utensil – see notes for 95/J/94 below)
69/J/94
Copper
adze: 9.3 × 2 cm, axe: 9.3 × 1.2 cm; both of them are 0.1 cm thick
Fifth Dynasty
These two items were found in the burial chamber in a layer of grey sand, mixed with both large and small chips of limestone. They were found 120 cm to the south from the large block that was still preserved in the former northern wall of the chamber. Both instruments were found below floor level.

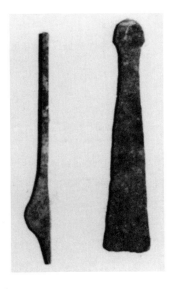

Fig. 4.84 Model awl or burin 95/J/94.

While the nature of the pointed instrument has sometimes been called a burin, that of the other utensil (somewhat skittle-shaped) has been usually called an adze.[115] It is, however, hard to imagine an adze of this elongated shape being able to do the sort of work an adze blade should do. It rather resembles another type of spatula, in author's opinion.

Models of tools (*fig. 4.85a*)
69/J/94a–b
Copper
a) L: 10 cm, max. W: 1 cm
b) L: 10 cm, W: 2 cm (at the blade edge)
Fifth Dynasty
These two pieces were found ca 15 cm under the level of the floor of the burial chamber, in a layer of grey sand mixed with limestone rubble, 120 cm to the south from the corner of the northern wall of the burial chamber.

Fig. 4.85a Models of tools 69/J/94a–b.
Photo MZ

Exc. no. 69/J/94a represents an awl or cosmetic spatula, whereas the second item (69/J/94b) is chisel. Both models are quite well preserved, only slightly corroded on the surface (*fig. 4.85b, pl. V*).

Once again, there is debate about exc. no. 69/J/94a, which Petrie[116] refers to as a "borer" or awl, but it could also be a cosmetic tool, either for cleaning nails, or mixing cosmetic colours etc. The author's preference is for an ancient version of a nail file (without the file). Registered together with 63/J/94, 64/J/94, 66/J/94, 70/J/94.

---

[113] S. Hassan, *Giza* III, 1941, 140 and fig. 117; and Shaft 559, part of the same tomb, 240–244 and pl. LXVII.
[114] Valloggia, *Balat* IV, 148 and pl. CVIII, *etc.*
[115] Petrie, *Tools and Weapons*, 30 and pl. XV, 45, 47. Petrie calls these varieties "necked adzes".
[116] Petrie, *op. cit.*, 52, and pl. LXV.47.

Needle

66/J/94c
Copper
L: 7.5 cm, W: 0.15–0.3 cm
Fifth Dynasty
Found together with other items exc. no. 66/J/94c ca 15 cm under the level of the floor of the burial chamber, in a layer of grey sand, together with other metal pieces under this number, just over 1 m from the northern wall of the burial chamber.

This needle is very well preserved: its point is still sharp and its eye is clear of oxidation. It is a very long needle (judging by present-day standards) and may have been originally used for thick material or even leatherwork (*fig. 4.86*).

It is rare to find a needle among copper artefacts because the slender nature of the material and the corrosive properties of copper usually destroy such small slender items. Needles of copper began to appear in the later Prehistoric period at Naqada.[117] They are seldom found in excavations because their fragile form and the usual presence of oxidation are susceptible to breakage and pulverisation in the majority of instances. However, they are documented in both male and female burial chambers. For the Old Kingdom, J. Garstang found examples in K.5 in Bet Khallaf,[118] while Flinders Petrie notes three from Meidum, also in the Third Dynasty, and H. Junker found a collection of nine (three without eyes in them), in the burial of Ptahhotep[119] – and there are many others.

Needle

82/J/94
Copper
L: 6.8 cm, W: 0.3 cm
Fifth Dynasty
This needle was found in the brownish layer resting on the floor of the temple, near its central part. It was 4.5 m to the west from the northern end of the preserved part of the eastern wall.

Copper needle, completely covered with a uniform coating of verdigris: the eye of the needle had been closed by the oxidation of the copper, but there was a depression where it had been.

Needles are seldom found in excavation sites, not only because of their fragile nature, but also because it is difficult to see them during the dusty conditions of excavation. The Abusir tombs have yielded a number of needles,[120] but several finely preserved examples from the late Sixth Dynasty have also been discovered at Balat.[121] H. Junker[122] remarks that the nine needles from the burial of Ptahhotep were very striking – not only because of the high number of such rare items, but also because three of them were without eyes for the thread. If the eyes were not present (verdigris can disguise their presence), then perhaps H. Junker's three examples were fine burins.

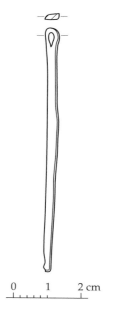

0   1   2 cm

Fig. 4.86 Needle 82/J/94c.

Needle and copper bead

89/J/94
Copper
Needle: L: 4.7 cm, W: 0.3 cm
Bead: diam.: 0.9 cm
Fifth Dynasty

---

[117] Petrie, *Tools and Weapons*, 53.
[118] Garstang, *Mahasna and Bêt Khallâf*, pl. XXIII, needles: 37, 38 – and a pin: 36.
[119] Junker, *Gîza* VII, Abb. 95: item nos. 2717 and 2705 are like the Abusir examples.
[120] Verner, Callender, *Djedkare's Cemetery*, pl. IX, Bf27: the needle lies in front of the copper dish.
[121] Valloggia, *Balat* IV, pl. CVII, Inv. Nos. 5792, 5793, 5392.
[122] Junker, *Gîza* VII, 228, Abb. 93, item nos: 2714a and b, and 2703.

The two small items were found in the filling of dark sand in the destroyed part of the floor in the room in the north-east corner of the pyramid temple. They were discovered ca 4 cm to the south-west from the north-east corner of this room.

The needle was badly corroded and had encrustations of verdigris, with only the suggestion of the eye position. The bead was without encrustations.

Fig. 4.87 Hemispherical spatula/razor 70/J/94. Photo MZ

Hemispherical spatula, blade or razor (?)
70/J/94
Copper
5 × 5 × 0.1 cm
Fifth Dynasty
Found in a layer of rubble mixed with sand and tiny limestone pieces, in the south-west corner (ca 1 m from the corner) of the burial chamber, ca floor level.

This is a semi-circular metal blade (*fig. 4.87*) whose identity is questionable. Petrie called them battleaxe blades.[123] H. Junker followed that choice with his reference to the *mibt* "Axtklingen" hieroglyph.[124] Most archaeologists refer to them as razors, but like the question of the spatulas above (see item 66/J/94a), there is still debate about the issue and some prefer to see them as hemispherical knife blades, others as axe blades. Given that both male and female ancient Egyptians cut or shaved their hair, razors would be a necessary item for the Afterlife and Junker inclines to this proposal.

Frequently, burials contain one or more of these instruments. One of the earliest is from the so-called Netjerikhet tomb at Bet Khallaf. In the great Third Dynasty mastaba there excavated by John Garstang,[125] a number of copper tools and instruments were found deposited with a collection of flint instruments. Two semi-circular blades (or razors) were among these items. For an untouched burial, thought to be that of an unnamed princess from the time of Khafre, there were two such razors.[126] In the Fifth Dynasty, the numbers of examples was larger. Hassan reports that Khnumbaf had three similar examples, which he refers to as axe-blades.[127] There is still uncertainty as to the identity of these thin metal objects, which look exactly like the axe blades that were wedged into the upper part of wooden axe handles.

Fishing hook (*fig.4.88*)
39/J/94
Copper
L: 2 cm
Fifth Dynasty
This was found among the debris in the western part of the temple, in the area of the presumed offering hall.

With the absence of a barb to the hook, this example is most likely to have come from the Old Kingdom period. Fish hook barbs are not recorded prior to the Eighteenth Dynasty. Petrie has many examples of fish hooks from all periods in *Tools and Weapons*.[128] This particular example is very similar to the First Dynasty examples, but an Old Kingdom period is more likely.

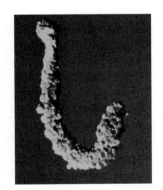

Fig. 4.88 Fishing hook 39/J/94. Photo MZ

[123] Petrie, *Tools and Weapons*, 30 and pl. II, No. 55 from the Third Dynasty.
[124] Junker, *Gîza* VII, 58.
[125] Garstang, *Mahasna and Bêt Khallâf*, 37.
[126] Hassan, *Gîza* VI/II, 8. The tools were still in position and the photograph of the burial chamber in pl. VI shows that they were deposited near the bone of an ox, but in the doorway leading into the tomb. In the Fifth Dynasty tomb of Ankhhaf at Giza – also an untouched burial – the instruments were deposited along one of the long sides of his sarcophagus (Hassan, *Gîza* III, 139, Fig. 117).
[127] Hassan, *loc. cit.*
[128] Petrie, *Tools and Weapons*, 37 and pl. XLIV for similar shapes. No. 61 on this plate comes from the First Dynasty, the time of King Den.

Workman's wedge
79/J/94
Heavily corroded iron
7.6 × 3.7 cm
Islamic Period
Discovered in the filling of sand and stone chips in the area where the western wall of the burial chamber once had been, approx. at floor level, close to the north-western corner.

The wedge is more or less rectangular on its front and back faces, but triangular on its sides: in fact, it is like a modern day wedge used to split timber. It is heavily encrusted with corrosion.

Rust has distorted this wedge, which may have been left behind by robbers who had used it to manoeuvre the blocks of limestone in the pyramid. See also corresponding finds from the Tomb Complex Lepsius no. 25 discussed in *chapter 5*.

4.5.6. Wood

A netting needle
80/J/94
Wood
L: 12.5 cm; W: 0.9 cm; thickness of the needle: 0.5 cm
Islamic Period (?)
It was found in the debris in the western part of the burial chamber.

This is a roughly shaped needle cut from a twig (*fig. 4.89*). The eye of the needle is it at one end.

Wooden needles like this are occasionally found, but Petrie has only examples from the Twelfth Dynasty. They are exactly like this.[129]

Such needles were used to make fishermen's nets. Together with the fish hook, they suggest the presence of a fisherman on the site of the pyramid. Even today, men fish in the nearby canals of Abusir, and in the period when the Lake of Abusir was functioning, it would not have been odd to find a fisherman wandering around the royal cemetery after he had made his catch.

Fig. 4.89 Netting needle 80/J/94.
Photo MZ

Fragments of a chest (furniture?) and obscure wooden objects
57/J/94
Wood, stucco
The largest piece: 8 × 2.5 cm, 6 × 3.6 cm
Fifth Dynasty
Found in the western part of the burial chamber, close to the destroyed western wall, in a layer of grey sand mixed with the limestone chips (found in the lower part of this layer), ca 0.75 cm above the foundation level.

Two fragments of worked wood, the surface of which is covered on one side with a layer of yellowish stucco, with faint traces of black colour on the surface. The larger piece has stucco on its outer face, while the inner surface is without stucco and is smoothed. Another worked, but thinner wooden fragment has the remains of a cross-piece, with part of a dowel protruding, somewhat like part of a chair. It, too, is covered with stucco on the outer side and its inner side is smoothed. The pieces perhaps come from a box or another piece of furniture, but the fragments are too badly preserved to suggest anything more concrete.

---

[129] Petrie, *Tools and Weapons*, 53 and pl. LXVI, nos. 118–122; LXV, nos. 88–101.

A part of a foundation deposit – possibly a chest (?)
72/J/94
Wood
Fifth Dynasty
This find was discovered in the north-eastern corner of the burial chamber, ca 0.75 cm below the foundation level of the floor (which has now been removed). The previously discovered bits were found in the western part of the burial chamber. These circumstances suggest a tertiary disturbance within the burial chamber.

One wooden piece was bigger than the other; both were covered with stucco. Now joined together with 57/J/94.

Fig. 4.90a Wooden fragment with inscription 77/J/94a. Photo MZ

Fig. 4.90b Wooden fragment with inscription 77/J/94a.

Fragments of a chest (?)
77/J/94a
Wood, stucco
4 fragments: 9.6 × 3 × 1 cm, 5 × 2.5 × 0.6 cm, 7.2 × 1.4 × 1 cm, inscribed piece: 7.3 × 0.8 × 0.7 cm
Fifth Dynasty

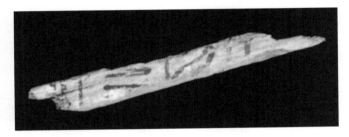

Found in a filling of greyish sand mixed with tiny chips of limestone, near the quarried eastern wall of the burial chamber, at ca 30 cm below floor level on some underfloor blocks.

These four wooden fragments were covered with a tiny layer of beige-brown stucco; one of them contained an inscription written black paint (*fig. 4.90a–b*).

Fig. 4.91a Wooden fragment with inscription 77/J/94b. Photo MZ

Fig. 4.91b Wooden fragment with inscription 77/J/94b.

Two fragments of a chest (?)
77/J/94b
Wood, stucco
9 × 3 × 0.4 cm (inscribed piece), 7 × 2.3 × 0.4 cm (anepigraphic fragment)
Fifth Dynasty
Found in the western part of the burial chamber (ca 2 m to the east from the destroyed west wall), in the filling of greyish sand mixed with limestone rubble.

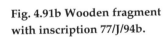

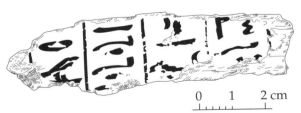

The inscribed piece is a thin wooden fragment, covered with a thin layer of beige-brown stucco, on which an inscription in columns has been written in black paint (*fig. 4.91a–b*). An anepigraphic fragment covered by a grey-green stucco was also found with the inscribed piece. We cannot rule out that exc. nos 77a–b/J/94 were originally part of one chest.

4.5.7. Stone tools

Blade
19/J/94
Flint
L: 8.3 cm, W: 2 cm
Fifth Dynasty.
This blade was found in the layer of sand mixed with ash in a hole below the foundation of the destroyed northern wing of the eastern wall of the temple.

Two blades
21/J/87b–c
Flint
L: 6.2 and 4 cm, W: 0.8, thickness: 1.5 cm
Fifth Dynasty
These two items were found on the floor level in front of the entrance to the temple.

The blades are finger length pieces of worked chert which have had a lot of previous use (*fig. 4.92*). Experiments with such pieces have revealed that stone knives were more efficient at cutting meat than copper or bronze knives, but like them, they needed sharpening. This consisted of flaking off more pieces of stone until the result (after many sharpenings) was no longer a knife, but a blade, like these ones.

In Nebtyemneferes's tomb another flint knife blade like this was found (6/M/87) in her storeroom in the north-western corner of the mastaba. That blade had been lying in the centre of the room, on the floor, below the layer of the mudbrick destruction and limestone detritus. Nebtyemneferes' knife has the same form as the blades found in Lepsius no. 24. Other flint blades (15/M/87) from her mastaba were discovered in the layer of mudbrick destruction to the east of the entrance to her mastaba (see *chapter 2.4.*). It is evident that such blades had been used in activities connected with the cult, which is why they were found in the outer parts of the respective tombs.

Flint knives and blades are commonly found in the tombs of members of the royal family: King Raneferef had 95, the Queen Khentkaus II complex recorded 20,[130] Princess Khekeretnebty had only two (56/B/76, 154/B/76).[131] An unnamed princess buried in Giza – probably early Fifth Dynasty – had two such blades as well.[132] All of these pieces had been resharpened, but only 154/B/76 retained something of its shape as a knife. All the rest had a similar form to the blades mentioned in the queen's collection.

A blade
76/J/94
Flint
L: 9.1 cm, W: 1.3 cm, thickness: 0.4 cm
Fifth Dynasty
This was found in the layer of drift sand on the floor of the descending corridor, 10 cm above the floor itself.

There is evidence of a little reworking on this example.

A tip of a knife
88/J/94

Fig. 4.92 Two flint blades 21/J/87.
Photo JB

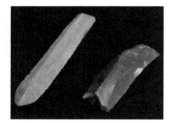

---

[130] J. A. Svoboda, in: Verner *et al.*, *Raneferef*, 509.
[131] Verner, Callender, *Djedkare's Cemetery*, 46.
[132] Hassan, *Gîza* VII, 5, pl. VI C; not far away from the doorway of this tomb, a large collection of these blades was found buried in a pit (Hassan, *Gîza* VII, pl. LVIII).

Flint
5.2 × 3.9 × 0.5 cm
Fifth Dynasty
This piece was found in the filling of dark sand in the room of the north-east corner of the temple, in the place where the floor has been torn out.

This is the only example of a knife, even though it is partial. Once again, there is evidence of retouching along the edge of the blade.

Stone knives were used throughout the pharaonic period as the material for such knives was readily available and flint knives were very effective in cutting meat, in particular. J. Svoboda[133] gives interesting details on the history and ritual relating to these blades. When the flint edges became blunt, the knife maker knapped the edges all round, thus making the knife much thinner and more rectangular with each episode of sharpening. Finally, only rectangular blades such as these were left. They are very frequently found in cemeteries, attesting to a series of visits to the cultic sites and making offerings of meat or other sorts of food that needed to be cut up.

Fig. 4.93a Stamp seal 21/J/87a.
Photo JB

4.5.8. Seals and clay sealings

Stamp seal
12/J/87
Limestone
H: 4.8 cm, base: 5.3 × 3.8 cm
Fifth – Sixth Dynasty
It was found near the entrance to the temple, on the floor level outside the eastern wall of the temple.

This object is an unfinished oval stamp seal with a pierced handle. The seal is not inscribed. Stamp seals have their origin in the late Fifth Dynasty, but they were seldom found by earlier excavators.[134] Uninscribed ones like this are also fairly common.

Stamp seal
21/J/87a
Limestone
H: 2.5 cm, base: 2.7 cm, thickness: 1.7 cm
Fifth – Sixth Dynasty
This stamp seal was found near the preceding no. 12/J/87, on the level of the floor of the temple, outside the eastern wall near the entrance to the temple.

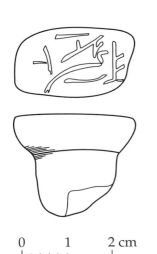

Fig. 4.93b Stamp seal 21/J/87a.

This is an oval stamp seal with a raised back for its owner to grasp (*figs. 4.93a–b*). On the base of the seal are incised a number of signs which might be interpreted as *Idf* and *mr*. The way in which the seal was made, together with the method of inscribing its base are very typical of Fifth and Sixth Dynasty stamp seals.

The discovery of this seal is extremely important for the stamp-seal corpus as,

---

[133] J. A. Svoboda, (in: Verner *et al., Raneferef,* 503ff.) gives a summary of the ritual significance of these flint knives and provides a very clear account of how these blades arrived at their final shape. In essentials, they are the remnants of many resharpening episodes, during which the knives lost their typical tangs and became side-scrapers, rather than knife blades (see *ibid.,* 506).
[134] Wiese, *Stempelsiegel-Amulette,* 27.
[135] *Ibid.,* 28 and 31, Abb. 3.

previously, no actual seals were known from Abusir: records consisted of just a few seal impressions (and then only four examples) which were dated to the Old Kingdom.[135] Stamp seals of a similar nature have been recorded for the Late Old Kingdom at Ayn Asil[136] and Elephantine,[137] and from the region of the pyramid complex of Queen Wedjebten (wife of Pepy II) from South Saqqara.[138] The meaning of these incoherent designs is unknown as yet. After the First Intermediate Period, the designs on the base plates of seal stamps become much easier to recognise.

Fragment of a cylindrical seal
34/J/94
Faience
2.6 × 1.6 cm, thickness: 0.2 cm
Date uncertain, possibly Middle Kingdom
The fragment was found in the ashy layer outside the entrance to the temple, to the east of the south-east corner of the mortuary temple.

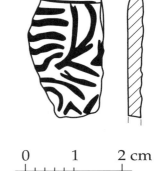

Fig. 4.94 Fragment of a cylindrical seal 34/J/94.

The piece is made of faience of a greyish-white colour inside, but it has a dark blue core, identifying the fabric as faience. On the exterior, the surface is a greenish colour. The fragment carries the remains of an incised but unidentifiable decoration consisting of lines (*fig. 4.94*). Too little of the decoration remains to be able to identify the subject matter, but it appears to be a more geometric sort of decoration than the one mentioned in the previous entry. This cylinder seal had once had its incisions filled in with a light green paste of some sort, which makes it likely that its origin is Middle Kingdom, when inlaid cylinder seals were more common.

G. Soukiassian[139] remarks that on the Ayn Asil site, the cylinder seals are less numerous than those of the stamp seals. He also notes that whereas it used to be considered that cylinder seals had a chronological horizon predating that of the stamp seals, in fact, this is not the case in the oasis, where the two co-exist in the same period. This discovery has implications for other Old Kingdom sites as well. Seals and their clay impressions are extremely important when one is analysing the economy of a site, for they record the circulation of products within a region or an administrative area.

Fig. 4.95 Seal impression 19/J/94a.
Photo MZ

Sealing 19/J/94a
Unfired clay
L: 1.5 cm
New Kingdom?
The sealing was found in the layer of sand mixed with ash on the foundation of the destroyed southern wing of the eastern wall of the temple; see *fig. 4.95*.

Scarab seal fragment
19/J/94b
Blue glazed faience
New Kingdom?
Found with 19a/J/94.

---

[136] Soukiassian *et al.*, *Balat* III, Pl. 46, 159.

[137] Other seals of the same genre have been discovered at Balat – Valloggia, *Balat* IV, 95: all except one of the 84 seals and sealings were found in the court septenrionale of the monument. M. Valloggia records that it was difficult to decide what the themes and figures on the seals might have been because they were broken and the signs themselves were difficult to interpret. Hieroglyphs, lizards, dogs and other animals were common themes, but many of these simple incised signs were illegible. G. Dreyer also records a similar incised unreadable design from this time: Elephantine VIII, 151, Abb. 60, which shows a small faience *Täfelchen* from the late Sixth Dynasty.

[138] Wiese, *Stempelsiegel-Amulette*, No. 810, Tafel 34.

[139] Soukiassian *et al.*, *Balat* III, 162.

Fig. 4.96 Scarab seal fragment 19/J/94b.
Photo MZ

A standard example of a small seal scarab dated to the New Kingdom (*fig. 4.96*). Unfortunately lower part of the scarab is destroyed and missing.

Fragments of a sealing bearing the impression of a plant motif
11/J/87
Clay
Largest fragment: 3.8 × 2 cm
Early Middle Kingdom
The sealing was found in the ashy clay layer on the floor level outside the entrance to the temple.

This is another testament to the revival of the cult of royal persons at Abusir during the Middle Kingdom.

Fragment of a sealing with the remains of a text (*fig. 4.97*)
19/J/87c
3 × 1.9 cm
Early Middle Kingdom ?
At the northern end of the eastern wall of the temple, in the south-east sector, this sealing was discovered.

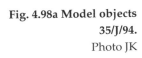

Fig. 4.97 Fragment of a sealing 19/J/87c.
Photo JB

This item is a fragment of a sealing with the remains of a text, the reading of which is not perfectly clear. In the text can perhaps be identified the signs
imy-r3 ꜥ Ptḥ ... n ? k3 pr ? Sn-pw-ꜥ3 ?...
"Overseer of the House of Records of Ptah ... *k3* (*pr* ?) Senpuaa".
Perhaps the signs before the last phrase might have been *ḥwt k3.*

4.5.9. Varia

Model objects
35/J/94
Unbaked clay
Decorated tablet: 9.5 × 5 × 2 cm

Fig. 4.98a Model objects 35/J/94.
Photo JK

Fifth – Sixth Dynasty
These various objects (*fig. 4.98a*) were found in the layer of sand outside the eastern wall of the temple, in the north-eastern part of the excavated area.
The models consists of a miniature rectangular chest, a rounded tablet, three rectangular tablets, miniature mudbrick (*fig. 4.98b, pl. V*) and several unidentifiable

objects. One of the rectangular tablets carries unidentifiable carvings in a frame.

These rough little models made of unbaked clay are occasionally found in burial structures. Similar models were found in several rooms in the temple of King Raneferef.[140] Apart from the round loaf and haunch of meat models and rough humanoid head models from this royal temple, there were also six oblong shaped objects of similar dimensions (10.5 × 5 cm) to the above-mentioned tablets. These were not engraved. In Balat,[141] other figurines of similar nature were found: they consisted of heads[142], animals[143] and other unidentifiable objects.[144] Some excavators have seen them as toys, but their real purpose has not as yet been defined.

Textile fragment
94/J/94
linen
19 × 4 cm
Islamic Period

Fig. 4.99 Textile fragment 94/J/94.
Photo MZ

This scrap of cloth was found among the debris in the burial chamber.

This fragment is decorated with a black geometric pattern (*fig. 4.99*).

4.6. Builders' marks and inscriptions

(The serial numbers in the catalogue of marks and inscriptions are followed by the excavation numbers in brackets. For the precise position of the individual marks and inscriptions, see *figs. 4.100–105*).

4.6.1. Eastern wall of the pit for the burial chamber (*fig. 4.100*)

1   (J/1/94-V)
The remains of a roughly vertical red line with two arrows pointing to the left (north) in red paint. In front of the arrows is a vertical inscription, also in red paint, which reads:
mḥ 2, šsp 5, ḏbꜥ 2
"2 cubits, 5 palms, 2 digits"
The measurement refers to the distance of the levelling line from the northern wall of the pit for the burial chamber.

0   10 cm

---

[140] See H. Benešovská, in: Verner *et al.*, *Raneferef*, 425–430. Many of these odd little items were found in Room R in the open columned courtyard: this room had been built up as the house of some later temple official – perhaps a priest – and judging by the coats of mud plaster that had been laid on the floor, it had been occupied for some time. These objects came from the lowest stratigraphical layer, so they seem to have been Old Kingdom in nature. (See Verner, in: Verner *et al.*, *Raneferef*, 71, for details. Fig. 1.3.5 has a photograph of other clay models that were found.)
[141] Valloggia, *Balat* IV, 155, pl. CXI–CXII.
[142] Valloggia, *op. cit.*, Nos. 2–5 in plate 44
[143] Valloggia, *op. cit.*, Nos. 9–15 in plate 44
[144] Valloggia, *op. cit.*, 122f. On p. 123 Vallogia remarks that identification of some of the pieces is difficult because they are so badly formed.

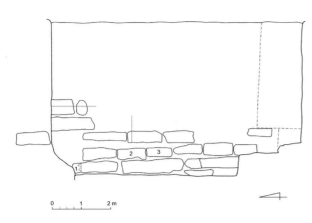

Fig. 4.100 Eastern wall of the pit for the burial chamber.

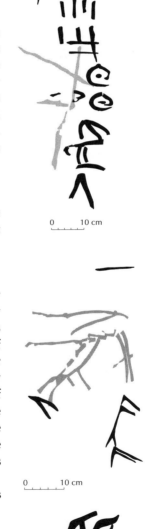

2   (J/4/94-V)

Vertical line of a cursive inscription, now face down, in black paint reading:

3bd 4 3ht, św 11 Ḏ ḥ. 3ḫ (?).

"4th month of inundation, 11th + x day. The shining (….. ?)."

The position of the inscription indicates that the latter had been written before the block was put in position. Unfortunately, the bottom part of the last sign is missing – precisely in this place a piece of the stone was chipped off. The last sign of a roughly triangular shape might be interpreted as a pyramid. However, the sign also might have represented a loaf of bread or walking legs and made part of a personal name.[145] After considering all the aforesaid circumstances, it seems that the inscription should probably be interpreted as a personal rather than a pyramid name.

3   (J/5/94-V)

The remains of a drawing face down, in red paint, the interpretation of which is not quite obvious. If an inscription, it may read:

ḥwt-wrt (?)

"Great House, temple (?)"

With regard to the position of the drawing (?), the block may have been reused from another building. *Ḥwt-wrt*, preceded by a surveying term *śm3ᶜ* "levelling", occurs among inscriptions found in the Tomb Complex Lepsius no. 25. The conjunction of *ḥwt-wrt* with the surveying term may indicate that the former referred to the pyramid or the pyramid and the mortuary temple. The term *ḥwt-wrt* is also attested from the pyramid of Raneferef (see below the text on p. 145), where it seems to have referred to the mortuary temple or its part. Due to the absence of a clear archaeological or epigraphic context, the precise meaning of the term *ḥwt-wrt* among the builders' marks thus remains elusive.

Besides the inscription, there are on the block also the remains of an unclear drawing and the signs *ii* in black paint.

4.6.2. Western wall of the pit for the burial chamber *(fig. 4.101)*

4   (J/2/94-Z)

Vertical line of a cursive inscription, now face down, in black paint. Across the inscription runs a horizontal levelling line in

---

[145] Though not attested among the personal names (Ranke, *PN*), the name might have read *3ḫ-di, Di-3ḫ, 3ḫ-iw,* etc.

Fig. 4.101 Western wall
of the pit for the burial
chamber.

red paint which is crossed by a vertical line referring to the axis
of the pyramid. The inscription reads:

Rš(wy): nḏś, wr.

"Two vigilant (pyramids): the small one and the big one."

The position of the inscription and the discontinuity of the
levelling line indicate that the block originally belonged to a
part of another building.

The interpretation of the first part of the name is not quite
obvious. Usually, a pyramid's name is formed by a short
phrase in which a king's name is a subject and the sign of a
pyramid at the end a determinative. But this is not the case
with the name under discussion. In this name, the two signs of
a pyramid can be taken for either a subject or a determinative
and the name interpreted as either *Rš mrwy* "Two pyramids
are vigilant" or *Rš(wy)* (with an omitted dual ending *wy*) "Two
vigilant (pyramids)".

5   (J/5/94-Z)

The remains of a levelling line in red paint at the edge of the
block, in addition to one cursive inscription and one builder's
mark in black paint. The inscription reads:

3bd 4 3ht, św 13.

"4th month of inundation, day 13."

The inscription with the date is superimposed by a large
sign *ꜥnḫ* in black paint. The sign might refer to the name of a

phyle division. On the block, there remain two crossing lines and one levelling horizontal line in red paint.

6   (J/6/94-Z)

A horizontal levelling line with an arrow pointing downwards, accompanied by the measurement *mḥ 4* "4 cubits", indicating the distance of the line from the ground level of the pyramid. The horizontal line is crossed by a short vertical line, also in red paint, which represents the final part of the vertical axis of the western wall of the pit for the burial chamber. Both the line and the measurement are in red paint. The measurement was written over a faded cursive inscription which reads:

3bd 4 3ḫt, św 12 + x

"4th month of inundation, day 10 + x"

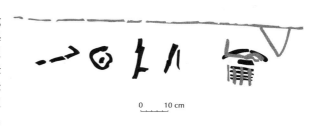

7   (J/8/94-Z)

A horizontal levelling line with an arrow pointing downwards, accompanied by a cursive inscription in red paint. The inscription, specifying the meaning of the line, reads:

mḥ 3 ḥr nfrw

"3 cubits above ground level"

8   (J/9/94-Z)

A horizontal line of an inscription in black paint reading

śmr-wˁty Ptḥ-ˁnḫw

"The sole companion Ankhuptah"

9   (J/15/94)

A vertical line with two arrows adjacent to each other: one pointing to the right and the other to the left. A cursive inscription is written over the line below the arrows. It reads:

wḏw

"axis"

The building term *wḏw* is, very probably, derived from *wḏ* "direct". We can meet with it among builders' inscriptions in some other buildings.[146] Under the inscription are the remains of an earlier inscription, the reading of which can not be reconstructed. Both the line and the inscriptions are in red paint.

Under the inscription are the unclear remains of another, earlier inscription in red paint, too.

4.6.3. Northern wall of the pit for the burial chamber (west of the descending corridor) *(fig. 4.102)*

10   (J/9/94-S)

The remains of a cursive inscription in black paint and a builder's mark in the shape of a circle divided by a cross in red paint. The inscription reads:

3bd 4 šmw, św ...

"4th month of summer, day ..."

The inscription seems to have been written on the block posterior to the mark.

146 M. Verner, Setting the Axis: an Ancient Terminus Technicus, in: *Homm. Lauer*, 433–436.

11 (J/11-12/94-S)

A horizontal levelling line accompanied by the measurement 8 *mḥ* – "8 cubits". The measurement indicates the distance of the line from the floor level of the burial chamber. The line and the measurement are in red paint.

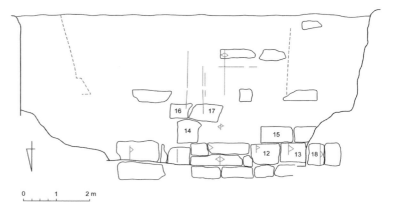

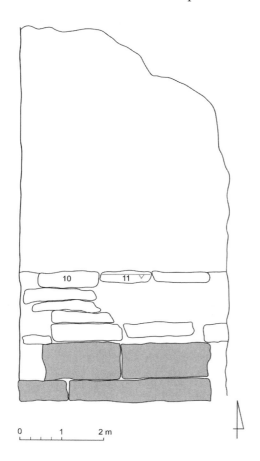

Fig. 4.102 Northern wall of the pit for the burial chamber.

Fig. 4.103 Southern wall of the pit for the burial chamber.

4.6.4. Southern wall of the pit for the burial chamber
(fig. 4.103)

12 (J/4/94-J)

A short vertical line with an arrow pointing to the right (westwards) and the sign *mn* "be enduring", possibly the name of a phyle division. Judging by their position, the line was drawn on the block already in position and so was the sign. Both the sign and the line are in red paint. The line might have been related to the position of the casing of the western wall of the descending corridor (see the previous remark in no. 11).

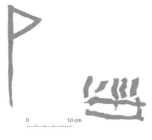

13 (J/5/94-J)

The block is adjacent to the right-hand side of the block with the preceding inscription, no. 12. The block bears the remains of two cursive inscriptions, one in black and the second in red paint, of which only the former one can be read as

(*Rš*)(*wy*): *nḏś wr – wȝḏt sȝ*

"Two vigilant (pyramids): the small one and the big one – phyle *wȝḏt*"

The previously cited inscription is upside down and its front part was cut away prior to the putting of the block in position. The sign *nḏś,* near the right-hand edge of the inscription, is upside down. Near the left edge of the block is a short vertical line with an arrow pointing to the right (westwards). The line may have related to the casing of the western wall of the descending corridor (see inscription no. 10).

14   (J/6/94-J)

The remains of two cursive inscriptions in black paint and a mark in the shape of a five pointed star in red paint. From one of the two inscriptions only unreadable traces have survived, while the second inscription can be read as:

Rś(wy): nḏś wr.

"Two vigilant (pyramids): the small one and the big one."

The mark seems to be superimposed on the inscriptions.

15   (J/7/94-J)

A charcoal line of a cursive inscription, lying upside down, which reads

ḥry-tp nśwt Ṯs(?)-ib.

"King's liegeman Tjesib (?)."

The inscription lies upside down, which means that it was not written on the block already in position. Moreover, the already inscribed block broke in two pieces under the pressure of the masonry.

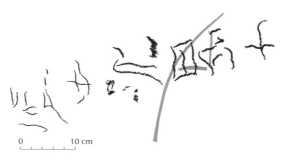

16   (J/9/94-J)

The remains of at least two cursive inscriptions, one mark and a vertical levelling line. The inscription and the mark are in black paint and are upside down which indicates that they were all put on the block prior to its placing in position. From one of the inscriptions survived the remnants of a date which reads:

3bd 1 šmw, św 2 + x

"month 1 of summer, day 2 + x"

The second inscription, which might have been the continuation of the preceding inscription with the date, reads:

Rś(wy)

"Two vigilant (pyramids)".

Under the preceding inscription there are the remains of the sign *ir* – the name of a phyle division? On the block are also unreadable traces of one more inscription.

17   (J/10/94-J)

Fragment of a cursive inscription with the date in black paint and the final part of a vertical line in red paint. The inscription, now on the block upside down, reads:

3bd tpy prt

"First month of winter"

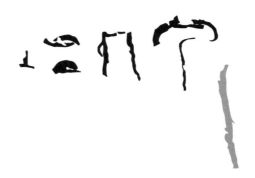

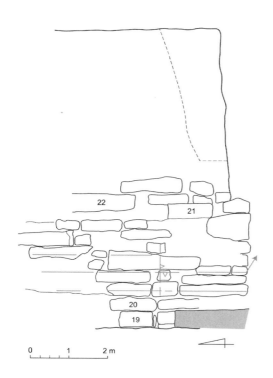

Fig. 4.104 Eastern wall of the trench for the descending corridor.

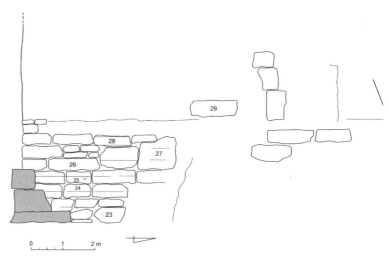

Fig. 4.105 Western wall of the trench for the descending corridor.

18   (J/15/94-J)

The sign *w3ḏ*, probably the name of a phyle. Next to the sign is a vertical line with an arrow pointing westwards. The line probably referred to the western wall of the burial chamber.

4.6.5. Eastern wall of the descending corridor *(fig. 4.104)*

19   (J/2/94-Vt)

A cursive inscription in black paint, written over an earlier mark in red paint, the meaning of which is not quite obvious. The inscription reads:

3bd 3 3ḥt, św 9

"3ʳᵈ month of inundation, day 9"

20   (J/4/94-Vt)

Cursive inscription in black paint written over a builder's mark in the shape of a five pointed star in red paint. The inscription reads:

... 3ḥt, św 26

"...of inundation, day 26"

21   (J/12/94-Vt)

Block with four cursive builders' marks in the shape of a five pointed star in black paint.

22   (J/13/94)

Builders' marks in the shape of a cross in red paint, written over the faded remains of an inscription from which survived only *św 1 + x*, "day 1 + x".

4.6.6. Western wall of the descending corridor *(fig. 4.105)*

23 (J/1/94-Zt)
Cursive inscription in black paint written over a builder's mark in the shape of a five pointed star in red paint. The inscription reads:
3bd 4 3ḫt, św 8 (?)
"4th month of inundation, day 8 (?)"

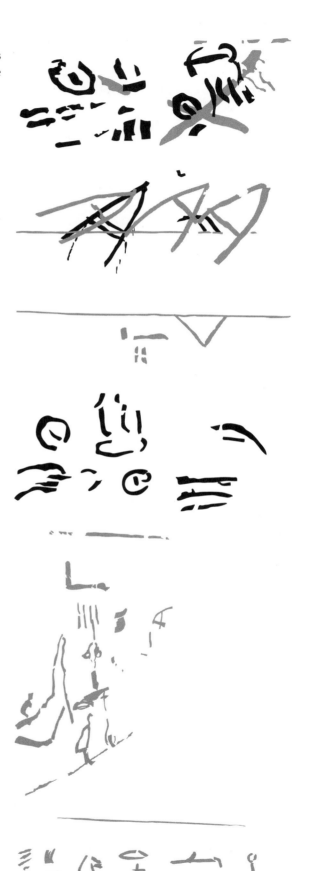

24 (J/3/94-Zt)
Four builders' marks in the shape of the sign *mr* crossed by a levelling line. The line and the marks are in red paint. Interestingly, some parts of the signs were additionally emphasized in black paint.

25 (J/5/94-Zt)
A levelling line with an arrow pointing downwards. Next to the arrow is written the measurement *mḥ 2* "2 cubits" indicating the distance of the line from the floor level of the corridor.

26 (J/8/94)
Cursive inscription in black paint which reads:
3bd 3 3ḫt, św 14
"3rd month of inundation, day 14"

27 (J/9/94-Zt)
The remains of two levelling lines (48 cm far from each other) in red paint between which is a cursive inscription which reads:
mḥ 4 ḥr nfrw
"4 cubits above the ground level"
To the left of the inscription lies the sign *ḥ3t* (part of the title *ḥ3ty-ᶜ* ?) in red paint and to the right of the inscription are the remains of unidentifiable marks in red paint, too.

28 (J/10/94-Zt)
The remains of a levelling line near the lower edge of the block and an irregular line following the upper edge of the block. Between the two lines are the remains of a cursive inscription, lying upside down, which reads:
śmr wᶜty, iry nfr-ḥ3t Ptḥ-špśś
"sole companion, keeper of the diadem Ptahshepses"
Both lines and inscriptions are in red paint.

0   10 cm

29   (J/15/94-Zt)
The remains of a builder's mark in the shape of a cross, over which is written a cursive inscription which reads:
ḥȝty-ʿ Ptḥ-špss
"count Ptahshepses"
Both the mark and the inscription are in red paint.

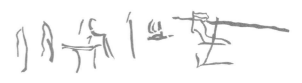

4.6.7. Loose stones found in and around the pyramid

30
A vertical line with an arrow, accompanied by a short cursive inscription which reads:
śmn
"establish (?)"
Both the line and the inscription, the meaning of which is unclear due to the intrusive character of the stone, are in charcoal.

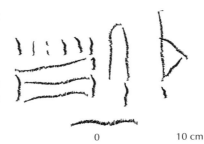

31
A builder's mark in the shape of the sign *śt* "seat (?)" in charcoal. The precise meaning of the mark is unclear (the name of a phyle division ?).

32
A cursive builders' inscription in charcoal which reads:
sȝb pr-ʿȝ
"judge and attendant of the Great House"

33
The remains of two cursive inscriptions, one in black and the second in red paint.

34
The remains of a cursive inscription in black paint which reads:
Rš(wy): ndś ...
"Two vigilant (pyramids): the small one ..."
The name, in which the sign of only one instead of two

pyramids survived, is followed by unreadable traces of a possibly earlier inscription.

35

The cursive sign *3ḥt* "inundation" in black paint, very probably a fragment of a date.

36

A cursive inscription *In* in red paint, possibly the personal name In.

37

A cursive sign *ḥwt-wrt* "temple (?)" in red paint. See above, inscription no. 3.

38

A cursive inscription in charcoal which reads:
Ptḥ-špśś
"Ptahshepses"

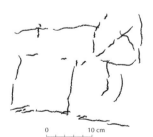

39

A very simple sketch in charcoal possibly representing a man facing a block (?).

40

A cursive inscription in red paint which reads:
ḥ3ty-ʿ Pt (sic!)*-špśś*
"count Ptahshepses"

41

A cursive inscription in black paint formed by two signs for a pyramid – very probably the remains of the name "Two vigilant (pyramids)". This bilder's mark probably comes from the Pyramid Complex Lepsius no. 24, but it was found in the area of the adjacent Mastaba of Nakhtsare – see Gr 2/Q/2004 in *chapter 3.5*.

42

A cursive inscription in red paint, with a fragment of the date,

ȝbd 1 + x šmw, sw 10 + x

"1ˢᵗ + x month of summer, day 10 + x"

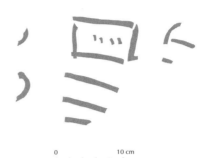

43

A cursive inscription in red paint which reads:

4. ỉswwt

"... (day) 4. Crews"

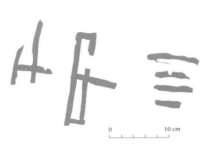

44

A cursive inscription in red paint, the reading of which is not quite obvious. It may read:

rdi tpt (?)

"instruction (?)"

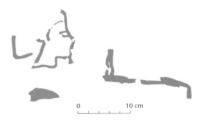

4.6.8. The pyramid's name

Among the names revealed in the pyramid Lepsius no. 24 four mention *Rš: nḏš, wr* "Two vigilant (pyramids): the small one and the big one" (nos. 4, 13, 14 and 34) and two refer to an abbreviated form of the former name namely, *Rš* "Two vigilant (pyramids)" (nos. 16 and 41). Judging from the archaeological situation in which the inscriptions were found, the Pyramid Complex Lepsius no. 24 was named "Two vigilant (pyramids): the small one and the big one". The name "big one" related to the pyramid tomb, whereas the name "small one" must have referred to the cult pyramid.

4.6.9. Dates

Unfortunately, among the dates revealed in the pyramid Lepsius no. 24 is not a single one which would refer to the occasion of the counting and which might help us date more precisely the building of the pyramid. However, some information can be deduced from the dates. Five of them refer to the inundation season (one to the third and four to the fourth month of the season), two to the winter season and three to the summer season (one of them to the last, or fourth month of the season). The dates thus seem to indicate that the work on the pyramid may have lasted from about one year up to one and half years.

4.6.10. Personal names

From the few personal names which occur among the builders' inscriptions found in the pyramid Lepsius no. 24 only one can be identified with certainty namely, the vizier Ptahshepses. His name occurs four times, once without any title (no. 38), once with the title of the "sole companion and keeper of the diadem" (no. 28) and twice with the title of the "count" (no. 29). For Ptahshepses, these titles are attested since at least the second building stage of his large mastaba in Abusir.[147] This chronological conclusion would date the building of the pyramid Lepsius no. 24 to approximately the mid reign (second decade ?) of Niuserre.[148] It is possible that only Ptahshepses was authorized to build the pyramid: among many significant titles he held, Ptahshepses was also the "overseer of all the works of the king".[149]

4.6.11. Builders' instructions

The inscriptions found in the pyramid Lepsius no. 24 containing builders' instructions do not basically differ from those known from other monuments in Abusir and elsewhere. The inscriptions confirm that on the outer face of the pyramid's core was drawn a grid of levelling lines which were one cubit apart from each other. To each line was added a short inscription with a measurement indicating how many cubits above the ground level of the pyramid the line lay. The same grid was also revealed inside the pyramid, on the walls of the pit for the burial chamber. In this case, however, the "ground level" referred to the floor of the burial chamber – *mḥ ... ḥr nfrw* "... cubits above ground level",[150] not the exterior ground level on which the pyramid stood.

Inside the pyramid, on the southern and western wall of the pit for the burial chamber, was found a vertical line relating to the east–west and north–south axis of the monument. On the western wall, the line ran from the bottom up to the top of the pyramid's core whereas, on the southern wall, it was formed by a short line only. Moreover, over the vertical line on the western wall was written a short inscription *wḏw* "axis" specifying the meaning of the line.

Somewhat mysterious among the builders' instructions is the writing of *ḥwt-wrt*, preceded by a surveying term *šmꜣꜥ* "levelling" (no. 3). The inscription is upside down, which indicates that the block may have been reused from another building. The term *ḥwt-wrt* also occurs among builders' inscriptions revealed in the monument Lepsius no. 25, in inscription no. 3, where it is preceded by a stylized pyramid. In the previously mentioned monument, the term *šmꜣꜥ ḥwt-wrt* occurs in two more inscriptions, nos. 43 and 62. The term appears in no. 43, beside the name of a phyle. All the aforesaid inscriptions from both Lepsius no. 24 and Lepsius no. 25 seem to indicate that *ḥwt-wrt* might have referred to the pyramid temple. The term *ḥwt-wrt* in Abusir is also attested from the pyramid of Niuserre, where L. Borchardt inclined to the attribution of this term to the pylon-like corner structure ("Eckbau") of the mortuary temple.[151] The term also occurs in the pyramid complex of Raneferef[152] where it seems to have referred to the mortuary temple or its part. Anyway, due to the absence of a clear archaeological or epigraphic context, the precise meaning of the term *ḥwt-wrt* among the builders' marks thus remains elusive.

Among the builders' marks found in the pyramid Lepsius no. 24 two in particular appear to have been prominent – a cross (nos. 5, 10, 22 and 29) and a five pointed

---

[147] See Verner, *Reliefs*, 34–42 (inscriptions nos. 30, 31, 41 and 42) and 90 (inscription no. 116) and *idem, Baugraffiti*, 189–191.
[148] For the reconstruction of the length of Niuserre's reign, see M. Verner, Once more to Niuserre's Dyad (München, ÄS 6794), in: *Egyptian Museum Collections* II, 1195–1204.
[149] Verner, *Reliefs*, 125.
[150] The term *ḥr nfrw* is attested in the Abusir monuments *e.g.* from the pyramids of Sahure and Neferirkare, see Borchardt, *Sahure*, I–II, 91 M 53, and *idem, Neferirkare*, 55. Borchardt interprets the term as "Nullinie". The term also occurs several times in the Mastaba of Ptahshepses, see Verner, *Baugraffiti*, 174.
[151] L. Borchardt, *Neuserre*, 145.
[152] Verner, in: Verner *et al., Raneferef*, 188f.

star (nos. 14, 20, 21 and 23). Unfortunately, neither from the statistics nor from the position of the marks, can any clear-cut conclusions be drawn. Less frequent are the marks in the shape of the four signs *mr* (no. 24) and *niwt* (a circle divided by a cross, no. 10). However, it can not be excluded that some of the marks helped the builders better distinguish one building step from the other. For instance, in the pyramid of Pepy I, the marks in the shape of a cross indicated the outer row of backing stones which were to be adjacent to the pyramid's casing.[153] All these signs are attested from a number of contemporaneous monuments in the pyramid fields[154] and both their origin and their meaning can differ with the different monuments. Some may have come from the quarries, others may refer to the different building stages.

4.6.12. Phyles and phyle divisions
It may be a mere chance that only two pieces of evidence of one phyle, *w3ḏt* (nos. 13 and 18) were found. As a matter of fact, among the builders' inscriptions found in the pyramid Lepsius no. 24 only three signs occur which very probably refer to phyle divisions: *ʿnḫ* (no. 5), *mn* (no. 12) and *ir* (no. 16). The number of divisions presupposes the existence of at least two phyles which might have been engaged in the construction of the pyramid.

4.7. Conclusions
4.7.1. Archaeological situation
Although the Pyramid Complex Lepsius no. 24 represents an interesting and important monument, it nonetheless must be said that its excavation did not bring any clear answers to questions concerning the pyramid owner and the dating of the monument. The complex is a typical example of the sort of pyramid complex built for a queen, which, following the prevailing opinion of Egyptologists, is likely to belong to a queen-mother. Such a monument in the later Old Kingdom consisted of a pyramid, a small mortuary temple and a cult pyramid. As has been already mentioned in this monograph, the inclusion of a cult pyramid was not an expected element of the architecture in the pyramid complexes of queens at this period. The Pyramid Complex Lepsius no. 24 was only the second example of such a complex (after the neighbouring Pyramid Complex of Khentkaus II) which includes this rather curious construction. This fact might have influenced also the name of the monument.[155]

4.7.2. Mummy and her royal ancestry
In the burial chamber of the pyramid Lepsius no. 24 was found a dismembered mummy of female, who died at an age of ca 25 years.[156] The gracile nature of the skeleton, whose stature was higher than was the mean for Ancient Egyptian females during the middle of the Old Kingdom suggests an adequate to better than average diet. At the same time, the skeleton displays a feeble muscularity. The fact that the lady had evidently not performed any strenuous physical work seems to indicate that this female mummy originated from the upper-most layers of the Egyptian society. Having in mind this supposition and also the chronometric dating of the

---

[153] V. Dobrev, Observations sur quelques marques de la pyramide de Pépi I, in: *Homm. Leclant* I, 149.
[154] For a more detailed discussion of these marks, see *e.g.* Verner, *Baugraffiti*, 163–169; V. Dobrev, Les marques sur pierres de construction de la nécropole de Pépi Ier. Étude prosopographique, *BIFAO* 96, 1996, 103–142, and *idem*, Les marques de la pyramide de Pépi Ier. Notes complémentaires, *BIFAO* 98, 1998, 151–170.
[155] We are reminded here that both the major and the cult pyramid probably had their own names *Rś: nḏś wr* (see *chapter 4.6.* and M. Verner's article on these builders' marks prepared for *Fs. Do. Arnold*). This idea might have been connected with the fact that the idea of a cult pyramid in a queen's pyramid complex was a new venture in architecture.
[156] See chapter 6.2. as well as E. Strouhal, V. Černý, L. Vyhnánek, An X-ray examination of the mummy found in pyramid Lepsius No. XXIV at Abusir, in: *Abusir and Saqqara 2000*, 543–560.

mummy, we can suppose that it was either the corpse of the pyramid owner, or the mummy belonged to another woman of a similar social rank.

In assigning the pyramid complex to a member of the royal family one is, however, also taking into account the nature of the monument (always a royal burial) and the location of its site – very close to other mortuary complexes which certainly belonged to members of the royal family – such as those of Khentkaus II and Raneferef. Beside these facts stand the remains of the rich burial equipment, all of which show that the occupant must have been a person of royal ancestry.

In contradiction to the theory[157] that pyramids belonged to the mothers of kings in the Old Kingdom, the lady buried in Lepsius no. 24 showed no clear signs that she had given birth to a child.[158] It could mean that the procedure through which the form of the tomb for the royal wives was selected,[159] was either different from earlier assumptions, or the person whose mummy was found in the burial chamber, was not the original pyramid owner.

4.7.3. When did the unknown lady live?

The dating of the period when the possible owner of the pyramid L24 lived and the assessment of her relationships inside the royal family is a complex task. Not only the location, but also the chronometric dating of the female mummified skeleton[160] enables us to come to the conclusion that the pyramid complex was built in the middle of the Fifth Dynasty, during the reign of either Raneferef or Niuserre.

For the purposes of our discussion, it seems to be important that the pyramid lies close to Raneferef's mortuary complex and there is thus a possibility that the owner of L24 might have been the wife of Raneferef. The chronometric dating of fragments from the mummies of the lady from L24 (see p. 244) and of King Raneferef shows that both individuals lived in a similar period. This fact enables us to hypothesize that if the female mummy from L24 had been the wife of Raneferef, it would be likely that this woman would have been buried close to the mortuary complex of her supposed husband.

Despite the youthful age at which Raneferef died,[161] the hypothetical royal couple was old enough to beget offspring. Nonetheless, there still remains the problem that her mummy did not bear clear marks of childbirth. In such case, the woman's importance might have lain in some significant role she played within the political and dynastic circumstances at the time. It could have been important for Niuserre to provide a pyramid tomb for her. This might have been underlined by the considerable size of the pyramid and, especially, the inclusion of the cult pyramid within her complex.[162]

Apart from this, a special position of the L24's owner might have influenced the simple architectural form of the mortuary temple of L24. If the owner was not a queen-mother, we can suppose that the rituals connected with her mortuary cult would have been different[163] from those belonging to women who ensured a continuation of the royal blood.

---

[157] For discussion on this topic, see P. Jánosi, The Queens of the Old Kingdom and their Tombs, *BACE* 3, 1992, 51–57.

[158] See p. 244. As follows from a personal communication with Martina Kujanová, childbirth process always leaves marks on the female pelvis. Therefore, it suggests that the woman from L24 had not delivered a child – since her skeleton did not show these marks of childbirth.

[159] *Cf.* doubts concerning the ascription of small pyramids to queen-mothers – P. Jánosi, *BACE* 3, 1993, 55–56.

[160] See p. 244.

[161] He was about 20–23 years old at the time of his death – Strouhal, Němečková, in Verner *et al., Raneferef*, 517.

[162] *Cf.* For the special dynastic and political position of Khentkaus II (who was the first queen in whose pyramid complex the cult pyramid was included) – Verner, *Khentkaus*, 170–171; idem, Khentkaus I, Khentkaus II and the title *mwt nśwt bity nśwt bity* (or: *nśwt bity, mwt nśwt bity*), GM 173, 2000, 215–218; idem, Was there a cult of Khentkaus I in Abusir?, GM 173, 1999, 219–224.

[163] See also Jánosi, *BACE* 3, 1992, 55–56.

We might also speculate on the possibility that Niuserre might also have married Raneferef's widow.[164] It would have been rational to utilise a pyramid that had already been commenced near the pyramid of her former husband and a great figure of the Fifth-Dynasty royal family, queen Khentkaus II.

Nevertheless, there is also a possibility that the lady was simply a wife of Niuserre and that she had not previously been married to Raneferef. In such case, location of the pyramid L24 could be influenced also by a lack of convenient building place in the vicinity of Niuserre's pyramid (see below).

The female in the burial chamber died at an age of about 25 years. Niuserre reigned, very probably, for up to thirty years.[165] Therefore, there is some reason to presume that Niuserre might have had at least one more spouse (she could have been Reputnebu or another queen – see below) with whom he would have had children.

4.7.4. The owner's name

The Pyramid Complex Lepsius no. 24 has not supplied a single clue regarding the name of its owner – either from a relief fragment or as a note in the collection of the *Baugraffiti* documented from the monument, the preference of the excavators has been for the owner of the pyramid to be Queen Reputnebu (Reputnub). This lady is the only queen who has been connected with Niuserre. This relationship between Niuserre and Reputnebu is based only on indirect archaeological evidence, above all, the discovery of fragments of two of her statues: in Niuserre's valley temple in Abusir and in Ptahshepses' mastaba in Abusir.[166] Reputnebu was also portrayed in the preserved relief decoration of the mortuary temple of Khentkaus II.[167]

The main problem connected with Reputnebu is the fact that we do not know where she was buried. Ludwig Borchardt was in error when he ascribed the pyramid structure located close to the south-east corner of Niuserre's pyramid to the tomb of a queen.[168] Due to its location to the south-east of king's major pyramid, within the temenos wall of Niuserre's pyramid, the monument's appearance and the absence of a mortuary temple for Borchardt's small pyramid,[169] it is almost certainly a cult pyramid. In the opinion of Peter Jánosi,[170] the pyramid of Reputnebu (as Niuserre's wife) might have been built to the south of Niuserre's mortuary temple and, therefore, one has to ask whether the Pyramid Complex Lepsius no. 24 might have been the resting place of Reputnebu. One then would wonder, what would have led Niuserre to build a pyramid complex for his spouse so far from his own pyramid?

4.7.5. Location again

Viewing the layout of the Royal Necropolis of Abusir, it is obvious that during the construction of his pyramid complex Niuserre was restricted in his construction site. Its border was created by the Pyramid Complex of Neferirkare from the south and south west, there was a slope from the plateau on which both monuments were built to the north and, to the east, there were very probably older mastabas.[171] There was another possible construction site for the pyramid complex: it was the

[164] Personal communication Miroslav Verner.
[165] M. Verner, Archaeological Remarks on the 4th and 5th Dynasty Chronology. *ArOr* 69, 2001, 401–4; *idem*, Once more to Niuserra's Dyad (München AS 6794), in: *Egyptian Museum Collections around the world*, 1195–1204.
[166] Borchardt, *Neuserre*, 25; B. Vachala, Ein weiter Beleg für die Königin Repewtnebu?, *ZÄS* 106, 1979, 176; Patočková, *Fragmenty soch*, 46–47, 58 and *idem*, Fragments de statues découverts dans le mastaba de Ptahchepses à Abousir, in: *Critères de datation*, 229.
[167] Verner, *Khentkaus*, 65, note 24, fig. on p. 83.
[168] Borchardt, *Neuserre*, 25.
[169] Borchardt, *op. cit.*, 25, 108–9, Bl. 1–2.
[170] Jánosi, *Pyramidenanlagen*, 35. Nevertheless, in the same place in his monograph, Jánosi, does not exclude the possibility that Reputnub was buried either in L24 or L25.
[171] Borchardt, *Neuserre*, 25–33, 109–34; Krejčí, *Ptahshepses*, 28.

unfilled area to the south-west of the Unfinished Pyramid of Raneferef. The main problem connected with this area, however, was its distance from the edge of the Nile cultivation. This would increase the costs for the transportation of the building material and the construction of a pyramid and its surrounding complex.

Niuserre and his engineers, decided to choose the place located right in the heart of the royal necropolis, which might have also been important factor during their decision-making process. This place had the advantage of the proximity of the unfinished causeway of Neferirkare, so that this access route was partially re-used as the causeway for Niuserre's pyramid complex. As a result, this decision caused changes in the layout of the pyramid complex, as in the distribution of the tombs of Niuserre's family members. An important fact concerning this situation was that around Niuserre's pyramid complex there was not a suitable space for the construction of a queen's pyramid complex.[172] Large-scaled terracing, on which the eastern part of Niuserre's mortuary temple was built, clearly illustrates the problems involved with the construction of a larger monument in the free area to the south of the king's mortuary temple. This area was bounded by the lowermost slope of the Libyan Desert. This situation therefore might have influenced the position of Niuserre's wife's monument to such a degree that it was built further from her spouse's pyramid.

The suggestion that L24 might have been built for Niuserre's spouse can also be explained in a different way. Chronologically important are the finds of masons' marks (see *chapter 4.6.*). Despite the fact that not a single one of the dates discovered in the pyramid Lepsius no. 24 refers to the counting of cattle, the builders' marks might help us to date, at least *relatively*, the building of the pyramid. The name of Ptahshepses is documented repeatedly among other personal names recorded in the collection of *Baugraffiti*. Ptahshepses' name appears either alone or preceded by his title of *iry nfr-ḥ3t, ḥ3ty-ꜥ*. In other inscriptions lacking the name of Ptahshepses, this man was very probably only mentioned by his title "count". The attestations of the title *iry nfr-ḥ3t* are (from a chronological point of view) important. Obviously, as the overseer of all the king's works, Ptahshepses was involved in the construction of pyramid Lepsius no. 24 and other monuments in the royal cemetery.[173] Ptahshepses obtained these titles in the later part of his life. It thus seems to indicate that the pyramid Lepsius no. 24 came into the existence – or was finished off – during a later stage in his long and successful career, *i.e.* in the same period as second (or third?) building stage of the large mastaba which Ptahshepses built for himself in the central part of the Abusir Necropolis.

This chronological deduction appears to correspond with the horizontal stratigraphy of the pyramid necropolis. Next to the work on his own pyramid complex during his up to thirty years long reign,[174] Niuserre had initially to complete three pyramid complexes which had been left largely unfinished due to the early deaths of their owners.[175] These tasks might have also delayed completion of the Pyramid Complex Lepsius no. 24 into the latter part of Niuserre's reign, or even after the majority of the work had been done on those large, unfinished construction projects in the necropolis.

Despite the fact that the masons' marks do not include any reference to the cattle counts, they bring some clue concerning the length of the pyramid complex's

[172] In P. Jánosi's opinion (*Pyramidenanlagen*, 34–35) the fact that Niuserre's cult pyramid was "pushed" further to the west from the standard position was due to the construction of Reputnebu's pyramid in this area. Nevertheless, it seems more probable that the area to the east from the cult pyramid was simply not suitable for a construction, due to the geomorphological situation in this area.

[173] Krejčí, *Ptahshepses*, 19–21.

[174] M. Verner, Archaeological Remarks on the 4th and 5th Dynasty Chronology. *ArOr* 69, 2001, 401–4; *idem*, Once more to Niuserra's Dyad (München AS 6794), in: *Egyptian Museum Collections*, 1195–1204.

[175] J. Krejčí, The origins and the development of the Royal Necropolis at Abusir, in: *Abusir and Saqqara 2000*, 480; *idem*, *Ptahshepses*, 28.

construction. As has been shown by M. Verner in this monograph (see *chapter 4.6.*), construction work on the pyramid complex might have taken circa one year to one and half years in duration.

4.7.6. Decline

Finds obtained through the archaeological excavations (see *chapter 4.5.*) show that the area of this pyramid complex already fell into disuse during the Late Old Kingdom.[176] Secondary burials and tombs started to arise on the grounds of the pyramid complex after this time. This decline did not stop during the First Intermediate Period, but it might have been partially retarded by an attempt to re-commence religious activity in the pyramid complex; this religious activity is well documented in some other royal monuments in the Abusir Pyramid Necropolis.[177] This supposition is based on the find of a Middle Kingdom sealing in the ashy layer of the floor at the entrance to the mortuary temple of L24. It seems that this revival was not particularly successful (we do not have any other clear marks of reactivation of the cult in the Pyramid Complex Lepsius no. 24) and the already ruined mortuary temple was re-used as a settlement as the finds of the Middle Kingdom settlement pottery show. Fragments of painted pottery as well as the ruined stone masonry (see *fig. 4.32*) suggest the existence of provisional shelters and habitation during the New Kingdom.[178] On the other hand, we also suspect the usage of the pyramid L24 as a stone quarry at that time.[179] These attacks culminated during the Medieval Period – as is shown by the glazed lamps, iron wedges and other finds used by stone-robbers.

4.7.7. Last remarks

Due to its very ruined state, the complex known as Lepsius 24 has not yielded all the answers we have sought. The name of the pyramid owner has not been pin-pointed. The form of the pyramid complex and the inclusion of a still new architectural feature – the cult pyramid – shows the elevated importance of its owner. The discrepancy between the aforesaid form of the tomb and the fact that the lady whose mummy was found in the burial chamber in all probability had not delivered a child could indicate the extraordinarily distinguished status of the owner of L24 (or there is also an uncertain possibility that the mummy doesn't belong to the owner). Despite these unanswered questions it seems that the chronological position of L24 is clearer than it was prior to the Czech excavation. The collection of the masons' marks date the Pyramid Complex Lepsius no. 24 to the second half of Niuserre's reign.

---

[176] *Cf.* Verner, in: Verner *et al.*, *Raneferef*, 106–110.

[177] *Cf.* Schäfer, *Priestergräber*, 18; L. Bareš, Eine Statue des Würdenträgers Sachmethotep und ihre Beziehung zum Totenkult des Mittleren Reiches in Abusir, *ZÄS* 91–94; *idem*, The destruction of the monuments at the necropolis of Abusir, in: *Abusir and Saqqara 2000*, 6; Verner, in: Verner *et al.*, *Raneferef*, 110–111.

[178] Bareš, in: *Abusir and Saqqara* 2000, 11; Verner, *ZÄS* 115, 1988, 169.

[179] *Cf.* the same situation in the neighbouring mortuary temple of Raneferef – Verner, in: Verner *et al.*, *Raneferef*, 111.

5. The Tomb Complex Lepsius no. 25

5.1. Location of the monument

The Tomb Complex Lepsius no. 25[1] is located on the south-eastern edge of the main, central pyramid necropolis of Abusir. It is bordered by a *wadi* running from the south-west to the north-east, towards the Nile valley. On the western side of the monument, there is the Mastaba of Nakhtsare (see *chapter 3.* of this monograph) and other mastabas aligned in a row extending to the south of Raneferef's mortuary temple. The distance between the Tomb Complex Lepsius no. 25 and this row of mastabas is about 20 m. At a distance of about 15 m, the Pyramid Complex Lepsius no. 24 is located and, to the north-east, lies the Mastaba of Nebtyemneferes. Thus it can be seen that the Tomb Complex Lepsius no. 25 was situated right on the edge of the Abusir Royal Necropolis.

This rather inconvenient location, which limited the building development of monuments in the area, was apparently one of the reasons for the unusual form of Lepsius no. 25.

As has been already mentioned, the monument consists of two tombs; in order to clarify the text of the monograph, the eastern tomb is designated as Lepsius no. 25/1 (or L25/1 in abbreviation) and the western one as Lepsius no. 25/2 (L25/2).

5.2. History of the exploration of Lepsius no. 25

No major archaeological work was made in the area of the monument prior to the year 2001[2] (*fig. 5.1*). Before the commencement of the Czech excavations, the monument appeared as two mounds lying close together (*figs.5.2–5.3*, and also *fig. 2.1*). The surface of the monument was covered by yellow-greyish sand, mixed with

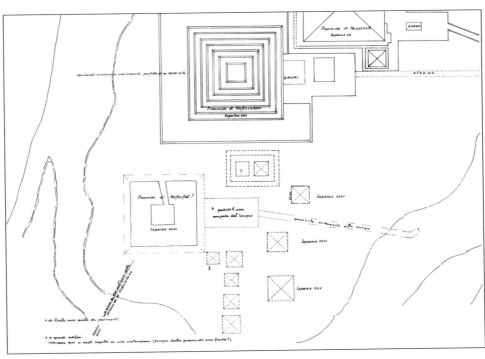

Fig. 5.1 Plan of the southern part of the Abusir Pyramid Necropolis before the excavations (*MRA*, Tav. 5).

[1] *LD* I, Bl. 32; *LD, Text* I 136–137.
[2] Borchardt, *Sahure* I, 145, plan B 1/2; Borchardt, *Neuserre*, 6.; *MRA* 190, Tav. 5.

the debris of smaller limestone fragments and several large limestone blocks. We have to underline here that apart from the location of the monument within the precincts of the royal necropolis, these enormous blocks also indicated that the monument had been built for either an honoured member of the elite, or else a member of the royal family. In the area of the monument and among these blocks, some small fragments of basalt and red quartzite were also scattered. Wind-blown yellow sand was filling the hollows located in the centre of the both parts of the monument at the time our investigation commenced. In some places, there were accumulations of weathered pottery sherds.

The eastern mound (L25/1) was higher (by 2 metres) and larger (by about 3–4 metres along its north–south axis). As far as the western mound (L25/2) is concerned, the middle of its eastern section featured depressions filled with wind-blown sand. On the surface, pottery sherds were scattered; they could be dated mainly to the horizons of the Old Kingdom and the late Graeco-Roman to Early Arabic (Coptic) Period.

The archaeological works were carried out in several stages.[3] The first, small-scale investigation was performed by the former Czechoslovak Institute of Egyptology during the archaeological season of 1990. A very limited *sondage* was made in the area of the north-eastern corner of L25/1.[4] Following the results of this work, together with the findings of a survey made on the surface of the monument, it was possible to put forward the tentative conjectures as to the character, orientation, and layout of this tomb complex with a non-standard orientation.[5] These original conjectures concerning the appearance of the monument supposed that the monument represented a pyramid complex for a queen with a pyramid built in its eastern sector and a mortuary temple situated in its western part. The main reason for this assumption was based on the fact that the eastern mound (L25/1), consisting of a part of the monument's debris, was larger and higher than the western part of the destroyed complex. Moreover, the morphology of the terrain in the area around Lepsius no. 25 was surmised to have affected the supposed reversal of the standard layout of a queen's pyramid complex, with the mortuary temple lying on the western

Fig. 5.2 Panoramic view of the southern part of the Abusir Pyramid Necropolis with minor tombs before the archaeological excavation.
Photo MZ

---

[3] For previous accounts concerning the Czech archaeological excavations of the Tomb Complex Lepsius No. 25 see: J. Krejčí, Pyramidové komplexy královen na abúsírském pohřebišti. Výzkum pyramidového komplexu Lepsius č. 25 (2001–2002, 2002–2003), *PES* 2, 2003, 64–78; *idem.*, Hrobový komplex Lepsius č. 25 v Abúsíru (Sezóna 2003–2004), *PES* 3, 2004, 203–213; J. Krejčí, M. Verner, Die „Zwillingspyramide" L 25 in Abusir, *Sokar* 8, 2004, 20–22; J. Krejčí, M. Verner, Twin Pyramid Complex „Lepsius no. XXV" in Abusir, in: *Fs. Sawy*, 159–165; J. Krejčí, The tomb complex "Lepsius No. 25" in Abusir, in: *Abusir and Saqqara 2005*, 261–273.

[4] M. Verner, Abusir pyramids "Lepsius no. XXIV. and no. XXV.", in: *Homm. Leclant* 1, 372.

[5] *Cf. op. cit.*, 374 and *idem., Pyramiden*, 321.

**Fig. 5.3 View of Lepsius
no. 24 and no. 25 before the
archaeological excavations.**
Photo MZ

**Fig. 5.4 Eastern part of
the tomb complex at
the beginning of the
archaeological excavations.**
Photo JK

side of the pyramid. The complex is not only from the south, but partially also from the east delimited by a short, steep slope on the edge of the Abusir Pyramid Plateau. This was seen as one of the main reasons for the non-standard appearance of the tomb complex.

The main excavation started in the spring of 2001 (*fig. 5.4*).[6] During this season, the archaeological mission of the Charles University concentrated its efforts on the

---

[6] During the archaeological seasons 2000–2001, 2002–2003, 2003-2004 and 2004–2005, the following members of the Czech Archaeological Expedition in Abusir took part in work during the excavations of the complex Lepsius no. 25 and in the study of individual found objects: Miroslav Verner, Jaromír Krejčí, Hana Benešovská, Vivienne Gae Callender (Macquarie University, Sydney), Viktor Černý (Institute of Archaeology of the Academy of Sciences of the Czech Republic, Prague), Dušan Magdolen (Institute of Oriental Studies, Slovak Academy of Sciences), Petra Vlčková, Vladimír Brůna (Jan Evangelista Purkyně University in Ústí nad Labem, Faculty of the Environment), Hana Vymazalová and Kamil Voděra. The excavation team co-operated with the following inspectors of the Supreme Council of Antiquities: Muhammad Nasser Ramadan, Nasrallah Fathy Killany, Abd el-Hamid Muhammad Rihan, Abd el-Ghaffar Abd el-Mu'an Ahmad, Mahruz Eid Mustafa, Azzam Ahmad Sallama. None of the work would have been successful without the co-operation given by the Saqqara Inspectorate, especially with its chief inspector Muhammad Kamal. The *reisin*, Talaal el-Kereti, Ahmad el-Kereti, Mitaal el-Kereti and Khaled el-Kereti directed both the excavation and restoration works at the complex Lepsius no. 25.

monument's eastern mound (L25/1). At first, layers of sand accumulated in the upper parts of the construction pit of the eastern tomb were removed. In addition to this, the eastern part of its superstructure was also cleared of wind-blown sand and stone rubble, which constituted, in fact, the destroyed core masonry of the tomb. Almost the whole area of the eastern part of L25/1 was covered by a layer of dark grey-brown sand mixed with disarticulated human bones, up to 3 m thick.

Fig. 5.5 The chapel during the archaeological excavations. Photo JK

Moreover, the excavation in this area yielded parts of reed mats and some items of burial equipment (faience beads) coming from the secondary cemetery that had developed in this area. The results of our work thus brought evidence that the tomb complex was destroyed in a great degree not only by stone robbers, but also by the secondary burials in the eastern part of the monument. During the works in the eastern part of the superstructure of L25/1, some remnants of the original masonry were unearthed. These remnants, including a corner of a room, produced evidence

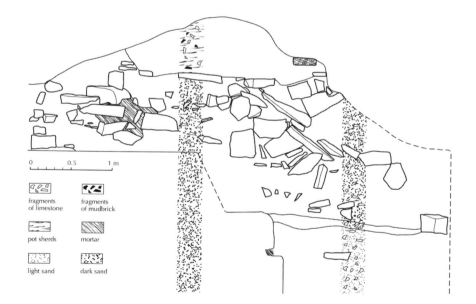

0   0.5   1 m

fragments of limestone	fragments of mudbrick
pot sherds	mortar
light sand	dark sand

Fig. 5.6a North-south section through the filling of the space above the southern outer wall of L25/2.

of the existence of an enigmatic space lined with limestone blocks (*fig. 5.5*). Thanks to the results of the subsequent archaeological works, this space was later attributed as a chapel for the building. A large part of the space of the chapel was filled with the above-mentioned layer with human bones. Beside the disarticulated human remains, fragments of a travertine statue of a female – probably a member of the elite – must be mentioned among the finds herefrom (6/N/2001; in the course of the season of 2003–2004 another fragment of a statue was found there – 57/N/2003).

During the autumn of 2002, the Czech mission focused on the excavation of the western part of the monument – Lepsius no. 25/2. This construction had been thought likely to be a mortuary temple for L25/1. Nevertheless, during the first days of excavation it emerged that this construction was of a different type. It became evident that the depression, in which we were working, was a construction pit of a pyramid-like tomb. The upper layers of the filling consisted of drifted sand; however, in the lower parts and then especially below the level of the terrain, the filling consisted of debris from this very badly destroyed construction.

The devastation of the monument had a rather complicated course. This situation is revealed by the fact that the debris and the sand filling the construction pit was to quite a high degree mixed with bones that had secondarily fallen down into the pit from the level of the secondary cemetery during the activities conducted by stone robbers.

After several days, the assumption that we were working in a construction pit for a burial apartment of a tomb was supported with new finds. We discovered that the side walls of the pit were made of a rather inferior masonry consisting of small limestone fragments joined by mud mortar (with the exception of the western wall; for the description of the masonry and architecture – see *chapter 5.3.*). In addition to these discoveries, blocks, which had once created a descending corridor that led to the burial apartment, were cleared. Nevertheless, the results of our work in the construction pit were quite disappointing: almost no part of the original casing or floor pavement of either the corridor or the burial chamber was found *in situ* – not even as loose blocks (see *chapter 5.3.*). On the other hand, the archaeological excavation brought an important discovery: it became evident that the western part of Lepsius no. 25 represented another tomb and, more interestingly, the construction pit of that tomb was designed in the same way as a burial apartment of a pyramid with an east–west oriented main pit for the cradle of a burial apartment and a descending corridor oriented along a north–south axis. In this way, our archaeological mission had found, curiously, a rather unusual second tomb, which we thought to be a pyramid. Despite the almost total destruction of the burial apartment, this archaeological season brought the discovery of some items coming from the burial equipment evidently belonging to a member of the Egyptian elite (model stone vessels 27/N/2002, 31/N/2002, 33/N/2002, copper model instruments 30/N/2002, 32/N/2002, and others).

The final season of the archaeological exploration in the area of the Tomb Complex Lepsius no. 25 was organized during the season of 2003–2004. We continued our work in the construction pit of the eastern tomb, L25/1, concentrating on the eastern part of its superstructure and the space in front of its eastern outer wall. The *sondage* at the south-west corner of L25/2 was enlarged (see *fig. 5.6a–b*), and three new trenches were excavated at the north-east corner of L25/1, in the area of the contact

Fig. 5.6b Section through the filling of the space to the south of the southern outer wall of L25/2.

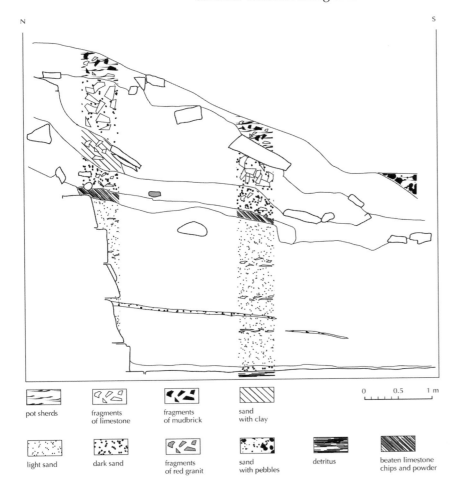

pot sherds fragments of limestone fragments of mudbrick sand with clay 0 0.5 1 m

light sand dark sand fragments of red granit sand with pebbles detritus beaten limestone chips and powder

Fig. 5.7 Workers dragging the collapsed large blocks. Photo JK

wall of both tombs (southwards of it), and to the north of L25/1. Unfortunately, due to safety reasons, lack of time and extreme hard labour involved in dragging away the large limestone blocks lying one over another in the areas of the destroyed outer walls of both tombs (*fig. 5.7*), the works had to be terminated without excavation of the major areas along the outer walls of the monument. Despite this fact, we were able to develop our ideas about the appearance of the tomb complex in antiquity: it consisted of two tombs with pyramid-like construction pit. The superstructures, however, were mastaba-like, each having different dimensions; only one cultic room, placed in the eastern part of the superstructure of the eastern tomb, was discovered.

Working in the construction pit of L25/1, we continued excavating the layers of yellow wind-blown sand and stone rubble – some of which had been partly removed already during the season of 2000–2001. Below the debris, remnants of white limestone walls of the funerary apartment were revealed. Regardless of the large-scale devastation caused by stone robbers, we were able to reconstruct the original, quite complicated plan of the burial apartment (see *chapter 5.3.*).

In the course of the excavation of the burial apartment, a number of items apparently coming from the burial equipment of the L25/1-tomb owner were unearthed. They included fragments of canopic jars (63a-b/N/2003), a set of travertine miniature bowls (65a-j/N/2003), a miniature basalt vessel (69/N/2003), as well as two model copper bowls (70a–b/N/2003), a copper model of a chisel (75/N/2003), several wooden objects: fragments of wooden vessels (gilded one 64/N/2003; 76a–c/N/2003), fragments of a case (66a–c/N/2003) and furniture, possibly of a box (?) (71/N/2003), and pottery – a vessel with pointed bottom (97/N/2003) and a number of pottery sherds coming from vessels that had been originally part of the burial equipment. The burial equipment clearly shows that the owner of this tomb was a person of a high social position within the Fifth Dynasty society. One has to underline, having in mind the destruction of the both collections, that the burial equipment from L25/1 is similar to the burial equipment found in the neighbouring pyramid, Lepsius no. 24 (see p. 97–134).

The excavation of this space in the above-described layers yielded a great many skeletal remains. They came mainly from the afore-mentioned secondary cemetery spreading out over the already partially destructed supestructure of L25/1. These scattered human remains were thus intrusive. Among these, however, we also found fragments of a mummified body. On the strength of their appearance and the clear traces of mummification, it was possible to distinguish these fragments from the other human remains found in this area. We can thus suppose that the mummified fragments originated from the tomb-owner's mummy. It was possible to date these mummified remains – which belonged to a woman[7] – using the chronometric dating to the Old Kingdom. This dating has yielded a conventional age of 4050 ± 40 BP and a dendrochronologically calibrated age range of 2660–2460 BC. This range corresponds with the dates obtained for the female mummy discovered in Lepsius no. 24[8] as well as for the mummy of King Raneferef.[9] An important fact is that these remains might have belonged to a person who was in a family relationship with another person buried in the burial chamber in the western tomb L25/2.[10] Tiny remains of a female mummy – mandible, right plantarum and other bones – could be also discerned very well during the archaeological excavation in the area of the burial chamber at the bottom of the construction pit of L25/2.

Besides the results achieved with respect to the architecture of the monument and in addition to the abundance and variety of items of the burial equipment unearthed, several other significant finds were made, including a large quantity of pottery sherds, with some almost complete vessels. Of major interest were masons' marks bearing the name of a building – $\triangle\triangle$, *Rš(wy)* – "The two vigilant (pyramids)". On the strength of these *Baugraffiti* we had at first supposed that Lepsius no. 25 consisted of two tombs, originally planned as pyramids, and that this monument was intended as a double-tomb, probably even a "double-pyramid" from the initial stages of the monument's construction. However, an intensive examination of the builders' marks from the pyramid Lepsius no. 24 showed, in M. Verner's opinion (*cf. chapters 4.6., 4.7.,* and *5.7.*), that these marks including the name *Rš(wy)* might be connected with the Pyramid Complex Lepsius no. 24 and might represent its name, and not the name of the double Tomb Complex Lepsius no. 25; for detailed discussion on this issue, see *chapter 5.8.*

During this last season in the Tomb Complex Lepsius no. 25, three additional *sondages* were made. The first one, conducted in the area to the south of the south-western corner of L25/2, revealed several levels of mudbrick masonry underneath a layer of brown sand. These levels contained numerous pottery sherds, several flint knives as well as mud sealings. Further to the south, we found a part of a construction built of inferior quality masonry: it appeared to be a rectangular inner room. A tiny mudbrick wall was revealed in the trench excavated to the south of the contact wall between the two parts of Lepsius no. 25. This mudbrick wall was overlaid with destroyed masonry of large limestone blocks and thick layers of sand. The similar situation was also found in the area around the north-eastern corner of L25/1, where small parts of two simple rectangular constructions had been built using the same type of inferior masonry (small, flat fragments of limestone joined by mud mortar), as was the case with the rectangular construction to the south of L25/2.

As has already been mentioned, the excavation of the monument also revealed an extensive secondary cemetery[11] in the vicinity and in the precinct of the tomb complex itself. This cemetery once almost completely covered the entire eastern face of the damaged monument. The stratigraphy of the site shows that the cemetery was established *after* the core masonry of the tomb complex had been stripped of its

---

[7] Personal communication Viktor Černý, autumn 2004.

[8] See *chapter 6.2.2.13.*

[9] E. Strouhal, A. Němečková, in: Verner *et al., Raneferef,* 518.

[10] Personal communication Viktor Černý, autumn 2004.

[11] Secondary cemeteries, dating to various periods of time, occur quite frequently in the Memphite area. One of such cemeteries had also developed in Abusir, where it covered vast areas of the Old Kingdom royal necropolis (see: Schäfer, *Priestergräber,* 111–133, Tafel 1; Strouhal, Bareš, *Secondary Cemetery, passim;* L. Bareš, The destruction of the monuments at the necropolis of Abusir, in: *Abusir and Saqqara 2000,* 14; K. Smoláriková, The Greek cemetery in Abusir, in: *Abusir and Saqqara 2000,* 67–72.

casing on the eastern side and in consequence of this the masonry collapsed (we can only suppose that this collapse can be dated into a long period beginning in the New Kingdom and ending in the Late Period). Later on, stone robbers attacked through their activities this cemetery, which resulted in the formation of a layer, about 0.5 to 3.0 m thick, made up of destroyed human remains, bandages, crushed mudbricks and brown sand. It has already been mentioned that some of these human remains were also found in the filling of the monument's two burial chambers. At least 76 individuals were identified in the course of an anthropological investigation. As four, unfortunately only partially preserved burials discovered 7.56 m from the eastern face of L25/1 show (see *fig. 5.8a, b, pl. VI*), the corpses were originally buried in matting made of palm leaf ribs[12] and, exceptionally, in frail wooden coffins, parts of which were also found (see catalogue of the finds – 98/N/2003 or 72/N/2003). Several fragments of decorated cartonnage were unearthed, too (see *fig. 5.9, pl. VI*). In addition to these items, some elements of the burial equipment – such as amulets and beads made of faience – were found (10–11/N/2001, 62/N/2003, 85/N/2003, 117/N/2003, and other). On the strength of these finds, the cemetery can be dated to the Late and Graeco-Roman Periods. The burials evidently belonged to lower-ranking inhabitants of the villages located in the immediate neighbourhood of the Abusir necropolis.

The *sondage* to the north of L25/1 made in the spring part of the 2003–2004 season revealed the existence of another secondary cemetery. The area is covered by a layer of grey sand mixed with debris coming from the neighbouring superstructure of L25/1, white limestone *raksha*, and yelow wind-blown sand. One section of this area was uncovered to reveal several burial pits. Some of these pits were equipped with simple low superstructures. The superstructures were constructed of larger fragments of unworked limestone joined together by mud mortar. Some of the stone blocks used in the construction of the superstructures had been acquired from the structures predating the secondary cemetery. In one case, for instance, we were able to identify and document a re-used block evidently coming from the casing of an Old Kingdom monument, possibly the neighbouring Pyramid Lepsius no. 24

Fig. 5.10 Secondary cemetery to the north of L25/1, a simple superstructure above a burial pit with a re-used limestone block from the casing of an earlier monument.
Photo JK

---

[12] *Cf.* Schäfer, *Priestergräber*, 114 and Abb. 183.

Figs. 5.11a Secondary cemetery to the north of L25/1 – view from the north. Photo JK

Figs. 5.11b Secondary cemetery to the north of L25/1 – view from the east. Photo JK

(*fig. 5.10*). The outer faces of these simple superstructures were neither coated nor decorated in another way (*figs. 5.11a, b*).

Altogether nine pits were excavated. These pits had been dug out in the layer of *dakka* – hard, beaten layer of mud mixed with limestone splinters and weathered pottery sherds, which appears to have been created already during the construction of Lepsius no. 25. It is apparent, that this layer should facilitate the transportation of building blocks and other material. The height of this layer varied from 35 to 50 cm. The excavation of this area revealed two burial pits with superstructures, two burial pits without superstructures, and five pits with no human remains or archaeological objects of any kind. The pits were oriented along the east–west, or northeast–southwest axis; in one case, a northwest–southeast orientation was recorded (*fig. 5.12*). Four of the pits contained human remains. The dead were buried with their heads to the west, and in most cases with their hands crossed over their abdomens (*fig. 5.13*). The results of the anthropological investigation of the human remains found in these four burial pits are summarised in *chapter 6.3.1*.

The secondary burial **111/N/2004** was the only burial pit with human remains in which at least some items were found. These objects – two flasks (113a–b/N/2004)

Fig. 5.12 Secondary cemetery to the north of L25/1.

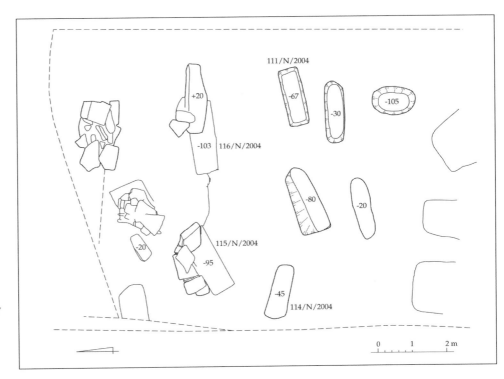

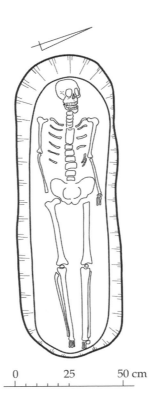

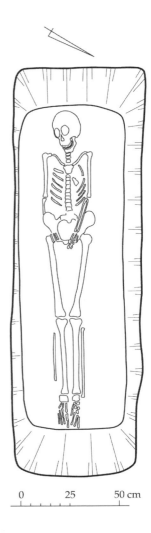

0   25   50 cm

0   25   50 cm

– were unearthed in the layer of wind-blown sand, in the depth of 30 cm below the level of the original terrain. It is thus very probable that these two vessels did not belong to the burial equipment of the deceased female buried in this grave and, instead, represented an intrusion brought to this place in consequence of subsequent human activities (such as stone-quarrying). The burial pit was 67 cm deep. The deceased female interred in the burial **114/N/2004** had her hands placed alongside her body (*figs. 5.14a–c*). The burial pit was 45 cm deep. The burial pit **115/N/2004** was covered by a superstructure, which was 57 cm high. In view of the fact that about 2/3 of its extent were found to have been removed, it is apparent that this secondary burial had been repeatedly disturbed by subsequent activities of stone robbers and tomb robbers (the same situation can be observed also in the case of the secondary burial 116/N/2004). This can be the reason why no burial equipment was found in the burial pit, which was 95 cm deep. The skeleton of the deceased female interred in this pit was in a good state of preservation. Her hands were crossed above her abdomen (*fig. 5.14b*). The secondary burial **116/N/2004** held a mummified body of a man, whose hands were crossed over his abdomen (see *figs. 5.14c* and *5.15*, *pl. VI*). The depth of the burial pit was 110 cm; it was the largest burial pit among those excavated in this area. The superstructure above the pit was 58 cm high.

No items were found in the remaining five burial pits excavated in this secondary cemetery. The mentioned pits were filled with wind-blown yellow sand, and we can only hypothesize that the elongated pits located to the south and to the south-west of the secondary burial 111/N/2004 had been only prepared for interment of the deceased. It does not seem probable that it would have been possible to remove bodies of the deceased from the burial pits and leave behind no traces of their

Fig. 5.13 Secondary cemetery to the north of L25/1, burial 111/N/2004. Photo JK

Fig. 5.14a Secondary cemetery to the north of L25/1, burial 114/N/2004.

Fig. 5.14b Secondary cemetery to the north of L25/1, burial 115/N/2004.

original interment, such as parts of the skeletons or other items connected with the secondary burials.

When studying the features of the individual secondary burials, we notice some differences. The two secondary burials which had been originally covered by superstructures were deeper than the other two. An interesting fact is that in both types of graves – in the burial pits with and without superstructures – both male and female were interred. Moreover, both types of graves were used for the interment of middle-aged persons. It is thus possible to suppose that, hypothetically, the persons buried in the pits covered by superstructures were of a different, possibly higher social status than the two persons interred in the burial pits exc. nos. 111/N/2004 and 114/N/2004. No relationship was detected between the bodies analysed during the anthropological investigation. Having in mind the orientation of the burials and almost no documented burial equipment, we can hypothesize that the burials might have belonged to early Christians and, therefore, we assign them to a late date.

Due to the deterioration of the monument, the Czech expedition had to undertake large-scale restoration works – the excavated space of L25/1 was refilled with blown sand, supporting walls were erected, and partial restoration works were carried out in order to prevent further destruction of the masonry: this was essential, for safety reasons. The mentioned works were performed both during the excavation and after the main excavation had been completed.

5.3. Description of Lepsius no. 25 and its architecture

The excavation of the monument revealed that it consisted of two tombs, now identified as L25/1 and L25/2. The tombs stand tightly together, their walls (the eastern one of L25/2 and the western one of L25/1) are touching each other (the western wall of L25/2 is actually partially resting on the masonry of L25/1). The entrances into the substructures of both tombs are located in the axes of their northern facing walls (*fig. 5.16*).

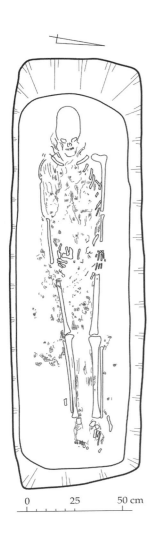

0   25   50 cm

Fig. 5.14c Secondary cemetery to the north of L25/1, burial 116/N/2004.

0   5   10 m

Fig. 5.16 Plan of the Tomb Complex Lepsius no. 25.

5.3.1. Lepsius no. 25/1

The eastern tomb, L25/1, represents a damaged monument, partially covered by destroyed masonry of large limestone blocks. The tomb is a rectangular structure oriented along its north–south axis. The dimensions of the tomb's superstructure are 24 × 11.5 metres.

The outer walls erected around the building shaft were constructed of large, rather regular blocks of local limestone joined together by mud but, in some instances, also quality lime pinkish mortar. These blocks were, however, only roughly worked (*fig. 5.17*). The interior of the core masonry is of a rather low quality, being made of smaller fragments of local limestone creating a kind of inner chambers filled with low quality masonry mixed with mudbricks and weathered pottery sherds (*fig. 5.18*). (The building techniques used in the construction of this monument are treated below.) In addition, a smaller part of the masonry's volume was made up of brown-grey sand.

As we can see, the builders of the tomb had depended on the massive outer walls and had not cared about the quality of construction for the inner masonry.[13] Therefore, once part of the large blocks of the façade had been removed by stone robbers, the masonry of the tomb collapsed to a large extent, thus creating the existing mound of the monument. A part of this destruction was removed during the archaeological excavations.

Fig. 5.17 South-eastern corner of L25/1, view from the south-east. Photo JK

Fig. 5.18 North-eastern corner of L25/1, view from the east. Photo JK

5.3.1.1. The doorway into the superstructure of L25/1

The chapel for Lepsius no. 25/1 lies in the eastern part of the tomb's superstructure. The entrance into the chapel is located to the south of the east–west axis of the tomb. The doorway had once been flanked by two low mudbrick walls. Now, the walls are only one, or two brick layers high (see *figs. 5.19–5.21*). The southern flanking wall is preserved up to the height of the first layer of mudbricks (8 cm), the northern one up to the height of the second layer of bricks (18 cm) (*fig. 5.22*). The format of the mudbricks was 32 × 15 × 9 cm.[14] Therefore, the reconstruction of the original height of these two walls is not possible and we can only conjecture it. Only faint remains of bricks at the eastern ends of both walls which were laid down crosswise to the main axis of the walls seem to indicate a kind of a more complex shape of both mudbrick walls. Nevertheless, due to their almost total erosion we do not have any direct idea concerning their original appearance. Moreover, the area between and around the two walls was covered by a mud lining (see *fig. 5.23*). Traces of white paint were clearly discernible, just as in

---

[13] A similar building technique was used also in the construction of other monuments in the Abusir Royal Necropolis, especially in the upper part of Raneferef's Unfinished Pyramid – Verner, in: Verner *et al.*, *Raneferef*, 9–12, figs. 1.1.5.–1.1.7. Nevertheless, this technique had gained ground in other royal pyramids in Abusir as well – *cf.* Verner, *Pyramids*, 93–100.

[14] *Cf.* mudbrick formats from Nakhtsare's mastaba and those used in Raneferef 's mortuary complex – Krejčí, in: Verner, *et al.*, *Raneferef*, 113–137 and especially tables 1.6.1–1.6.6 and figs. 1.6.22–1.6.26.

Fig. 5.19 Southern part of the superstructure of L25/1 and entrance into the chapel from the east. Photo JK

Fig. 5.20 Plan of the area to the east of the entrance to the chapel in L25/1.

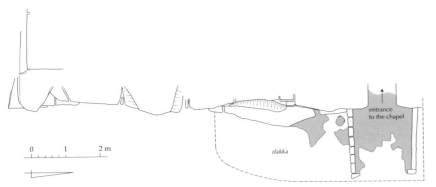

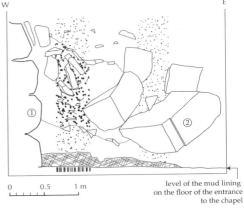

dakka

entrance to the chapel

W   E

level of the mud lining
on the floor of the entrance
to the chapel

fragments of limestone

organic remnants

light sand

dark sand

mud coating

mudbrick

>>**Fig. 5.21 Section through the filling of the area to the north of the entrance to the chapel in L25/1.** *1* – Northern flanking wall in front of the entrance to the chapel; *2* – loose block of white limestone from the casing of L25/1.

Fig. 5.22 Two walls flanking the entrance into the chapel of L25/1. Photo JK

Fig. 5.23 The *dakka* layer and remains of the mud lining in the area along the eastern face of the L25/1. Photo JK

the area between the walls and along their outer foot. These areas were also – as is the case with the chapel – painted white.[15]

Not only the area to the north of L25/1 (see *chapter 5.1.*), but also the area in front of the entrance to the chapel was literary "paved" by a layer of *dakka*. It was made up of mud mixed with limestone splinters and small fragments of weathered pottery sherds.

5.3.1.2. Cultic room

The entrance into the cultic room – the chapel – or, more precisely, the small part creating a kind of a vestibule, is 0.89 m wide (see plan on *fig. 5.24*). Its side walls had been built of large smoothed blocks of white limestone (up to dimensions of 2 × 1.5 × 0.5 m) (*figs. 5.25a–b* and *fig. 5.26*). It is very probable that the doorway had not been closed by a door-leaf. No piece of direct evidence – no hinge holder, nor latch hole, or imprints of a door leaf on the floor – of the door leaf(s) was found. We can speculate on the reasons for this fact. Unfortunately, it was not possible to excavate the area further to the east, where another part of the cultic room may have been located.[16] If such a hypothetical building had existed there, it could also have prevented direct access to the main chapel in the superstructure of L25/1. This hypothesis is also supported by the fact, that no threshold was found in the entrance. This also seems to show that another building had been constructed in front of the entrance to the chapel.

The walls of the doorway had been cased with flat slabs of fine white limestone.

Fig. 5.24 Plan of the chapel in L25/1.

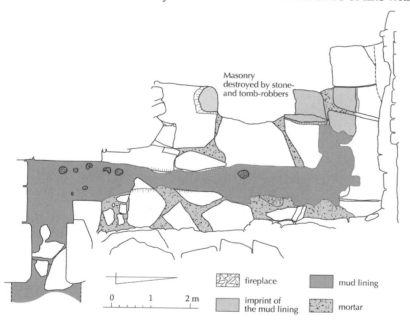

Masonry destroyed by stone- and tomb-robbers

0   1   2 m

fireplace   mud lining

imprint of the mud lining   mortar

Three petroglyphs were found and documented on its northern wall (see *figs. 5.27* and *5.28a–b*). One of the petroglyphs represented a bird (a goose/duck?), the second one depicted a Coptic cross, and the third one a cross-like sign, only partially preserved (we cannot exclude that this sign also represented a Coptic cross). In addition, we recorded yet another sign – it seems to be a hieroglyphic sign *šw*, a sign connected with royal ideology. This sign shows a different patina and surface weathering (it is almost the same as the surface of the rest of the entrance wall). It thus seems that this sign had been made in the same, or slightly later period as was the construction of the Lepsius no. 25 complex and that it predated the first group of petroglyphs. As a matter of course, we can connect this sign with the royal ancestry of the tomb

---

[15] The remains of white paint seem to provide evidence that the area outside the chapel itself had been considered as a cultic area as well.

[16] This fact seems to be supported by the unearthing of a part of an inferior masonry to the east of the north-eastern corner of L25/1 – see p. 179–180.

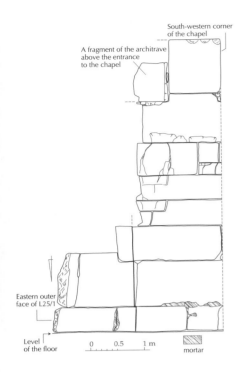

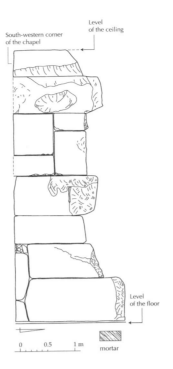

Fig. 5.25a Southern wall of the chapel in L25/1 and the doorway.

Fig. 5.25b Preserved part of the western wall of the chapel in L25/1.

Fig. 5.26 Southern wall of the chapel in L25/1, view from the north. Photo JK

Fig. 5.27 Northern wall of the doorway to the chapel in L25/1.

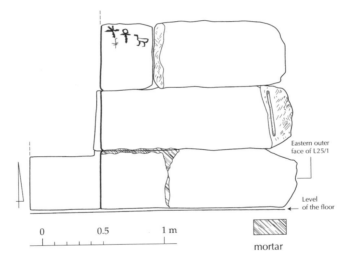

Fig. 5.28a Detail view of the petroglyphs. Photo JK

>>Fig. 5.28b Detail view of the petroglyphs.

owner. The other petroglyphs were apparently later (their patina is much lighter, and the technique of execution of the signs differs from that of the *św*-sign). The Coptic cross among the signs would allow us to hypothesize that the group of these later signs were incised into the surface of the wall during Coptic times. Thus, we could use them as one of the relative dating criteria: the overall destruction of the entire Lepsius no. 25 complex, especially of its eastern part with the secondary

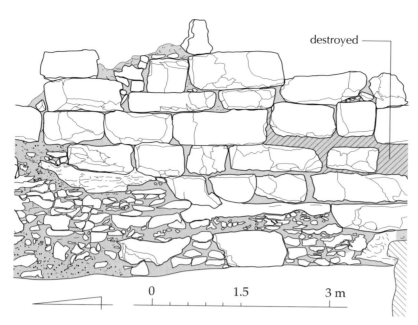

destroyed ⎯⎯⎯

0   1.5   3 m

Fig. 5.29 Chapel, the core masonry of the eastern wall.

cemetery. In the time of their execution the construction of the chapel and its doorway was certainly still standing free of the layers of sand and debris.[17] A tiny room represented the "vestibule" of the chapel: its dimensions were 1.15 × 1.65 × 5.12 m. A small fragment of a roofing beam was preserved in the south-western corner of the room. It shows that the vestibule had been roofed by flat slabs of limestone, resting on the side walls of the room. We can suppose, also on the basis of the exceptional layout of the whole vestibule and chapel area with very narrow spaces, that the entire area was roofed by transversely laid limestone beams. Nevertheless, we are not able to reconstruct the format of the ceiling blocks and their dimensions, because the fragment was too small.

The vestibule gave access to a north–south oriented room. Numerous finds of cultic pottery and pottery sherds in the lowermost part of the filling of this area indicate that this room once served as a chapel. Unfortunately, it is not entirely clear whether there had been a doorway between "the vestibule" and the chapel itself. The degree of destruction of the chapel is even higher, and there is no clear evidence of the existence of a door pilaster between the vestibule and the chapel. No traces of a door-leaf were found either on the preserved side walls or on the mud lining of the room, not even a kind of pivot holder in the floor of the room. It is thus very probable that the doorway was not provided with a wooden leaf. The chapel's casing, which had been made up of finely smoothed larger blocks of white limestone, was almost totally missing (it was preserved only in the southernmost part of the eastern wall). The core masonry consisted of large, only roughly worked blocks (*fig. 5.29*). The roof of the chapel was not preserved at all. As has been already suggested, we can suppose that it was constructed in the same way and at the same (or similar) level as that in the vestibule with the ceiling blocks laid crosswise to the longer axis of the room. We also assume that the height of the chapel was the same as in the case of the vestibule – *i.e.* 5.12 m above the pavement of the room. The pavement of the chapel was made of large, flat blocks of limestone. This layer of blocks also created a foundation layer for erecting the side walls of the chapel. Therefore, the area of the chapel proper is indicated quite roughly on the surface of the pavement blocks, while it disappears in the western part of the chapel. The

---

[17] The area of the Pyramid Complex of Khentkaus II bears signs of activities during Coptic times (Verner, *Khentkaus*, 22–23); they have been documented in other places of the Abusir Royal Necropolis as well (W. B. Oerter, Remains of Coptic Settlement at Abusir, in: *Secrets of the Desert and the Pyramids*, 183–191). Unfortunately, we cannot date the secondary burials excavated to the north of L25/1 – *cf.* p. 158–161 more precisely. Nevertheless, there is a possibility that they can be dated to the Early Christian Period.

Fig.5.30a–d Mud lining of the floor preserved in the chapel. Photos JK

a	b
c	d

pavement blocks were covered by a partially preserved mud lining showing, just as in the case of the vestibule, that the chapel's floor had been cleaned on a regular basis (*fig.5.30a–d*). As faint remains of white paint were found on the mud lining, we know that also the floor in the main cultic room of L25/1 had been painted white. On the surface of the mud lining, there are clear marks of burning (the colour of the mud lining shifts from grey-brown to red-brown and red) and, in the area of the chapel's axis, we can see a small fire-place (see *fig. 5.31* on *pl. VII* and plan on *fig. 5.16*). These fire spots might have come into the existence in connection with the cultic rituals which were running in the chapel.[18]

As was already mentioned, the masonry of the chapel's side walls was destroyed to a large scale. The western part of the chapel had been totally demolished by stone robbers. Therefore, the reconstruction of the original chapel's layout and groundplan is very problematic and, on the basis of our present knowledge, it cannot be made in its entirety. There are two possibilities, however, of visualising the original appearance of the chapel.

1. Following the preserved parts and imprints of mud lining noticeable on the floor blocks, the ground plan of the chapel might have turned its direction to the south, creating quite a bizarre and unusual kind of *en chicane* layout.[19] In this way, the easternmost part of the chapel – the area into which the doorway from the vestibule was leading – represented a narrow corridor which would have led in our reconstruction to the chapel proper. This passageway was oriented along the north–south axis. This best preserved part was connected with only faint imprints of mud lining which show that this corridor might have turned to the west and then again to the south (*fig. 5.32*).

This best preserved part of the corridor had the same width as the vestibule, *i.e.* 1.15 m. Its length, deriving from the extent of the preserved mud lining of the floor in the northern part of the space, equated to 7.20 m. It is very probable that the short passage leading to the west was also 1.15 m wide. Its length, however, is not easy to ascertain. Following the width of the better preserved part of the room as well as the imprints of the mud lining in its north–south oriented part, we can establish that the length of this east–west passage would have come to 3.20 m. The corridor then might have turned its direction again – to the south. The destruction in this supposed western part of the chapel is even worse than in its eastern part: only several large limestone blocks of the pavement layer survived the attacks of stone

Fig. 5.32 The northern part of the chapel with imprints of mud lining. Photo JK

---

[18] Nevertheless, we cannot rule out that these fire spots are relics of some secondary activities which were made inside the chapel.

[19] This kind of arrangement of a cultic installation can be observed, in the Meidum pyramid complex in the form of *en chicane* layout of the entrance passageways leading to the courtyard with stelae in the cultic edifice of the complex (*MRA* III, 24, figs. 5. and 6).

robbers. Only faint imprints of the mud lining were preserved on this limestone pavement. It seems that also in this case the corridor had the same width as in its easternmost part – 1.15 m. Its length, however, is problematic to ascertain – the imprints of mud lining disappear at a distance of about 4.00 m from the northern wall of the corridor (with the preserved edge of the floor mud lining – see above). One can only hypothesize that the cultic place proper – or a deep niche with a false door (no fragments of such a false door were found during archaeological excavation) or an offering room – was located in this area. The offering room might have been oriented along the east–west axis.[20]

2. On the other hand, the imprints of mud lining on the floor pavement are not entirely clear, therefore, a different layout can be proposed here. Also in this reconstruction we suppose the existence of a south–north oriented chapel represented only by the easternmost part of the hypothesis presented above. In this case, no other rooms would have been added to this space. We can then assume that a deep niche might have been located already in the western wall of the chapel. Such an arrangement would not necessarily appear in the ground plan of the chapel, and the false door could once have been located in the western wall of such a niche. In this hypothesis, then, the faint remains of mud lining discussed above might have emerged secondarily, as a consequence of attacks from stone robbers and secondary burying.

In view of the existence of imprints of mud lining on the floor and the low elevation in the area of the supposed western part of the chapel, we tend to reconstruct the original appearance of this place following the first hypothesis. We cannot explain why the chapel should have had such a strange and, in the context of the Old Kingdom tomb architecture, non-standard layout. Nevertheless, seeing the layout of the substructure of L25/1 (see p. 170–174), one can observe that it and the proposed ground plan of the chapel are strikingly similar. In both cases, we notice an *en chicane* layout. This arrangement might have been influenced by the endeavour to protect the offering place as much as possible from the outside world, which constitutes one of the characteristic traits of the ancient Egyptian cultic architecture (we can suppose a similar approach to these problems also in the case of the subterranean part of the tomb).

As has been mentioned earlier in this chapter, it is apparent that neither the vestibule nor the chapel (or the access corridor) were equipped with a door-leaf(s).[21] We can hypothesize that the layout of the chapel with an *en chicane* access and with missing door-leafs at least in the entrance from the outside was intentional and that it was a part of the overall religious and architectonic concept which we cannot follow, mainly due to the level of destruction of the monument.

Seeing the results of the archaeological excavation done in the Tomb Complex Lepsius no. 25 which was able to be done only in a limited area, we cannot exclude that this cultic room might have served as an offering place not only for L25/1, but also for L25/2. In this case, we should then suppose that not one, but two false doors might have been originally located there – both in the first and in the second hypothetical reconstruction of the chapel's layout as proposed above. As has already been mentioned, the archaeological investigation in the area of the chapel

---

[20] This orientation of non-royal offering chapels started to spread in the Memphite area during Niuserre's rule. In the opinion of P. Jánosi, the first example of such an offering room in non-royal tombs can be found in Persen's tomb in Saqqara – Les tombes privées »des maisons d'éternité«, in: *L'art égyptienne*, 62; for the original publication, see Petrie, Murray, *Seven Memphite Tomb Chapels*, 9, pl. XIX:4; for the dating of Persen's tomb see Harpur, *Decoration*, 107; for the situation in the Mastaba of Ptahshepses, see also P. Jánosi, in: *Abusir and Saqqara in 2000*, 454, note 40, and Krejčí, *Ptahshepses*, 55 and 183. This development was preceded by the progress in the royal mortuary architecture. East–west oriented offering chapels can be detected in the kings' mortuary temples from Sahure's reign onwards – see P. Jánosi, Die Entwicklung und Deutung des Totenopferraumes in den Pyramidentempeln des Alten Reiches, in: *Ägyptische Tempel*, 156f.

[21] There are no traces of the typical hinge holder in the preserved pavement.

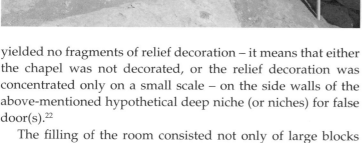

yielded no fragments of relief decoration – it means that either the chapel was not decorated, or the relief decoration was concentrated only on a small scale – on the side walls of the above-mentioned hypothetical deep niche (or niches) for false door(s).[22]

The filling of the room consisted not only of large blocks of limestone, but also of crushed mudbricks, grey-brown sand, totally destroyed disarticulated human remains coming from the secondary cemetery, mixed with linen bands, parts of wooden coffins and palm-leaf mat wrappings, crushed by stone robbers and the destruction(s) of the monument. Besides, numerous pottery sherds were found in the course of investigation of this area. Of special importance are two sets of finds brought to light during excavation in the eastern part of the chapel. The first one of these is represented by a few fragments of a papyrus roll with records of offerings (see *chapter 5.6.*). This roll was probably an account-list mentioning amounts of meat and pastry. The second group of finds, fragments of a travertine statue, portrayed a standing woman dressed in a simple robe and adorned with a necklace. There is a possibility that the statue depicted a woman of royal origin, the fact of which is indicated by the statue's reconstructed height (60–65 cm), high quality of craftsmanship, and the type of material used (for further description, see p. 189–190). In addition, several other fragments, originally coming from a travertine statue(s), were found. If these fragments really came from statues, we can start to conjecture about the function of these statues. If they had been part of the original layout of the chapel, it might be possible to connect with the cultic purpose of this part of the tomb's superstructure. Nevertheless, despite that fact, both of these discoveries are dated to the Old Kingdom or, more precisely, to the Fifth Dynasty but, due to subsequent intrusions caused mainly by stone robbers and secondary burying, it is not clear whether they can be connected with the original equipment, or whether they have to be taken as an intrusive find. For ascribing the items to the original owner of L25/1, we can argue that the papyrus fragments and some of the fragments of the travertine statues were found in the lower levels of the room's filling, and in the case of the fragments of the papyrus roll even below the level of the chapel's floor.

Fig. 5.33 Descending corridor in L25/1 from the south.
Photo JK

Fig. 5.34 Descending corridor in L25/1, remains of blocks of the eastern side wall.
Photo KV

5.3.1.3. The burial apartment of L25/1

The burial apartment of the eastern tomb of Lepsius no. 25 was found in a better state of preservation as compared with the one of L25/2 (see *chapter 5.2.2.2.*). But still, the underground rooms of L25/1 had been severely damaged. Despite this fact, we

---

[22] We can see such an arrangement in the case of Inti's tomb – see Bárta *et al.*, *Qar*, in press.

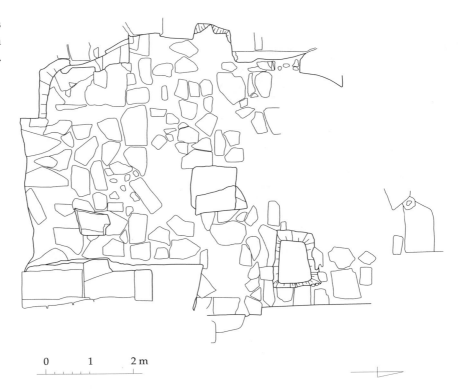

Fig. 5.36 Plan of the remains of the burial apartment in L25.

0   1   2 m

can reconstruct its groundplan, as opposed to the situation in L25/2. Unfortunately, the exact dimensions of its individual rooms cannot be ascertained with precision.

The entrance into the substructure of L25/1 was located in the middle of the northern wall of the tomb. It seems that the entrance was situated at the level of the foot of the tomb's outer wall, or slightly above it (0.25 m). The entrance led into the descending passage of the access corridor, of which only a layer of the under-pavement limestone blocks remained *in situ* (*fig. 5.33*). The side walls and the ceiling of the descending corridor had completely disappeared – only the rear parts of large blocks of white limestone which had once formed the side walls of the corridor had been preserved (*figs. 5.34*). The exposed faces of the blocks bore clear cutting marks left behind by stone robbers. In this way, the original width of the corridor was not preserved in its masonry, which was also the case with the corridor's height. Nevertheless, the width can be reconstructed using the masons' marks observed on the surface of the under-pavement blocks. The preserved layer of these blocks declined at an angle of 26.8°. We can suppose that this angle is very probably a little steeper than the angle of the actual pavement layer. The corridor's floor had presumably to link itself up with the horizontal part of the entrance corridor. The angle of the corridor's floor might have been about 25.5°.

The preserved under-pavement layer, however, bore builders' marks made in red and black ink (see *fig. 5.35, pl. VII*). They show that the corridor might have been ca 1.10 m wide and we can only suppose that the height of the corridor was the same, *i.e.*, that the corridor was square in its section. As has already been mentioned, at its lower end, the descending corridor opened out into a horizontal part of the access to the burial chamber. Unfortunately, this part had been devastated even more than the descending corridor – a portion of the under-pavement layer and part of the casing of individual sections of the accessing corridor were all that were preserved. The casing consisted of the blocks of fine limestone, which was also shown by two "pillars" of the original casing stones that had survived in the middle of the construction pit (*figs. 5.36 and 5.37a–b*). The casing of the corridor still remained *in situ* in the southern part of the eastern wall and in the southern wall of the construction pit. The casing blocks, however, had not been fully smoothed, and quite large portions of the blocks' surface showed protrusions of material remaining to be cut off, with marks left behind by tools (*fig. 5.38*). The casing of the western

wall of the burial chamber did not survive well and it was partially cut up by stone robbers.

On both of the well-preserved walls in the eastern wall of the horizontal passage, two horizontal lines painted in red ink remain – the lower one marked the level of 0.60–0.63 cm and the upper one the level of 0.63–0.72 cm above the under-pavement layer. We can assume that these lines indicated the level of the pavement of the access corridor's floor. The two lines might have been created upon later adjustment of measurements. These lines were supplemented by two vertical lines located 1.30 m and 1.84 m to the north of the southern cased wall of the corridor. It is highly probable that we can link this reading with the length of the second, north–south oriented partition of the access corridor, whereas the first reading might have been connected with the width of the third, east–west oriented section of the same corridor. The second reading can be connected with the first horizontal part of the access corridor.

Interesting masons' marks were preserved below the above-mentioned lower horizontal line on the eastern wall (*fig. 5.39a–c*). The masons' mark, documented on the northern part of this wall, appears to have been very probably upside down (*fig. 5.40a, pl. VII; fig.5.40b*). It reads *mḥ 2* – "two cubits [above, below? …]". The second builders' mark was preserved to the south of the first one, almost in the south-eastern corner. As is the case with the first mark, this *Baugraffito* is upside down. We can read it as follows: *mḥ 1, šsp 2 (?) [dbꜥ x]* – "1 cubit, 2(?) palms, [x digits]" (*fig. 5,41a, pl. VII, 5.41b*). It is very probable that this mark was not in its original position (on a re-used block of white limestone), we can, therefore, follow the interpretation of a similar mark found in the Pyramid Complex Lepsius no. 24. M. Verner associates this similar mark with the distance of a certain builders' line to a wall (see p. 134 in this monograph). Not only the fact that both marks were discovered in an upside-down position, but also the spot where the second mark was located (only about 30 cm from a side wall of the corridor) seems to show that both blocks on which the discussed graffiti were preserved, were reused. Thus the graffiti do not seem

Fig. 5.37a Remains of the burial apartment in L25/1. Overall view from above.
Photo JK

Fig. 5.37b Remains of the burial apartment in L25/1 and the descending corridor.
Photo JK

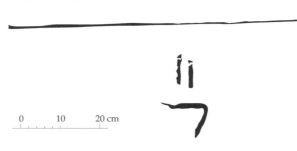

0   10   20 cm

0   5   10 cm

to relate to the actual situation in the substructure of L25/1.

Nevertheless, coming back to the descending part of the access corridor, the masons' marks on the under-pavement blocks show us that the descending passage of the corridor was originally 1.10 m wide. As mentioned above, we can suppose that this part of the corridor was square in section, which means this passage was 1.10 m high. The same situation is in the case with the height of the horizontal parts of the access corridor. We can only theorize that these parts were higher, hypothetically ca 1.60–1.70 m.[23] These parts might have made it possible for an upright

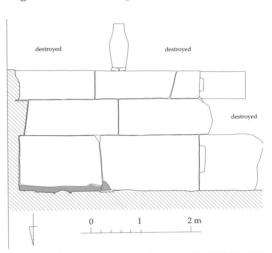

Fig. 5.38 Tool marks left on the casing in the construction pit in L25/1. Photo JK

Fig. 5.39a Remains of the eastern wall in the burial apartment of L25/1. Photo JK

Fig. 5.39b Remains of the southern wall in the burial apartment of L25/1

Fig. 5.39c Remains of the western wall in the burial apartment of L25/1 Photo JK

<< **Fig. 5.40b Masons' mark on the casing of the eastern wall.**

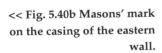

<< **Fig. 5.41b Masons' mark at the south-east corner of the horizontal passage of the accessing corridor in L25/1.**

person to enter. As has already been mentioned, the masonry of the access corridor as well as of the burial chamber had been almost totally destroyed, however, we can reconstruct the original layout on the strength of the remainig masonry and of the builders' marks. The horizontal part was originally formed of three spaces – a north–south oriented room which gave access to the adjacent space oriented along the east–west axis, and another, short passage oriented along the north–south axis.

---

[23] This height was also documented in the case of complicated burial apartment in the Mastaba of Werkaure – J. Krejčí, Several remarks on the Abusir pyramid necropolis – its minor tombs and their place in the chronology of the royal cemetery, in: *Chronology of IVth and IIIrd Millenium*, 124–125.

This last, short passage gave access to the burial chamber. In this way, the access corridor turned twice – to the west and then to the north.

It seems that the descending corridor continued in the form of a horizontal passage. This room might also have had a small slope of a few degrees. Its western wall was delimited by the already mentioned larger casing block of white limestone. The southern end of this first horizontal room was marked by another "pillar" of the casing. The dimensions of the individual parts can be ascertained only approximately. The length of the first, north–south oriented passage, which was 1.20 m wide, could not be reconstructed, however, we suppose that it was at least 6.5 m long. The entrance between this and the second, east–west oriented space was 0.64 m wide and 0.52 m long; the following section of the corridor measured 2.25 × 1.30 m. The third partition of the access corridor was oriented along its north–south axis. Unfortunately, we cannot reconstruct whether or not there was another doorway between this and the preceding east–west oriented passage. The last, north–south oriented space measured 1.10 × 1.36 m.

At the end of this complex set of four parts of the access corridor, a north–south burial chamber was located. Just as with the other rooms in the subterranean part of the tomb, the burial chamber was destroyed to a great extent. Only parts of the side walls' casing and quite a large part of the under-floor layer of flat limestone blocks remained *in situ*. However, the ground plan can be reconstructed with the help of the tiny red masons' marks still remaining on some blocks of the under-floor layer and on the side walls. We can thus assume that the burial chamber was 4.5 m long and, together with its sarcophagus niche, it was 2.7 m wide.[24] Taking account of the state of preservation of masonry in the area of the burial apartment and the horizontal masons'marks, we can reconstruct the height of the burial chamber in the range of 2.44–2.84 m.[25] There is no direct evidence of how the chamber was roofed. We can only suppose that, in compliance with the practice documented in other minor tombs in the Abusir Royal Necropolis, this burial chamber was covered by a flat roof constructed of limestone slabs laid down transversally, just as the access corridor mentioned above.

The area of the burial chamber and of the individual parts of the access corridor, which together made up the burial apartment, was filled with layers of collapsed masonry of the side walls of the pit, mixed with grey sand. Despite all the effort, no fragment of granite which could have been attributed definitely to a sarcophagus, was found. Moreover, there is no evidence of any other equipment of the chamber, *e.g.*, the pit for a canopic chest.[26] A shallow shaft (67 cm deep) which was unearthed during the archaeological excavation (*fig. 5.42*) and which was partly located below the original eastern wall of the first horizontal corridor, apparently came into the existence through action of tomb robbers and stone robbers.

Fig. 5.42 Construction pit in L25/1, a shallow shaft in its bottom.
Photo JK

[24] Discussing the theories that the owner of L25 was a royal lady (or two royal ladies) (see *chapter 5.8*), we have to mention that this burial chamber was quite small – the burial chamber of Neferhetepes measured 4.20 × 3.15 × 3.15 m (4.5) m, that of Neit 6.30 × 3.15 × ? m; that of Iput II 6.30 × 3.15 × ? m; that of Wedjebten 7.40 × 3.15 × 3.60 m. Does the fact that the burial chamber in L25/1 (the dimensions of the chamber in L25/2 cannot be estimated due to its total destruction) is smaller than the cited examples indicate a lower social status of the tomb owner(s)?).
[25] *Cf.* the height of the burial chambers in this part of the Abusir pyramid necropolis – for the pyramid Lepsius no. 24 see p. 82 in this monograph; the burial chamber in the pyramid of Khentkaus II was 2.57 m high (Jánosi, in: Verner, *Khentkaus*, 148) – we can suppose that the height may have been more than 2.60 m from the pavement of the chamber.
[26] *Cf.* Jánosi, in: Verner, *Khentkaus*, 148.

Fig. 5.43a Southern outer wall of L25/2.
Photo JK
Fig. 5.43b North-western corner of L25/2 with the core masonry.
Photo JK

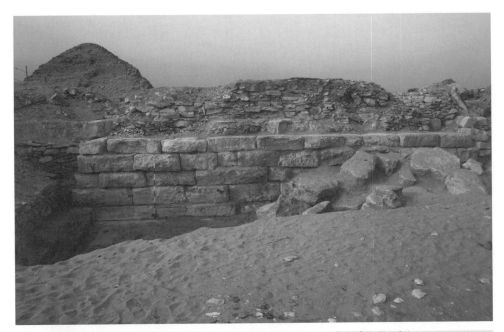

5.3.2. Lepsius no. 25/2

In contrast to L25/1, the western part of the Tomb Complex Lepsius no. 25 is even in a worse state of preservation. Stone robbers destroyed the burial apartment of L25/2 almost entirely, with the destruction taking place in a number of stages. The core masonry and especially the casing of the inner rooms were damaged to a large extent. In some parts, *e.g.* in the case of the western wall of the construction pit, only the outer walls were preserved.

5.3.2.1. The superstructure of L25/2

The core of this part of the tomb complex was built, not surprisingly, using a similar building technique as in the case of L25/1. The outer walls were constructed of large, roughly worked blocks of local limestone. The blocks were regular, as in the case of L25/1 and had dimensions similar to the blocks from the eastern tomb (*fig. 5.43a*). The blocks were joined together by mud and pinkish lime mortar. The inner core masonry was partially built of smaller fragments of local limestone,

Fig. 5.44 Construction pit for the burial apartment in L25/2; view from the south. Photo JK

creating a kind of inner chamber. These chambers were filled with low-quality masonry mixed with mudbricks and weathered pottery sherds. A part of the core masonry was represented by limestone fragments not very well joined by mud mortar, mudbricks, weathered pottery sherds and brown sand (*fig. 5.43b*). It is apparent that the builders of the tomb had depended on the massive outer walls and had not cared about the quality of construction of the inner masonry. Consequently, once some of the large blocks of the façade were removed by stone robbers, the masonry of the tomb collapsed for the most part, thus creating the mound that marks the monument in our times.

5.3.2.2. The burial apartment of L25/2

As follows from the above, the burial apartment of L25/2 is damaged even more so than in the case of L25/1 (*figs. 5.44–5.45*). No block from the side walls, nor from the corridor or the burial chamber, remained *in situ*. The only exception is, possibly, the area of the entrance into the descending corridor. In this place the blocks of the casing of the tomb's outer walls seem to delimitate the side walls of the corridor (see *figs. 5.46a–b*). The pavement of the burial chamber is not preserved, except for two blocks of white limestone below the western wall of the construction pit. They seem to show that the level of the burial chamber's floor was 48–58 cm above the bottom of the construction pit (see *fig. 5.51*).

Fig. 5.45a Construction pit for the burial apartment in L25/2; view from the east. Photo JK

Fig. 5.45b Construction pit for the burial apartment in L25/2; view from the north. Photo JK

Fig. 5.46a L25/2 upper end
of the descending corridor
with the entrance filled with
a (plugging?) limestone
block; view from the south.
Photo JK

Fig. 5.46b Northern wall of
L25/2 with the entrance to
the descending corridor.
Photo JK

Fig. 5.47 Descending
corridor to the substructure
of L25/2, view from the
south-west. Photo JK

Fig. 5.48 Plan of the burial
chamber in L25/2.

In contrast to the situation in L25/1, there is a possibility that the pavement of the descending corridor survived, at least in its upper part. In this section of the corridor, several blocks of the pavement layer created a low elevation oriented along the north-south axis. This elevation almost certainly represents a junction for the side wall (see *fig. 5.46a*). However, we cannot fully rule out that there was another layer of the actual pavement blocks of the corridor and that the preserved layer of flat blocks constitutes a layer of under-pavement blocks[28]. As for the side walls of the corridor, their state of preservation is worse than in the case of L25/1 (*fig. 5.47*).

In general, the reconstruction of the original appearance of the burial apartment is very complicated, if not – in some respects (see below) – impossible (*fig. 5.48*). Nevertheless, as mentioned above, distinct remains of the descending corridor were found in the axis of the northern wall of the tomb (see *fig. 5.46a–b*). The entrance into the corridor originally opened, as in the case of the corridor in L25/1, at the foot of the wall. Despite the fact that no helping masons' lines or marks remain on the surface of the (under-)pavement blocks, we can, thanks to the situation at the upper end, reconstruct the width of the corridor. The entrance delimited by the casing

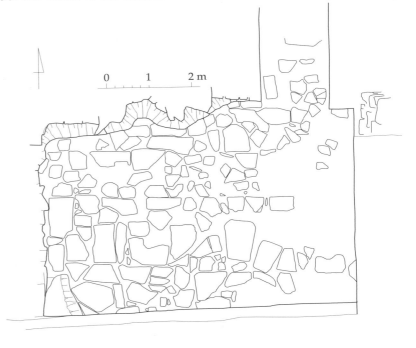

0   1   2 m

---

[28] *Cf.* the similar situation in the northern part of the descending corridor in Raneferef's pyramid. For information on this descending corridor – see Verner, in: Verner *et al.*, Raneferef, 15–22.

blocks of the outer wall was 0.96–1.00 m wide. The situation further to the south (see above) makes it posssible to reconstruct the width of the corridor similar to the corridor in L25/1, *i.e.*, 1.10–1.15 m. We can only hypothesize that the corridor was square in the section, which means its height would be the same as its width (1.10–1.15 m). The angle of the (under-)pavement blocks corresponds to that from the neighbouring tomb, varying slightly between 25° and 25.5°.

Only parts of the lining of the construction pit for the burial apartment remained (*fig. 5.49*). This lining was made of small limestone fragments and splinters, but the lining also documented the way in which the burial chamber was constructed: after the tomb had been laid out and the construction of the core masonry of the tomb had begun, the builders started digging out the pit. The bottom of the pit was covered up with under-pavement blocks. As a small trial excavation underneath the under-pavement blocks showed, there was only one layer of these blocks laid in the layer of dark-brown sand. Thereafter, the lining of the pit (which had been dug out in the not-too-stable subsoil of sand and gravel) was added to the side walls of the pit as the construction of the tomb's core progressed.[29] The inferior quality of the construction methods used seems to indicate both haste in which the tomb(s) were constructed and the lower rank of the tomb owner(s).

In the western wall of the lining several masons' lines survived (*figs. 5.50a–b, pl. VII*, and *fig. 5.51*). They indicated the level of the underfloor blocks. The northernmost of the marks (see *fig. 5.50a*) seems to have pinpointed the position of the northern

Fig. 5.49 Lining of the western wall of the pit for the burial apartment, view from the east.
Photo JK

Fig. 5.50a Northern arrow sign on the blocks in the western wall of the construction pit in L25/2.
Photo JK

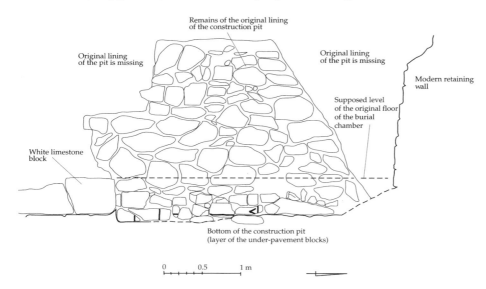

Fig. 5.51 View of the remaining part of the original lininig in the western wall of the construction pit; the masons' marks and lines are indicated, too.

---

[29] We have to underline the great difference between the quality of construction of the pit lining in the pyramid L24 and that in both L25/1 and L25/2.

wall of the burial chamber. Two other vertical signs were located at quite a short distance from the arrow-sign (1.20 and 1.35 m), therefore, it is almost certain that they did not mark the place of the southern wall. Instead, they could have, *e.g.*, set the east–west axis of the burial chamber.

Even with the masons' marks, it is almost impossible to reconstruct the original appearance of the burial apartment. We cannot say whether the burial apartment in L25/2 had been designed to have as complicated a layout as the one in L25/1; however, it cannot be excluded. There is also a possibility that the burial apartment had been designed in a way similar to that of the pyramids of kings and queens, with a north–south oriented descending corridor and a burial chamber oriented along the east–west axis (*cf.* the situation in L24). Due to security reasons, we could not excavate the construction pit of L25/2 in its entirety. Some of the masonry belonging to the burial apartment remained, unfortunately, in the unexcavated part of the tomb. Thus it remains unsolved whether the above-mentioned *Baugraffiti* delimited the dimensions of the burial chamber. As is the case with L25/1, the filling of the area of the burial apartment consisted of debris, grey sand, white limestone *raksha*, scattered human bones, and fragments of granite and basalt. We could not discern any fragments of a sarcophagus for the deceased. Nevertheless, as mentioned in the chapter 5.1.1., it is possible that parts of the mummified body hypothetically dated to the Old Kingdom were found during our works in this area.

5.3.3. Structures excavated outside the Tomb Complex Lepsius no. 25.

Beside the work inside the tombs themselves, we carried out three *sondages* outside the tomb complex. The first one was excavated by the north-east corner of the monument (or, more precisely, of L25/1). This narrow trench was cut through the filling consisting of large limestone blocks fallen from the destroyed outer wall of L25/1 and the sand. At the distance of 4.75 m eastwards from the north-east corner of L25/1, it revealed a part of a construction consisting of large flat blocks of yellow local limestone topped with mudbricks. This construction, which was excavated only to a limited extent (4.10 × 3.00 m), consisted of two rectangular structures separated by a narrow gap (0.65 m wide) (*figs. 5.52* and *5.53a–b*). The

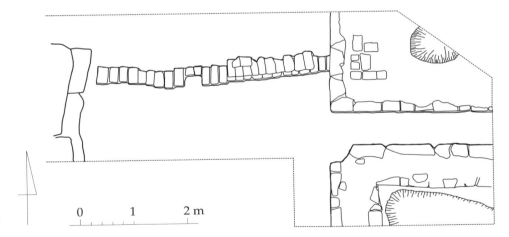

Fig. 5.52 Plan of the structure at the north-eastern corner of L25/1.

0   1   2 m

limestone blocks made up the outer faces of the southern part of the construction. In both cases, we detected a depression in the middle of the respective structures. The mudbricks used in the structures were badly weathered, so that it was not possible to determine their format and binding. We know only that they were 15–16 cm wide. On the basis of the inferior quality, position and level at which the construction had been built we are able to suppose that it formed the lowermost level of a building of unknown function. On the western face of the northern structure, the builders' mark no. Gr. 166/N/2003 bearing the title and name of Princess Hanebu (see *chapter 5.7.*) was revealed.

This structure was connected with the outer wall of L25/1 by a narrow mudbrick wall running in a east–west direction and slightly deflected. No more than three layers of bricks were preserved. As far as their bonding is concerned, we can state that the preserved layers show only headers. The format of the bricks is similar to the bricks used in the previously mentioned construction: 35–38 × 16–17.5 × 10–11 cm. The bricks were made of dark-brown material with a mixture of limestone detritus and, surprisingly, only a low amount of straw.[30] The mortar is of almost the same composition.

Another trench was excavated by the south-west corner of L25/2 and along part of its southern wall. In the western sector of the *sondage* a complex stratigraphy of mudbrick walls could be observed (*figs. 5.54–5.56*). At least two, but more probably three stages of development can be traced in this area. The earliest phase consisted of two walls with the orientation shifting slightly off the rigid north–south axis. The wall in the second level was shifted even more to the east. The uppermost level of the brick masonry was represented by a wall connected with the blocks of the outer wall of L25/2 and was oriented along the north–south axis. The following table sets forth the basic characteristics of these mudbrick walls.

Fig. 5.53a Structure at the north-eastern corner of L25/1 – view from the north-west.
Photo JK

Fig. 5.53b Structure at the north-eastern corner of L25/1 – view from the east.
Photo JK

Phase	Format	Material	Bonding[31]
First phase	27–28 × 14–17 × 10 cm	Dark-brown mud material with higher addition of chaff, limestone detritus, and weathered pottery sherds	Not discernible
Second phase	26–28 × 16–18 × 10–11.5 cm	Greyish-brown mud material with addition of chaff and limestone detritus	A2
Third phase	30–34 × 13–16 × 10.5–11 cm	Two different materials: 1. dark-brown mud material with addition of white limestone detritus, 2. light brown-yellowish material with a substantial addition of *tafla* and with limestone detritus	A3

Another structure was uncovered in the eastern part of the trench. This construction was similar to that revealed by the north-east corner of L25/1 (see above). It also appears to represent the lower part of a building, which consisted of a layer constructed of limestone blocks of inferior quality topped with mudbrick masonry. The unearthed mudbricks were weathered, and only two dimensions

[30] The format of the bricks used in this wall is surprisingly large – *cf.* Krejčí, in: Verner *et al.*, *Raneferef*, 115–136.
[31] Spencer, *Brick Architecture*, pl. 1–4.

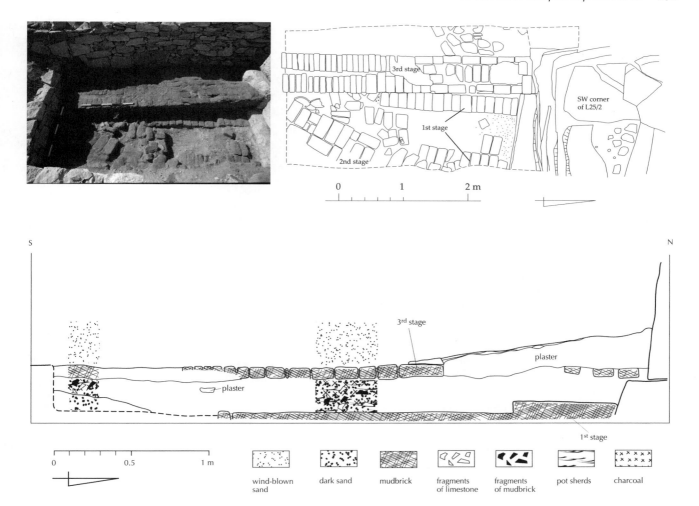

0   1   2 m

0   0.5   1 m

wind-blown   dark sand   mudbrick   fragments   fragments   pot sherds   charcoal
sand   of limestone   of mudbrick

Fig. 5.54 Mudbrick masonry to the south of the south-western corner of L25/2. Photo JK

Fig. 5.55 Plan of the mud masonry to the south of the south-western corner of L25/2.

Fig. 5.56 Section through the mudbrick masonry in the trench to the south from the south-western corner of L25/1.

can be mentioned here: length 30 cm and width 14–15 cm. It seems that (*fig. 5.57* and *figs. 5.58a–c*) there was a kind of enclosed space that was 1.10 m wide and at least 1.80 m. Only part of this construction (3.20 × 4.20 m) was excavated as it was partially covered by large limestone blocks from the outer wall of L25/2. During the excavations, we found miniature pottery, fragments of cultic pottery and flint knives. These finds suggest cultic use of this space. One can only hypothesize that these cultic activities were connected with the Lepsius no. 25 complex, but the minimal preservation state of structures makes it difficult to say more than this.

A third *sondage* was conducted in the area of the join between the two tombs. In its upper part it revealed that the eastern tomb L25/1 was older than L25/2 (*fig. 5.59*). In its lower part the *sondage* uncovered two small portions of mudbrick masonry. The smaller one, which has been connected directly with the outer wall of L25/2 consists of only a few mudbricks made of dark mud material and with the following format 35 × 19 × 11 cm. Another, which is located further to the south (precisely 3.05 m from the outer wall L25/2) is a larger portion of a construction. Only three layers of a north-eastern corner (?) of a mudbrick structure remained *in situ*. The format of bricks made of brown mud material with addition of straw, sand and limestone detritus was a little bit smaller than was the case with the previously mentioned bricks: 32–35 × 16–17 × 10–10.5 cm. It thus seems probable that these two constructions do not belong to the same structure (see also *fig. 5.60*). As a larger number of objects connectable with cultic activities were unearthed in this area as well, we need to mention the wooden inscribed stele 93/N/2003 found in the level of the original terrain, we can suppose that this area had some cultic function, too.

5.3.4. Technology of the tombs' construction

Not only the architectural appearance, but also the way in which the monument was built, show non-standard features. After the monument had been laid out, it

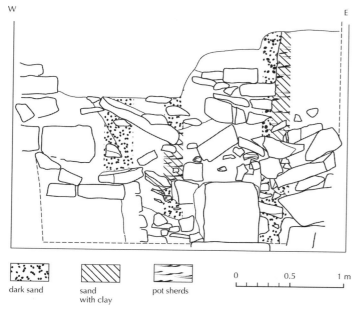

Fig. 5.57 Plan of the foundations of a structure to the south of L25/2.

Fig. 5.58a Foundations of a structure to the south of L25/2, general view from the south-west. Photo JK

Fig. 5.58b Foundations of a structure to the south of L25/2, view from the south. Photo JK

Fig. 5.58c Foundations of a structure to the south of L25/2, view from the north. Photo JK

Fig. 5.59 Section through the filling and masonry in the upper part of the join of the western wall of L25/1 and south-eastern corner of L25/2.

>>Fig. 5.60 (above left) Mudbrick constructions found at the bottom of the *sondage* in the area of the join between L25/1 and L25/2.
Photo JK

>>Fig. 5.61 (above right) Layer of the brown sand as revealed in the construction pit in L25/2. Photo JK

seems that the layer of *dakka* was created which certainly facilitated the progress of construction works. Possibly together with this, the excavation of the construction pit (in the form of a letter "T") of the respective tomb was begun. It is surprising that the core masonry of both tombs was built on a layer of dark-brown sand, which was up to 1.5 m thick (*fig. 5.61*). The core masonry of the tombs, constructed on this layer, was laid around the construction pits for the burial apartments. As became apparent during the excavation, the layer was not sufficient to support the solid masonry of the tombs (*fig. 5.62*). The reasons for the use of this method are not clear

Fig. 5.62 Masonry of the western wall of the construction pit in L25/2.
Photo JK

Fig. 5.63 Re-used white limestone block built in the eastern face of L25/1.
Photo JK

– it could be the result of haste in which the monument was built, or, it could have had some ritual meaning.[32]

The archaeological excavations in L25/2 showed that the pit for the burial apartment was lined with a layer of small fragments of limestone and mud mortar. The situation in L25/1 enables us to assume that at first the side walls of the internal rooms of the tomb were constructed and then the pavement was laid down. In the case of L25/2 the procedure might have been reversed, as is shown by the preserved white limestone blocks (see above) of the pavement. The free space between the blocks of the casing of the side walls and the face of the lining of the construction pit was filled with rubble. In both cases, we suppose the use of a flat ceiling in the burial chambers and in other rooms of the substructures.

The core masonry which in the meantime developed around the construction pit is of indifferent quality. The outer face consisted of large, roughly worked blocks of local grey limestone.[33] This masonry contained a filling of small limestone fragments, crushed mudbricks, pottery sherds and sand. The core masonry of both tombs contained some of chamber-like spaces filled with rubble, weathered pottery sherds and sand. This *caisson* technology was attested nearby, in Raneferef's unfinished pyramid, too.[34] We can notice the use of this method especially in the case of the trenches in which the descending corridors

---

[32] *E.g.*, connected with the idea of a Primeval Hill.
[33] In the use of these large blocks in the tomb cladding, the Lepsius no. 25 complex, together with the neighbouring Mastaba of Werkaure, differs markedly from other monuments in the Abusir royal necropolis.
[34] Verner, in: Verner *et al.*, *Raneferef*, 9–12, fig. 2.1.2.

were constructed. In an effective way, these chamber-like constructions filled the free space of the tombs' superstructure. The low quality of the construction work became apparent after the attacks of the stone robbers. A large part of outer face of tomb L25/1, in which stability was impaired by the robbers, collapsed.

It was not unusual within the framwork of the ancient Egyptian architecture for building material to be reused. We can prove it also in the case of the Tomb Complex Lepsius no. 25. The most prominent examples of recycling are two blocks of white limestone which were once built in the masonry of L25/1. The first block is still embedded into the eastern face of L25/1 (dimensions: 25–50 × ? × 120 cm; see *fig. 5.63*). The second block was found in the debris filling the space to the east of the tomb (42–50 × 30–53 × 108 cm, *fig. 5.64*). Taking into our account their form, it is very probable that both blocks were originally part of a drum piece above an entrance. In regard to the fact that their dimensions do not differ very much (especially in their maximum thickness) and that both blocks were made of the same type of limestone, we can suppose that the blocks had originally formed one piece. If it were so, then the construction would have represented a large structure: the width of the hypothetical entrance would have been at least 153 cm. High quality white limestone seems to show that the blocks were originally used in a construction connected with a higher social stratum, or even with the royal family. Even if this had not been the case, then the presence of these two blocks enables us to suppose the existence of an older building dismantled (?) before (but not certainly because of) the construction of Lepsius no. 25. Unfortunately, no remains of inscriptions were documented on the surface of the blocks.

Fig. 5.64 Re-used white limestone block found in the debris to the east of L25/1.
Photo JK

5.3.5. The reconstruction of the original appearance of the tomb complex

An important question concerning the Tomb Complex Lepsius no. 25 is the reconstruction of its original appearance (*fig. 5.65, pl. VIII*). We cannot exclude the possibility that the construction was not finished according to its original plan. An important detail in this respect is the fact that no block which would have belonged to the casing of one of the two tombs was found – even on the outer walls that had been excavated (*i.e.*, the western and the eastern walls of the tomb). Moreover, no loose-block which might have come from the original casing of the tomb, was found. We can thus – as has already been mentioned – suppose that the side walls had not been cased.

Because of this fact it is not an easy task to ascertain the slope of the outer walls of the tombs – which we can only estimate to have been around 80°, the typical angle of the side walls of a mastaba.

As has already been said in this chapter several times, the tomb superstructures had the form of two, north–south oriented, tightly attached mastabas, both built on a rectangular groundplan. The eastern tomb (L25/1) was larger and was 27.7 m (53 cubits) long and 21.53 m (41 cubits) broad; the western tomb (L25/2) had dimensions of 21.68 × 15.65 m (42 × 30 cubits). Due to the fact that the masonry of L25/1 was preserved to a higher level – 6 m above the present terrain – than the masonry of L25/2 and by the simple fact that L25/1 is larger than L25/2,[35] it is possible to suppose that L25/1 was higher than L25/2. Having in mind the large-scale destruction we can suppose that both tombs were in respect of their dimensions quite high. If we would count together the height of the fallen blocks of the eastern outer face of L25/1, we can assume that this tomb was ca 8.00 m high. The twin tomb (L25/2) was, then, comparatively lower and we only guess that its height was about 6.00 m (above the original terrain).

There is also a possibility that the superstructures of the tombs were designed as stepped structures. Nevertheless, there is no direct proof for such a hypothesis.[36]

---

[35] We can suppose, having in mind the length/height ratio of the mastabas, that the tomb with the larger horizontal dimensions was also higher than the one with a shorter length.
[36] *Cf.* Khentkaus' I tomb in Giza (Hassan, *Gîza* IV, 15, pl. II:A, III) and the stepped >>

Despite the fact that the possible association of the name  *Rš(wy)* with the Tomb Complex Lepsius no. 25 was rejected by M. Verner in this monograph,[37] it is important to note that the tombs' substructures were built in the same way as burial apartments of pyramids – in large construction pits. It leads us to suggest that the tombs were initially to be constructed as two pyramids. However, we are unable to reconstruct the reasons for their subsequent development.

Due to the large-scale destruction of the entire twin-tomb monument, we could not excavate the area around this complex in its entirety. As a consequence of this fact, we can only hypothesize whether the constructions built beside both tombs (see *chapter 5.3.3.*) were functionally connected with them. Nevertheless, as there was only one, quite tiny cultic room in the eastern part of L25/1, we can suppose that these simple constructions might have been used for cultic purposes.[38]

Fig. 5.66a Fragment of a canopic jar 63a/N/2003.
Photo JK
Fig. 5.66 b Fragment of a canopic jar 63b/N/2003.

5.4. Finds from Lepsius no. 25/1
5.4.1. Stone vessels

Fragments of canopic jars
63a–b/N/2003
Limestone
a) H: 11.5 cm, max. W: 10 cm, max. thickness of the wall: 2 cm
b) H: 6 cm, max. W: 4 cm, max. thickness of the wall: 2.5 cm
Fifth Dynasty
Found within the white limestone *raksha* in the layer above the under-pavement blocks of the burial chamber in L25/1, 0.40 m to the north of the southern wall of the burial chamber and 0.80 m to the east of the western wall of the burial chamber.

These two fragments probably come from two different canopic jars.[39] The inside walls on both of the jars are concave, as compared with their rims. The rim of 63a/N/2003 is protruding outwards, whereas the rim of 63b/N/2003 is more vertical (see *figs. 5.66a–b* and *A.7*). In both cases, the rim is visibly marked off from the outer walls of the canopic jars. The outer walls of the vessels had been smoothed, not polished. The fragments of the vessels were too small to ascertain the diameter of their mouths. See also *chapters A.3.2.* and *A.4.*

Miniature bowls
Travertine
65a-j/N/2003
a) diam.: 5.8 cm, H: 2.1 cm, thickness of the walls: 0.4–1.2 cm

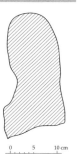
0   5   10 cm

>> pyramids of queens south of Menkaure's pyramid in Giza (Reisner, *Menkaure*, Plan VII; Jánosi, *Pyramidenanlagen*, 25–28, Abb.6, and discussion on pp. 82–87 and Abb. 33). If this hypothesis was correct, then we could suppose two steps in the case of the superstructures of both tombs.
[37] For discussion on this problem – see p. 66, 136, 137, 139, 142, 144, 146, 227–231 in this monograph, and Krejčí, *PES 2*, 2003, 64–78; *idem.*, *PES 3*, 2004, 203–213; Krejčí, Verner, *Sokar 8*, 2004, 20–22; Krejčí, Verner, in: *Fs. Sawy*, 159–165; Krejčí, in: *Abusir and Saqqara 2005*, 261–273.
[38] The building of the cultic structures outside the tomb itself was one of the typical features of the private tomb architecture of the period. We can enumerate some of them located at the Abusir Necropolis – *i.e.* the tombs of Djadjaemankh (Borchardt, *Neuserre*, Bl 22) and that of Userkafankh (*op. cit.*, Bl. 20), in the "Complex of funerary cult structures" in front of the mastaba of Khekeretnebty – Verner, in: Verner, Callender, *Djedkare's Cemetery*, 77–84 and figs. G1 and F1; we can document the same approach and in a way also in the case of the Mastaba of Ptahshepses – Krejčí, *Ptahshepses*, 78–144. Such constructions outside the tombs are attested in all Old Kingdom cemeteries.
[39] We can suppose that there was a standard number of four canopic jars. See also p. 272 in this monograph and P. Vlčková, Royal canopic jars from Abusir, *ArOr 70*, 2002, 147–162; *idem*, in: Verner et al., *Raneferef*, 338–341; *idem, Abusir XV. Stone Vessels from the Mortuary Complex of Raneferef at Abusir*, 53–54.

b) diam.: 5 cm, H: 1.6 cm, thickness: 0.4-0.7 cm

c) diam.: 4.9 cm, H: 1.7 cm, thickness: 0.5-0.8 cm; marks of an *off-axis* drilling

d) diam.: 5.9 cm, H: 1.4 cm, thickness: 0.3-0.6 cm

e) diam.: 5.3 cm, H: 1.5 cm, thickness: 0.5-1.0 cm

f) diam.: 5.3 cm, H: 1.8 cm, thickness: 0.5-0.7 cm

g) diam.: 5 cm, H: 1.2 cm, thickness: 0.4-0.9 cm; very obvious marks of drilling; flat bottom

h) diam.: 5.8 cm, H: 1.6 cm, thickness: 0.6 cm

i) diam.: 5.4 cm, H: 1.4 cm, thickness: 0.4-0.9 cm; marks of an *off-axis* drilling

j) diam.: 5.2 cm, H: 1.5 cm, thickness: 0.6–0.8 cm

Fifth Dynasty

Found in the area of the burial apartment of L25/1, in the area of the first horizontal part of the accessing corridor. The miniature bowls lay in the layer of *raksha* mixed with, blown sand and brown sand, just above the floor; the items were scattered in the area of the whole room: from the point ca 0.40 m to the west of the south-western corner of the room as far as 2 m to the north of the south-eastern corner of the room.

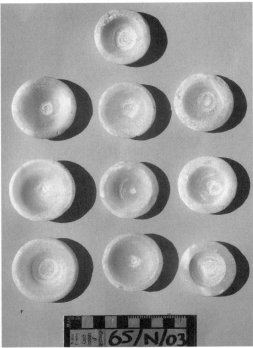

All the items represent simple miniature bowls made of travertine[40], polished on the outside. Their interiors bear clear marks of drilling, and the vessels are also smoothed there (*figs. 5.67a–b* as well as *fig. A.13.*).

a) Not very well articulated rim, slightly bevelled toward outside

b) Not very well articulated rim, slightly bevelled toward outside

c) Not very well articulated rim, slightly bevelled toward outside, below the rim, there is a vertical part of the bowl's wall

d) Flat, not very well articulated rim, slightly bevelled toward outside

e) Well articulated rim, bevelled toward outside

f) Well articulated rim, bevelled toward outside

g) Flat rim, well articulated vertical part on the wall from exterior below the rim.

h) Well articulated rim, bevelled toward outside

i) Quite flatly articulated rim, bevelled toward outside; below the rim an uneven vertical part of the bowl's wall

j) Quite flatly articulated rim, bevelled toward outside, below the rim a short vertical part of the bowl's wall

Such model bowls are the standard part of the burial equipment dated to the Old Kingdom.[41] For the evaluation of the items from L25/1, see *Appendix* in this monograph.

Fig. 5.67a Miniature bowls 65/N/2003.
Photo KV

Fig. 5.67b Side-view of five bowls of the exc. no 65/N/2003.
Photo KV

Miniature vase
69/N/2003
Basalt
H: 6.5 cm, diam.: of the mouth 4 cm, diam. of the bottom: 1.4 cm, W: 3.1 cm
Fifth Dynasty

---

[40] *Cf.* J. A. Harrel, Misuse of the term "alabaster" in Egyptology, *GM* 119, 1990, 37–42; R. and D. Klemm, Calcit-Alabaster oder Travertine? Bemerkungen zum Sinn und Unsinn petrographischer Bezeichnungen in der Ägyptologie, *GM* 122, 1991, 61–70.

[41] P. Vlčková, *Abusir XV. Stone Vessels from the Mortuary Complex of Raneferef at Abusir*, 68–69.

Fig. 5.68 Miniature vase 69/N/2003. Photo KV

This item was found in the above-ground layer of *raksha* in the area of the burial apartment of L25/1, 2.50 m to the south of the south-eastern corner of the east-west oriented part of the access corridor and 0.80 m to the west of the eastern wall of the space.

This miniature of a vase has its interior partially drilled – to the depth of 1 cm. The walls of the interior bear clear marks of drilling. The outer walls are polished. The rim of the vase is flat and the vessel's wall below it is concave. The bottom of the vase is flat (see *fig. 5.68*).

Fig. 5.69a Lid of vessel (?), exc. no. 99/N/2003. Photo JK

Fig. 5.69b Side view of the lid, exc. no. 9/N/2003. Photo JK

Lid?
99/N/2003
Reddish limestone
Diam.: 7.1 cm, thickness: 2.6 cm
Fifth Dynasty
The item was found during excavations in the southern half of the burial chamber, in its north-south axis, 2.75 m from the southern wall of the preserved southern wall of the access corridor. The object was unearthed in the layer of blown sand above the floor of the chamber.

The object is partially destroyed; about 40 per cent of its volume is missing. The reverse side of the lid(?) is well worked, smoothed, with two scratches creating a cross-like pattern made slightly off the lid's axis. There are remains of two colour coats – light, pinkish-red colour and dark, brownish-red colour (*fig. 5.69a*). The obverse of the lid is more roughly worked than is the case with the reverse and it has the form of a segment of a circle (see *fig. 5.69b*). The function of the object is not certain; however, it might have functioned as a lid of a stone vessel or, taking account of its discovery in the burial chamber, even of a canopic jar.

5.4.2. Stone Implements

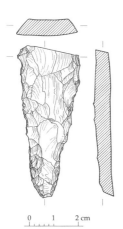

0   1   2 cm

Fig. 5.70 Flint blade 112/N/2004.

Blade
112/N/2004
Flint
L: 6.1 cm, W: 2.5 cm, thickness: 0.7 cm
Fifth Dynasty
Found in the layer of wind-blown sand to the north of the entrance into the descending corridor of L25/1, 14.5 m to the north and 1.25 m to the west of the north-western corner of the entrance to the tomb's substructure.

A blade with a pointed tip, fine retouching, and with a ridge on the obverse and a flat reverse (*fig. 5.70*).[42]

5.4.3. Metallic objects

Model of a hoe
2/N/2001
Copper
L: 5.5 cm, W: 1.7–2 cm, H: 1.6 cm
Fifth Dynasty

---

[42] For the same type of a blade see Svoboda, in: Verner *et al.*, *Raneferef*, 507, fig. 2.11.11:4.

Found during the cleaning of the area around the north-eastern corner of the tomb L25/1, in a layer of wind-blown yellow sand in between the large blocks of limestone, 3.25 m to the east of the north-eastern corner of the tomb, ca 1 m below the preserved masonry.

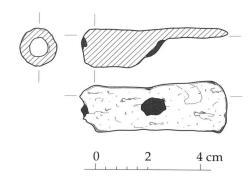

A corroded model made of copper, showing a hoe.[43] The model features a circular mounting designed for the fastening of a handle. There are small remains of a wooden handle still in position in the mounting; these remains are corroded because of the long deposition of the object in unsuitable conditions (*fig. 5.71*) Due to the find-conditions, we are unable to ascertain whether this model instrument was originally a part of the burial equipment belonging to the owners of L25/1 or L25/2 (in this case it might have been brought to its find spot by tomb robbers). It is also possible that it was brought to the place of its discovery from one of the neighbouring tombs – Nebtyemneferes', Werkaure's mastaba, or another tomb.

Fig. 5.71 Copper model of a hoe 2/N/2001.

Rolled sheet
49/N/2003
Copper
L: 5 cm, max. W: 0.5 cm
Date unknown, possibly Old Kingdom
Found in the loose brown sand, 2.60 m to the north of the southern wall and 0.54 m to the east of the western wall of the chapel in L25/1.

A fragment of a copper sheet rolled into the shape of a cornet, the surface of the sheet is corroded. As a matter of course, on the basis of the find-position of this object we can suppose that it came originally from Lepsius no. 25/1, nevertheless, this hypothesis cannot be proved due to the fact of the repeated disturbance of this area. There is a question of the function of this item. It seems to be a kind of a semi-finished object, or an unfinished model.

Model bowls
70a–b/N/2003
Copper
a) H: 1.6 cm, diam.: of the mouth 5.4 cm, diam.: of the bottom: 2.7 cm
b) H: 1.5 cm, diam.: of the mouth 5.0 cm, diam.: of the bottom: 2.3 cm
Fifth Dynasty
The model bowl 70a/N/2003 was found in the above-ground layer of *raksha* in the area of the burial apartment of L25/1, 1.50 m to the east of the east wall of the east–west oriented part of the accessing corridor and 0.80 m to the west of the east wall of this space.
The bowl 70b/N/2003 was unearthed below the south-eastern corner of the preserved masonry of white limestone blocks in the east-west corridor, at the same level as the bowl 70a.

Fig. 5.72b Copper model bowls 70a–b/N/2003.

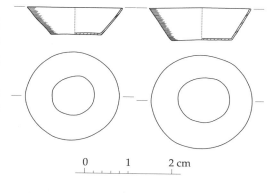

Two simple miniature bowls made of high quality copper plates. Sand grains adhere to their surfaces. The bowls are of the same form – their bottom is flat and their side walls flare from a narrower bottom to a broader rim (see *figs. 5.72a, pl. VIII* and *fig. 5.72b*). It is apparent that both model vessels were originally part of the burial equipment of the tomb owner.[44]

---

[43] Cf. Petrie, *Tools and Weapons*, pl. XIX: 1–3, 24.
[44] Cf. Hassan, *Giza* III, 140, pl. XLIV; idem, *Giza* VII, 9, pl. XI.

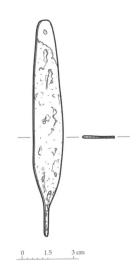

0   1.5   3 cm

**Fig. 5.73b Model instrument
75/N/2003.**

Model of a chisel
75/N/2003
Copper
L: 11.5 cm, max. W: 1.5 cm, thickness: 0.12 cm
Fifth Dynasty
Due to the find spot of this copper model – in the layer of *raksha* filling the gaps between the limestone blocks of the underpavement layer in the burial chamber – it is apparent that it came from the original burial equipment. The chisel was found below the blocks of the casing of the original western wall of the chamber, 4.30 m to the north and 0.15 m to the west of the south-western corner of the burial chamber or, more precisely, of the last, east–west oriented part of the access corridor leading to the burial chamber.

A model of a chisel (or a spatula? – see *chapter 4.5.5.*) with a pointed end to be inserted into a wooden handle; the opposite end is straight-cut. The surface of the chisel is corroded (*fig. 5.73a, pl. VIII* and *fig. 5.73b*). A typical example of this kind of model instrument has been documented in Giza.[45]

5.4.4. Fragments of statues

Fragment of a statue
6a–b/N/2001
Travertine
a) L: 12.7 cm, W: 7 cm, depth: 2.4 cm
b) L: 9 cm, W: 3 cm, H: 3.7 cm
Fifth Dynasty
Found in the layer of grey sand mixed with fragments and blocks of limestone and limestone detritus, 6 m to the north from the south wall of the chapel (room no. 1) at a depth of 3.20 m from the level of the ceiling of the chapel.

**Fig.5.75 Fragments of statue
6a–b/N/2001.**

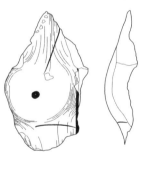

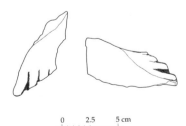

0   2.5   5 cm

Fragment of a torso 6a/N/2001 belonging to the travertine statue of a lady, with the left breast preserved. The surface of the fragment (except for the surfaces originated by the breaking of the statue, which are clean) is well polished. The surface is covered with a dark brown colour which has undergone decay during the fragment's length of time in the sand mixed with the broken mudbricks. This layer represents the original colouring of the close-fitting dress in which the lady was clothed. On the upper part of the fragment, there are imprints of a whitish beige colour representing a necklace. On the fragment, we can see only one chain of small globular beads; however, we cannot fully rule out, that the lady wore a broader necklace. Her nipple, as well as the edge of her robe, are marked by lines of black colour (*fig. 5.74, pl. VIII* and *fig. 5.75*). On the fragment no. 6a/N/2001, no part of a wig is depicted; we can therefore suppose that the lady wore a short wig and not a tripartite wig.

Object exc. no. 6b/N/2001 represents a fragment of the instep of the left leg of a statue. Individual toes were separated by cuts, which deepened towards the ends of the toes. This separation has been accentuated by lines of black colour (*fig. 5.76, pl. VIII* and also *fig. 5.75*).

Not only due to the corresponding measurements, but also due to the technique used in working the stone surface, exc. no. 6b/N/2001 very probably comes from the same statue as is the case with 6a/N/2001. If this statue had been preserved completely, then it would have been ca 55–60 cm high. It is apparent also, that, because of the high degree of workmanship and the type of robe in which the lady was clothed (a close-fitting dress very probably with broad straps) we can suppose that the lady depicted in the statue belonged to the upper social stratum and there

---

[45] *Cf.* Hassan, *Giza* III, 140, fig. 118, pl. XLIV.

is every probability that it belonged to a member of the royal family.[46] We have to underline here that the fragments were found in a sand layer mixed with fragments of limestone, about 1.5 m above the pavement of the chapel. Therefore, we cannot rule out the notion that the fragments were brought to this place by the stone robbers and tomb robbers from another part of the tomb complex, or even another monument located around this complex.

Fragment of a statue
57/N/2003
Travertine
L: 15 cm, W: 8 cm, depth 3 cm
Found in the layer of brown sand and fragments of limestone (in which the disarticulated human corpses – exc. no. 48/N/2003 – were scattered), 5.80 m to the north from the south-east corner of the chapel, at a level 3.10 m below the original ceiling level of the chapel, above its eastern wall.

Unfortunately, only a small fragment of a statue was found. The surface of the statue was well polished. The features of the statue are marked with black lines (*fig. 5.77*). Despite the fact that the fragment is small, it is possible to say that it represents the outer part of a left leg (below the knee?). There are also some remains of red colour.

Only the fact that the statue from which the fragment originated was made of travertine allows us to suppose that this fragment might have been connected with the statue fragments exc. no. 6a–b/N/2001. Due to the fragmentary preservation of the all three fragments, however, it was not possible to join them successfully and therefore it remains only a hypothesis.

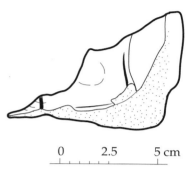

0   2.5   5 cm

Fig. 5.77 Fragment of a travertine statue 57/N/2003.

5.4.5. Wood

Stele
93/N/2003
Wood
H: 15 cm, W: 7 cm, depth: 2.7 cm
Fifth-Sixth Dynasty
Found during the work in the *sondage* located in the area between L25/1 and L25/2 under a large block near the base of L25/1, 1 m to the south from the southern wall of L25/1

A small, neatly made wooden stele with the figure of a striding male, apparently an official, on the *verso*. Only the face and frontal part of the torso have broken away, otherwise, the wooden plank is in fairly good condition. The man is depicted in a long kilt belted by a band; his right hand is depicted hanging alongside his body. On the *recto*, there are discernible outlines of a male striding figure, also wearing a long kilt. That man also wears a wig, of which the rear side has been preserved. Unfortunately, the facial part of this person's head, neck and the whole right part of body

Fig. 5.79a–b Votive wooden stele 93/N/2003, *verso, recto.*

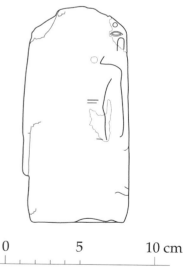

0   5   10 cm

[46] Personal communication by H. Benešovská. For further reading concerning the date, see: P. Jánosi, The Queens of the Old Kingdom and their Tombs, *BACE* 3 (1992), 51–57; B. Fay, Royal Women in Sculpture, in: *L'art de l'Ancient Empire égyptien*, 101–147; *idem*, Royal Women as represented in Sculpture During the Old Kingdom, in: *Critères de datation* 159–186; N. Cherpion, La statuaire privée d'Ancien Empire: Indices de datation, in: *Critères de datation* 97–142; B. Fay, A Royal (?) Woman, in: *Eternal* Egypt, 70–72.

is missing. His left hand hangs alongside his body. The fact that the figure was accompanied by hieroglyphic texts is revealed by faint remains of a few hieroglyphic signs among which only the sign *r* can be deciphered (see *fig. 5.78, pl. VIII* and *figs. 5.79a–b*). Unfortunately, the stele's decoration is almost destroyed, the dating of the stele is thus almost impossible. Nevertheless, the fine features of the male figure, as well as the way, the remaining *r* sign was executed, we can date the stele to the end of the Fifth Dynasty or to the Sixth Dynasty.

We can suppose that the stele was votive in its function; however, due to its find spot, outside the tomb-complex itself, there is a possibility that it was brought to the find spot from a neighbouring tomb during the later period of the development of the area. It seems that the stela was dedicated to the mortuary cult of an unknown person. As good quality wood was used, and as the craftsmanship was of a high standard, this person clearly did not come from a low social stratum.

Fragment of a vessel
64/N/2003
Wood, golden foil
L: 3.4 cm, H: 1.1: m, depth: 0.8 cm
Fifth Dynasty
Found 1.40 m to the north from the south-eastern corner of the door frame (one of the spaces of the access corridor to the burial chamber) at a level of 0–1.50 m above the under-pavement layer of limestone blocks.

A small fragment of a vessel made of wood with golden foil on both its walls. The fragment contains part of the rim, which was rounded. Under the golden foil there was a brown-beige slip which may have helped to adhere the foils onto the surface of the vessel (*fig. 5.80, pl. IX*). It was not possible to ascertain the diameter of the vessel's mouth – the fragment is too small. Due to the find spot of the fragment in the lowermost level of the filling of the burial chamber, we suppose that this item came from a vessel once belonging to the burial equipment of the original tomb owner.

Fragments of a vessel?
76a–e/N/2003
Wood
a) W: 2.6 cm, H: 3 cm, depth: 1 cm
b) W: 2.2 cm, H: 3 cm, depth: 1 cm.
c) W: 6.4 cm, H: 2.5 cm, depth: 0.7 cm
d) W: 1 cm, H: 3.3 cm
e) W. 0.75 cm, H: 4 cm
Fifth Dynasty
Found in the layer of *raksha* in the under-pavement layer of the limestone blocks in the burial chamber, below the casing of the original western wall of the chamber, 4.30 m to the north and 0.15 m to the west from the south-western corner of the burial chamber, respectively the last part of the access corridor leading to the burial chamber.

Fragments of possibly one votive(?) vessel (a bowl?) made of wood. On the surface there are remains of white slip. The individual parts of the vessel are joined together by means of small tenons, which still remain in position (*fig. 5.81*). The rim of the vessel is distinctly rounded from the outside and it is slightly flattened at the top.

Fig. 5.81 Fragments of a wooden vessel(s) 76a–d/N/2003. Photo KV

Fragments of a case
66a–c/N/2003
Wood
a) L: 6 cm, W: 3.9 cm, depth: 1 cm
b) L: 6 m, W: 2.2 cm, depth: 0.6 cm
c) L: 4.2 cm, W: 1.2 cm, depth: 0.7 cm
Fifth Dynasty
Fragments 66a–b/N/2003 found in the area of the burial chamber in a layer of grey-brown sand with the fragments of limestone. Item 66c/N/2003 found in the south-eastern corner of the burial chamber, in a slot between a casing block and a block of the under-pavement layer of limestone blocks.

Three fragments of a wooden case(s?) with beige colour on the surface on which decoration made of golden foil has been adhered. Also these fragments come very probably from the original burial chamber. The fragment 66c/N/2003 which includes a part of a small circular hollow (diam. 0.9–1.0 cm, see *fig. 5.82, pl. IX*) resembles similar internal parts to the toilet boxes dated to the later periods[47]. The hollows were used for cointaining of the toilet containers and flasks. We were not able to connect the three fragments together, so that there is a doubt whether they were part of one box or more pieces of furniture.

A fragment of a box
71/N/2003
Wood
L: 20 cm, W: 6 cm, depth: 0.5 cm
Fifth Dynasty?
Found in the layer of *raksha*, 1.20 m to the north and 0.20 m to the west from the most northern preserved part of white limestone casing of the eastern wall of the access corridor to the burial chamber.

Fig. 5.83 A fragment of a toilet box.
Photo KV

Very much weathered fragment of a wooden plank with one completely preserved oval opening and at least five others only partially preserved. There were apparently two sizes of the openings: one larger had a diameter 3.0–3.3 cm (as we can see in the preserved one example), the other three were possibly smaller, but their diameter is not possible to ascertain (*fig. 5.83*). The function of this piece is the same as in the case of exc. no. 66c/N/2002. This plank was apparently an internal part of a toilet box (see note 47). It is apparent that the box originally contained two rows of openings for the placing of cosmetic flasks.

Part of a coffin
72/N/2003
Wood
W: 21–26 cm, H: 19.5 cm, depth: 3 cm
Late Period, Graeco-Roman Period
Found in the level of clear, blown sand, 1 m to the east from the secondary burials exc. no. 73/N/2003, 0.30 m above the level of the floor of the doorway to the chapel.

A part of a coffin, very probably of a trough. The wooden plank on the outer (?) side is covered by a thick black colour, on which we can see decoration made in

---

[47] Killen, *Furniture* II, 28, pl. 14 and 26–28, fig. 46, pl. 12.

**Fig. 5.85 Part of a coffin
72/N/2003.**

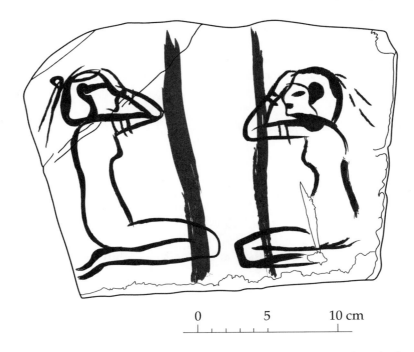

light yellow colour. The decoration consists of two kneeling female figures (Eset and Nebthet?) posed in a lamenting gesture, with hands raised in front of their faces. The figures are depicted as kneeling and looking at each other from their respective sides of the board. Each woman is dressed in a tight robe and on their arms they have circlets and bracelets. They wear bag wigs on their heads on which are tied bands of fabric which end in knots at the backs of their heads (see *figs. 5.84, pl. IX* and *fig. 5.85*).

A face mask from a coffin
98/N/2003
Wood
Max. H: 22 cm, max. W: 19 cm, max. depth 3 cm
Late Period, Graeco-Roman Period
Found in the same archaeological situation as the anthropological material (exc. no. 74/N/2003) in the layer of wind-blown sand and large white limestone blocks, to the east from the chapel of L25/1 in the level 0–1.50 m above the pavement of the doorway between vestibule and the chapel.

This object represents part of a wooden coffin – a face mask, very possibly of a female. The person wears a simple wig. Below it, we can see two amygdaloidal eyes with an edge indicating an eyebrow, a symmetrical nose and full lips. Cheeks are full and the chin is rounded. These facts enable us to assume that the coffin belonged to a woman. The surface of the mask is covered by a calcareous white plaster, but no other piece of decoration, *e.g.*, lines defining features of the female's face, remained (see *fig. 5.86*).

**Fig. 5.86 Face mask
98/N/2003.**

5.4.6. Pottery

Vessel
97/N/2003
H: 19 cm, max. diam.: 12 cm
Fifth Dynasty
Found during the excavation of the above-ground layer in the area of the burial chamber of L25/1.

A vessel thrown on the potter's wheel (in the interior, there are marks of turning). The bottom of the vessel is pointed. The vessel was made of well fired pottery. On the surface of the vessel there are remains of light red slip.

Bottle
50/N/2003
Pottery
H: 9.70 cm, diam.: max. 5.6 cm, diam.: min. 2.7 cm, thickness of the wall: 0.1–0.9 cm
Fifth Dynasty
Found in the layer of loose brown sand in the vestibule – 1.08 m to the east of the south-western corner of the vestibule and 1.09 below the level of the room's roof.

Bottle made of quality pottery: the rim is rounded, slightly everted. The outer walls were smoothed and covered by red slip (*fig. 5.87*).

Vessel
96/N/2003
Pottery
New Kingdom
Found in the same archaeological situation as the anthropological material (exc. no. 74/N/2003) in the layer of wind-blown sand and large white limestone blocks, to the east from the chapel in the level 0.00–1.50 m above the pavement of the doorway between vestibule to the chapel and the chapel itself.

A vessel thrown on the potter's wheel (in the interior, there are marks of the turning) made of a high quality fired material. The mouth of the vessel, which is preserved only partially, is open, however, the rim itself is missing. The bottom of the vessel is egg-shaped (see *fig. 5.88*).

Fig. 5.87 Vessel 50/N/2003.
Photo JK
Fig. 5.88 Vessel 96/N/2003.
Photo JK

Bowl
100/N/2003
Pottery
H: 6.5 cm, diam.: 10.4 cm
Third Intermediate Period
Found in the same archaeological situation as the anthropological material (exc. no. 74/N/2003) in the layer of wind-blown sand and large white limestone blocks, to the east from the chapel in the level 0.00–1.50 m above the pavement of the doorway between the vestibule and chapel. However, due to the large-scale destruction of the area of the secondary cemetery, it is not possible to connect this find with the excavated secondary burials and other anthropological material excavated in this area.

Fig. 5.89 Bowl 100/N/2003.
Photo JK

A bowl thrown on the potter's wheel (on both the interior and exterior wall of the bowl, there are marks of turning). The rounded rim of the bowl is drawn slightly into the interior of the bowl. The bottom is tapered. A high quality fired material (see *fig. 5.89*).

Sherd
92/N/2003
Pottery, paint – blue, red ochre, black
5.8 × 5.0 cm
New Kingdom
Found in the layer of wind-blown sand and white limestone blocks during the excavation of the south-eastern corner of the tomb L25/1.

A small fragment of unglazed buff pottery with a striped decoration in blue, red ochre and black colour. The decoration consists of a horizontal band of blue and white and vertical stripes of interchanging buff and stripes of black, blue and red colour (see *fig. 5.90, pl. X*).[48]

Flask
113a/N/2004
Pottery
H: 11.1 cm, max. diam.: 5.1 cm, diam.: of the bottom 3.8 cm, diam of the mouth: 2.1 cm
Late Roman Period
Found during the excavation of the burial pit 111/N/2004 in the layer of wind-blown sand, ca 0.30 m below the surface of the hard, beaten layer of mud and pottery sherds (*dakka*) in which the pit has been excavated. The finding circumstances show that this find does not belong to the burial equipment of the deceased person as the burial itself was put deeper (0.90 m).

A small flask made on the potter's wheel with a handle and tall thrown neck. The material is fine with an addition of sand and is of beige colour. On the surface, there are clear marks of smoothing. The bottom of the flask has been cut by means of a string, leaving typical marks on the base (*fig. 5.91*).

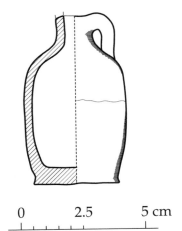

0   2.5   5 cm

Fig. 5.91 Flask 113a/N/2004.

Flask
113b/N/2004
Pottery
H: 7.3 cm, max. diam.:4.3, diam.: of the bottom 3.6 cm, diam.: of the mouth 1.4 cm
Late Roman Period
Its find spot was the same as 113a/N/2004.

A small flask made on the potter's wheel with a handle and long neck. The material is fine and is of orange-red colour. On the surface, there are clear marks of smoothing (*fig. 5.92*). On the bottom there are typical marks made from cutting off the wheel by means of a string.

5.4.7. Varia

Fragments of a papyrus roll
56/N/2003
Papyrus
Fifth Dynasty
Tiny fragments of a papyrus roll were found in the area of the doorway between the vestibule and the chapel of L25/1, in the layer 35–40 cm below the crown of the preserved masonry of the doorway, in the area of 3.60–4.20 m to the north from the south-western corner of the vestibule and 0.60 m to the east from the western wall of the chapel.

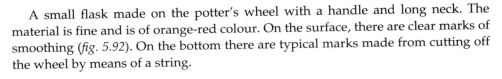

0   2.5   5 cm

Fig. 5.92 Flask 113b/N/2004.

Several fragments of a papyrus roll with a hieroglyphic text on the *verso* and *recto*. For the detailed description and for the evaluation, see the report and the analysis in *chapter 5.6*.

---

[48] Fragments of similar blue painted pottery dated to the New Kingdom were found in the Ptahshepses mastaba (Charvát, *Pottery*, 181–182 and Benešovská, Vlčková, *Secrets of the desert*, 304–305); for further information on blue decorated pottery from the New Kingdom – see Hope, *CCÉ* 1, 1994.

A false door stele
8/N/2001
Limestone
L: 27 cm, W: 16 cm, H: 5.3 cm
Late Old Kingdom

This object was found during the archaeological excavation in the *sondage* between the pyramid L24 and the tomb L25/1, in the axis of the descending corridor of the latter monument, 10.40 m to the north from the preserved northern face of the outer wall of L25/1, in the layer of wind-blown sand and large limestone blocks from the destroyed outer wall of the tomb. It lay at 2.05 m below the preserved crown of the northern face of the tomb.

A small stele of the false door with quite a weathered surface. No trace of an inscription is detectable. Despite the fact that the surface of the false door is badly weathered, it does not seem that it bore any inscription or other decoration (*fig. 5.93a, pl. X, fig. 5.93b*). The stela, following its style and the artwork, can be dated to the Sixth Dynasty. It is likely that this small stela was built in a minor tomb belonging to a member of a lower social stratum. Such a tomb might have been built in this area during the period when the original cults had been already declining and the monuments started to decay. It is possible that the stela, due to its find spot, came from the area of the Pyramid Complex Lepsius no. 24 where secondary burying is attested during the late Old Kingdom (see *chapters 4.5.1.* and *4.7.*).

Beads
53a–b/N/2003
Cornelian and shell
a) L: 2 cm, max. diam.: 0.8 cm
b) L: 1.8 cm, max. W: 1.3 cm
Late Period

Found in the layer of brown sand with fragments of limestone and limestone detritus and the anthropological material filling the northern part of chapel of the tomb L25/1, in the level 0-2.50 m above the pavement of the chapel's area.

a) Cornelian bead of the tear-drop shape with a hole for the string and a flat bottom (see *fig. 5.94, pl. X*).
b) A white shell partially drilled for inserting a string (for both beads, see *fig. 5.95*).

Bowl
16/N/2001
Limestone
Diam.: 12–12.3 cm, H: 5.5 cm, W: of the wall 1.6–3.5 cm
Fifth Dynasty or Late Period

This item was found in the layer of wind-blown sand, which filled the upper level of the construction pit of L25/1, in the middle of the pit, and its date is problematic.

A semi-finished half-globular bowl, roughly worked, made secondarily from a piece of white limestone. The rim of the bowl is flat with no further decoration (*fig. 5.96*).

Fig. 5.93b A small false door stele 8/N/2001.

0   10   20 cm

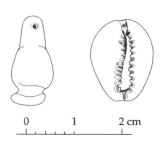

0   1   2 cm

Fig. 5.95 Beads exc. no. 53a–b/N/2003.

Lid
17/N/2001
Quartzite
Upper diam.: 5.3 cm, middle diam.: 3.8 cm, lower diam.: 4.7 cm, H: 1.5 cm
Late Period, Graeco-Roman Period?
The lid was found to the east of the tomb L25/1, in the surface layer of wind-blown sand and fragments of limestone, 3.5 m to the east from the western wall of the vestibule and 1 m to the north from the southern wall of the same room, 0.30 m below the modern surface.

A lid made of close-grained quartzite with a mixture of iron oxide, used together with a container (for *kohl*?). On the surface, some remains of colour (*kohl*?) were found. There are also remains of a layer of bandage on the outer surface of the lid (see *fig. 5.97*). Very probably, it belonged to a small toilet vessel. Due to the find spot of this item, we can suppose that it originated during the later period of the Egyptian history – most probably during the Late Period or Graeco-Roman Period. The lid might It can be a part of the burial equipment of one of the secondary burials which filled the whole eastern side of L25/1.

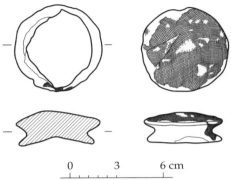

0   3   6 cm

Fig. 5.96 Limestone bowl 16/N/2001.
Photo KV

Fig. 5.97 Quartzite lid 17/N/2001.

Scarab
5/N/2001
Faience
L: 1.8 cm, W: 1.2 cm, H: 0.7 cm
New Kingdom – Late Period
This scarab was found in the area of the chapel, in the level of of 1.90 m above the floor of the chapel and 3.12 m from the southern wall of the vestibule and in the line of the face of the destroyed western wall of the chapel. The item lay in the layer of grey sand, fragments of limestone and limestone detritus.

On the lower side of the scarab a stylised scene is depicted, consisting of a figure of a king wearing the Lower-Egyptian crown kneeling in an adoration gesture in front of an obelisk. The height of the obelisk is the same as the king's figure. Above the king, two hieroglyphic signs have been incised, namely *nfr nṯr*. Below the whole scene, a hieroglyphic sign *nb* is located. Along the longer axis of the scarab's base plate, a narrow tunnel was made which was circular in its section. It was apparently used for the insertion of a string by which the scarab was hung (see *fig.5.98a–b, pl. X*).Unfortunately, this type of scarab decoration of with the king adoring the obelisk is not easy to date. This type might have been dated to a long period covering time span from the reign of Thutmose III till the First Millenium BC.[49]

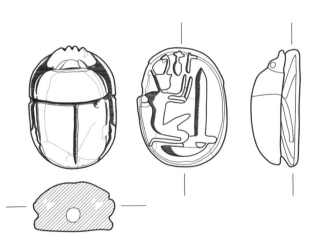

Fig. 5.98b Scarab 5/N/2001.

Bead
10/N/2001
Faience
L: 0.9 cm, W: 1.7 cm, H: 1.5 cm
Late (Saite) Period
Found 4.5 m to the east from the eastern wall of the vestibule in L25/1 and 3.75 m to the north from its southern wall, at the level 3 m below the original roof of the vestibule.

---

[49] *Cf.* Hall, *Royal Scarabs*, 143; Hornung, Staehlin, *Skarabäen Basel*, 189–190, 253–254, Tafel 31:315, Tafel 32: 314, 316; Regner, *Skarabäen und Skaraboide*, 17–18.

Fragment of a pendant representing a crown of the goddess Hathor/ Eset with horns and a sun disk in between.[50] On the rear side of the pendant, one can see a small loop for an attachment string. Material, of which the bead was made, is light blue (*fig. 5.99, pl. XI* and *fig. 5.100*).

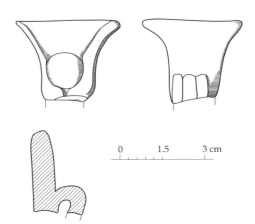

Pendant?
11/N/2001
Faience
L: 3.5 cm, W: 1.7 cm, H: 0.6 cm
Late or Ptolemaic Period
Found in the surface layer of wind-blown sand and fragments of limestone 3 m to the east from the western wall of the vestibule in L25/1 and 1.5 m to the north from the southern wall of this room.

Fig. 5.100 Faience bead 10/N/2001.
Fig. 5.101 Faience pendant 11/N/2001.

An oblong fragment of a faience object which could probably be described as a pendant. This seems to be supported by a partially preserved hollow running along the long axis of the object which was used for the insertion of a string. This object might have been used as a pendant. The glaze is blue and on the preserved edge of the object, there is the 3 mm wide black band. The object is flat with no other decoration (see *fig. 5.101*).

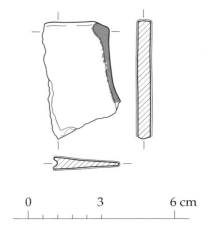

Beads
54/N/2003
Faience
Various dimensions, max. L.: 3.5 cm, max. diameter: 0.28 cm, min. diameter: 0.15 m
Late Period
Found in the layer of brown sand mixed with fragments of limestone, ca 3 m to the north from the south-western corner of the vestibule.

Various sizes of tubular faience beads with various glazes on the surface.[51] They apparently originated from the secondary cemetery covering the eastern part of the superstructure of L25/1.

Amulet
55/N/2003
Faience
L: 3.5 cm, W: 3 cm, depth: 0.7 cm
Late Period
Found in the debris layer in the area of the burial chamber, near the preserved masonry of white limestone.

This object represents a part of an *udjat* amulet with multicoloured decoration (*fig. 5.102, pl. XI*). Due to its appearance[52] we can date this bead to the Late Period. The bead can be connected with intrusive secondary burials which were also found scattered in the area of the burial chamber.

Bead
59/N/2003
Faience
L: 1.2–1.6 cm, depth: 0.4 cm, diam. of the bead's eye: 0.17 cm
Late Period – Twenty-fifth Dynasty

---

[50] *Cf.* Andrews, *Amulets*, fig. 82:f – this example which is similar to our exc. no. 10/N/2001 – has been dated to the Saite Period.
[51] *Cf.* Callender, in: Verner, *et al.*, *Raneferef*, 442–449, figs. 2.2.8–10.
[52] Müller-Winkler, *Objekt-Amulette*, 151–156, Taf. VIII: 150, 155.

Found in the layer of grey-brown sand 2.30 m to the west from the core masonry of the eastern wall of chapel and 6.80 m to the north from the south-western corner of the vestibule.

Faience bead in the form of an *udjat* eye with black colour decoration made on the green-blue faience glaze. Along the longer axis of the bead, an aperture was drilled for inserting of the string (*fig. 5.103, pl. XI*).[53]

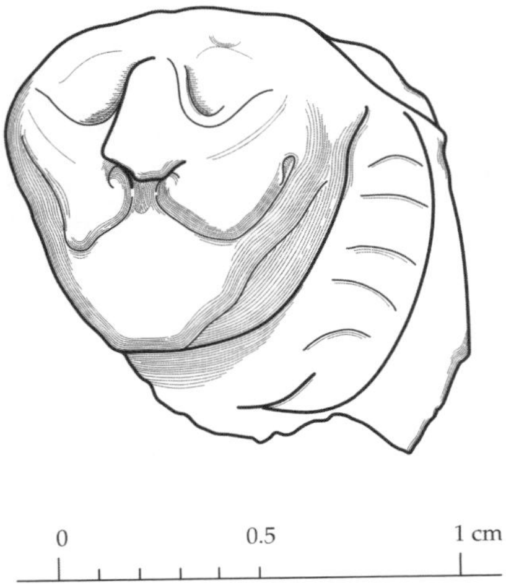

Fig. 5.104 Fragment of a faience bead in form of a lioness.

0   0.5   1 cm

Bead
62/N/2003
Faience
L: 1 cm, H: 1 cm, depth: 1 cm
Late Period
This faience bead was found in the layer of wind-blown sand and large white limestone blocks fallen from the outer wall of L25/1, ca 1 m below the present surface, in the east-western axis of L25/1, 4 m to the east from the eastern wall of L25/1.

Fragment of a faience bead in the form of a lioness. A part of a bead with the left part of the animal's face is missing (*fig. 5.104*).[54]

Ring
15/N/2001
Glass
Diam. of the ring: 1.8 cm, diam. in cut: 0.35 cm
Late or Arabic Period
The ring was found during the excavation of the blown sand layer mixed with the burials (3/N/2001) in the east part of the superstructure of L25/1, 4 m to the east from the south-eastern corner of the vestibule and 1.60 m to the north from the southern wall of this room.

Fig. 5. 105 Glass ring 15/N/2001.
Photo KV

A glass ring with a very short break (see *fig. 5. 105*).

Beads
85a–c/N/2003
Glass
Late Period
a) H: 0.4 cm, diam.: 0.7 cm, diam. of the hollow: 0.3 cm
b) H: 0.5–0.8 cm, diam.: 1.0 cm, diam. of the hollow 0.3 cm
c) L: 2.0 cm, diam.: 1.0 cm, diam. of the hollow: 0.25 cm
Found in the area of the skull of a child exc. no. 73/N/2003 unearthed to the east from L25/1.

Three colour beads with hollows for inserting a string to which they were attached. Two beads (85a–b) are discoidal, the exc. no. 85c/N/2003 is a cylinder (see *fig. 5.106, pl. XI*).

Band of fabric
4/N/2001
Linen fabric
L: 22 cm, W: 4.4 cm
Coptic Period

[53] *Cf.* Müller-Winkler, *Objekt-Amulette*, 151–156, Taf. VIII: 150, 155.
[54] Cf. Andrews, *Amulets*, fig. 30:a and d, dated to the Third Intermediate Period.

Found during the excavation of the supporting wall to the west of the vestibule in L25/1, 0.40 m to the north from the last surviving block and 0.20 m to the west from the western wall of the chapel and 3 m below the roof of the chapel in the layer of yellowish-grey sand mixed with larger fragments of limestone.

Fig. 5.107 Piece of fabric.
Photo KV

A part of a fabric band, or a belt with fastened knot. The design of the belt is simple and consists of a broader (2.0 cm) band of white colour and several narrow bands (0.1–0.7 cm) of lighter green-blue colour interchanging with the bands (0.1–0.2 cm) of white colour (*fig. 5.107*).

5.5. Finds from Lepsius 25/2
5.5.1. Stone Instruments

Scraper
20/N/2002
Flint
L: 6.5 cm, W: 3.3 cm, H: 0.8 cm
Fifth Dynasty
Found in the layer of the ruined filling masonry (grey sand and fragments of limestone) of the tomb L25/2 in the level 1.80 m below the preserved crown of the western wall of L25/2, 1.30 m to the south from the northern wall of the construction pit of L25/2.

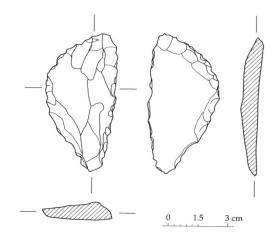

A flint scraper with raised obverse quite roughly worked and a flat reverse with edges sharpened by fine retouching. This is also the case of obverse (*fig. 5.108*).

**Fig. 5.108 Flint scraper
20/N/2003.**

Knife
82/N/2003
Flint
L: 10.2 cm, max. W: 3.8 cm, depth: 0.8 cm
Fifth Dynasty
Found in the level of the yellow sand with the limestone debris, 0.30 m below the crown of the tomb L25/2 and 0.50 m to the north from the south-western corner of the monument, closely to the western wall of L25/2.

A large blade knife made of flint with a slight retouching on its rounded tip on its obverse side. The reverse side is flat. The whole blade is curved in its section (*fig. 5.109, pl. XI and fig. 5. 110*).

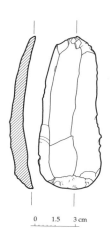

**Fig. 5. 110 Flint knife
82/N/2003.**

Blade
91/N/2003
Flint
L: 7.7 cm, W: 2.0 cm
Fifth Dynasty
Found on the surface of the contact layer in the area of the *sondage* in the area of the south-western corner of L25/2, ca 0.20 m to the south from the southern wall of the tomb L25/2 and 1.20 m to the west from the south-western corner of L25/2.

A brown flint blade (knife) with flaked surfaces and chipped edges: the obverse has a raised, flat central ridge but the reverse has a single flat surface (*fig. 5.111*). There is slight retouching on the edges of the implement.

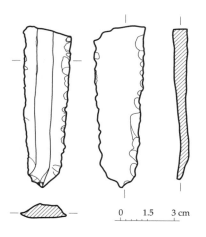

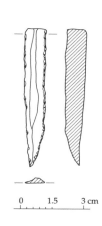

Fig. 5.111 Flint blade 91/N/2003.

Fig. 5.112 Flint blade 101/N/2003.

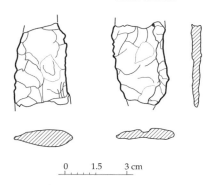

Fig. 5.113 Fragment of a knife 105/N/2004.

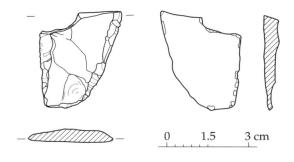

Fig. 5.114 Fragment of a flint scraper 106/N/2004.

Blade
101/N/2003
Flint
L: 6.9 cm, W: 1 cm, depth: 0.3 cm
Fifth Dynasty
This blade was found during the excavation of the surface layer of wind-blown sand and limestone detritus above the mudbrick structure lying to the south-west from the Tomb Complex Lepsius no. 25.

The narrow blade has a very fine retouching on the edges and a raised, flat central ridge on the obverse and no mark of the working on the reverse, which represents a single flat surface (*fig. 5.112*).

Fragment of a knife(?)
105/N/2004
Slate?
L: 4.1 cm, W: 2.6 cm, depth: 0.4–0.7 cm
Fifth Dynasty
This implement was unearthed in the *sondage* laid to the south from the join of L25/1 and L25/2, 3 m to the south from the southern wall of L25/2, in the level of its preserved masonry, in the layer of grey-brown sand, broken mudbricks and pottery sherds.

A fragment of a stone blade (originally of a knife?), quite roughly worked with retouching on the edges (*fig. 5.113*).

Scraper
106/N/2004
Flint
L: 3.2 cm, W: 2.9 cm, depth: 0.45 cm
Fifth Dynasty

Found during the enlarging of the *sondage* to the south of L25/2, 3.70 to the south from the southern wall of L25/2, 0.5 below its preserved crown and 2.50 m to the east from the brick wall running to the south from the south-western corner of L25/2, in the waste layer of brown sand, pottery, broken mudbricks and small limestone fragments.

A fragment of a dark flint scraper with a very fine retouching on its edges. On one side, we can see a deep notch used for inserting the scraper into the wooden handle (*fig. 5.114*). On the obverse, there is a thick ridge, whereas on the reverse only sparsely made retouching.

5.5.2. Stone vessels

Model vessel
27/N/2002
Travertine
Max. H: 4.8 cm, diam. of the neck: 2.2 cm, max. diam. of the vessel: 3.8 cm, max. diam. of the bottom: 1.5 cm
Fifth Dynasty
This fragment of a model vessel was unearthed in the layer of wind-blown sand in the space of the descending corridor of L25/2.

A fragment of a model vase – its lower part and the neck are missing. The surface of the vessel has been polished. The material on the break is weathered and the surface of the vessel is exfoliating (*fig. 5.115*). For discussion on this model vessel, see also *chapter A.3.2.*

Fig. 5.115 Fragment of a model vessel 27/N/2002. Photo KV

Model of a bowl
31/N/2002
Travertine
Diam.: 5.3 cm, H: 2.3 cm, thickness of the wall: 0.5–0.75 cm
Fifth Dynasty
Found in the layer of limestone debris, fragments of mudbricks and sand, in the area of the eastern "niche" in the construction pit of L25/2.

Quite a deep model of a bowl with un-articulated rounded rim. From outside, there are marks of drilling on its walls (see *fig. A. 11*). For further discussion on this model vessel, see also *chapter 6.3.2.*

Model of a cup
33/N/2002
Basalt
Diam. of the mouth: 3.6 cm, diam. of the bottom: 1.8 cm, H: 3.3 cm, thickness of the walls: 0.6–1.3 cm
Fifth Dynasty
Found in the layer of *raksha* in the burial chamber of L25/2, in the level above the preserved layer of the under-pavement blocks.

Figs. 5.116a–b Basalt model of a bowl 33/N/2003. Photos KV

Model of a cup with funnel-like walls, was originally part of the set for the Opening of the Mouth ritual.[55] The outer walls are polished, the interior walls bear clear marks of the drilling (see also *chapters A.3.2* and *A.4.2*, *figs. 5.116a–b*).

Fragment of a bowl
83/N/2003
Basalt
Max. H: 7.4 cm, max. W: 7 cm, max. thickness of the bowl's wall: 1.5 cm
Fifth Dynasty
Found in the *sondage* with the south-western corner of L25/2, 2.80 m to the south from the southern wall of the tomb and 1.15 to the east from the south-western corner of L25/2 in the layer of the yellow sand with limestone detritus, 50 cm under the preserved crown of the southern wall of the tomb L25/2.

A fragment of a bowl's rim, the surface has been polished. The rim is slightly separated from the inside of the vessel by a kind of a groove (see *fig. A.5* and discussion in *chapters A.3.2* and *A.4.2* as well as *fig. A.5*).

Fragment of vessel
110/N/2004
Travertine
Max. L: 13 cm, max. W: 6.7 cm, thickness of the vessel's wall: 0.75–1.15 cm
Fifth Dynasty
Found during the detracting of the layer of wind-blown sand to the south of L25/2, 4.70 m to the south of the southern wall of L25/2, 4.75 m to the west from the south-western corner of L25/2 in the level of the preserved crown of the southern wall of the tomb L25/2.

---

[55] *Cf.* Verner, in: Verner *et al.*, *Raneferef*, fig. 1.2.49.

A fragment of a travertine cylindrical vessel with a slightly outwards drawn rim. The rim is detached from outside from the wall of the vessel. The walls as from the exterior as in the interior of the vessel have been polished. We can reconstruct the diameter of the vessel's mouth as 17 cm (see also *chapters A.3.2.* and *A.4.2.*).

5.5.3. Metallic objects

Model of a chisel
30/N/2002
Copper
L: 7 cm, max. W: 0.5 cm
Fifth Dynasty
Found in the layer of *raksha* in the lower part of the descending corridor to the burial chamber.

Model of a chisel with one end rounded and the other pointed. The model is made of quality material, however, its surface is corroded with sand grains adhered (*figs. 5.117* and *fig. 5.118*).

Model implements
32a–c/N/2002
Copper

a) L: 6.4 cm, W: 1.1–2.0 cm, depth: 0.075 cm
b) L: 7.5 cm, W: 1.3–2.1 cm, depth: 0.1 cm
c) L: 6.2 cm, W: 1.0–1.6 cm, depth: 0.075 cm
Fifth Dynasty
Found in the almost the same position as chisel exc. no. 30/N/2002, 0.50 m to the south from this position.

Three models of chisels. In all the cases, both ends of the chisel are even. In one third of the body of the models, there is a constriction. The models are made of quality material; on the surface they are corroded and sand grains stick to the surface of the implements (*fig. 5.119, pl. XI* and *fig. 5.120*).

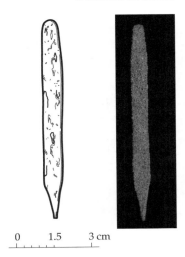
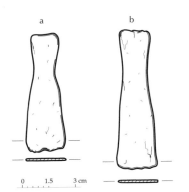

Fig. 5.117 Copper model of a chisel 30/N/2002. Photo KV
Fig. 5.118 Copper model of a chisel 30/N/2002.

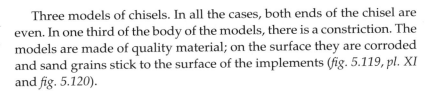

Fig. 5.120 Coper model implements 32a–c/N/2002.

Arrow
36/N/2002
Copper
L: 4.5 cm, W: 1.0 cm
Arabic Period
Found in the layer of the clean blown sand in front of the northern wall of L25/2, about 1.5 m below the preserved crown of the tomb's masonry.

Slightly deformed arrow, triangular in section and with concave sides. There are distinct ribs in the intersections of the individual sides. In the lower part, there is a circular mounting for inserting of the wooden part of the arrow (*fig. 5.121*).

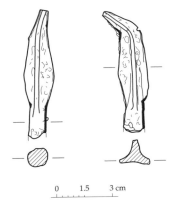

Fig. 5.121 Copper arrow 36/N/2002.

Arrow
38/N/2002
Copper
L: 2.8 cm, W: 1.0 × 1.0 cm
Arabic Period
Found in the layer of the clean blown sand 4.30 m to the north from the northern outer wall of L25/2, 0.90 m to the east from the entrance to the descending corridor and 1.75 m below the preserved crown of the tomb's masonry.

Copper arrow, triangular in section, corroded to a high degree on the surface. The sides of the arrow are concave. There is a small circular mounting for inserting of the wooden part of the arrow (*fig. 5.122*).

Arrow
39/N/2002
Copper
L: 2.0 cm, W: 1.35 cm, H: 0.20 cm
Arabic Period
This arrow was found at the same find spot as 38/N/2002, to the north from the northern outer wall of L25/2.

Fragment of a middle part of an arrow, flat in section, and with a distinct rib running along the longer axis of the arrow.

Arrow
84/N/2003
Copper
L: 1.9 cm, W: 1.0 cm
Arabic Period
Found in the layer of the clean blown sand by the south-western corner of the outer wall of the tomb L25/2, 2.90 m below the preserved crown of the tomb's masonry.

Copper arrow, triangular in section, corroded to a high degree on the surface. The sides of the arrow are concave. There is a small circular mounting for inserting the wooden part of the arrow (*fig. 5.123*).

Wedges
43a–d/N/2002
Iron
a) L: 14.3 cm, W: 5 cm, depth: 3.2 cm
b) L: 14 cm, W: 4.5 cm, depth: 3.2 cm
c) L: 13.5 cm, W: 4.3 cm, depth: 4 cm
d) L: 13.2–13.5 cm, W: 4.7 cm, depth: 3 cm
Arabic Period
Found in the layer of *raksha* in the eastern part of the construction pit of L25/2 in the level of the project zero, 4.15 m to the east from the western end of the substructural layer of large flat limestone blocks below the eastern outer wall of the tomb L25/2.

The wedges are heavy made of iron (now much corroded on the surface) and with additions of sand grains. The tip of the wedges is not sharp. The blunt end has signs of much use and is splayed at it perimeter from being hard and often hit (*fig. 5.124*).

***Warak*-pieces**
44/N/2002
Iron
Arabic Period
a) L: 16.1 cm, W: 4 cm
b) L: 15 cm, W: 4.1–4.5 cm
c) L: 12.4. W: 4.2 cm
d) L: 17.5 cm, W: 8.2 cm
Max. thickness of all pieces is 0.5 cm
Arabic Period

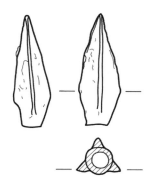

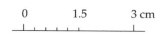

| 0 | 1.5 | 3 cm |

Fig. 5.122 Copper arrow 38/N/2002.

Fig. 5.123 Copper arrow 84/N/2003.
Photo KV

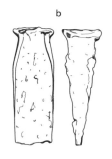

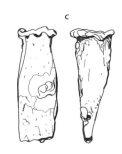

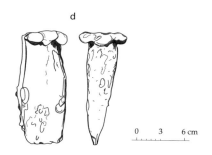

Fig. 5.124 Iron wedges 43a–d/N/2002.

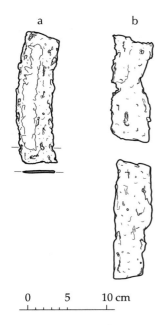

a   b

0   5   10 cm

**Fig. 5.125 Iron *warak*-pieces
44a–c/N/2002.**

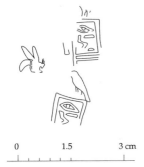

0   1.5   3 cm

Fig. 5.126 Sealing 22/N/2002.

0   0.5   1 cm

**Fig. 5.127 Sealing
23a/N/2002.**

0   1   2 cm

**Fig. 5.128 Sealing
23b/N/2002.**

Found in the layer of *raksha* in the eastern part of the construction pit of L25/2 in the level of the project zero, 4.15 m to the east from the west end of the substructural layer of large flat limestone blocks below the eastern outer wall of the tomb L25/2.

The *warak*-pieces (used to guide the direction of wedges being hammered into the stone) are all of similar size and shape but in differing states of preservation. Like the wedges (43/N/2002), they are made of iron and have become badly corroded (*fig. 5.125*).

5.5.4. Sealings

22/N/2002
L: 3.5 cm, W: 3.10
Fifth Dynasty
Found in the debris filling the construction pit of L25/2, in the level of the well worked limestone blocks of the core masonry of L25/1, *i.e.* in the eastern part of the construction pit, in the area of a "niche".

This item is a fragment of a sealing with remains of two seal impressions (see *fig. 5.126*).
   A:
Ḥr ʾIr-mȝꜥt
Ḥr ʾIr-mȝꜥt
B
…bity….

23a–c/N/2002
a) L: 3.1 cm, W: 2.1 cm
b) L: 4 cm, W: 3 cm
c) L: 3.3 cm, W: 2.7 cm
Fifth Dynasty
These broken mud sealings were found during the clearing of the north-eastern corner of the construction pit of L25/2, in the layer of grey sand and limestone debris, 1.90 m to to the south from the northern wall of the pit and 1.30 m to the west from the eastern wall of the pit (respectivelly well worked blocks of limestone belonging to the core masonry of L25/1 – see find spot of exc. no. 22/N/2002), in the level of 0.50 cm above the preserved crown of the eastern wall of the construction pit of L25/2.

23a/N/2002 (*fig. 5.127*)
1 *Ḥr Št-ib-tȝwy*
2 *ḥry-ḥbt, irr [wḏt]*

23b/N/2002 (*fig. 5.128*)
A
Ḥr [Št-ib-tȝwy]
B
1 *mry, Ḥr […], ḥm-nṯr, Ḥr […]*
2 *štp-šȝ, wḏt*
3 *pr…*

23c/N/2002 (*fig. 5.129*)
A
Ḥr […]
wꜥb…
ḥry šštȝ

B

Ḥr [Št-ib-t3wy], mrr

80a-b,d/N/2003

a) W: 2 cm, L: 3.5 cm

b) W: 2.2 cm, L: 2.5 cm

d) W: 2.5 cm, L: 2.5 cm

Found in the filling consisting of blown yellow sand and limestone rubble, *ca* 1.5 m to the south of the southern outer wall of L25/2 and 1.75 to the east from the south-western corner of L25/2, in the level of 2.00 m below the crown of the outer wall.

Fig. 5.129 Sealing 23c/N/2002.

80a/N/2003 (*fig. 5.130*)

A

1 *Ḥr [...]*

2 *Mn-iśwt-[Ny-wśr-rˁ]*

3 *...rt, pr-ˁ3, ś...*

B

n Ny-wśr-rˁ

0   1   2 cm
Fig. 5.130 Sealing 80a/N/2003.

80b/N/2003 (*fig. 5.131*)

Only faint remains of the hieroglyphic imprints in white colour are preserved.

Ḥr Št-ib-t3wy

0   1   2 cm
Fig. 5.131 Sealing 80b/N/2003.

80d/N/2003 (*fig. 5.132*)

1 *[Ḥr] Št-ib-t3wy*

2 *df3w*

90b/N/2003 (*fig. 5.133*)

L: 4.5 cm, W: 3.5 cm

Found in the above ground layer in the *sondage* at the south-western corner of L25/2.

0   1   2 cm
Fig. 5.132 Sealing 80a/N/2003.

A

1 *Ḥr Št-ib-t3wy*

2 *... ḫnty-š ...*

B

1 *Ḥr Št-ib-t3wy*

2 *... t m pr-ˁ3*

103d /N/2003 (*fig.5.134*)

Found to the south of L25/2, between the *sondage*s at the south-western corner of L25/2 and *sondage* at the join of L25/1 and L25/2, in the level of 0–1 m below the preserved crown of this wall, in the layer of pottery, mud brick and fragments of limestone.

0   1   2 cm
Fig. 5.133 Sealing 90b/N/2003.

On the surface of the partially preserved sealing we can read:

1 *...[mr] r nb.f*

2 *Ḥr Št-ib-[t3wy]*

3 *...śb3ty [mr] r [nb.f]*

4 *Ḥr Št-[ib-t3wy]*

107/N/2004 (*fig. 5.135*, pl. XX and *fig. 5.136*)

2.7 × 2 cm

Found during the clearing of the area to the south from the south-western corner of L25/2, in the level of 1.50 m below the preserved crown of the southern wall of L25/2 and 1 m to the east from the south-western corner of L25/2.

0   1   2 cm
Fig.5.134 Sealing 103d /N/2003.

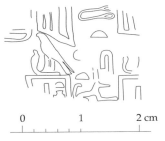

Fig. 5.136 - Sealing 107/N/2004.

Fig. 5.138 Sealing 108a/N/2004.

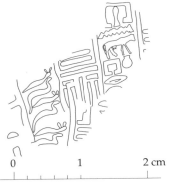

Fig. 5.140 Sealing 108b/N/2004.

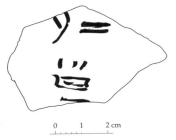

Fig. 5.141b Jar docket 104/N/2004.

Fig. 5.142 Pottery bowl 35/N/2002.

On the surface of the partially preserved mud sealing we can read:
1 *Ḥr Št-ib-tȝwy*
2 …*tt*… *šḥt rw* (?)

108a/N/2004 (*fig. 5.137, pl. XX* and *fig. 5.138*)
Found during the archaeological excavation in area between the *sondage* at the south-western corner of L25/2 and the *sondage* located to the south of the join between L25/1 and L25/2, found in the level of 1.80 m below the preserved crown of the southern outer wall of L25/2, 3.5 metres to the east from the south-western corner of L25/2. The sealing was found close to the wall.

Quite well readable sealing reads:
1 *Ḥr-[Št-ib-]tȝwy*
2 … *[m]rr wḏ nb.f*
3 … *ḏȝ*
4 *šmȝ᷄ wḏ᷄-mdw n ḥ*…
5 … *ḫnty* …

108b/N/2004 (*fig. 5.139, pl. XX* and *fig. 5.140*)
Find spot of this sealing is the same as in the case of 108a/N/2004.
1 [*Ḥr-Št-ib*]-*tȝwy*
2 *pr-ḥḏ n ḫnw* [*m*]*rr*
3 [*Ḥr-Št-ib*]-*tȝwy*
4 *ḏfȝw*
5 … *št* …

5.5.5. Pottery

Jar docket
104/N/2004
Pottery, black ink
L: 9 cm, W: 5.5 cm, thickness of the wall: 0.4 cm
Fifth Dynasty
Found 3 m to the south and 1 m below the preserved crown of the southern wall of L25/2 and 1.70 m to the east from the brick wall running southwards from the south-western corner of L25/2, in the waste layer of brown sand, pottery, broken mudbricks and small limestone fragments.

Fragment of a vessel, well burnt with white slip on the outer wall. In the interior, there are marks of the turning on the potter's wheel. On the outer wall, there is a hieratic inscription (*fig. 5.141a, pl. XX* and *fig. 5.141b*):
ȝbd 2 ȝḫt
"second month of the period of inundation"

Bowl
35/N/2002
Pottery
Upper diam.: 23 cm, lower diam.: 7.6 cm, H: 15 cm
Ptolemaic Period
This bowl was found to the north from L25/2, in the layer of wind-blown sand (below a layer of the *raksha*), ca 1.20 m below the present surface.

A deep bowl, upwards drawn and gently indented from outside rim, (*fig. 5.142*). The base of the bowl is articulated by means of a potter's knife. There are clear marks of using of rapid potter's wheel.

Flask
37/N/2002
Pottery
H: 15.0 cm, diam.: 2.6 cm (lower) and 2.8 cm (upper)
Graeco-Roman Period
The flask was found in the *sondage* along the northern outer wall of L25/2 to the east from the beginning of the descending corridor, 1 m below the present surface, 0.5 m to the north from the tomb's wall in a layer of the clean yellow blown sand.

Tall flask made of very fine material. The flask was made by the sticking on of a many pieces of the potter's clay and then smoothed. The form of the vessel is slightly asymmetric. The bottom is provided by a narrow rounded and outwards drawn rim, the same is the case of the rim along the flasket's mouth (*fig. 5.143*).

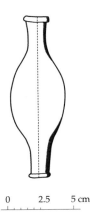

Fig. 5.143 Pottery flask 37/N/2002.

Flask
109/N/2004
Pottery
H: 11.8 cm, diam. of the mouth: 2.2 cm, diam. of the bottom: 2.2 cm, max. diam.: 3.3 cm
Late Roman Period
This small vessel was found during the enlarging of the *sondage* by the southwestern corner of L25/2, 3.30 m to the south from the southern wall of L25/2, 1.80 m below its preserved crown and 1.55 to the east from the brick wall running southwards from the south-western corner of L25/2, in the layer of yellow blown sand.

The vessel was thrown on the potter's wheel (on the bottom, there are marks of cutting by means of a string from the wheel). The body is slim and it connected with a high, slim neck with horizontal slightly raised bands. The rim of the flask is rounded from inside and flat from above (*fig. 5.144*). The flask was made of fine well burned material of light-beige colour.

5.5.6. Varia

Fragment of a statue
24/N/2002
Diorite
L: 5.5. cm, W: 3 cm, depth 1.5 cm
Old Kingdom (Fifth Dynasty?)
The diorite fragment was found during the archaeological works in the construction pit for the burial apartment, in the layer of the grey sand with small fragments of limestone, 3 m to the south from the north-west corner of the pit and 3.25 m from the eastern wall of pit, 50 cm below the preserved crown of this wall.

A fragment of a statue with one polished surface – possible (right?) shoulder (see *figs. 145a–b*). Due to the finding circumstances – not deep in the filling of the construction pit for the burial chamber of L25/2 – it is very probable that it was brought to this place from another monument in the vicinity during the frequent actions of the tomb- and stone-robbers in this part of the Abusir pyramid cemetery.

Beads
117a–b/N/2004
Faience
a) L: 0.9 cm, W: 0.7 cm, depth: 0.3 cm
b) L: 0.9 cm, W: 0.6 cm, depth: 0.28 cm
Ptolemaic Period?[56]

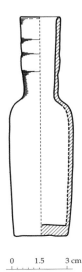

Fig. 5.144 Pottery flask 109/N/2004.

Figs.5.145a–b Fragment of a diorite statue.
Photo KV

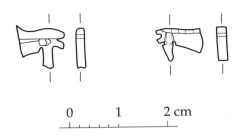

0   1   2 cm

**Fig. 5.146 Two *udjat* beads
117a–b/N/2004**

Beads were found in the layer of wind-blown sand, 6.7 m to the east from the south-western corner of L25/2, 4.70 m to the south from the southern wall of L25/2 in the level of the preserved crown.

Two beads in the form of an *udjat* eye, treated in a simplified way (see *fig. 5.146*). Both beads were drilled along their longer axis. On the surface, there is a green-blue glaze. These two *udjat* eyes are standard examples of mass production for the period.

5.6. Fragments of papyrus from Lepsius 25/1

Hana Vymazalová

5.6.1. Introduction

In 2003, several fragments of papyrus were discovered in the chapel of the eastern tomb, L25/1, in the level below the floor of the room (see *chapter 5.4.8.*). The fragments have now been deposited in two glass frames labelled by the excavation numbers 56A/N/03 and 56B/N/03 (no reg. no. was given to the find), and are in the storeroom of the Czech expedition in Abusir.[57]

The fragments are very small and badly preserved and it is first of all doubtful whether the papyri originally belonged to an archive of the Tomb Complex Lepsius no. 25, or whether the find represents an intrusive element that might have come to the chapel in many possible ways during the long centuries of its existence. The fact that the fragments were discovered in the level below the floor of the room of the chapel proffers no solution to this question. No other indications have been found concerning the existence of a papyrus archive in this tomb; on the other hand, the surroundings of the tomb have not been completely cleared, and the structures around the tomb still might provide some evidence on this subject.[58]

Concerning the fragments themselves, it is hard to estimate whether they belonged to a single scroll or to several documents. Most of the fragments bear the remains of account-tables. This form of the record is well known from the papyrus archives found in the mortuary temples of Kings Neferirkare and Raneferef, and was used for recording neat overviews of the revenues and expenses of these funerary temples.[59]

The account-tables which are partly preserved on these fragments seem to be drawn with the use of a ruler; however, the rows of the tables are not always of the same width. Some fragments show an alternation within the rows: some are less narrow than others (fragments X, V, W *recto*), while other fragments show clearly regularly drawn tables. This small difference might indicate that not all the fragments belonged to the same document. What the arrangement of the account-tables concerns, we can say with certainty – knowing the accounting records from the archives of Neferirkare and Raneferef – that the columns of these account-tables correspond to different products, while the rows most probably refer to the days of a month.[60]

---

[56] Müller-Winkler, *Amuletobjekte*, 160–162, Taf. VIII.

[57] The fragments were deposited in two glass frames more or less randomly during the process of conservation. The catalogue below gives for each fragment the information in which frame it is deposited.

[58] Some minor work has been done in 2003 south of L25/2. However, the excavation was not extensive enough to affirm the existence of a cult place similar to the funerary temples of the kings and queens in the neighbouring funerary complexes. If such a cult place / temple existed at L25, we might also consider the possibility of the existence of an administrative archive. If on the other hand L25 operated as a mastaba dependant on one of the royal funerary complexes, the possibility of an independent archive can be excluded.

[59] Posener-Kriéger, de Cenival, *Abu Sir Papyri*; Posener-Kriéger, *Les papyrus d'Abousir*; Posener-Kriéger, Verner, Vymazalová, *Papyrus Archive*.

[60] See the account-tables from the papyrus archives of both kings.

5.6.2. Catalogue of fragments
(*figs. 5.147a–b* and *5.148a–b; figs. 5.149a–b* and *5.150a–b*, see *pls. XII–XIX.*)

<u>A (1.3 × 1.8 cm; frame A)</u>
Recto: small fragment of a table. Only the sign *nṯr* is preserved, written in a row made by two horizontal lines. Before the sign, on the right side of the small fragment starts a double vertical line, and it runs further below. The sign *nṯr* might have opened a heading of a section of text.
Verso: empty.

<u>B (2.8 × 7.8 cm; frame A)</u>
Recto: part of a column of an account-table. It contains the heading *dbḥt ḥtp* "offering consumption, offering meal"[61] to which the number 69 is ascribed in every preserved row of the table. This column of the table is separated from the following entries by means of a vertical double line.
Verso: in the middle of the fragment, the remnants of ...*wꜣ*[62] "...boat *wꜣ*" are preserved. Below them follows the sign of a sack, probably designating packages of goods.

<u>C (6.5 × 6.8 cm; frame B)</u>
Recto: fragment of an account-table. Parts of four columns of numbers are preserved on this fragment. The first column is preceded by a double vertical line which might indicate the beginning of a new section of the record. One of the horizontal lines in the table is drawn in red ink. Such red lines mark decades of a month, and we can find many examples of this feature in the papyri of Neferirkare and Raneferef.[63] Thus, the red line on this fragment indicates either the 10th or the 20th day of a month. The columns of the table contain the numbers 5, 69, 23(?) and 5 respectively, written in every preserved row. Taking into consideration the number 69 in the second column, we might possibly relate this fragment to the fragments B and F where the same number occurs. On the other hand, this suggestion cannot be proven because none of the latter fragments B and F shows clearly any of the other numbers in their other columns.
Verso: empty.

<u>D (1.6 × 1.7 cm; frame A)</u>
Recto: small fragment of an account-table. Two preserved rows of the table contain the number 5. To the right of them, a double vertical line can be recognised. This fragment might have belonged to fragments C and E to which it is very similar.
Verso: empty.

<u>E (1.3 × 2.4 cm; frame A)</u>
Recto: small fragment of an account-table. Four rows of the table are preserved, each of them containing the number 5. A double vertical line runs on the right edge of the fragment. This feature together with the number 5 indicates that the fragment might have originally belonged to fragments C and D.
Verso: traces of a sign at the top right of the fragment.

<u>F (7.3 × 5.0 cm; frame A)</u>
Recto: part of an account-table; the fragment is badly damaged. Parts of about 10 rows of a table survived. The line below the last row is drawn in red and probably

---

[61] *Wb* V, 440–441: *dbḥt ḥtp* "Speisenbedarf für das Totenmahl"; W. Barta, Die altägyptische Opferliste von der Frühzeit bis zur griechisch-römischen Epoche, *MÄS* 3, Berlin 1963.
62 The writing of the boat is a bit unusual, more common is the ⬡ writing which can be observed in the papyrus archive of Neferirkare, documents 41c1, 44A, 50 1a, 87 C and 97A⁴, see Posener-Kriéger, de Cenival, Abu Sir Papyri; Posener-Kriéger, *Les papyrus d'Abousir* 669.
63 Posener-Kriéger, *Les papyrus d'Abousir*, 255–256.

marks the end of the account-table; most probably it was the thirtieth row of the record. No entries are written in the columns in the right part of the fragment while the number 69 can be recognised in some of the rows of the column in the left part of the fragment. The extreme left-hand column probably contained numbers over 20. This fragment might be related to fragment B and possibly also to fragment C, and might represent the bottom of the same account-table.

Verso: empty.

G (0.7 × 1.0 cm; frame A)

Recto: tiny fragment containing part of the number 9, and some traces of a vertical line on the left edge of the fragment. The fragment might have belonged to fragments B, C or F which contain numbers ending with the numeral 9, namely the number 69.

Verso: empty.

H (7.6 × 4.2 cm; frame A)

Recto: part of a table. The fragment bears several horizontal lines. Traces of writing are preserved only at the bottom of the fragment. These were probably headings of some records. The right-hand part of the fragment shows the sign *t* and a determinative of legs, followed by the sign *sb*. The left part of the fragment is divided by means of a double vertical line, behind which the top of the sign *rnpt* is partly preserved. This part of the fragment might possibly be related to fragments I and J, even though no clear connection can be made.

Verso: empty.

I (1.0 × 2.6 cm; frame A)

Recto: small fragment with remains of a record. A double vertical line is preserved on this small fragment. Possibly, the fragment might belong to fragments J and H, see also the *verso*.

Verso: the sign *t* and the determinative of a papyrus roll survived at the bottom of this fragment; to the right of them seem to be the remnants of *ḥ*. The signs might possibly represent the final part of the word *k3ḥt* "shoulder of beef" from fragment J *verso*, should these two fragments have originally belonged together.

J (1.15 × 3.0 cm; frame A)

Recto: small fragment with remains of a record. Part of a name of a product (?) is preserved, of which the sign *n*, the determinative of a jar, and a plural determinative consisting of three dots, can be clearly recognised. The first sign of the name is not preserved completely; it might however be related to another incomplete sign that is written on fragment H. The meaning of the writing, however, remains unclear. Small traces of a vertical line are visible at the left bottom edge of the fragment. The fragment might possibly belong also to fragment I, see the *verso*.

Verso: the name *k3ḥ[t]* (?) "shoulder of beef(?)" is partly preserved at the bottom of the fragment. This fragment might possibly belong to I *verso*, which would then show the last part of the word.

K, L (3.5 × 4.7 cm; frame B)

Recto: fragment of a table, the two fragments originally belonged together. The cells of the table contain no entries. The rows are wider than in the other fragments; in this respect, the fragment resembles fragment H.

Verso: traces of a sign on the edge of the fragment.

M (2.4 × 3.9 cm; frame B)

Recto: part of an account-table. The heading is only partly preserved; most of it is very unclear but it seems to contain an ending of a cartouche followed by *mnꜥt*(?), and the determinatives of a pregnant woman and of a city. This heading might be interpreted as a funerary domain *mnʿt* "wet-nurse" of a king whose name is not preserved,[64] and we might suppose that the domain in this heading stands for the provenance of the products listed below in the table. Below the heading, two columns of the table are partly preserved, ascribed to beer and the bread *psn*. In this type of texts, beer is usually named after bread, but in this case it is mentioned first. Such an arrangement is however not without a parallel, as a similar example can be found in one document of Neferirkare.[65]

Verso: empty.

N (4.3 × 5.7 cm; frame A)

Recto: part of an account-table. Part of a heading of the table is preserved in two lines of text: ...[*š*]*ḫppt*... "...delivered/supplied..." survived from the first line, while the second line specifies the character of the delivered products as *iwf* "meat". Below a horizontal double line the table divides into columns, each of which is ascribed to a different meat product. The preserved columns show: *ḫpš* "beef foreleg" and *tpy-ḫpš* "the best of beef foreleg". Interestingly, the word *ḫpš* in *tpy-ḫpš* is spelled with a mistake. This seems somehow striking considering the fact that the scribe managed to write it in the right way in the previous column. Nevertheless, this unusual writing seems not to relate to any other known meat product than *tpy-ḫpš*. Some traces of a third product are visible on the left edge of the fragment. No numbers are written in the preserved rows of the table that correspond to these products. It seems that *ḫpš* might have been the first of a number of butchery products mentioned in the account, and some of the products that might have followed after it are preserved on other fragments. Above every name of the product, a red oval-shaped mark is made. The meaning of this red mark is not clear but we can notice that similar red marks occur also on the fragments O and S. These marks seem to be written above the names of the products listed in the account-table. This reminds us of check marks used in the papyrus archives of Neferirkare and Raneferef[66] which possibly helped the scribes not to make mistakes in their accounts. However, those check marks were written as short, oblique strokes, and thus we cannot be certain that the stroke-marks known from the other archives represent a parallel to the thick-dot-marks in this manuscript.

Verso: in the bottom part of the fragment, the writing *rȝ-pr* "sanctuary" is preserved. The sign of a sack is written below it.

O (4.6 × 7.1 cm; frame B)

Recto: part of an account-table. Part of a heading of the table is preserved in the small remnants of two lines of text: ...*im* "...there" survived from the first line while in the second line is a determinative of meat. Possibly, fragment O might be related to fragment N, and the heading on O *recto* might be a continuation of the heading on N *recto*, so that the first line of text would read ...*šḫppt im*, and the second line would show the name *iwf* with three plural determinatives of which the first and the last survived. A very small part of papyrus is missing between fragments N and O if these indeed belonged together.

The columns at the bottom part of the fragment below a horizontal double line are ascribed to butchery products. The product in the first column is not preserved, although some remnants of it are apparent at the edge of the fragment N. The following columns relate to *iwʿ* "beef hind thigh", and *ḏrrw* "flank". The name of the last product is also lost. Above the names of the products, red marks are added. No numbers are given in the preserved rows of the table for neither of these products.

---

[64] The Old Kingdom domains *mnʿt* + name of a king are known for kings Snofru and Khufu and several non-royal persons; see Jacquet-Gordon, *Domaines funéraires*, 134, 333, 382, 415, 443. The recent excavation of the SCA at Abusir brought about new evidence of the funerary domains *mnʿt Sȝḥw-Rʿ*, see the Ph.D. thesis of Mohamed Ismail Khaled, at Charles University in Prague, see also note 73.

[65] Neferirkare's document 40a, see Posener-Kriéger, *Les papyrus d'Abousir*, 289–291.

[66] *Op. cit.*, 219–220; Posener-Kriéger, Verner, Vymazalová, *Papyrus Archive*, 395, 401.

Verso: remnants of a text survived, which mention a festival, and *r3-dt* "gate of eternity(?)".[67] The rest of the text is not clearly understandable. The sign of a sack is added below the writing.

P (2.3 × 5.0 cm; frame B)
Recto: part of three columns of an account-table. A determinative of meat is preserved in the middle column, while some traces of signs are recognisable in the left column. No numbers are written in the preserved rows of the table. This fragment is similar to N *recto* and O *recto*, and might have originally followed after them, being part of an account-table concerning butchery products.
Verso: the top edge of the fragment shows the remnants of the numeral 3, and the sign *t* is written below.

Q (1.7 × 2.5 cm; frame A)
Recto: part of a table. The preserved cells of the table contain no entries.
Verso: empty.

R (1.5 × 2.0 cm; frame A)
Recto: part of a table. The preserved cells of the table contain no entries.
Verso: empty.

S (1.7 × 2.4 cm; frame A)
Recto: small fragment of an account-table. Below a horizontal line at the top of the fragment, the last part of a heading is preserved, namely, *t* and a determinative of a house. Red marks are visible at the bottom of the fragment, similar to those from fragments N and O *recto*. This fragment might have belonged to the same record, being a continuation or an ending of the heading of an account of butchery products.
Verso: traces of writing at the left edge of the fragment. The sign *r* can be recognised.

T (2.1 × 2.2 cm; frame A)
Recto: part of a table. The preserved cells of the table contain no entries.
Verso: empty.

U (1.5 × 2.4 cm; frame A)
Recto: part of a table. The preserved cells of the table contain no entries.
Verso: empty.

V (4.8 × 4.2 cm; frame B)
Recto: fragment of a table. One of the horizontal lines is drawn in red ink. The cells of the table contain no entries.
Verso: empty

W (1.9 × 3.1 cm; frame A)
Recto: fragment of a table. The rows of the table do not have the same width; no vertical lines are preserved. The bottom part of the fragment is damaged. The fragment might have belonged to fragments X and Y to which it is very similar.
Verso: empty.

X (5.0 × 6.9 cm; frame B)
Recto: fragment of a table. The rows of the table on this fragment have different widths. The cells of the table contain no entries. The fragment can be related to Y and W.
Verso: empty

---

[67] The meaning of the term *r3-dt* is not completely clear. It might designate some part of a funerary monument or an associated place, possibly an entrance into a tomb, which is sometimes called *pr-dt*. See also the term *dt* in *Wb* V, 509–510.

Y (1.8 × 1.8; frame B)
Recto: tiny fragment of a table, originally belonging to X. The cells of the table contain no entries.
Verso: empty

Z (1.2 × 1.7 cm; frame A)
Recto: small fragment with a line, possibly part of an account-table.
Verso: tiny traces of ink.

5.6.3. Concluding remarks on the papyrus fragments

Although it is not clear whether the fragments discovered in L25/1 originally belonged to one papyrus scroll or to several documents, we can see that all of the fragments show traces of a table-type record in which the width of the rows are not always the same (*e.g.* fragment X).

All of the account-tables obviously concern the delivery of different products. Besides bread and beer, we can find here various butchery products. The meat is referred to with the general term *iwf* in the heading, while the columns of the table contain specific names for different parts of the slaughtered animal. This is typical for specific accounts of meat.[68] Above the individual names (and columns), red signs are added, the function of which is not completely clear – one calls to mind the use of check marks in accounts we use today. They might be similar to the oblique strokes used in other Abusir records, such as Neferirkare's and Raneferef's.[69] There is, however, a striking difference between the accounts in these papyri because those texts are more revealing; the L25 fragments provide no details, and thus the meaning of the red signs cannot be safely determined.

Some of the fragments show numbers, and these range from 5 to 69 (fragments B–G). The relatively high number 69 is on one fragment (B) associated with "offering consumption", and we might suppose that it is a sort of sum. However, no indication of the items to which the number 69 is related is preserved on the other two fragments (C, F) where it occurs. It is possible that all three fragments with this number belong together, and cover a large part of the one-month-record of the "offering consumption". On the other hand, these fragments cannot be joined directly, so it is impossible to prove such a supposition. It is also possible that the number 69 was mentioned in several different columns on the papyrus. This seems to be supported by the entries in the other columns on the fragments C and F: we can notice that there are differences between the numbers written in the columns on these fragments. The column preceding the column with the number 69 contains numbers on fragment C, whilst the same column on fragment F seems to be empty. Thus, merely the existence of the number 69 on all of these fragments is not enough to prove that the fragments B, C and F belong to the same part of the record.

Most of the preserved fragments in the L25 papyri contain no numbers (fragments A, H–Z). This holds even for the fragments listing the butchery products where no numbers are given for the products. The fragments are too small to provide any satisfactory explanation of this fact. We can however notice that the lines of the table are carefully drawn, and the handwriting of the hieratic signs is particularly nice. It is possible that the prepared account-table was never used for recording, or that the numbers were inscribed only in the bottom part of the table which is now lost. The record might relate to a festival, as indicated by fragment O *verso*. In that instance, the numbers would be written only in rows corresponding to the celebration of the festival.[70]

---

[68] Posener-Kriéger, Verner, Vymazalová, *Papyrus Archive*, 400.

[69] See, *e.g.*, Raneferef's document 49–50, *op. cit.*, 267. See also above note 66.

[70] See the records in the archive of Neferirkare, e.g. 5A is the table of priestly duties for individual days of a month, and its section f which refers to a festival, shows the names of the priests only for the festival days. On the other hand, e.g. Raneferef's document 47–48 A1–4 contains a table written specifically for the days of a festival and refers to no other days in month. See Posener-Kriéger, *Les papyrus d'Abousir*, Posener-Kriéger, Verner, Vymazalová, *Papyrus Archive*.

The numbers preserved on fragments B–G can hardly relate to the butchery products enumerated on fragments N–P because the numbers are too high in comparison with the preserved accounts of butchery products in the archives of Neferirkare and Raneferef where usually a very few pieces are mentioned for each cut of meat.[71]

The numbers here, however, might refer to a sum of the products, as the "offerings consumption" on fragment B indicates. If we take into consideration all the information we have from the archives of Neferirkare and Raneferef, high numbers might also indicate that the preserved fragments from L25 refer to revenues, rather than expenses.[72] In relation to this, it is very interesting to find on one of the fragments (M) the name of *mnꜥt ...w* which might refer to a funerary domain of a king whose name is not preserved; it might possibly have been *mnꜥt Sꜣḥw-Rꜥ*.[73] It is not clear whether this name of a funerary domain can be understood as the provenance of the products mentioned in the record. If this funerary domain was indeed the provenance of the goods listed on the preserved fragment from L25, it would be interesting to note that in Raneferef's funerary temple, the butchery products were delivered from the slaughterhouses of Sahure's palace,[74] while here we might possibly have Sahure's funerary domain.

There is still one important question which could not be answered until now. Did these recently discovered papyri fragments belong to an archive for the tomb L25? Or, were they brought to the chapel of L25 from another tomb complex at the necropolis by the wind or some other possible means? If the latter situation, then most probably the papyri would have come from one of the royal pyramid complexes and would have belonged to one of the other papyri archives.

We are still not completely sure of the identity of the tomb owner of L25. Apparently, it was a member of the royal family of the Fifth Dynasty. The anthropological examination of the remnants of two bodies discovered in the two burial chambers of L25 indicated that probably two related women were buried in this tomb (see *chapter 6.3.2.1.*). This seems to be confirmed also by builders' inscriptions (see *chapter 5.7.* and the conclusion *chapter 5.8.*)

If the twin tomb belonged to a king's spouse (L25/1) and her daughter (L25/2), we could find a parallel for the papyrus archive of a queen in the temple of Khentkaus II. The fragments of papyri discovered in the temple of Khentkaus in the 1970s show clearly that the queens' complexes might have had their own archives.[75] However, the Khentkaus' text related to cult statues and not related to the economic running of her funerary temple, and we know from the archive of Neferirkare that the queen's cult was connected to the cult of her deceased husband. This parallel cannot be considered as proof that the small fragments of accounts discovered in L25/1 actually belonged to the archive of this particular tomb.

Despite these suggestions, the fragments provide no clear identification about the tomb owner to whom those records originally related. The question of the origin cannot be answered properly from the evidence so far extant. Possibly, a future cleaning of the space around L25 might reveal some more evidence about the cult of the owners of the twin tomb. Then we might be able to clarify whether the tomb had a specific archive, or whether it was economically dependent and supplied by one of the royal funerary temples.

Considering all the available evidence, and the circumstances of discovery of the fragments, at this stage it is most probable that the papyrus scroll appeared intrusively in the chapel of L25/1.

---

[71] Posener-Kriéger, *Les papyrus d'Abousir*, 310–323; Posener-Kriéger, Verner, Vymazalová, *Papyrus Archive*, 400–401.

[72] The experience is that revenues usually consist of high numbers of products because they represent a totality of goods, from which smaller allocations of items are given out as "expenses".

[73] M. I. Khaled, H. Vymazalová, The funerary domain *mnꜥt* in the Fifth Dynasty, *Times, Signs and Pyramids,* (in press).

[74] Posener-Kriéger, Verner, Vymazalová, *Papyrus Archive*, 358–359, 386, 400.

[75] P. Posener-Kriéger, in: Verner, *Khentkaus*, 133–142.

5.7. Builders' marks and inscriptions

5.7.1. Builders' marks *in situ*

1   (Gr 118/N/02)

The remains of a cursive inscription in black paint found on a block in the core of the eastern wall of the offering room. The reading of the inscription – which lies upside down - is not quite clear. At both the beginning and the end of the inscription is the sign *št*, the meaning of which is not quite obvious (the name of the phyle division ?).

2   (Gr 134a/N/03)

Builder's mark in the shape of a triangle - very probably a stylized pyramid.[76] Found on a block in position in the core of the north-eastern corner of the burial chamber.

3   (Gr 134b/N/03)

On the same stone as the preceding no. 2 is another builders' inscription in charcoal, formed by the stylized pyramid, followed by *ḥwt-wrt* "temple".[77]

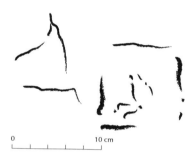

4   (Gr 159/N/03)

The remains of different marks and crossing lines in red and black paint on a block in position in the core of the eastern wall of the offering room (lowest row of blocks). From all the marks only the sign *wr* (the name of a phyle?) can be read.

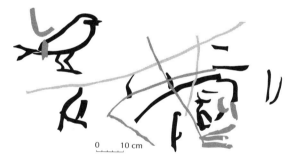

5   (Gr 160/N/03)

Builder's mark (upside down) in red paint on a block in position in the core of the eastern wall of the offering room (third row of the blocks above the floor).

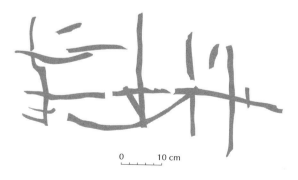

---

[76] The symbol of a stylized pyramid occurs, for instance, among the builders' marks in the pyramid complex of Senusret I in Lisht where it seems to have had the meaning of a team mark, see Arnold, *Control Notes*, 140 (E 29b.1) and 151 (S 3).

[77] For a more detailed discussion, see p. 227.

6   (Gr 166/N/03)

Cursive inscription in black paint on a block in position built in a minor construction (foundation platform of the larger, eastern monument) located near the north-eastern corner of the twin tomb. The inscription reads (see *fig. 151, pl. XX*)

s3t nśwt Ḥ3-nbw

"king's daughter Hanebu"

The princess is so far not known, neither is the name Hanebu as yet attested among Egyptian personal names.[78]

5.7.2. Loose stones

7   (Gr 1/N/01)

Cursive inscription in red paint, the reading of which is not quite clear:

s3b ...

"judge ....."

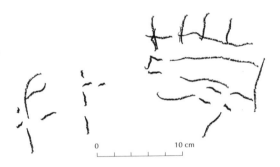

8   (Gr 3/N/01)

Cursive sign *mn* "be enduring", possibly the name of a phyle division (or, a wish concerning the tomb ?), in charcoal.

9   (Gr 6/N/01)

The unreadable remains of an inscription in black paint, over which is written in red paint an inscription, of which survived only the remains which read:

Ḫnmw (?).... . [św] 13.

"Khnum. 13th Day (?)."

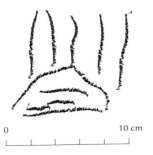

10   (Gr 8/N/01)

Cursive sign *ḫˤ* "appear", in charcoal, the meaning of which is not quite obvious. It may be the name of a phyle division.

---

[78] See Ranke, *PN.*

11   (Gr 2/N/02)

The unreadable remains of a cursive inscription in red paint and a cursive inscription in charcoal which reads

št w3dt s3 (?)

"the division *št* of phyle *w3dt*" (?).

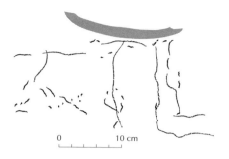

12   (Gr 16/N/02)

A cursive inscription in red paint which reads

s3b Š...

"judge S... (?)"

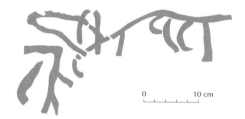

13   (Gr 15b/N/02)

A cursive inscription in charcoal which reads

mn w3dt

"division *mn* of phyle *w3dt*""

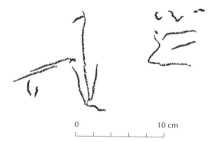

14   (Gr 17/N/02)

A cursive builder's mark in the shape of the labrys in black paint.

15   (Gr 21a/N/02)

A builder's mark in the shape of a labrys in black paint, over which is written a cursive inscription in three lines in black paint. The inscription reads (see also *fig. 5.152*, on *pl. XX*):

ḫnt 6

wh3t

štst

"front part (?) 6

cauldron (?)

box (on the offering sledge) (?)"

Over the labrys mark and the inscription, which does not seem to give much sense, was sketched in charcoal a cursive mark in the shape of a trident, the meaning of which is not quite obvious.

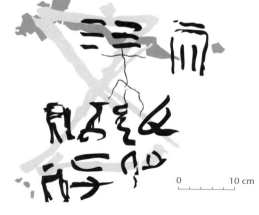

16   (Gr 21b/N/02)

On the side wall of the stone with the preceding inscription and marks there is a fragment of a cursive inscription which reads

prt, św 20

"winter, day 20"

On the stone are unreadable traces of an inscription in black paint.

17   (Gr 25/N/02)
The remains of a cursive inscription in red paint which
reads
št.š (*?*)
"its place (?)"

0   10 cm

18   (Gr 26a/N/02)
Fragment of a cursive inscription in charcoal, the reading
of which is not quite obvious (*šmnt m3... ?* "establishment of
..... "?).

"...?"

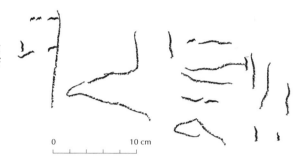

0   10 cm

19   (Gr 27/N/02)
A cursive inscription in black paint, which reads
ḥ3ty-ꜥ
"count"

0   10 cm

20   (Gr 28/N/02)
A cursive inscription in charcoal, the reading of which is
not certain. A part of it may read *nšwt ...* "king's ..... (?)".

0   10 cm

21   (Gr 29/N/02)
A cursive inscription in charcoal, the reading of which is
not obvious.

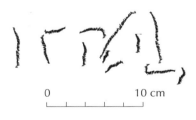

0   10 cm

22   (Gr 29a/N/02)
A cursive inscription in black paint, which reads (see *fig.
5.153, on pl. XX*)
Ršꜣ(wy)
"Two vigilant (pyramids)"
Under the inscription are the remains of a double line in

0   5 cm

black paint.

23 (Gr 29b/N/02)
A cursive inscription in black paint, which reads
(*Wꜥb*)-*išwt*-(*Wšr-kꜣ.f*) (?)
"(Pure are) the cult places of (Userkaf) (?)"

24 (Gr 142/N/03)
A cursive inscription in charcoal, which reads
išwt
"places, seats"
The remains of the name "Pure are the places of Userkaf"?

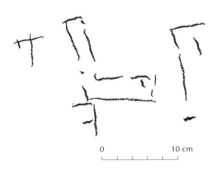

25 (Gr 143/N/03)
A cursive inscription in red paint, which reads
šmꜣꜥ ḥwt-wrt
"levelling of the temple"
See the text below no. 43

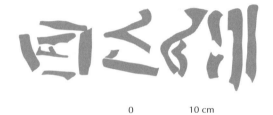

26 (Gr 147/N/03)
A cursive inscription in black paint with a date, which reads
(see *fig. 5.154*, on *pl. XX*):
ꜣbd 4 prt, sw 20 (?)
"4th month of winter, day 20 (?)"
On the stone are the remains of another, earlier inscription.

27 (Gr 34/N/02)
A cursive inscription in black paint which reads
mn wr sꜣ
"division *mn* of phyle *wr*."
The meaning of the inscription is not quite clear. Does the numeral refer to the number of divisions of the phyle?

28   (number is missing)
A cursive inscription in red paint which reads
wḏȝ (ḏȝ ?) 3
..... ?"

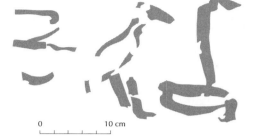

29   (Gr 36/N/02)
A cursive inscription in black paint, the reading of which is
not quite obvious
wḏȝ (?) or *ḏȝ (?)*
"storeroom (?) ... (?)"
Above the inscription is a rectangular shape sketched in
charcoal.

30   (Gr 39/N/02)
Builder's mark in the shape of the labrys, in black paint.

31   (Gr 39/N/02)
Two cursive inscriptions in black paint. From the first
inscription only unreadable remains survived. The second
inscription, written additionally in much smaller signs at the
lower edge of the stone, reads
Wˁb iśwt (Wśr-kȝ.f)
"Pure are the (cult) places of (Userkaf)"

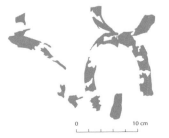

32   (Gr 45/N/02)
A damaged cursive inscription in red paint, of which only
one sign can be read
śṯ ..... (?)
"phyle *śṯ* ..... (?)"

33   (Gr 47/N/02)
A cursive inscription in charcoal, which reads
mn ..... (?)
"division *mn ..... (?)."*

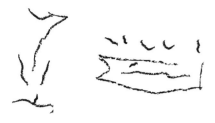

0   10 cm

34   (Gr 154/N/03)
A cursive inscription in black paint with the name of Userkaf's pyramid complex
Wˁb-iśwt-Wśr-kȝ.f
"Pure are the (cult) places of Userkaf."

0   10 cm

35   (Gr 51/N/02)
A cursive sign *śt* "seat" in red paint. A builder's mark?

0   10 cm

36   (Gr 53/N/02)
A cursive inscription in black paint, which reads
mn sȝ wr
"division *mn* of phyle *wr*"

0   10 cm

37   (Gr 54/N/02)
The remains of the sign *nbw* "gold" followed by the remains of two signs, the reading of which is unclear, all in red paint.

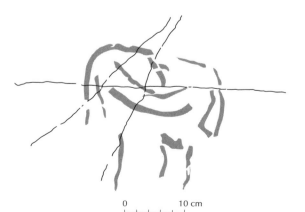

0   10 cm

38   (Gr 56/N/02)

A builder's mark in the shape of a labrys in black paint, over which was written another builder's mark in the shape of the cross in red paint. Finally, over the two marks was written a cursive inscription in black paint, the meaning of which is not quite clear

wr b3 7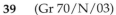

The meaning of the inscription is unclear. Is it division *b3* of phyle *wr* ? Or a personal name Werba?

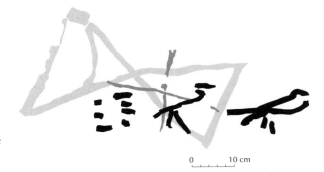

39   (Gr 70/N/03)

A cursive builder's mark in charcoal in the shape of the sign *nfr* whose meaning is not quite clear. It can be the name of a phyle division.

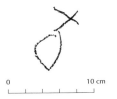

40   (Gr 75/N/03)

A cursive builder's mark in the shape of the sign *ir* (the name of a phyle division?), in red paint.

41   (Gr 77/N/03)

A cursive builder's mark in charcoal in the shape of the sign *ḫꜥ* (?) (the name of a phyle division?). Over the mark is written the sign of a pyramid (upside down).

42   (Gr 80/N/03)

A cursive builder's inscription in charcoal, which may read *Ptḥ*.

43   (Gr 86/N/03)

The remains of a cursive inscription in red paint which reads

Šm3ꜥ(?) ḥwt-wrt. Št.

"Levelling (?) the temple. Phyle *št*."

44   (Gr 87/N/03)
A cursive inscription in black paint, which contains the
name of Userkaf's pyramid complex (see *fig. 5.155, pl. XXI*):
W^cb-iśwt-Wśr-k3.f
"Pure are the (cult) places of Userkaf."

0   10 cm

45   (Gr 92/N/03)
A cursive builder's mark in charcoal, in the shape of the
sign *ḫ^c* (?) (the name of a phyle division?).

0   10 cm

46   (Gr 95/N/03)
A cursive inscription in black paint, which reads
ḥ3ty-^c
"count"

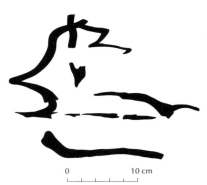

0   10 cm

47   (Gr 96/N/03)
A cursive inscription in black paint, with the remains of the
name of Userkaf's pyramid complex
W^cb-iśwt-(Wśr-k3.f)
"Pure are the (cult) places of (Userkaf)."

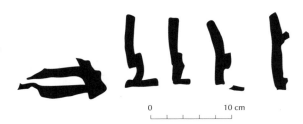

0   10 cm

48   (Gr 97/N/03)
A cursive inscription in black paint, which reads
ḥ3ty-^c
"count"

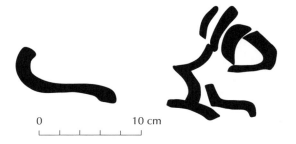

0   10 cm

49   (Gr 99/N/03)
A cursive inscription in black paint, which reads
ḫ3ty-ʿ
"count"

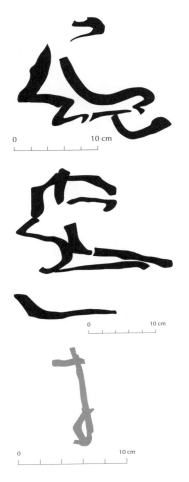

50   (Gr 103/N/03)
A cursive inscription in black paint, which reads
ḫ3ty-ʿ
"count"

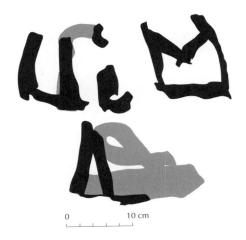

51   (Gr 104/N/03)
A cursive mark in the shape of the sign *nfr* (the name of a phyle division?)

52   (Gr 105/N/03)
A cursive inscription in black paint with the remains of the name of Userkaf's pyramid complex
Wʿb-iśwt-(Wśr-k3.f)
"Pure are the (cult) places of (Userkaf)."
The inscription is superimposed on the remains of an unreadable inscription in red paint.

53   (Gr 116/N/03)
The remains of a horizontal line, with an arrow pointing downwards in red paint. Below the line, also in red paint, is a short inscription which reads
mḥ 1
"1 cubit"
The inscription was written over the charcoal builder's mark *mr* (the name of a phyle division?). On the stone are the traces of red paint which may come from the remains of another inscription.

54   (Gr 117/N/03)
A stylized builder's mark in the shape of a five pointed star.

55   (Gr 124/N/03)
A cursive inscription in black paint, which reads (see also *fig. 5.156*, on *pl. XXI*):
Rš(wy)
"Two vigilant (pyramids)."

56   (Gr 126/N/03)
A cursive mark in the shape of a seated figure, written over the mark in the shape of a cross. Both marks are in charcoal.

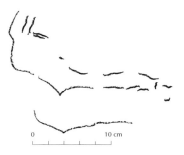

57   (Gr 127b/N/03)
A cursive inscription in black paint, which reads
ḥȝty-ʿ
"count"

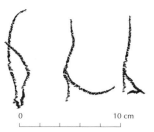

58   (Gr 130/N/03)
A cursive inscription in charcoal, which reads (*fig.5.157, pl. XXI*)
Bbi
"Bebi"[79]

59   (Gr 140/N/03)
A cursive inscription in charcoal, formed by four vertical strokes followed by the personal name *Bbi* "Bebi".

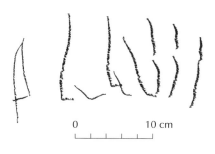

---

[79] Bebi is a relatively common name attested since the Old Kingdom, see Ranke, *PN* I, 95/16.

5.7.3. Personal names

Among the builders' inscriptions found in the twin tomb Lepsius no. 25, the personal name of the king's daughter Hanebu (inscription no. 6) occupies a very prominent place. It is the only personal name which was found in position (in fact, on one of the blocks of a collapsed wall but – unequivocally – the block bearing the name had once made up part of the wall). The king's daughter Hanebu thus represents a candidate for the owner of the bigger tomb of the twin tomb. For a more detailed discussion of Hanebu, see *chapter 5.8.*

5.7.4 Builders' instruction

In the set of builders' marks from the monument Lepsius no. 25 (nos. 43) the term *šmꜣꜥ ḥwt-wrt* occurs only once. Interestingly, in inscription no. 3 the term *wrt* is preceded by a stylized drawing of a pyramid. Unfortunately, the precise archaeological (architectural) context of both no. 3 and the no. 43 is missing since all the inscriptions occur on loose stones.

5.7.5. Builders' marks

Besides the rarely attested builders' marks formed by two crossing lines (no. 4) and a five pointed star (no. 54), in the twin tomb Lepsius no. 25 there more frequently occurs the mark in the shape of a labrys (nos. 14, 15, 30 and 38) which represents a stylized sign *hꜣ* and is an abbreviated form of the name of the king's daughter Hanebu. Chronologically importantly, the mark is also attested from the cult pyramid of Khentkaus II. For a more detailed discussion on the name and the chronological meaning of its occurrence in the three previously mentioned monuments, see chapter 5.8.

5.7.6. Phyle / division

The names of three phyles – *wr* (nos. 27 and 36), *št* (no. 32) and *wꜣḏt* (nos. 10, 11, 13, 31, 33 and 34 – are attested among the builders' inscriptions in the monument Lepsius no. 25. Most frequently is attested the name of the phyle *wꜣḏt*. Much more uncertain is the situation as far as the names of the phyle divisions are concerned. Theoretically, six[80] names could be attributed to the divisions namely, *ir* (no. 40), *mn* (nos. 8, 13, 27, 33 and 36), *mr* (no. 53), *nfr* (nos. 39 and 51), *ḫꜥ* (nos. 10, 41 and 45) and perhaps also *št* (no. 11). However, some of the marks can be setting marks (*e.g. st*), some others can have a building meaning (*e.g. nfr* „end"). The signs *ir* and *ḫꜥ* are attested as the names of the phyle divisions in the papyri from both Neferirkara's[81] and Raneferef's[82] archive.

5.7.7. Dates

Only two builders' inscriptions with a date survived in the pyramid Lepsius no. 25. Both of them refer to the *prt* season. Unfortunately, such insufficient evidence does not enable us to come to any chronological conclusions.

5.7.8. Pyramid names

The name *Ršꜣ(wy)* (nos. 22 and 55), followed by the determinative formed by a pair of pyramids, refers to the pyramid Lepsius no. 24. For a more detailed discussion, see concluding *chapter 5.8.* Interestingly, in several inscriptions (nos. 23, 24 (?), 31, 34, 47 and 52) on the loose stones, occurs the name of Userkaf's pyramid complex *Wꜥb-*

---

[80] For the discussion on the number of the phyle divisions, see E. Edel, *Die Kalksteintäfelchen*, in: Ricke, SH Userkaf, 12.

[81] Posener-Kriéger, *Les papyrus d'Abousir*, 566.

[82] Posener-Kriéger, Verner, Vymazalová, *Papyrus Archive*, 366. For the theory that the phyles who built a pyramid complex stayed on after the complex was completed in order to maintain it and carry out the mortuary cult of the king to whom the complex belonged, see Roth, *Egyptian Phyles*, 119.

išwt-Wśr-k3.f "Pure-are-the-(cult)-places-of-Userkaf." For a more detailed discussion of the problem, see *chapter 5.8.*

5.7.9. Titles

Surprisingly, the only two titles attested in the builders' inscriptions in the twin tomb Lepsius no. 25 are ḥ3ty-ꜥ "count" (nos. 25, 46, 48, 49, 50 and 57) and s3b (nos. 7 and 12). All the pieces of evidence occur on the loose stones found in the remains of the monument and none of them is followed by a personal name. The interpretation of this strange situation is rather difficult. Can we surmise that the title, attested also in the adjacent pyramid Lepsius no. 24 in conjunction with the name of the vizier Ptahshepses, referred to the same person? If so, the vizier might have largely contributed to the construction of the twin tomb and, as the case might be, supervised the work on the monument.

5.8. Conclusions

5.8.1. Appearance of the monument

This unusual complex consists of two tombs built one beside each other and representing a particularly massive mastaba. Consequently, this tomb complex can be classified as one of the most peculiar tomb constructions of the period. There is a strong likelihood that both tombs were started as pyramids during the construction of their subterranean parts. Their builders then changed the monuments' layout with a curious alteration to their superstructures. As a result, the tombs were finally completed as modified mastabas.

The layout of the core masonries of both tombs was similar to the layout which we can see in the case of pyramids of queens for that period, with a descending corridor oriented along the north-south axis and a large building pit for the construction of the burial apartment; the "U-shaped rim" of the core masonry was built along the edge of that pit.[83] However, the subterranean part – at least of L25/1 – has a non-standard, complicated layout, with a double bend in an access route to the burial chamber (see fig. 5.16).[84]

For our evaluation of the architecture of the Lepsius 25 complex we can also take into consideration the unusual layout of the underground part of the not far-distant Mastaba of Werkaure (the so-called Pyramid Lepsius no. 23) which is presently under excavation.[85] It seems that there are probably three tombs with a similar non-standard layout and appearance in the southern part of the Abusir Royal Necropolis. In this regard we can probably speak about a new tomb sub-type.[86] This sub-type would link together the layout of a pyramid (namely the layout of the subterranean part and of the core masonry) with the superstructure of a mastaba. We can thus suggest that this layout of these minor tombs at the Abusir Royal Necropolis was influenced by local conditions – such as an unstable subsoil (see *chapter 5.3.*), a difficult terrain (regarding the position of these tombs on the very edge of the plateau) and, probably, elements of an orientation towards the main communication lines within the necropolis. Neither can we exclude the possibility that this exceptional layout may have been a factor of the high social standing of the tomb owners. Results of the recent archaeological excavations of the Mastaba of Werkaure seem to confirm that those special constructions could be used for high-ranking members of the king's family.[87]

---

[83] *Cf. chapter 4.4.1.* in this monograph.

[84] We are reminded here that the situation in the case of the burial apartment in L25/2 is not clear and we can suppose that the same room layout was used also in this instance.

[85] J. Krejčí, Several Remarks on the Abusir pyramid necropolis: its minor tombs and their place in the chronology of the royal cemetery, in: *Chronology and Archaeology in Ancient Egypt*, 127–129, 135–136.

[86] The architectural evaluation of this "new type" of tomb will be shortly forthcoming.

[87] However, regarding the uncertainty of the identity of the tomb-owners for L25, we must admit that this supposition is tentative in their case.

situation with many other funeral monuments in the Memphite Necropolis and it therefore remains a possibility that it might have been the engineers' intention not to smooth the casing of the tombs.[88]

We have also to keep in mind that no piece of the relief decoration – even of a false door (as is also the case with the pyramid L24 and Nakhtsare's mastaba) – which could be attributable to this tomb complex was ever found. Moreover, the cult room located in the eastern part of L25/1, whose side walls were preserved up to its roof around its entrance, does not possess any piece of original decoration. We could explain these omissions as being the result of the large-scale destruction of the monument; however, we would expect to have unearthed at least some small fragments of such decoration or pieces of a false door, but none were found. This situation might be explained as well by the unusual plan of this chapel, marked out by an *en chicane* layout, possibly with a deep niche for the false door in the westernmost part of the room. We expect that only this niche (and by definition also the false door) was decorated and that the widespread destruction made in this area of L25/1 deprived the monument of its meagre decoration.

Despite the lack of the relief decoration, there is enough archaeological data to suggest that quite a long period elapsed, during which cultic activities took place in the area of the chapel. Finds consisting of fragments of cultic pottery as well as repeated cleaning and covering of the chapel's floor with mud linings clearly document this supposition. Unfortunately, papyrus fragments (*chapter 5.6.*) – even though connectable with a mortuary cult – may well have been an intrusive find brought to the place of its unearthing by the tomb- and stone-robbers in the later periods of the development of the necropolis (see below). The unearthing of remains of a female statue (or more statues) are unfortunately also inconclusive, shedding no further light on the problems of the monument – other than to suggest that the fragments may offer some confirmation of a female burial in this tomb.

5.8.2. Masons' marks

Among the most important finds from the area of L25 are the builders' marks. The problem of the name of this unusual tomb complex has already been analysed by M. Verner (chapters *4.6* and *5.7*).[89] It is very probable that the name, *Rš(wy)* – "Two vigilant (pyramids)", which we originally attributed to Lepsius no. 25[90] actually represents the name of the Pyramid Complex Lepsius no. 24.

The masons' marks also play some role in our attribution of the tomb complex to specific persons and also in our dating of both tombs.

5.8.3. Owners and dating

Despite all the efforts made through several archaeological seasons in regard to the names and dates associated with this monument, we do not have any direct clue concerning the owners of this very atypical mortuary complex. The position of the double-mastaba on the edge of the royal necropolis seems to show that the tomb owners might have been of lower status in the hierarchy of the royal family. On the other hand, this position also could show that either the construction was built before all the other minor tombs in the royal necropolis or, *vice versa*, they might have been built at the end of the development of this part of the royal necropolis.

The identification of the tombs' owners is not facilitated by the find of two sets of masons' marks: those mentioning the name of Userkaf's pyramid complex and that mentioning the name of Princess Hanebu. The name of the Pyramid Complex of Userkaf is problematic because this complex is located ca 3 km from the Abusir cemetery. This builders' mark with the name *Wˁb šwt Wśr-kȝ.f* thus represents a

---

[88] Perhaps this strange option may have been made with the intention of giving such tombs an approximate similarity to the rocks appearing on both sides of the Nile Valley?
[89] *Cf.* also M. Verner's article for *Fs. Do. Arnold*, in press.
[90] J. Krejčí, *PES* 2, 2003, 64–78; *idem.*, *PES* 3, 2004, 203–213; J. Krejčí, M. Verner, *Sokar* 8, 2004, 20–22; J. Krejčí, M. Verner, in: *Fs. Sawy*, 159–165; J. Krejčí, in: *Abusir and Saqqara 2005*, 261–273.

that mentioning the name of Princess Hanebu. The name of the Pyramid Complex of Userkaf is problematic because this complex is located ca 3 km from the Abusir cemetery. This builders' mark with the name *Wˁb śwt Wśr-k3.f* thus represents a dating criterion *post quem* – the double-tomb complex might date to the range of time beginning with Sahure's reign. Secondly, all the attestations of this name have been always found on loose blocks, indicating that these blocks were not used in the originally intended building. Unfortunately, we do not know very much about the circulation of the building material on royal building sites, so we do not know what the practices were at the time of the complex's construction. However, having in mind the large number of attestations for the use of construction blocks with the names of buildings used in "wrong" monuments, we can suppose that this was quite a frequent practice. Due to the location of the site being mainly connected with the middle part of the Fifth Dynasty, and due to the tomb's location on the edge of the royal necropolis of Abusir, as well as some archaeological finds (especially mud sealings), we can argue that these attestations of the name of Userkaf's complex, are not directly connectable with the person of this king.

In *chapter 5.3.4.* we discussed the large, re-used blocks of white limestone coming from an architrave with a drum which were built into the eastern façade of L25/1. If we would combine the re-usage of these blocks in L25 with the above discussed graffiti mentioning the name of Userkaf's pyramid complex, we cannot rule out that, before the construction of L25, a conjectural monument, hypothetically a tomb, stood somewhere in the area of the southern part of the royal necropolis and, not being needed any more, it was dismantled.

The question of the ownership of the tombs can be also answered on the basis of the available archaeological and epigraphical material, both of which supply different data concerning this problem.

As it stands, the only directly mentioned name connected with L25 is the name of Princess Hanebu, an as-yet-unknown member of the royal family.[91] This mason's mark was found on the masonry of a small portion of the building of uncertain character at the north-east corner of L25/1 (see p. 179–180). This construction might have been part of another tomb squeezed between Lepsius no. 25 and the Mastaba of Nebtyemneferes, or, it might have served as a kind of cultic or subsidiary building (with a storeroom?) belonging to the Tomb Complex Lepsius no. 25 – *cf.* the similar construction located to the south of L25/2.[92] Thus it is that we cannot rule out the proposition that Hanebu herself was the tomb owner of L 25. If this person were really buried in this tomb complex, we might then assume that the princess would have been interred in the eastern tomb, which was the larger of the two. The western tomb might have been used for the interment of another lady as the results of the archaeological excavation shown to us (see below).

A find of very fragmentarily preserved, female mummified corpses in both the burial chambers of L25/1 and L25/2 is important in our argumentation on the original owners of both these tombs. Following the anthropological investigation we cannot fully rule out that these were two related females. (See *chapter 6.3.2.1.*). However, due to the damaged state of both corpses, this report is really a tentative assessment. As has been mentioned in *chapter 5.1.*, both burial chambers were largely destroyed and, moreover, parts of the original mummies were mixed with parts of other cadavers from the secondary cemetery. Nevertheless, during the course of the archaeological excavation, it was possible to sort out the separate body parts coming from the secondary cemetery from those supposedly belonging to the original tomb owners. As a result of the widespread and repeated devastation of the tombs, parts

---

[91] *Cf. chapter 5.7.* In J. Krejčí's account, in: *Chronology and Archaeology in Ancient Egypt*, 133–135, the name Hanebu was wrongly attributed to a prince, not to a princess.

[92] Unfortunately, due to the layer of large limestone blocks lying on top of this curious little building, we were not able to further excavate either of these constructions.

[93] Due to financial constrictions and the pressure of time, chronometric dating was done only in the case of one fragment of the mummy found in L25/1.

women were actual relatives (the bone analysis implied that there was a kind of relationship between the two women whose mummified body-parts were found, see *chapter 6.3.2.1.*), the fragments of the mummy found in L25/2 would have dated to the same period. Following all these results we could therefore suggest that the double mastaba belonged to a princess (or perhaps a queen) and her daughter, or maybe two sisters (of royal origin) who were interred here. As we proposed above, the eastern tomb – the larger one – might have been used for the interment of the more important of these two possible female tomb owners, the Princess Hanebu and the western tomb – the smaller one – for her supposed daughter or sister.

This hypothesis seems also to be supported by the items belonging to the burial equipment of both the deceased. These finds prove that the owners of the both tombs were members of the upper social strata of the Egyptian society and these grave goods are comparable, *e.g.*, with the burial equipment of the owner of the pyramid Lepsius no. 24, Prince Nakhtsare and other members of the royal family.[94] The archaeology thus also endorses our suggestion of ascribing Lepsius no. 25 to the members of the then ruling elite.

Whatever the identity of the owners of the tombs, there is still the question as to which ruler of the Fifth Dynasty they were connected. As has been already indicated, the masons' inscription mentioning the name of Userkaf's pyramid complex can be used only as a dating criterion *post quem*. In this case, the *labrys* signs and *Rš(wy): nḏś wr* inscription that were found within the double-tomb would play an important role in assigning a relative date. The *labrys* signs found on the loose blocks from L25 are, very probably, an abbreviation of the name of Princess Hanebu.[95] They are also attested on the loose blocks found in the enclosure of the cult pyramid of Khentkaus II.[96] We know that the sector of Khentkaus' II cult pyramid was part of a later building phase of this pyramid complex (called MBT II by M. Verner), and that its construction belongs to a later part of Niuserre's reign.[97] Another role is played by *Rš(wy): nḏś wr* the suggested name of pyramid L24: one of these graffiti records was built into the masonry of L25/1. As a result, we can suppose that this block, located in the lowermost masonry of the construction pit of L25/1, was (re-)used. This would mean that L25/1 (and the whole L25) was *very probably* built relatively later than the pyramid Lepsius no. 24. If so, it would have been erected simultaneously with the MBT II phase of Khentkaus II, respectively with the enclosure wall of its cult pyramid. The same situation is also the case with the Mastaba of Nakhtsare. During the unearthing of this tomb a large limestone loose-block with two pyramid signs (which apparently are remains of the name *Rš(wy): nḏś wr* (*cf.* p. 65 in this monograph) were discovered.

Unfortunately, we are unable to establish a more precise relative chronology in connection with L24, L25, Nakhtsare's mastaba and some parts of the Pyramid Complex of Khentkaus II. As has been proposed by M. Verner, the construction of Khentkaus' II pyramid was started already during the reign of Neferirkare[98] and it was continued in further phases during the reign of Niuserre.[99] As has been established in *chapter 4.7.*, the Pyramid Complex Lepsius no. 24 had very probably been built during the second part of the reign of the same king. Viewing the location of the monuments, we suppose that the Tomb Complex Lepsius no. 25 was built later than Lepsius no. 24. This seems to be supported by the find of *Rš(wy): nḏś*

---

[94] *Cf.* V. G. Callender's account on stone vessels found in the Abusir minor tombs in this monograph (*Appendix. Stone Vessels from the Cemetery of Members of the Royal Families of Abusir*).

[95] The *labrys* sign is also found in the name of Princess Hanebu – see *chapter 5.7* – and the isolated signs are probably an abbreviation of her name.

[96] Verner, *Khentkaus*, 50–51.

[97] Verner, *Khentkaus*, 40–41 and fig. 55b.

[98] Verner, *Khentkaus*, 170.

[99] Verner, *Khentkaus*, 38–40, several additions were made even during the late Fifth and in the Sixth Dynasty.

wr inscriptions in L25 and Nakhtsare's tomb. In these two cases, the blocks very probably might have been left-overs remaining on the site after the construction of the L24 pyramid.

The situation with the blocks with the *labrys* signs is more complicated as, *e.g.*, in the cult pyramid of Khentkaus II they were also used as left-overs. Nevertheless, if the MBT II phase of Khentkaus' II pyramid complex is dated to Niuserre's time, we can – with some degree of caution – date the construction of both parts of Lepsius no. 25 to the later part of Niuserre's reign.[100] Discussing the relative chronology, we can figure out that at first the major part of the MBT II phase of Khenktaus' II pyramid complex was built, then, in a swift sequence L24, L25 and Nakhtsare's tomb (together with other mastabas lying to the south from this monument). The works might have been finished through some minor changes and additions in Khentkaus' complex (*e.g.*, the construction of the enclosure wall of the queen's cult pyramid).

As has been already discussed in regard to the pyramid Lepsius no. 24, there was not enough space for the construction of additional tombs in Niuserre's cemetery. Having in mind the horizontal stratigraphy of the site, it thus seems logical to assign the construction of the Tomb Complex Lepsius no. 25 to Niuserre's reign.

We should also discuss another possible family connection – that the persons buried in Lepsius no. 25 were relatives of Raneferef. Unfortunately, we have no other clue to offer for this suggestion – apart from the location of the structure (it is closer to Raneferef's mortuary complex than to Niuserre's pyramid complex). In this case, the tomb owners might have been descendants of Raneferef. Nonetheless, the construction of L25 is very likely to have been erected during Niuserre's reign, as this king seems to have been obliged not only to finish the construction of his brother's complex, but also other monuments connected with Neferirkare's family line.

To sum up: a precise date for the Tomb Complex Lepsius no. 25 is not possible to affirm. Our dates range from the reign of Sahure (due to the find of builders' inscriptions with the name of Userkaf's pyramid) to Niuserre. However, having in mind all the data, the location and the situation of this largely destroyed monument, we prefer dating it to the later part of Niuserre's reign.

5.8.4. Later activities

Concerning the consecutive development in the area of the tomb complex Lepsius no. 25, it shared a partially different fate from the Pyramid Complex Lepsius no. 24 (see *chapter 4.7.*) It seems that its area was not used as a settlement, nor was it used as a cemetery for the interring of secondary burials during the late Old Kingdom, First Intermediate Period and Middle Kingdom. However, the find of a New Kingdom scarab as well as the New Kingdom pottery shows that (as was the case for the entire Abusir Necropolis), the area of the monument belonging to bygone kings was a definite focus for the New Kingdom and later inhabitants of the Nile Valley, even though the nature of activities in this period is not known. As the voluminous layers of smashed secondary burials show, it seems that these activities started during the Late Period (probably during the Twenty-sixth Dynasty). At this time, the secondary cemetery covered the entire eastern part of L25/1's superstructure. The next phase

---

[100] We do not know precisely, whether the masons' mark *s3t nśwt H3-nbw* (which was found on the masonry of a small portion of the building of uncertain nature in the north-east corner of L25/1) and the *labrys* signs are certainly connected with one of the original tomb-owners of L25. This construction might have been part of another tomb built in the area between Lepsius no. 25 and the Mastaba of Nebtyemneferes. In that case, then, this hypothetical tomb would be older than L25 and also older than the MBT II phase of the Pyramid Complex of Khentkaus II. We can thus suppose that two already discussed drum-piece blocks made of white limestone (see p. 164) might have come from this older, hypothetical tomb. If this is the case, Princess Hanebu might have been an owner of this structure and been connected with one of the kings who reigned before Niuserre, so the tomb owners of L25 must then have remained unknown.

of smashed secondary burials show, it seems that these activities started during the Late Period (probably during the Twenty-sixth Dynasty). At this time, the secondary cemetery covered the entire eastern part of L25/1's superstructure. The next phase of activities – another secondary cemetery – was carried out in the area to the north of the monument. Due to the orientation of the burial pits and the omission of burial equipment, we can suppose that these burials can be dated to even later periods (hypothetically, to the Early Christian Period?). As is well documented in the case of a Kufic inscription on the eastern wall of Raneferef's Unfinished Pyramid, dating to the ninth and tenth centuries[101] the Abusir pyramids were also visited in the Middle Ages. This last-mentioned visitation has been supported by finds of copper arrow heads in the area of Lepsius no. 25. During the same period, widespread destruction of the monument was also going on: the finds of stone-robbers' wedges certainly document this destruction. These activities contributed to the lamentable state of preservation of this monument which also, unfortunately, made worse its excavation, as well as the architectural and archaeological evaluation of this particular monument.

---

[101] B. Vachala, F. Ondráš, An Arabic inscription of the pyramid of Neferefra, in: *Abusir and Saqqara 2000*, 73–76.

6. Anthropological Material

6.1. Human skeletal remains from the Pyramid Complex Lepsius no. 24 and the Mastaba of Nakhtsare

Martina Kujanová

This chapter deals with the human skeletal remains from the excavation of the Czech Institute of Egyptology at the Abusir Pyramid Necropolis in the season 1994. The skeletal remains came from the pyramid complex of an anonymous lady marked Lepsius No. 24 dated to the Fifth Dynasty (area J) and from the Mastaba of Prince Nakhtsare, dated to the Fifth Dynasty (area Q). The discovered skeletal material from secondary burials however represents a population sample of local inhabitants from the Graeco-Roman Period. The osteological analysis of human skeletal remains can provide a wide range of information (sex and age profile, stature, diseases, demography etc.). Demography, which is the study of populations concerning the statistics of populations, is based on sufficient number of skeletons. In this current work, these or other comparative analyses were restricted regarding a very low number of individuals in this sample. The primary object of this chapter is therefore to provide a basic osteological description and anthropological assessments of the human remains. However, this sample could be enlarged in future seasons and used for further analyses.

6.1.1. Methodology within this current work

The investigation covered both metrical and descriptive characters of preserved skeletons. The descriptive cranial and pelvic morphological features were evaluated according to scale by Buikstra and Ubelaker (the cranial features were evaluated against a six point scale).[1] The primary sex diagnosis was obtained from the pelvic morphological features[2] and the metrical approach of a hip bone.[3] The age determination is based on the age-related degeneration of the skeletons. The age of adult skeletons are difficult to evaluate accurately and as a result adult individuals are only divided into broad categories of age using the fusion data according to Todd (the pubic symphysis was assessed against a ten point scale),[4] Lovejoy (the analysis dealt with the auricular surface that was assessed against an eight point scale)[5]. For assessment of dental abrasion, which is also one of the more accurate indicators of age, the method of Lovejoy was applied.[6] In addition, the evaluating of the sternal end of ribs was recorded.[7] As it is anticipated for the following seasons that more burials will be excavated, all of the long bones and selected cranial dimensions[8] were measured for further analysis. The estimated living stature of the

---

[1] Buikstra, Ubelaker, *Standards for Data Collection.*

[2] J. Brůžek, A Method for Visual Determination of Sex, Using the Human Hip Bone, *Amer. J. Phys. Anthropol.* 117, 2002, 157–168.

[3] P. Murail, J. Brůžek, F. Houët, E. Cunha, DSP: A Toll for Probabilistic Sex Diagnosis Using Worldwide Variability in Hip Bone Measurements, *Bull. soc. anthrop.* 17, 2005, 3–4, 167–176.

[4] *Cf.* McKern, Stewart, *Skeletal Age Changes.*

[5] C. O. Lovejoy, R. S. Meindl, T. R. Przybeck, Chronological Metamorphosis of the Auricular Surface of Illium: A New Method for the Determination of Adult Skeletal Age at Death, *Amer. J. Phys. Anthropol.* 68/1, 1985, 47–56.

[6] C. O. Lovejoy, Dental Wear in the Libben Population: Its Pattern and Role in the Determination of Adult Skeletal Age at Death, *Amer. J. Phys. Anthropol.* 68/1, 1985, 15–28.

[7] M. Y. Iscan, J. R. Loth, K. K. Wright, Age Estimation from the Rib by Phase Analysis, *J. Forensic Sci.* 30/3, 1985, 853–863.

[8] Martin, Saller, *Lehrbuch der Anthropologie.*

individuals was calculated on measurements taken on the long bones and using equations derived by M. Trotter and G. C. Gleser.[9] Skeletal pathology was based on Buikstra's and Ubelaker's formulae.[10]

The burials are briefly described below in a following sequence: preservation, morphological characters of skeletons, sex determination, estimation of age, skeletal pathology, stature estimation, and other descriptions.

6.1.2. Osteological description of the skeletons

74/J/94

For these human remains, only fragments of a gracile skull were preserved. Bone material present consists of the maxilla, with frontal, right parietal and partly sphenoidal bone. Only the first molars and unerupted third molars were preserved. The aging techniques used to estimate the age of this skeleton were thus the degree of calcification in the preserved teeth showing subadult dentition, and suture closures which were open. No further analysis could be done.

Conclusion: skeleton of immature individual, ca 14–15 years old.

9/Q/94

This was a badly damaged skeleton of robust construction with marked muscular development. As all skeletal elements were fused, it can be concluded that this individual was older than 25 years of age. The individual probably was not much older as no osteoarthritic changes affected the skeleton.

Conclusion: skeleton of adult individual older than 25 years.

10/Q/94

Despite the mostly bad bone preservation, some descriptions and conclusions can be made in this case. The cranial remains contained here only consisted of a fragmentary skull. These fragments were: the frontal, the parietal and the occipital bones, the intact, right temporal bone and part of the mandible. All these fragments were of gracile construction, with slight muscular relief. The damaged postcranial skeleton was also of gracile construction with traces of slight muscular relief. The upper limb bones, sternum and pubis bone were preserved in some parts.

Regarding the bad preservation of the skeleton, only a few morphological features could be described. On the skull, the mastoid process was small and as for the postcranial skeleton, at the distal end of humerus the presence of fossa olecranii, one of usual anatomic variants, was registered. Some of the other characters are mentioned below.

The measurements and morphological characters of pelvis used in the determination of sex of this skeleton indicated, with a high probability, that this individual was female. These helping characters were the feminine form of ventral arch of pubic bone, narrow ischiopubic ramus ridge, symmetric and wide greater sciatic notch, double arc compose (a separate arch was formed in the area of auricular surface) and overall gracility of the pelvis. There was no clear evidence of preauricular sulcus, a feature more commonly present and better marked in the female than in the male.

The aging techniques used to estimate the age of the skeleton were epiphyseal fusion, dental attrition and suture closure. All of these observations indicate that the remains belonged to a person not yet fully mature. As for the postcranial skeleton, the proximal epiphysis of humerus was not fused. The fusion had just occurred in these cases: the distal epiphysis of the radius, the distal epiphysis of ulna, the distal epiphysis of the femur and the proximal epiphysis of tibia

---

[9] M. Trotter, G. C. Gleser, Estimation of Stature from Long Bones of American Whites and Negroes, *Amer. J. Phys. Anthropol.* 10, 1952, 463–514.

[10] See note 1.

and fibula. The proximal epiphysis of the femur, the distal epiphysis of the tibia, fibula and the epiphysis of the metatarsal bones were also only just on the point of unifying. On the pelvis, the ischial tuberosity was only partly fused, and the crista iliaca was also not yet fully united. For the vertebrae, a furrowed surface on their body was observed and, the first vertebra of the sacral bone was not being fused as well as the fourth with the fifth vertebra. The body of the sternum was still not completely united. The sternal end of the ribs registered degree 1–2 and the sternal end of the clavicle registered as degree 1, which generally occurs at an average age of about 17–20 years. As for the skull, the cranial sutures were open. Eleven mandible teeth with no abrasion were present in the jaw. The third molars were not completely erupted, and the right second molar had evidence of caries.

The computed stature of the individual was 155.1 ± 3.41 cm according to measurements of long bones of the skeleton.

Obvious traces of the mummification process (a perforated cribriform plate in the ethmoid bone and a partly in the sphenoidal bone, with probably an ancient resin in the posterior part of the cranial cavity, together with remnants of mummified tissue) were also observed.

Conclusion: skeleton of female, ca 18–19 years old.

37/Q/94 *(figs. 6.6–6.12, pls. XXIII–XXIV)*

The preservation of this skeleton as a whole was good. The cranium of this individual was well preserved, except for the separated and incomplete maxilla. Well preserved dentition was noticed for this skull, but two teeth had been lost ante-mortem. The postcranial skeleton itself was very well preserved. Both skull and postcranial skeleton were of middling robust construction and had the marks of a medium muscular development.

Cranial morphology showed pentagonoid outline, upright forehead, a minimal prominence of glabella and supra-orbital ridge, medium frontal tubers, and a middle sharp supra-orbital margin. The nuchal crest was registered as degree 1 and the mastoid process was small. On the mandible, there was a small mental eminence. The cranial index was 81.1 which shows the head of the individual was rather short.

For the postcranial skeleton, the presence of fossa olecranii on the humerus was noted. The sacrum was wide and following pelvic characteristics were used in the determination of sex. The pelvis as a whole was rather wide and low. The preauricular sulcus was registered under degree 1 (very smooth, with no evidence of its presence) and there was a separate arch formed in the area of auricular surface which is a feminine form of arc compose. The metrical assessment of the pelvic bone asserted unequivocally a member of the female sex.

The age estimation assessed mainly from the morphological changes in the pubic symphysis surface, dental attrition, and suture closure revealed that the individual was between 30–40 years of age at the time of death. The indicators are described bellow. The pubic symphysis registered changes between phases VI–VII which is within the 30–40 age category. The dental abrasion belonged to the phase F–G category which generally occurs also at age category of 30–40 years. The cranial sutures showed a significant closure. The epiphyses of bones of postcranial skeleton were fully united.

As for the skeletal pathology, some pathological changes were registered. On the skull, only the right first molar in the maxilla had evidence of caries. For the postcranial skeleton, the epiphyses of the long bones and the scapula with clavicle had initial indications of a degenerative-productive process. Small enthesopathies were visible on the patella of both sides. There were small arthritic changes on the lumbar and cervical vertebra, and the same changes were also, but less pronounced on the thoracic vertebra. The thoracic vertebrae had depressions known as "Schmorl's nodes" which is a result of pressure on the vertebral bodies and commonly appears with other types of degenerative changes. There is a sacralisation of the fifth lumbar vertebra – with corresponding changes on the pelvic bones which could be congenital or connected with physical stress or trauma.

The computed average stature of this individual was 157.8 ± 3.41 cm.

Conclusion: skeleton of female, ca 30–40 years old.

38/Q/94 (see *fig. 6.1–6.5, pl. XXII*)

The skeleton as a whole was well preserved. The intact cranium with separated and incomplete maxilla was of a medium robust construction with the muscular development in the medium range. The robust postcranial skeleton was almost complete (except for the fragmentary upper limb long bones) with evidence of a medium range muscular development.

Morphological characters of the skull were recorded as follows: the outline of the skull was ovoid, the nuchal crest as well as the mastoid process was in the range of degree 3. The forehead was slightly slanting with small frontal tubers. The supra-orbital ridge and the glabella were assessed to be degree 2 while the supra-orbital margin was registered as degree 3. The middle mental eminence was recorded. The cranial index was 75.4 which shows that the head was of middle length.

There was a narrow and middle bend sacrum. The pelvis as a whole was narrow and high with asymmetric and middling wide greater sciatic notch. The preauricular sulcus was not present and the arc compose was in the form of a fluently joining arch. These pelvic features together with the metrical assessment of the pelvic bone reveal that, with a high probability, the skeleton was of the male sex.

As for the age estimation, the pubic symphysis changes of phase VIII–IX were noticed, as well as the auricular surface changes of phase 6 which show the age category of 40–50 years. Using the cranial morphological changes to estimate the age, there was an almost complete obliteration of the sagittal suture, and middle obliteration of coronal and lambdoid sutures. The dental abrasion registered as degree H (both mandible and maxilla) which is within the 40–50 age category. The seven maxillary and eleven mandible teeth were lost before death.

The skeleton was affected by some pathological changes also referring to an age category. The postcranial bones revealed some traces of degenerative joint diseases, which generally afflicts most of the population over 45 years of age. As for this individual, the long bones articulations were observed to have slight arthritic changes. There were also markedly extensive arthritic changes on the right calcaneus, and slight arthritic changes on the navicular bone of both sides as well as in the metatarsal bones. The vertebrae showed very pronounced degenerative and productive changes, and osteophytes (in particular lumbar vertebrae). The thoracic vertebrae had Schmorl's nodes. There was no evidence of fractures but there was an extending productive change (exostosis) on the shaft of the left tibia under the lateral condyle on the posterior side (ossification of muscular or ligamentous attachment) indicating some evidence of repetitive stress or activity. As for the skull, there was dental caries present in the second right incisive tooth and right canine tooth of the maxilla.

The measurements of the long bones of the lower extremities were used to compute stature of the person, which was in average 171.3 ± 3.91cm.

Obvious traces of the mummification process (perforated cribriform plate of the right ethmoidal bone) were present on the skull, and there was a firm and dark substance – probably an ancient resin – in the posterior part of cranial cavity, together with the remnants of mummified tissue). On the postcranial skeleton, some remains of mummified tissue with cloth fibers clinging to the surface were also found, adding to the evidence for mummification in these human remains.

Conclusion: skeleton of male, ca 40–60 years old.

6.1.3. Summary

The secondary burials found in the area of the pyramid complex Lepsius no. 24 and of the mastaba of Nakhtsare can be connected with lower-rank occupants living in the near neighborhood of the Abusir Necropolis during the Graeco-Roman Period. The human skeletal remains recovered in 1994 were anthropologically processed and included five individuals. The good bone preservation was registered only in two burials (37/Q/94 and 38/Q/94); three burials were not complete due to disturbances on a previous occasion (74/J/94, 9/Q/94, and 10/Q/94). Regarding the very low number of studied skeletons, only individual conclusions could be made, with no possibility of any general characteristics analysis of the sample. The analyses determining sex and age of individuals revealed that the remains were of those individuals:

74/J/94: skeleton of immature individual, ca 14–15 years old
9/Q/94: skeleton of adult individual
10/Q/94: skeleton of female, ca 18–19 years old
37/Q/94: skeleton of female, ca 30–40 years old
38/Q/94: skeleton of male, ca 40–60 years old

The analyses of the skeletons also revealed that some pathological findings were recorded. In one case (38/Q/94) extensive degenerative changes (above all in the vertebrae) and arthritic changes in the bones of the foot (38/Q/94) were recorded. This supports the estimation of the bones being from older adult. Only mild degenerative joint disease was present on the postcranial bones from the skeleton 37/Q/94. Both individuals (38/Q/94 and 37/Q/94) displayed Schmorl's nodes on the vertebral bodies indicating either age-related changes or occupational stress caused by heavy manual labour during adolescence. In one case (38/Q/94), there was also evidence of a bony exostosis on the tibia which could be in connection with repeated stress (or a single incident) and strain on the muscles, possibly as result of the individual's occupation. Small enthesopathies were visible on the patella of both sides of one individual (37/Q/94) which is also an indicator of biomechanical stress affecting the organism. The caries were noted in both maxilla and mandible (38/Q/94, 10/Q/94, and 37/Q/94) but not in high rates.

As for the morphological variants, a sacralisation, common variance in the number of vertebrae, was registered in one case (37/Q/94). The occurrence of this trait is either congenital or caused by physical stress.

The only nonmetric traits noted was the presence of *fossa olecranii* in two cases (10/Q/94, 37/Q/94) which is not as rare. In this small sample, it can not be used to determinate whether the interred individuals were relatives or from the same population group.

The craniofacial measurements showed that there was one head that was medium long (38/Q/94) and one that was rather short (37/Q/94).

Two individuals showed obvious traces of the mummification process (38/Q/94, 10/Q/94) where perforated bones were present on the skull, and there with a firm and dark substance – probably an ancient resin – in the posterior part of cranial cavity. Some remains of mummified tissue with separated cloth fibers clinging to the surface were also found on the skull as well as on the postcranial skeleton.

The study of Strouhal and Bareš[11] could serve as a suitable comparative sample, but at present no confrontation with that evidence can be carried out, because this sample consisted of only five individuals.

---

[11] Strouhal, Bareš, *Secondary Cemetery.*

6.2. Human remains found in Pyramid Lepsius no. 24 and the Mastaba of Nebtyemneferes

Eugen Strouhal, Viktor Černý

6.2.1. Introduction

This report describes human remains found by the Czech (up to 1992 Czechoslovak) Institute of Egyptology in two neighbouring burial edifices – the Mastaba of Nebtyemneferes which was excavated in the 1987 season[12], and Pyramid Complex Lepsius no. 24, from the excavation season of 1994,[13] both at the Abusir Royal Cemetery.

From the anthropological point of view, a preliminary report on the find of a dismantled mummy in the pyramid Lepsius no. 24 was published[14]. A shorter paper was delivered at the Eighth International Congress of Egyptologists in Cairo in the year 2000.[15] The finds of skeletal remains in the Mastaba of Nebtyemneferes were not as yet published.

In the present chapter we shall firstly deal with the mummy from the pyramid Lepsius no. 24.

6.2.2. The mummy from the pyramid Lepsius no. 24 (49/J/94)

6.2.2.1. Stratigraphy of finds of the dismembered mummy

Parts of the disintegrated mummy were found in the western half of the destroyed burial chamber of the pyramid. Only fragments of the uppermost region of the skeleton lay on the original floor at the base of a layer of greyish sand and limestone fragments with remnants of dispersed wrappings nearby. They included parts of the skull (right parietal and zygomatic bones), the cervical and upper half of the thoracic spine, the upper half of the sternum, a few upper ribs and fragments of the lower ones, as well as both clavicles. In the same layer, pieces of a destroyed sarcophagus of red granite and remnants of burial equipment were found. The left half of the mandible was revealed 18–20 cm below the floor level, in a flat depression where a floor block had been torn out.

Other cranial fragments (the remaining bones of the calva, and the right half of the mandible), the neck, and most of the entire lower half of the body was oriented southeast to northwest and the upper right extremity was dislocated upwards. The fragments were found at the top of a 1.4 m thick layer of clean blown sand, which contained a limestone block coming from the destroyed casing of the burial chamber and there were, in addition, some organic remains, comprising the cut off right hand of the mummy.

The other upper extremity was found 1.5–2 m above the floor level in a secondary recess in the southwest corner of the burial chamber, created by pulling out an original casing block of the chamber.

The dismantling of the mummy and dispersal of its fragments to different places can be attributed to repeated robberies and activities of burial stone cutters in various periods following the burial.

6.2.2.2. Methods of examination

During the season of 1994, the constituents of the mummy were cleaned of sand, their original places determined and joined together. They were examined and described macroscopically by us.

---

[12] M. Verner, Excavations at Abusir. Season 1987, *ZÄS* 115/2, 1988, 165–171.
[13] M. Verner, Excavations at Abusir. Seasons of 1994/95 and 1995/96, *ZÄS* 124/1, 1997, 71–85.
[14] E. Strouhal, V. Černý, L.Vyhnánek, An X-ray examination of the mummy found in the Pyramid Lepsius No. XXIV at Abusir, in: *Abusir and Saqqara 2000*, 543–555, pls. 88–97.
[15] E. Strouhal, Three mummies from the royal cemetery at Abusir, in: *Egyptology at the Dawn of the 21 century* I, 478–485.

In 1998, it was possible to examine the mummy parts by X-ray, thanks to the permission granted by the Supreme Council of Antiquities of Egypt[16] and with the kind co-operation of the X-ray laboratory of the National Research Centre in the Pyramid Zone of Giza.[17] The radiographs were examined in collaboration with the late Czech radiologist and palaeopathologist, Luboš Vyhnánek, who became post mortem co-author of another paper on the same topic.[18]

6.2.2.3. The state of preservation of the mummy

The lower part of the body (from the horizontal break in the middle of the fifth lumbar vertebra down) and both upper extremities have been preserved as separated mummified pieces. The upper third of the trunk, also comprising the skull, was fragmented intentionally by robbers searching for valuables. All the remnant fragments fit together and to the lower part of the body in perfect contact points. By joining them together, the presence of *a single* body could be demonstrated (*fig.6.13, pl. XXIV*).

6.2.2.4. Embalming techniques

The mummy was originally well embalmed by desiccation (probably using natron) and copious coating with resin. During the millennia which elapsed after throwing the mummy out of its sarcophagus and coffin, dry sand drifted into the burial chamber from the surrounding desert, and the skin, with the underlying soft parts of the mummy, became folded and wrinkled.

Brain removal (excerebration) has been suggested by finding remnants of brown meningae alternating with a coating of black resin on the inner surface of the cranial cavity. Several compact fragments of filling, composed of numerous layers of folded linen soaked with resin, were found in the vicinity of the cranial fragments at the top of a 1.4 m thick layer of clean blown sand. One of them displayed a regular convex surface and a flat base with crevices caused by folding the linen. This mass of fabric could have easily fitted into one of the fossae cerebelli as an occipital filling of the evacuated cranial cavity (*fig. 6.14, pl. XXIV*). Because the nasal cavity did not survive, we have no proof of an embalming opening within it.

6.2.2.5. Demographic data

Concerning the individual age of the mummified body, the synchondrosis sphenooccipitalis of the cranial base is completely fused. All the third molars (except for the missing upper left one) are erupted up to the occlusal level, but not yet abraded. The first molars show just tiny dots of dentine. All preserved teeth are healthy; there are no traces of intravital tooth loss and the alveolar process displays no retraction (*fig.6.15, pl. XXVI*).

All of the preserved cranial sutures are open if viewed from both sides (*fig.6.19, pl. XXIV*), except for the right half of the lambdoid suture which was in an anomalously progressed fusion viewed from inside, but appears open when viewed from the outside.

A running fusion is shown by the epiphysis of the right clavicle (transition between stages II to III, according to Szilvássy).[19] The sacrum still has a slit between bodies of S_{1-2}.

The epiphyses of the other bones are firmly fused with the pertinent diaphyses. On the distal femora and both ends of the tibiae, transversal lines of density of the bone shadow represent short-term remnants of the fused growth fissures. According to these features, the individual died as a young adult, with an age in the range of 21–23 years.

---

[16] We extend our thanks to the former Director General Professor Dr. Mohammad Gaballah and the Director of the Pyramid zone of Giza Dr. Zahi Hawass.

[17] We appreciate the kind co-operation of Dr. Azza Mohammad Sarry El-Din, Dr. Mohammad Al-Tohany Suleiman and Dr. Aiman Ahmad Abd El-Ghani.

[18] E. Strouhal, V. Černý, L. Vyhnánek, in: *Abusir and Saqqara 2000*.

[19] J. Szilvássy, Age determination of the sternal artcular faces of the clavicula, *J. Hum. Evol.* 9, 1980, 609–611.

The female sex of the body is obvious. It is evidenced by a flat, completely desiccated left mamma, and remnants of the right one on the anterior side of the lower chest. To these sexual features, the excellently preserved labia maiora of the vagina has to be added (*fig. 6.16, pl. XXV*). In addition, the sexually dependent descriptive features and the anthropometric values (*table 6.1*) fit well into the ranges of ancient Egyptian females of the Late Period to the Ptolemaic-Roman Period[20].

The description which follows has been combined from the macroscopic and radiological points of view (the later marked by *X-rays* in italics) according to the examined body parts.

6.2.2.6. The skull

The skull, smashed post mortem by the robbers, is defective. A calva was reconstructed except for missing anterior part of right half of the frontal bone and the left temporal bone (*fig. 6.17*, pl. XXV). Of the face, only the zygomatic bones and the alveolar parts of the maxilla survived. A few parts of the cranial base survived separately. The mandible was broken into two halves: the left condyle is missing (see *fig. 6.15, pl. XXIV*).

Soft tissues covered with skin survived only on the right temporal and occipital bones, together with the right auricle deformed by drying out. The mummy also possessed a bunch of straight hair – somewhat dark brown to rusty in colour (*fig. 6.18, pl. XXV*).

From the *X-rays*, the calva in axial projection is quite gracile. Its thickness on both tubera frontalia is 6 mm, on the tubera parietalia left 6 mm, right 7 mm (*fig.6.19, pl. XXVI*). The upper edge of the left orbit is thin and sharp, the tubera frontalia and parietalia are well pronounced. The forehead slopes perpendicularly and the tubercula marginalia are of medium size. The mandible is relatively more robust, but the chin has a well rounded protuberantia with slight tubercula mentalia.

From the upper dentition, the C-M_1 teeth are on both sides in situ, from the left I_{1-2} only the roots survived; the right M_3 remains in situ. From the lower dentition, the left P_2–M_3 and right M_1 and M_3 remain in situ. The other teeth lost their crowns post mortem and only their roots or root tips survived inside the alveoli (*fig. 6.15, pl. XXIV*).

6.2.2.7. The neck and loose parts of the upper thorax

On the cranial end of the neck fragment, the broken-off right occipital condyle of the skull adheres, while, on the left side, the upper joint surface of the atlas has been exposed. Both joint surfaces of the atlas and the interior of the spinal channel are coated with black resin.

Viewed from the anterior side, the neck fragment preserves the pharyngeal cavity which lacks the anterior wall. In its posterior wall, the contours of the bodies of the removed upper cervical vertebrae are displayed in outline. In the lower third of the neck, the fibrous septum between the pharynx and the larynx has been preserved. Their respective cavities have been narrowed by desiccation antero- posteriorly to 3 and 2 mm broad crevices. The mucosae of both cavities are coated with resin. On the anterior side of the larynx soft tissue, permeated by resin, has survived in which the thyroid cartilage retained a prominence of 9 mm.

The dorsal side of the neck is covered by skin and the underlying neck muscles are folded lengthwise (*fig. 6.20, pl. XXVI*). In the midline, the spinal processes of the removed cervical vertebrae retained their outlines.

From the *X-rays* of the neck, the entire, isolated cervical spine can be inspected. The small and gracile vertebral bodies reveal fine spongiotic structure. The intervertebral spaces are regular and narrow and the edges of the bodies as well as the apex dentis of the epistropheus do not show any osteophytes. On the dorsal side of the spine, remnants of the neck muscles are visible, on the ventral side, at the level of C_{3-6}, soft tissues can be discerned (*fig. 6.20, pl. XXVI*).

---

[20] Strouhal, Bareš, *Secondary Cemetery*, 156–160.

A separate fragment consisting of vertebrae T_2 to T_7 (except for the posterior edge of the arch of T_4) is covered by remnants of ligaments and muscle, strongly permeated by resin. According to the *X-rays*, the vertebral bodies are small and square, a typical feminine feature. The resinous flow has coated all sides of the spinal channel suggesting that resin was poured inside via the empty braincase (*fig. 6.20, pl. XXVI*).

Another separate fragment consists of the manubrium sterni covered by soft tissue on both sides and partial fusion with the preserved upper third of the corpus sterni, coated with resin. The upper and left edge of the manubrium has an irregular outline without exostoses (*fig. 6.21, pl. XXVI*).

Several wholly or partially preserved gracile upper ribs show fine spongiotic structure and thin compactae (*fig. 6.21, pl. XXVI*).

6.2.2.8. The lower thorax

The lower part of the thorax has been preserved as a whole between the eighth thoracic and upper half of the fifth lumbar vertebral body, which broke horizontally at mid-height. The chest has a cylindrical and elongated shape, with the widest diameter in its upper reach, tapering towards the waist.

In the anterior surface of the thorax, skin resembling parchment has been preserved with the remains of completely dried out, flat mammae. Inside the open, broken lower edge of the thoracic cavity, numerous layers of folded linen fillings in bundles can be observed. They are penetrated by resin and the interior walls of the thoracic cavity are coated by the same substance (*fig. 6.22, pl. XXVII*).

The dorsal side of the thorax is almost completely covered by ochre-brown skin, in the right half straight, in the left half irregularly folded, with occasional fissures or cracks, without resinous coating. The spine projects by its spinal processes (*fig. 6.23, pl. XXVII*).

According to the antero-posterior *X-rays*, the thoracic cage consists of nine left and four right ribs, some of them broken post mortem. The last ribs on either sides have wavy shapes. The lower thoracic and lumbar sections of the spine are almost straight and their intervertebral discs are regular and narrow (except for a hint of the commencement of dextroconvex scoliosis at T_{12}–L_2, with slightly opening right edges of intervertebral spaces). Not even incipient osteophytes on vertebral bodies can be distinguished (*fig. 6.24, pl. XXVII*).

Both halves of the thoracic cavity have been stuffed with textiles folded haphazardly and partly soaked in resin. In the right hemithorax they are in less contrast to those in the left hemithorax. A still more contrasting globular bundle, permeated by more resin, can be discerned in the lower part of the cavity (*fig. 6.24, pl. XXVII*).

In the oblique projection by the *X-rays*, the spine shows only a slight thoracic kyphosis and a pronounced lordosis. The described fillings, permeated by more resin, are mostly placed in the posterior part of the thoracic cavity, while they are sparse and exhibit less contrast in its anterior part (*fig. 6.25, pl. XXVIII*).

6.2.2.9. The upper extremity girdles

Both the separately found gracile clavicles have broken off ends, for the left, it is the medial one, for the right, the lateral one. The preserved right epiphysis was in fusion, between stages II and III of Szilvássy's scale (see note 19 and *fig. 6.28, pl. XXIX*).

Both the isolated gracile scapulae are almost complete. The left one is still covered on the dorsal side by folded soft tissue coated with resin. On the ventral side, in the upper half, it retains remnants of the subscapular muscle, in the lower half the bone is exposed. The right scapula is almost entirely bare except for the remains of soft tissue on the acromion and resinous coating on the cavitas glenoidalis (*fig. 6.28, pl. XXIX*).

Both fragments of the free extremities consist of the humeri and antebrachial bones, embalmed in an extended position (*fig. 6.22, pl. XXVII*). The axes of the humeri, with the axes of the antebrachial bones, include deviation angles 160° right and 170° left. This is a typical feature of gracile young females. Soft tissues have been preserved throughout the whole extent, folded longitudinally, in places with a thin resinous coating, except for the proximal and distal ends. White stains of moulds are apparent on both arms. The exposed humeral heads are small and smooth. The distal joint surfaces have been preserved except for that of the left ulna (*fig. 6.26, pl. XXVIII*).

By *X-rays* the bones are slender. The humeral heads are completely fused without remnants of growth fissures. Distal ends of the humeri have largely perforated septa between the fossae coronoideae and olecrani in harmony with the gracile body build and female sex of the individual. All joint surfaces except that of the broken off left distal ulnar are smooth, without arthritic changes. On the diaphyses, muscular attachments appear indistinct in the radiographs (*fig. 6.28, pl. XXIX*).

6.2.2.10. The right hand

This separately found fragment (except for the middle and distal phalangae of the second finger) has been preserved from the proximal row of the carpal bones to the tips of the fingers with the well set nails. The hand is small, elongated, narrow and gracile. The skin and the underlying tissue are longitudinally folded, especially in the palms, in places transversally cracked, by the drying up of the flesh. White spots of moulds are present in the palm (*figs. 6.26–6.27, pl. XXVIII*).

From the *X-rays* we can tell that no remnants of growth fissures, post mortem breakage or pathologies can be revealed (*fig. 6.28, pl. XXIX*).

The left hand, cut off, thrown away and perhaps destroyed by the robbers, was not found in our excavations.

Bone	No.	Name of the measurement	Value/Range (mm)
Calva	1	Maximum length	165–170
	8	Maximum breadth	138
Mandible	65	Bicondylar breadth	126–128
	66	Bigonial breadth	97
	68(1)	Length of mandible	91
	69	Symphyseal height	32–33
	69.1	Height of mandibular body (L)	30
	69.3	Thickness of mandibular body (L)	12
	70(2)	Minimum height of ramus (L)	48
	71	Minimum breadth of ramus (L)	33
	79	Mandibular (gonial) angle (L)	118°?
Sternum	2	Length of manubrium	43
	–	Breadth of upper edge of corpus	22
Scapula	2	Breadth (L)	93
Clavicle	6	Circumference (L)	29
	6	Circumference (R)	30
Humerus	9	Transversal diameter of caput (L)	36
	10	Vertical diameter of caput (L)	37
Radius	5 (6)	Breadth of the distal end (L)	26
Pelvis	2	Bicristal breadth	235
	5	Bispinal breadth	180
Fibula	1	Maximum length (L)	358
	1	Maximum length (R)	357

Table 6.1
Measurements of the skeletal parts of the anonymous female mummy 49/J/94

Numbers of measurements by Martin, Saller, *Lehrbuch der Anthropologie*.
(L) = left, (R) = right

6.2.2.11. The lower extremity girdles

The lower half of the body has been preserved as a whole. This reflects a lack of interest on the part of the robbers to dismantle it – in distinction to the marked fragmentation of the upper parts of the body, the possible repository of valuable objects (*figs. 6.29–6.30, pl. XXIX*).

On the outer sides of the pelvis, well preserved skin with underlying soft tissue is longitudinally folded. It has a dark brown colour as a result of the thin resinous coating. In some areas, remnants of light brown to ochre wrappings of finely woven textile adhere, stuck on by resin. Similar wrappings were found in the vicinity, dispersed there after unwrapping the mummy (*fig. 6.31, pl. XXX*).

The anterior wall of the abdominal cavity is deeply sunken in the dorsal direction, betraying a lack of firm fillings in the pelvis under the partly preserved islets of skin. In the concavity of the left iliac wing some textile rags permeated by resin and partly covered by white moulds have been laid bare. Near the dorsal edge, exposed spongiosa of the broken vertebral body L_5 can be found (*figs. 6.29, pl. XXIX and 6.31, pl. XXX*). In the pubic region, the labia majora of the vagina have been excellently preserved (*fig. 6.16, pl. XXV*).

On the back part of the pelvic region, partly straight and partly folded skin with gluteal muscles, projecting tubera ischiadica, and the gluteal groove with the anus can be observed. There are many white spots of mould, not only in the gluteal region, but also under the knees and on the heels, and in places where the resting body had touched the sometimes humid sand base (*fig. 6.30, pl. XXIX*).

From the *X-rays*, textile fillings in the small pelvis together with a few contrasting shadows of irregular rod-like lumps, probably of resin, can be discerned. The pelvis reveals female features – apart from the vertically oval shape of the pelvic inlet probably due to distortion by the X-ray projection. The preauricular grooves are still shallow, a sign that the female had not borne a child. The sacrum still has an open slit between the bodies of segments S_{1-2} confirming the young adult age of the individual. Both hip joints have a regular smooth shape with very narrow slits. The femoral heads are fused without remnants of any epiphyseal fissures. The same applies to the completed fusion of the greater and smaller trochanters (*fig. 6.32, pl. XXX*).

Table 6.2 Measurements of the mummified parts of the anonymous queen 49/J/94. [1] from the most proximal edge of the carpus to the tip of the 3rd finger [2] between the heads of the 2nd and 5th metacarpals [3] between the posterior side of the heel and the tip of big toe. (L) = left (R) = right

Region	Name of the measurement	Value (mm)
Upper arm	Circumference in the middle (L)	77
	Circumference in the middle (R)	79
Forearm	Circumference in the middle (L)	92
	Circumference in the middle (R)	91
Hand	Length (R)[1]	167
	Breadth (R)[2]	56
Hips	Bitrochanteric breadth	253
Leg	Length (L)	838
	Length (R)	834
	Circumference in the middle of thigh (L)	122
	Circumference in the middle of thigh (R)	125
	Maximum breadth of the knee (L)	72
	Maximum breadth of the knee (R)	75
	Circumference of the calf (L)	120
	Circumference of the calf (R)	118
Foot	Length (L)[3]	204
	Length (R)[3]	203

The lower extremities are very thin and possess desiccated and longitudinally folded skin with underlying muscles (*figs. 6.29–30, pl. XXIX*) . On the other hand, femoral compactae appear from the *X-rays* to be relatively solid, compared with the spongiosa of the medulla (*fig. 6.32, pl. XXX*).

In the *X-rays*, there is a curious asymmetry of the femoral necks, the left one appearing shorter than the right one. It is connected with a difference in the colodiaphyseal angles, the left one being smaller than the right one. It could have been a distortion caused by the projection. The dessicated and longitudinally folded gluteal and femoral muscles can be only faintly discerned in the radiographs (*fig. 6.32, pl. XXX*).

The surfaces of both knee joints are well contoured and smooth, with narrow slits, without even incipient arthritic changes. The transversal linear density of the bone shadow at the femoral condyles and partly on the tibial heads and distal ends are remnants from fused growth fissures. Over the lateral half of the proximal end of the left fibula, shadows of two rod-like objects, possibly cylindrical beads, can be discerned (*fig. 6.33, pl. XXXI*).

Both crural bones revealed in the *X-rays* are thin to medium compactae. The complete absence of Harris lines in the distal quarters of the tibial diaphyses reveals that the young female did not suffer from any chronic disease or a long period of famine. The joint surfaces of both talocrural joints are also well contoured and smooth with narrow slits and no pathological changes (*fig. 6.34, pl. XXXI*).

The feet are in dorsal semiflextion. Only both big toes have all the pertinent phalagae preserved, while the other toes lack some or all of them . The preserved nails are deeply inserted under the edges of the surrounding soft tissues (*figs. 6.35–6.36, pl. XXXII*).

The skin and underlying soft tissues of the soles are dried and adhere tightly to the foot bones. The deeply excavated longitudinal and slightly developed transversal vaults of the feet are well apparent (*fig. 6.36, pl. XXXII*).

From the *X-rays*, the joints of the feet are smooth, without pathological changes. There are no growth fissure or lines of increased density (*fig. 6.34, pl. XXXI*).

6.2.2.12. The anthropometric examination

A few skeletal measurements of the individual which could be determined in some of the fragments are assembled in *table 6.1*. Several important data are lacking because the presence of soft tissues did not permit us to view the underlying structures. On the other hand, we measured some regions of the mummy to show the slenderness or shapes of some of them (*table 6.2*).

All measurements are small, in accordance with the female sex of the individual. They fit into the variation range of ancient Egyptian females of the Abusir region from the Late Period to the Ptolemaic–Roman Periods (see note 20).

Measures taken on mummified parts express the results of combination of small osteometric values of the individual with a great amount of shrinkage of the soft tissue by dessication during the past millennia.

According to the length of the left and the right fibula, the stature was reconstructed using tables for Afro-American females by Trotter and Gleser as about 160 cm.[21] This roughly equals the assessed length of the mummy joined together from its fragments (*fig. 6.13, pl. XXIV*).

6.2.2.13. Discussion

The stratigraphic evidence of finds of the single fragments reveals that the mummy was firstly thrown out of its coffin and sarcophagus by the tomb robbers. They unwrapped it on the floor of the burial chamber. Searching for valuables in the uppermost parts of the mummy, they dismantled it into fragments and unwrapped them, smashing the skull. Most of these disrupted parts, except for the neck, had subsequently lost organic remains by the influence of intermittent atmospheric moisture.

The remaining parts of the mummy were dissected into larger constituents (upper extremities, hands, lower trunk with the lower extremities and feet), which were of not enough interest to the robbers for them to unwrap these pieces and break them into smaller fragments. After a long period, when a thick layer of dry desert sand accumulated on top of these remains, stone cutters and/or other gangs of robbers moved these pieces up together with some of the fragments from the upper region of the body. In spite of these vicissitudes, the mummy parts could still be joined together almost entirely in various contact places, except for the missing pieces of the skull, distal joint of right ulna and left hand, as well as the phalangae of some fingers and toes.

---

[21] Trotter, Gleser, *Amer. J. Phys. Anthropol.* 10, 1952, 463–514. Tables for Afroamericans suit better to ancient Egyptians than the ones for White Americans.

According to morphoscopic, anthropometric and radiographic examination, the mummy belonged to a young female, who died as a 21–23 year old. She was the sole occupant of the burial chamber of a small pyramid Lepsius no. 24, which was obviously built for a queen. It is curious that her mummy remained the only burial in the ruined substructure of the pyramid during the elapsed millennia. No other remains of a secondary burial, which are frequently found in the royal cemetery at Abusir, were found during the excavations.

The mummification technique applied to the mummy was perfect in securing the survival of the body for millennia. The body was eviscerated, dried up, coated richly by resin inside and outside, packed with linen, permeated by resin and wrapped by linen coated by resin. Therefore, it could successfully resist mishandling during repeated robberies and climatic influences especially after dismantling the roof of the burial chamber by stone cutters.

Moreover, in spite of the fact that the nasal cavity did not survive and no inspection for the presence of an embalming hole could be made, we found indirect evidence for a possible brain removal (excerebration and textile filling of the brain cavity as well as application of hot resin which coated the spinal channel; see p. 239). This embalming intervention was attested up to date as starting no earlier than at the beginning of the Middle Kingdom.[22] It must have been then an *exclusive innovation*. There is not yet certain proof for its existence in the Old Kingdom.

Because no other features of the embalming techniques of the periods later than Fifth Dynasty were revealed in the mummy (as, for example, the presence of amulets or scarabs in wrappings, of a heart scarab, visceral parcels, subcutaneous stuffing etc.), the brain removal evidence cannot be taken for an argument against the Fifth Dynasty date of the mummy. On the contrary, the possible excerebration suggests a hypothesis of a still earlier date for beginnings of this procedure.

For the sake of certainty, chronometric dating of a fragment of a hand phalanx with remnants of skin (ETH-18817) was performed, yielding conventional age 4070 years ± 55 years BP and dendrochronologically calibrated age range of 2701–2465 years BC.[23] Its upper limit is 201 years, the lower one 45 years and its mean (2583 years BC) 83 years higher than the usually accepted date of the Fifth Dynasty (2500–2350 years BC). The dating range for the female's mummy is on both ends 72–73 years higher than the one obtained for the King Raneferef (2628–2393 years BC).[24] In view of the well known fact that chronometric dates after 2000 BC are usually higher than the data accepted by Egyptologists, there can be no doubt that both individuals lived during the Fifth Dynasty.

The high status of the female has been supported also by the absence of any pathological changes in her dentition and skeleton, especially in the spine and joints. Moreover, according to the lack of Harris lines for retarded growth, occurring often in Ancient Egypt in the remains of common people, she was exempt from chronic diseases or longer periods of hunger during her childhood and adolescence.

Her body build was slender, with a gracile skeleton, feeble muscularity and "aristocratic" elongated hands. She had a stature of about 160 cm, higher than the mean for Ancient Egyptian females. Her physical features according to skeletal and mummy measurements fall into the range of ancient Egyptian women. She clearly had not exerted herself in any strenuous physical work. Moreover, it is probable that she did not give birth to a child.

Concerning the identification of the mummy who was buried in the pyramid Lepsius no. 24, it is precluded by the fact that no name survived either in the

[22] E. Strouhal, Embalming excerebration in the Middle Kingdom, in: *Science in Egyptology*, 141–154.
[23] Our thanks for this information to Dr. G. Bonani and prof. Dr. Willy Woelfli from the Eidgenössische technische Hochschule, Zürich, Switzerland.
[24] E. Strouhal, A. Němečková, Identification of King Raneferef according to human remains found in the burial chamber of the Unfinished Pyramid, in: Verner *et al.*, *Raneferef*, 513–518.

Bone	No.	Name of the measurement	Value (mm)	
Vertebrae	1	Anterior body heights C5–7	12 12 14	
	1	Anterior body heights T1–12	15 16 17 18 18 18 19 19 19 21 22 25	
	1	Anterior body heights L1 and L4	26 28	
			L	R
Clavicle	1	Maximum length	131	–
	6	Circumference of the middle	30	–
Humerus	1	Maximum length	–	291
	7	Minimum circumference of diaphysis	51	51
	8	Head cicumference	–	115
	9	Transversal diameter of humeral head	–	35
	10	Sagittal diameter of humeral head	–	37
Radius	1	Maximum length	215	215
	3	Minimum circumference	33	34
Ulna	1	Maximum length	230	232
	3	Minimum circumference	30	30
Hip bone	1	Height of the pelvis	120	–
		Height of ischium including acetabulum	83	83
	22	Maximum diameter of acetabulum	44	43
	33	Pubic angle	90	90
Femur	1	Maximum length	–	410
	6	Sagittal diameter of mid-diaphysis	–	26
	7	Transversal diameter of mid-diaphysis	–	20
	9	Upper transversal diameter of diaphysis	–	27
	10	Upper sagittal diameter of diaphysis	–	21
	18	Vertical diameter of femoral head	–	37
	19	Transversal diameter of femoral head	–	37
Tibia	1b	Medial length	340	–
	8a	Maximum diameter at foramen nutritium	27	27
	9a	Transversal diameter at foramen nutritium	20	20
	10b	Minimum circumference	60	60
Fibula	1	Maximum length	341	–
	4a	Minimum circumference	31	–
Talus	1	Maximum length	–	47?
	2	Breadth	–	37?
	3	Height	27	–

pyramid temple or on any of the graffiti on the stone blocks from the core of the pyramid[25]. We can only conjecture according to the small size of the pyramid and the female sex of its user that the burial belonged to a queen of the Fifth Dynasty. The application of the still rare excerebration seems obviously connected with her higher status, as does the presence of advanced mummification, known only for the upper social classes during the Fifth Dynasty. From the known queens of the middle part of the Fifth Dynasty, Niuserre's consort Reputnebu[26] could be a candidate as suggested by M. Verner.[27]

6.2.3. Skeletal remains from the Mastaba of Nebtyemneferes

6.2.3.1. Finding circumstances

The Mastaba of Nebtyemneferes (labelled by M), located east of the Pyramid Complex Lepsius no. 24, was excavated in the season 1987. It possesses two oblong north–south oriented chambers in its substructure. The western one is filled to its capacity with a coarse white limestone sarcophagus, around which lay the

Table 6.3

Measurements of the postcranial skeleton of Princess Nebtyemneferes (2/M/87).

Numbers of measurements by Martin, Saller, *Lehrbuch der Anthropologie I*.
L = left, R = right

---

[25] Verner, *ZÄS*, 1997.
[26] B. Vachala, Ein weiterer Beleg für die Königin Repetnebu, *ZÄS* 106, 1979, 176.
[27] M. Verner, Abusir Pyramids "Lepsius no. XXIV. and no. XXV", in: *Homm. Leclant*, 371–378.

remnants of textile wrappings from a body that had been unwrapped. In the eastern chamber, remains of the burial equipment, originally deposited here but plundered in antiquity, were found in the chamber, together with skeletal remains (2/M/87) thrown out from the sarcophagus, which, with the highest probability, belonged to Princess Nebtyemneferes.[28]

In the subsidiary shaft near the southwest corner of the mastaba, 36–40 cm below the level of its orifice, under a sand layer in its southeast corner, a small wooden coffin with a lid sunk inside was found (length 102 cm, breadth 47 cm, height 27 cm). Into it a child's skeleton (13/M/87), lying in situ stretched out on its left side, with the lower extremities flexed 120° at the hip joint and 80° in the knee joint was squeezed. The head was oriented north, the face looking east, the right upper extremity stretched along the side of the coffin, the left one flexed backwards, pointing towards the chin. The flexed skeleton was in situ 92 cm long, while the reconstructed length of the body according to length of the femora (see note 28) was 135.5 cm; the outer length of the coffin, however, was 102 cm. Because of this, the lower extremities had to be flexed to accommodate the body.

Partial remains of a swept adult burial (8/M/87) were found in a layer of brick destruction inside the serdab of the mastaba.

6.2.3.2. The postcranial skeleton of Nebtyemneferes (2/M/87)

6.2.3.2.1. State of preservation

All the discovered bones were devoid of wrappings. Remnants of soft tissue survived on several bones. The skull and mandible with cervical vertebrae C_1 and C_2 are missing. Of the postcranial skeleton, the right clavicle, humerus and ulna, both radii and hand bones, right patella, both tali and calcanei as well as the small feet bones have been preserved entire. All the other preserved bones as cervical vertebrae $C_{3,5-7}$, thoracic T_{1-12} and lumbar $L_{1,3,4}$, sacrum, sternum, ribs, both scapulae, left humerus and ulna, both innominate bones, right femur, both tibiae and fibulae are defective.

6.2.3.2.2. Demographic data

According to the sexually dependent features of the pelvis and a few other postcranial bones, the slender gracile body build and small values of metric features, the female sex is unambiguous (*table 6.3*).

Osteophytes of the spine are only in the initial grade 1, except for vertebra C_5 which is recorded at grade 2 (length under 3 mm). Degenerative spondylarthritis is apparent in $C_{3/4}$ right, $C_{4/5}$ left and L_{4-5} on both sides. The upper terminal plate of L_3 is depressed to a maximum depth of 4 mm, sloping to an unhealed linear crack at the anterior edge (10 mm long), probably a traumatic compression.

The manubrium sterni has long osteophytes at the joint surfaces, which are in other locations absent. The manubrium has been fused with the corpus. Sacral segments S_{1-2} are fused without the remnants of a fissure. No degenerative arthritic changes are patent in any of the big joints. Age at death points to the range of 30–40 years.

6.2.3.2.3. Osteoscopy

The postcranial skeleton is gracile to medium robust and the muscular relief medium developed.

The clavicles are only slightly curved and have only small flat tuberositates costoclaviculares. The humeri display feeble tuberositates deltoideae and have no perforations at the distal ends. There are still no ageing changes on their proximal ends. The radii are medium, the ulnae slightly curved. Both bones have only slightly developed cristae interosseae.

The cristae iliacae are medium large and the incisura ichiadica major is broadly open. The sulcus praeauricularis is large and deep, but there are no pits on posterior

---

[28] Verner, *ZÄS*, 1988, 167–168.

sides of the pubes. The foramen obturatum is small and triangular. The pubes form a subpubic arch.

The right femur shows a pilaster of grade 3, the tuberositas glutea is grade 3, a fossa hypotrochanterica is present no ageing changes are apparent. On the tibiae, the lineae musculi solei form slight ridges, the fibulae are medium deeply grooved.

6.2.3.2.4. Osteometry

The postcranial measurements of Nebtyemneferes fit also well into the ancient Egyptian female range[29] (*table 6.3*). Comparison with the skeletal measurements of the anonymous female mummy from the pyramid Lepsius no. 24 (49/J/87) is unfortunately possible only in four of them. The circumference of the left clavicle, and the transversal and vertical diameters of the humeral head are almost the same in both persons, while the maximum length of the fibula is 17 mm smaller in the princess than in the queen (*cf. table 6.1* and *table 6.3*).

The stature of Nebtyemneferes can be reconstructed with a greater reliability than the stature of the anonymous female, because it is based on the maximum lengths of eight long bones. The resulting value of 154.2 cm is 5.8 cm lower than that of the anonymous female, and approaches the assessed common mean of 155 cm for ancient Egyptian females.

6.2.3.2.5. Blood groups

With the help of the navicular bone and one of the cuboid bones of Nebtyemneferes, it proved possible to determine her blood group[30]. The results yielded on repeated assays determined that she had group 0. The same blood group was determined in the remains of the educator/tutor Idu, in distinction to groups A of King Djedkare Isesi and the princesses in the Djedkare's Family Cemetery at Abusir[31]. This has to be considered a matter of chance because of the relatively big distance of the Mastaba of Nebtyemneferes from the aforementioned family cemetery. No blood group could be determined, for technical reasons up till now, in the anonymous mummy of the supposed queen from L24 (6.2.2).

6.2.3.2.6. Discussion

Like the anonymous female from pyramid Lepsius no. 24, Princess Nebtyemneferes also had a slender figure with a gracile body build. She was smaller than the queen, died older than the former and gave birth to more than one child. Comparison of the two females, because of the missing skull of Nebtyemneferes and the still mummified majority of the body of the queen, was possible only in four measurements. Such evidence is too meagre to permit any contingent argument for their eventual blood relationship.

6.2.3.3. The child's skeleton in the dummy shaft (13/M/87)

6.2.3.3.1. State of preservation

Small remnants of coarse textile wrappings adhering to the calva have been preserved, without traces of resin. No resinous filling of the cranial cavity was observed. The bones are ochre coloured, slightly rotten and partly disintegrating because of the atmosphere, but they are without the spots that result after resin has been used, precluding embalming.

Of the skull there are a defective calva, fragments from the base, the left maxilla with left zygomaticum and a defective mandible. The spine is complete (except for the right half of the atlas). The sacrum and pelvis are well preserved.

---

[29] Strouhal, Bareš, *Secondary Cemetery*, 158–160.
[30] We are indebted for this to Assoc. Prof. Dr. Přemysl Klír of the Postgraduate Medical Institute in Prague.
[31] E. Strouhal, P. Klír, A. Němečková, The anthropological evaluation of human skeletal remains from the mastabas of Djedkare Isesi's family cemetery at Abusir, in: Verner, Callender, *Djedkare's Cemetery*, 119–132.

The bones of the upper extremity girdle (both scapulae, claviculae, humeri, radii and left ulna) as well as the lower extremity ones (both femurs, tibiae and, fibulae) are defective, while both tali, calcanei and small feet bones are preserved entirely. In addition, almost all isolated epiphyses survived.

6.2.3.3.2. Demographic data

There is a defective deciduous dentition with the fully erupted lower permanent incisors (root length 7 mm, a narrow slot at the tip of the root) and erupting upper ones (root length 6 mm, tip of the root still open).

The bodies and arches of the vertebrae are fused (except for the unfused anterior and posterior arches of the atlas, which fuse around 9 years). The adjoining apex dentis epistrophei is not yet fused with the dens (these fuse around 12 years).

The sacral segments are not united and they still lack the apophyses of the massae laterales. Constituents of the hip bones are still free. The ischia are also not fused with the pubic bones in their lower contact points where they unite between 7–12 years.[32] The tubercula majora and minora of the humeri were in fusion, which happens between 6–8 years. The epicondyli laterales are unfused (they fuse at 14 years). Epiphyses and apophyses of all other bones are not yet fused with their pertinent diaphyses. The resulting age at death points to 7–8 years.

Sexing by morphology is unreliable for this age.

Table 6.4
Measurements of the
postcranial skeleton of child
13/M/87.

Numbers of measurements
by Martin, Saller, *Lehrbuch
der Anthropologie* I.
L = left, R = right

Bone	No.	Name of the measurement	Value (mm)	
			L	R
Clavicula	1	Diaphyseal length	96	–
Hip bone	9	Iliac height	87	86
	12	Iliac breadth	95	94
	15	Height of ilium	55	53
	17	Pubic length	40	39
Femur	1	Diaphyseal length	279	278
Tibia	1	Diaphyseal length	232	232

6.2.3.3.3. Osteometry

Measurements of some pelvic and long extremity bones show values slightly above the assessed age interval (*table 6.4*). According to the mean length of both femurs, the stature was about 135.5 cm,[33] somewhat higher compared with the determined dental and epihyseal age.

6.2.3.3.4. Discussion

The burial belonged apparently to a poor child whose body length had to be squeezed into a much smaller and very simple wooden coffin. It was wrapped in coarse textiles, without proper mummification of the body and no resinous filling of the cranial cavity. The location of the burial within a subsidiary shaft precludes its dating to the Fifth Dynasty mastaba built for a princess. The skeleton remained in situ, overlooked or ignored by later robbers. It was evidently a burial belonging to a period between the Late Period to the Ptolemaic-Roman secondary cemetery, which favoured the use of older burial premises.

6.2.3.4. The swept adult skeleton in the serdab (8/M/87)

6.2.3.4.1. State of preservation

Only a few remains of the upper part of the skeleton survived. The skull, preserved except for a mandible, is nearly intact. Of the postcranial skeleton, only seven thoracic vertebrae ($T_{1-2, 4-8}$), fragments of six ribs, the right scapula without the medial edge and the right clavicle have been preserved with several defects.

---

[32] Schinz *et al.*, *Lehrbuch der Röntgendiagnostik*, Tabs. 4–7.
[33] Olivier, *Pratique anthropologique*, 259 (table based on a curve by T. D. Stewart).

6.2.3.4.2. Mummification techniques

The skeleton was mummified. On the surface of the ochre coloured bones many black spots of resin and remnants of dried soft tissue are present. A filling by poured hot and later hardened resin has been preserved inside the cranial cavity. The nasal cavity is devoid of all left conchae and of two thirds of the nasal septum. The opening in the cribra ethmoidea communicates with the one in the medial wall of the left orbit. There is even an opening in the anterior aspect of the left half of the corpus sphenoidis (8 × 12 mm).

6.2.3.4.3. Demographic data

According to the calvarium which is big and robust, with both glabella and external occipital protuberance of Broca's grade 3,[34] the deceased had a very sloping forehead, absence of tubera frontalia and slightly developed tubera parietalia, strong lineae temporales and strong muscular relief on the planum nuchale: the male sex of the individual is indisputable.

Concerning the age at death, abrasion of the preserved upper teeth is progressed (on both M_{1-2} almost to the half height of crown, on both P_1 with slight remnants of enamel, on the right P_2 with large spots of dentine and on the right C abraded almost to half of the crown. A mesial caries (24 mm, depth 3 mm), without open pulpar cavity was present in the left M_1, while the other teeth and their alveoli are healthy. Retraction of the alveolar process is medium. All the cranial sutures are open from outside. The thoracic vertebrae show no osteophytes or spondylarthritis. These features point to an age in the range of 25–35 years.

6.2.3.4.4. Cranioscopy

The calvarium is long and narrow, drawn backwards and up, with the vertex 2.5 cm dorsally of the bregma, followed by a short slope to an obliquely flattened occiput. In vertical norm the calvarium has an ovoid outline, in occipital norm, it has a house form.

No.	Name of the measurement	Value (mm)
1	Cranial lenghth	188
8	Cranial breadth	138
5	Basis length	94
9	Minimum frontal breadth	94
10	Maximum frontal breadth	109
11	Biauricular breadth	123
13(1)	Maximum mastoideal breadth	123
17	Basion-bregma height	133
40	Facial length	86
23	Horizontal circumference	530
24	Transversal arch	297
25	Median sagittal arch	376
43	Breadth of upper face	104
44	Biorbital breadth	95
45	Bizygomatic breadth	130
46	Breadth of middle face	103
48	Height of upper face	67
50	Anterior interorbital breadth	18
51	Orbital breadth	40
52	Orbital height	36
54	Nasal breadth	26
55	Nasal height	52
60	Maxilloalveolar length	51
61	Maxilloalveolar breadth	63

Table 6.5
Cranial measurements of male 8/M/87.

Numbers of measurements by Martin, Saller, *Lehrbuch der Anthropologie* I.
L = left, R = right

---

[34] Martin, Saller, *Lehrbuch der Anthropologie* I

Table 6.6
Cranial indices of male
8/M/87.

Numbers of measurements
by Martin, Saller, *Lehrbuch
der Anthropologie* I.
L = left, R = right

No.	Name of the index	Value
I 1	Length-breadth of the skull	73.4
I 2	Length-height of the skull	70.7
I 3	Breadth-height of the skull	96.4
I 13	Transversal frontoparietal	68.1
I 39	Upper facial	51.5
I 42	Orbital	90.0
I 46	Interorbital	18.9
I 48	Nasal	50.0
I 54	Maxilloalveolar	123.5
I 60	Gnathic (alveolar)	91.5

6.2.3.4.5. Craniometry
All values are large, in harmony with the male sex of the individual (*table 6.5*). In indices (*table 6.6*), the calvarium is dolichokranic, orthocranic and metriocranic, with a mesosemic forehead. The upper face has a mesen form with mesoconchic orbits which are relatively close. The apertura piriformis displays mesorrhiny, the alveolar process with the palate a strong brachyurany and the facial profile an accentuated orthognathy shape.

6.2.3.4.6. Discussion
The few bones of a young adult male found in a disturbed and swept burial in the serdab was well mummified comprising excerebration. Resin was used for filling the cranial cavity and coating the body. These findings, together with the location of the parts of a mostly destroyed skeleton reveal that it is a question of a secondary burial, one of the numerous ones dispersed over the territory of the Royal Cemetery of Abusir. They have been dated in the era that extends from the Late Period to the Ptolemaic–Roman Periods.

6.2.4. Conclusions on the anthropological material from the Mastaba of Nebtyemneferes and Pyramid Complex Lepsius no. 24

Pyramid Complex Lepsius no. 24 was built for a queen whose name has not been found during the excavations and remains therefore uncertain (see discussion in chapter 4). The body found within this pyramid was well mummified and most probably excerebrated. She was 21–23 years old, slender, gracile, with a stature above the ancient Egyptian female mean. Her body was without any pathological changes in the teeth or skeleton. She was the sole occupant of the pyramid. There is every possibility that she was a queen, a consort of one of the kings of the middle part of the Fifth Dynasty. The dating of her mummy to that period has been ascertained by the chronometrical methods.

The headless skeleton found thrown out from its coffin and sarcophagus and displaced to an adjoining chamber was the sole original occupant of the mastaba designed for Princess Nebtyemneferes. She was a 30–40 year old female with gracile to medium build body and medium developed muscular relief. Because her skull had been cut off and was not able to be retrieved, it was not possible to establish any links with the anonymous queen.

The burial of a poor 7–8 years old child in the upper part of a dummy shaft of the same mastaba was found in situ, squeezed, with flexed legs, into a coarse wooden coffin that was too small for the body. It was found in the sand fill of the shaft. Its body was not mummified and therefore preserved only as a bare, wrapped skeleton. It was most probably a burial within a secondary cemetery dated from the Late Period to the Graeco-Roman Periods.

The partial remains of a swept burial of a 25–35 year old anonymous male belonged to the same secondary cemetery.

6.3. Human remains from the Tomb Complex Lepsius no. 25

Viktor Černý

Important number of human remains was unearthed from the Tomb Complex Lepsius no. 25. Together with smaller number of osteological material, which can be dated to the Old Kingdom, the majority of the bones comes from the Late Period. Unfortunately, overwhelming majority of the burials has been heavily disturbed by past interventions during the quarrying of building material from the pyramid itself. Aside from five burials have been spared from such destroying activity only osteological material without anatomical connections was at our disposal.

6.3.1. Skeletons with anatomical connections

All of these skeletons come from the secondary cemetery situated to the north of L25/1. (For further details concerning the archaeology of this area, see pp. 158–161).

111/N/2004

Medially preserved skeleton belongs to an adult individual. The pelvis as a whole very gracile with wide sciatic notch; the sacrum wide and low; the cranium very fragmentary; cranial sutures with minimal or middle closure; dental abrasion of middle degree; vertebra and other articulations without arthritic changes; marked changes on pubic symphysis.

Outcome: skeleton of female, middle age category (35–55 years old).

114/N/2004

Highly damaged skeleton belongs to an adult individual. The skull in fragments; the cranial sutures with middle closure; preserved vertebra without arthritic changes; an osteolytic lesion on posterior side in distal part of left femur.

Outcome: it is not possible to determine the sex or to estimate the age at death with more credibility – perhaps skeleton of male (?) of middle age category (?).

115/N/2004

Slightly damaged skeleton belongs to an adult individual. Open and symmetric sciatic notch together with metrical assessments shows unambiguously female morphology. The dental abrasion of middle degree; the cranial sutures of middle closure in all parts; pubic and auricular symphysis with middle developed changes; the articular changes are of mild degree detectable only on some thoracic vertebra (backbone preserved completely).

Outcome: skeleton of female, early middle age category (35–45 years old).

116/N/2004

Relatively well preserved skeleton belongs to an adult individual. The sciatic notch very narrow; the pubis short; the sacrum narrow and long; the mastoid processes of heavy appearance; the significant closure of cranial sutures; the advanced dental abrasion; the sternal parts of the ribs with marked degenerative changes; the small arthritic changes of completely preserved backbone only on lumbar vertebra; pubic and auricular symphysis heavily changed; osteophytic border round head of femur and ossified ligaments on *linea aspera*.

Outcome: skeleton of male, middle or older age category (45–65 years old).

118/N/2003

Heavily damaged skeleton belongs to an adult individual. Because of very poor state of preservation, no any outcome can be drawn on the sex and the age at death.

6.3.2. Bones without anatomical connections

As noted above overwhelming majority of the anthropological remains lacked anatomical connections during the excavation. Some of these bones were unearthed directly in the funeral chamber of pyramid Lepsius no. 25 and thus could eventually be dated to the Old Kingdom; much bigger part comes from the Late Period.

6.3.2.1. Bones from the burial chambers of the Tomb Complex Lepsius no. 25

A question of possible anatomical connections arises from finding context. There are five locations numbered **28N** (partially mummified bone fragment of pelvis probably of young female), **67** (a – right femur, b – distal fragment of right fibula, c – fragment of right mandible, d – right *os petrosum*, e – right patella, f – occipital), **77** (a – fragment of right scapula, b – right clavicle, c – left parietal, d – fragment of right parietal, e – two left ribs, f – four right ribs, g – thoracic vertebra, h – diaphysis of left femur of immature individual, i – distal fragment of tibia of immature individual, j – proximal fragment of humerus of immature individual, k – phalange of hand), **87** (a – fragment of proximal part of left humerus, b – left radius, c – left ulna, d – two left ribs, e – fragment of occipital) and **88** (distal fragment of right fibula).

From osteological point of view only three anatomical units can be distinguished in the material listed above – A) left forearm (87b + c), B) part of a skull (87e + 67f + 77c + 77d) and C) proximal part of right low extremity (67a + 28N). Unfortunately, it is not possible to decide if these three anatomical units belong to one or more individuals.

Fig. 6.37 Maximal length of diaphysis of immature femora.

Fig. 6.38 Maximal length of mature femora.

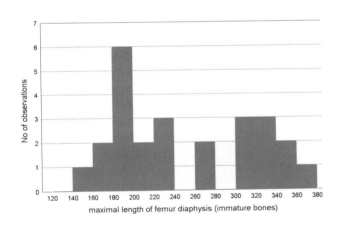

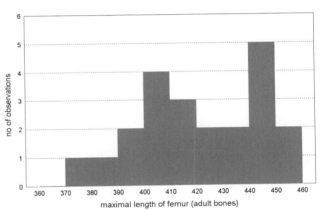

6.3.2.2. Dispersed bones from the Late Period

The bones were secured in 29 finding contexts. The best preserved bone is right femur (53 whole bones and 31 fragments of proximal epiphysis) indicating the minimal number of individuals as 84. However, an important number of left femora (whole bones and fragments as well), which are not possible to easily complete with their right counterparts, indicates that the number of individuals buried in pyramid 25 might be greater.

The measurements of maximal length of diaphysis of immature femora and measurements of maximal length of mature femora have subsequently been undertaken. The diaphyses lengths of 180–200 mm (representing the category of 3–4 years old children) prevail in the sample of immature individuals (*fig. 6.37*). The others age categories are represented with similar frequency of about 10 %. The scantiness of age category of 7–12 years old individuals (diaphyses length of 240–300 mm) should also be noted. These findings are, however, in broader accordance with mortality pattern seen in others skeletal samples.

The length of femora of adult individuals (*fig. 6.38*) varies from 374 to 457 mm with the average 421.1 mm what corresponds with stature approximately 160 cm. A validity of the estimate could be biased by an overweight of female or male skeletons in the sample. Unfortunately, because of the absence of anatomical connections of the measured bone it was not possible to answer this question directly. We thus tried to estimate the sex ratio by using sufficiently preserved pelvic bones. The analysis which takes in consideration human worldwide sexual dimorphism of pelvic bone has been applied. The results based on 11 pelvises showing 5 males, 5 females and 1 undetermined individual do not advance the above mentioned hypothesis of female or male overweight in the sample.

Craniofacial characteristics of the ancient Egyptians from Late Period can be undertaken on the base of 15 measurable skulls. Because of the lack of the anatomical contexts (same as in the femora measurements) the sex determination of the skulls would be very unreliable so that we provide here the cranial indices reducing the influence of sexual dimorphism. It was shown that the cranial index attains the values between 70.2 and 77.4 what corresponds with the dolichocrane up to mesocrane skulls with the average value (73.7) still within dolichocrane category. As to the breadth-height index the skulls fall in the interval from 69.1 to 76.6 with the average value (72.4) in the middle category. As to the face only four skulls have been sufficiently preserved for the measurements. The index of the upper face with its average value (53.5) shows on the middle face with some tendency to narrower values.

6.3.3. Conclusion

The human remains from Tomb Complex Lepsius no. 25 contain great number of bones, however, mostly without anatomical connections. The anthropological analysis of such material is thus heavily reduced. Moreover, the state of preservation of various bones or anatomical parts is not sufficient – it is evident that later interruptions have damaged the Late Period burials with very different intensity. Minimal number of individuals buried on the cemetery was calculated as 84 according to the right femur appearances (whole bones plus fragments of proximal epiphyses). However, in regard of a high number of left bones and left fragments that have not been possible to unfailingly complete with their right counterparts it is highly possible that the number of individuals buried in the place of Tomb Complex Lepsius no. 25 was higher perhaps for tens and could extend beyond 100. Measurements of the diaphyses of immature femora showed more important proportion of 4 years old children what could be otherwise expected in regards of mortality profiles of past populations. Although it is not possible to draw any conclusion about sexual dimorphism of the osteological characteristics of the population in question it is obvious that stature was in average of 160 cm. The craniofacial measurements showed the head of the population from Abusir Late Period was in average long with middle face.

**Fig. 3.28b Model vases 18
and 33/Q/94.**
Photo MZ

**Fig. 3.45 Copper models of
instruments 25/Q/94.**
Photo MZ

**Fig. 3.52a Masons' mark
Gr 1/Q/94.**
Photo MZ

**Fig. 3.53a Masons' mark
Gr 2/Q/94.**
Photo MZ

**Fig. 3.54a Masons' mark
Gr 3/Q/94** (*avers*)**.**
Photo MZ

**Fig. 3.55a Masons' mark
Gr 3/Q/94** (*revers*)**.**
Photo MZ

Fig. 4.18 Satelite image of the Abusir Pyramid Necropolis with minor tombs indicated.

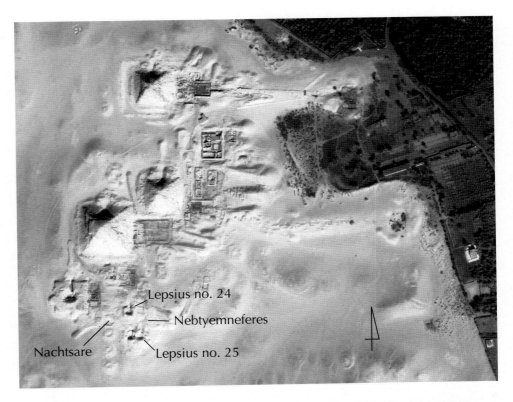

Lepsius no. 24
Nebtyemneferes
Nachtsare
Lepsius no. 25

Fig. 4.19 Three-dimensional computer reconstruction of the Pyramid Complex Lepsius no. 24 and its surroundings.

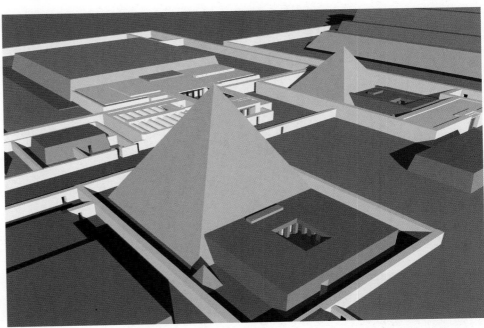

Fig. 4.39a–b North-eastern part of the mortuary temple of L24 – imprints of the side walls and of red colouring remaining on the flat limestone blocks.
Photo JK

Fig. 4.48 Masons' marks and lines on the lower part of western wall of the building pit of L24.
Photo JK

Fig. 4.49 Masons' marks and lines on the lower part of western wall of the building pit of L24. Detail.
Photo JK

Fig. 4.74 Jar with handles 33/J/87.
Photo MZ

Fig. 4.77 Islamic lamps 52/J/94 and 62/J/94.
Photo MZ

**Fig. 4.81a Copper models
66/J/94c and 69/J/94.**
Photo MZ

**Fig. 4.81c Spatula from the
set of models 66/J/94c.**
Photo MZ

**>Fig. 4.82b Two fine chisels
66/J/96c.**
Photo MZ

**Fig. 4.85b Models of awl/
borer 69/J/94a.**
Photo MZ
**>Fig. 4.98b Model
mudbrick.**
Photo MZ

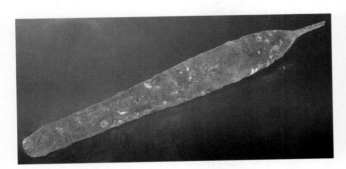

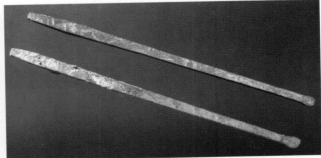

Fig. 5.8a Partially preserved burials to the east from L25/1.
Photo JK

Fig. 5.8b Detail of a child burial with glass beads – exc. nos. 85a–c/N/2003.
Photo JK

>>Fig. 5.15 Secondary cemetery to the north of L25/1, mummified body in the burial pit 116/N/2004.
Photo JK

Fig. 5.9 Fragment of decorated cartonnage found in the area of the secondary cemetery.
Photo JK

Fig. 5.35 Builders' marks on the under-pavement blocks in the descending corridor of L25/1.
Photo KV

Fig. 5.31 Fire place in the mud lining of the floor, preserved in the chapel of L25/1.
Photo JK.

>Fig. 5.40a Masons' mark on the casing of the eastern wallof the horiyontal passage of the accessing corridor in L25/1.
Photo JK

Fig. 5.41a Masons' mark at the south-east corner of the horizontal passage of the accessing corridor in L25/1.
Photo JK

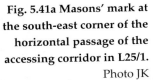

Fig. 5.050b Arrow-signs and masons' lines on the blocks in the western wall of the construction pit in L25/2.
Photo JK

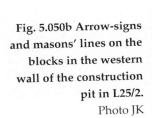

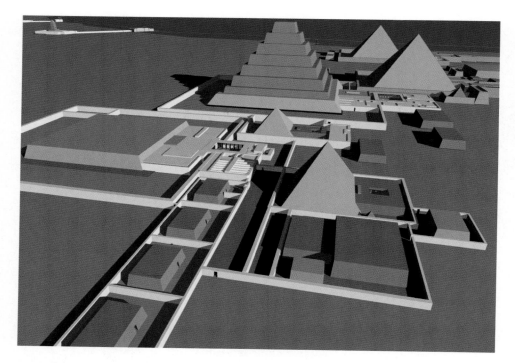

Fig. 5.65 Three-dimensional computer visualisation of the Tomb Complex Lepsius no. 25 and neighbouring minor tombs in the Abusir Pyramid Necropolis as seen from the south-east.

Fig. 5.72a Model bowls 70a–b/N/2003.
Photo KV

4 cm

Fig. 5.73a Model instrument 75/N/2003.
Photo JK

Fig. 5.78 Votive wooden stele 93/N/2003.
Photo JK

Fig. 5.74 Fragment of a statue 6a/N/2001.
Photo KV

Fig. 5.76 Fragment of a statue 6b/N/2001.
Photo KV

**Fig. 5.80 Fragment of a
wooden vessel 64/N/2003.**
Photo KV

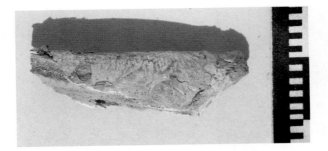

**Fig. 5.82 Fragments
of a case (box).**
Photo KV

**Fig. 5.84 Part of a coffin
72/N/2003.**
Photo KV

Fig. 5.90 Decorated sherd 92/N/2003.
Photo JK

Fig. 5.93a A small false door stele 8/N/2001.
Photo KV

Fig. 5.94 Cornelian bead 53a–b/N/2003.
Photo JK

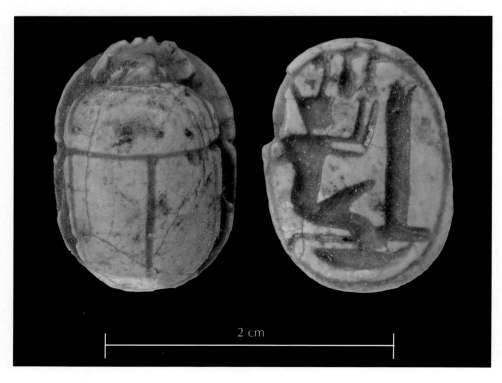

Fig. 5.98a Scarab 5/N/2001.
Photo JK

Fig. 5.99 Faience bead 10/N/2001.
Photo KV

>**Fig. 5.102 Fragment of an** *udjat* **amulet, 55/N/2003.**
Photo KV

>>**Fig. 5.103** *Udjat* **bead 59/N/2003.**
Photo KV

>**Fig. 5.106 Three glass beads 85a–c/N/2003.**

Fig. 5.109 Flint knife 82/N/2003.
Photo JK

>**Fig. 5.119 Coper model implements 32a–c/N/2002.**
Photo KV

Fig. 5.135 Sealing 107/N/2004.
Photo JK

>**Fig. 5.137 Sealing 108a/N/2004.**
Photo JK

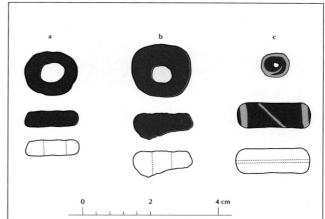

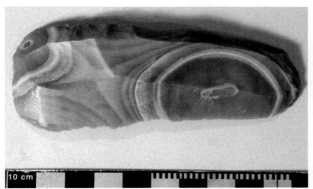

Fig. 5.147a,b Fragments of papyrus from Lepsius 25/1 – *recto*.

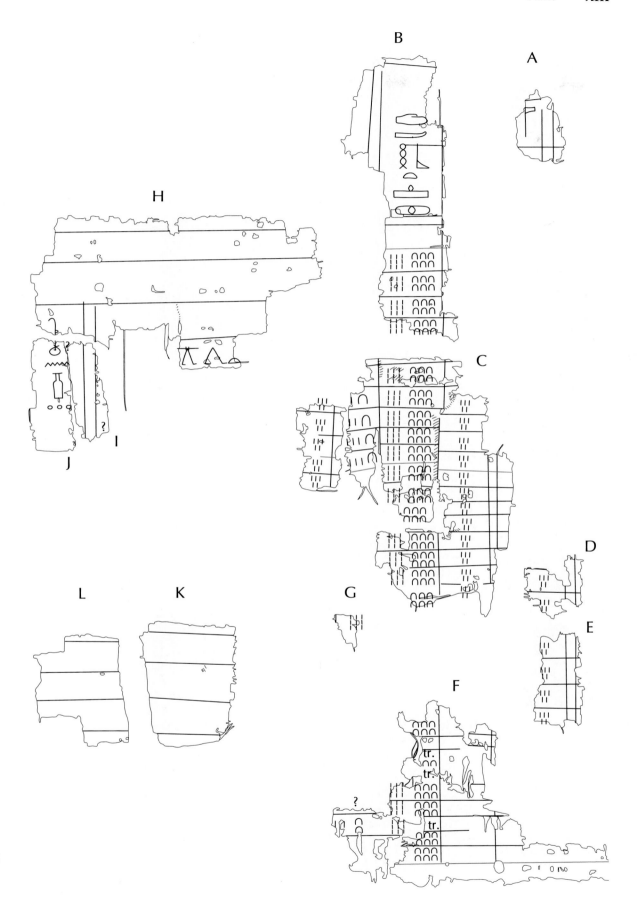

Fig. 5.148a,b Fragments of papyrus from Lepsius 25/1 – *verso.*

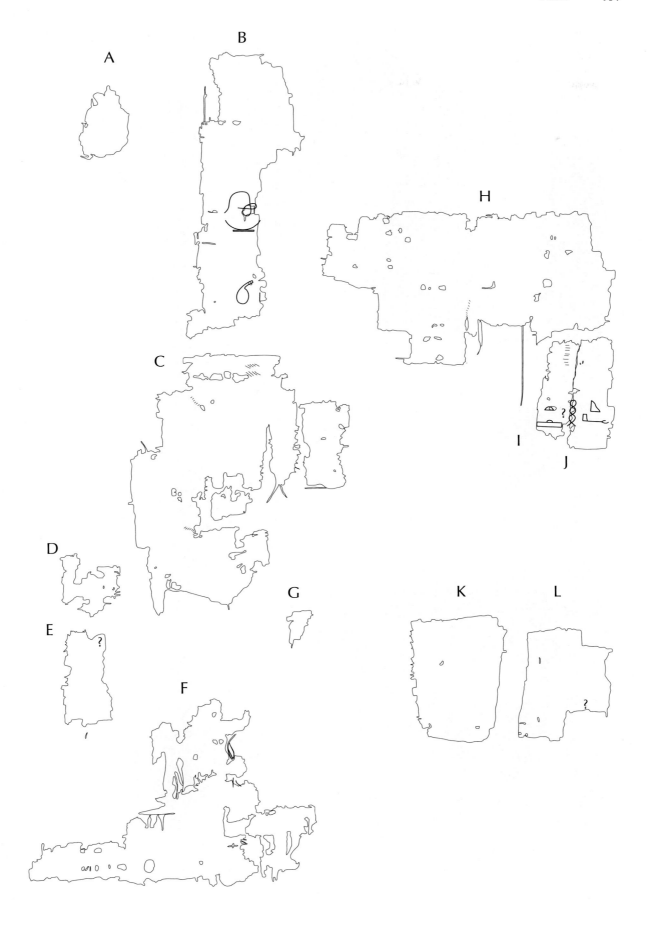

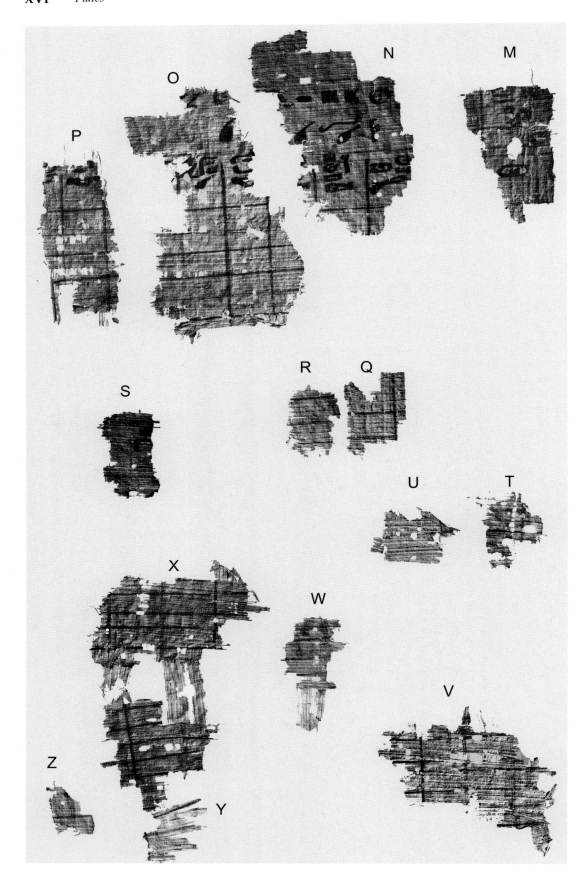

Fig. 5.149a,b Fragments of papyrus from Lepsius 25/1 – *recto*.

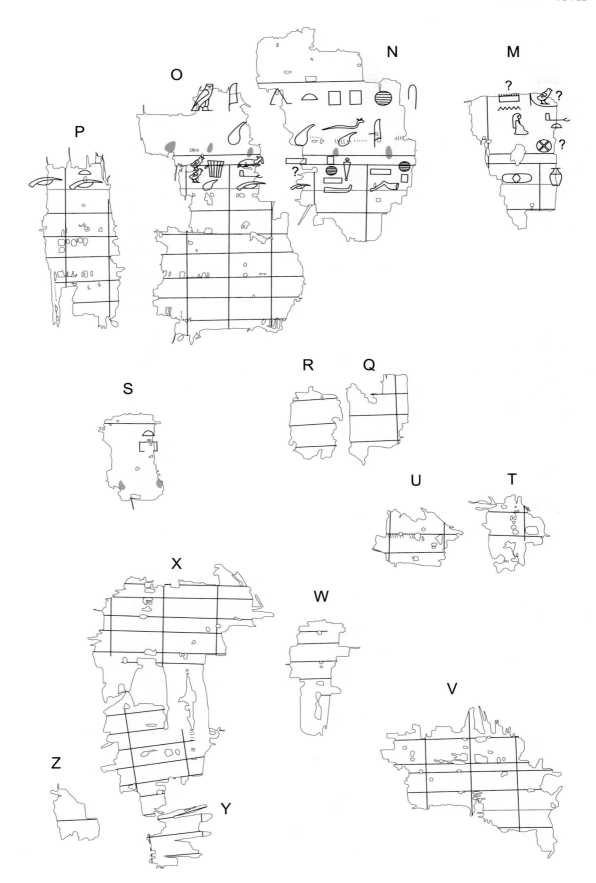

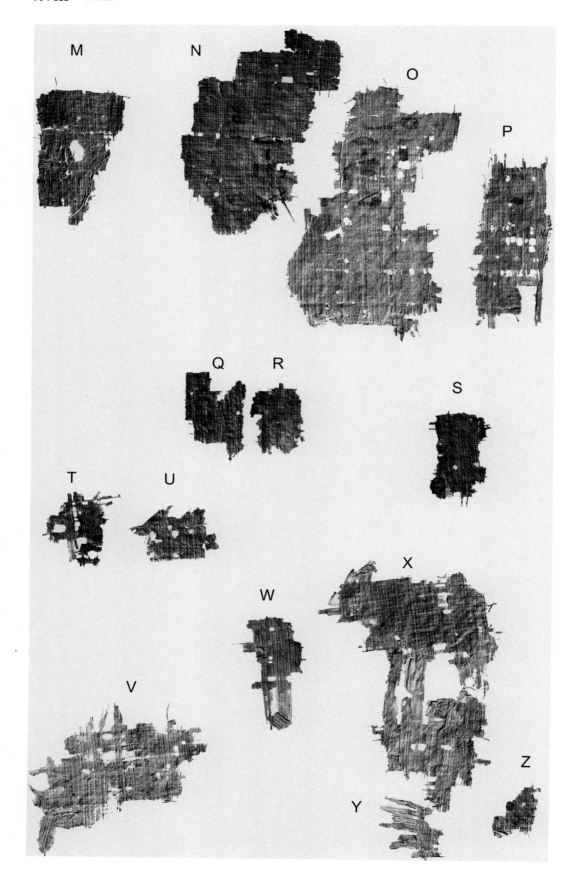

Fig. 5.149a,b Fragments of papyrus from Lepsius 25/1 – *verso.*

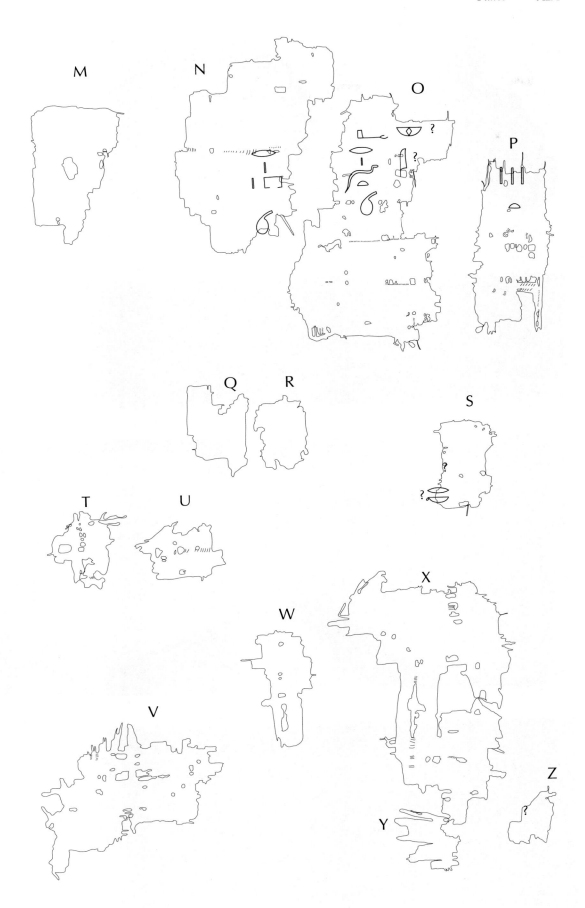

Fig. 5.139 Sealing 108b/N/2004.
Photo JK

Fig. 5.141a Jar docket 104/N/2004.
Photo JK

Fig. 5.151 Builders' mark Gr 166/N/03.
Photo JK

Fig. 5.152 Builders' mark Gr 21/N/02.
Photo KV

Fig. 5.153 Builders' mark Gr 29a/N/2002.
Photo KV

Fig. 5.154 Builders' mark Gr 147/N/2002.
Photo JK

**Fig. 5.155 Builders' mark
Gr 87/N/03.**
Photo KV

**Fig. 5.156 Builders' mark
Gr 124a/N/2003.**
Photo JK

**Fig. 5.157 Builders' mark
Gr 130/N/2003.**
Photo JK

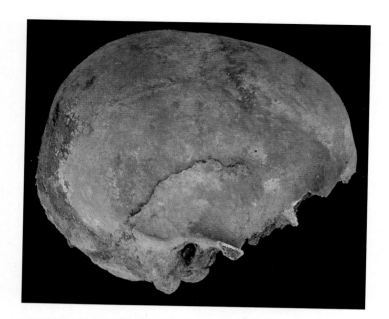

Fig. 6.1–6.5 Skull
of 40-60 years old male
(38/Q/94).
Photo MK

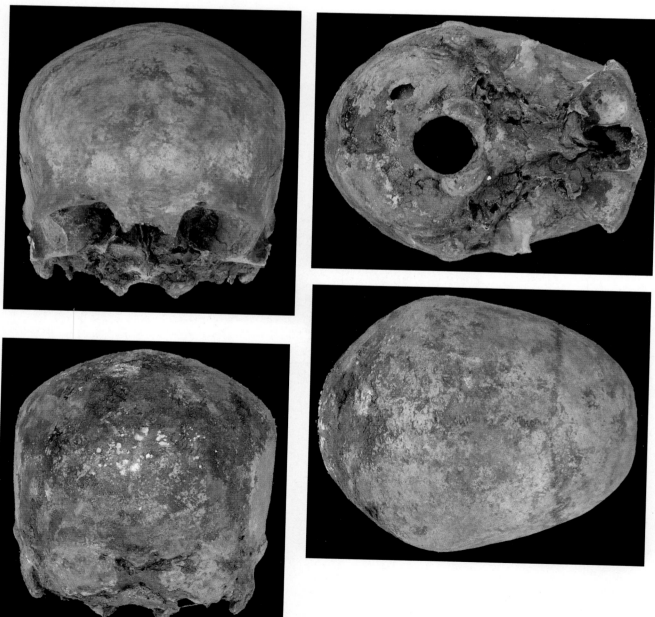

Fig. 6.06–6.10 Skull of 30–40 years old female (37/Q/94). Photo MK

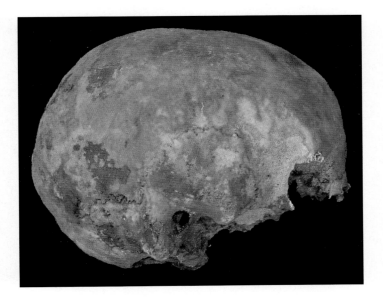

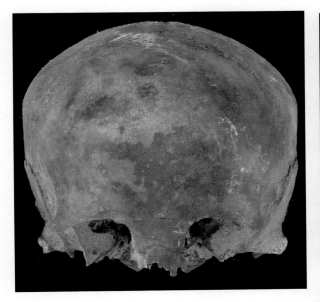

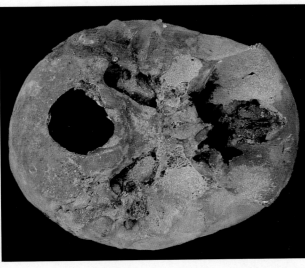

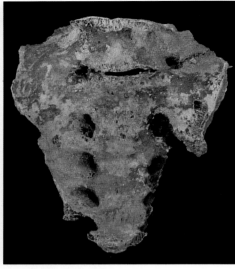

Fig. 6.11–6.12 Sacralization of L₅ (37/Q/94).
Photos MK

Fig. 6.13 Mummy 49/J/94 joined together from the discovered skeletalized or mummified fragments.
Photo VČ

Fig. 6.15 The upper and lower dentition with incipent attrition.
Photo ES

Fig. 6.14 Most probably, the filling of the occipital part of the cranial cavity made of textiles soaked in liquid resin.
Photo ES

6.16 The well preserved labia maiora attesting the female sex.
Photo ES

Fig. 6.18 The calva and neck with remnants of soft tissue in right lateral view. The right lateral quarter of the frontal squama was removed intentionally to show a lump of resinous filling still present inside the cranial cavity.
Photo ES

Fig. 6.17 The defective calva with missing right anterior edge of the frontal squama in frontal view. Post mortem breaks by smashing the skull.
Photo ES

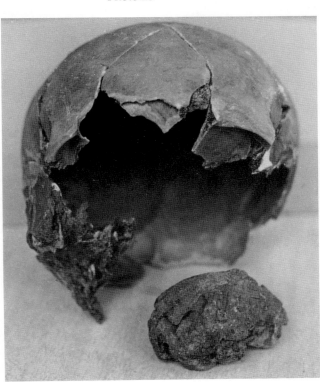

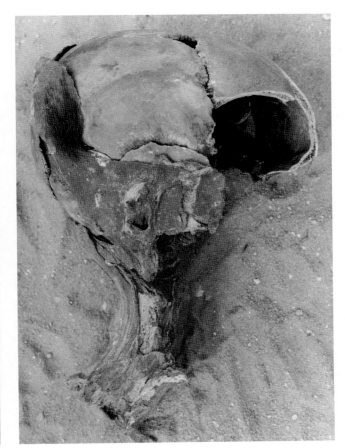

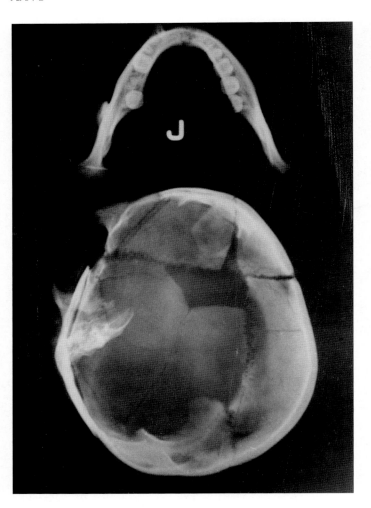

Fig. 6.19 X-rays of the calva in a distorted axial projection, showing the open sutures.
Photo AMS *et al.*

Fig. 6.20 X-rays of the cervical and thoracic spine in right lateral projection.
Photo AMS *et al*

Fig. 6.21 X-rays of upper ribs and the defective sternum (below left).
Photo AMS *et al*

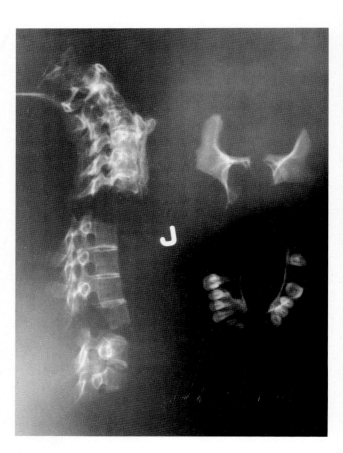

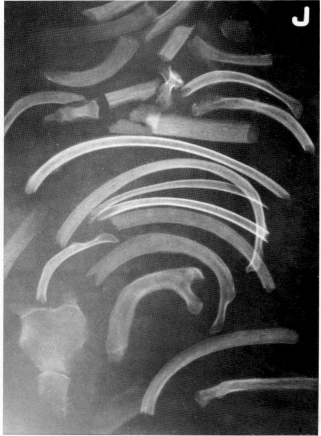

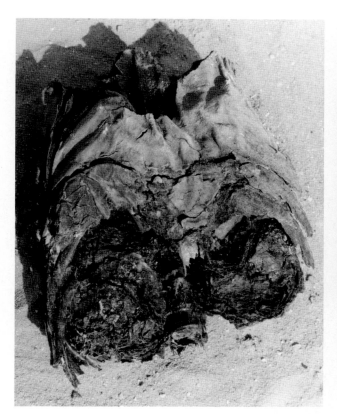 

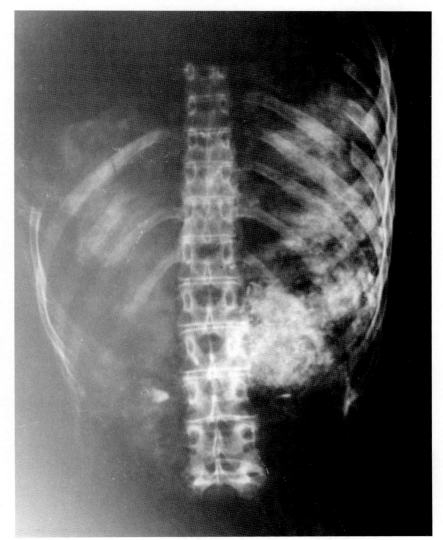

Fig. 6.22 The lower thorax in distorted view from below, showing fillings of the thoracic cavity. Photo ES

Fig. 6.23 Dorsal side of the lower thorax with preserved skin. Photo ES

Fig. 6.24 Anteroposterior X-ray projection of the lower thorax with the lower thoracic and lumbar spine and textile fillings in the left hemithorax. The right hemithorax has a decreased density. Photo AMS *et al*

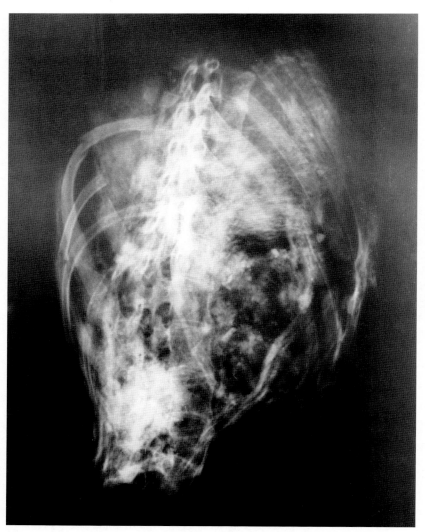

Fig. 6.25 Oblique X-rays projection shows accumulation of the fillings in the dorsal parts of the lower thorax.
Photo AMS *et al.*

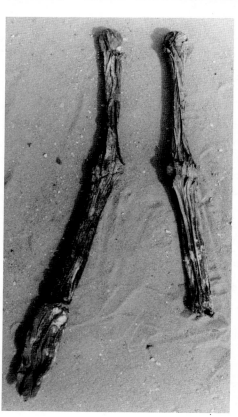

Fig. 6.26 Both arms with deviating forearms and the right hand with palm up.
Photo ES

Fig. 6.27 The right hand in dorsal view.
Photo ES

Fig. 6.28 X-rays showing both clavicles (left above, right lower), the scapulae (left and right), both arms and the right hand (left).
Photo AMS *et al.*

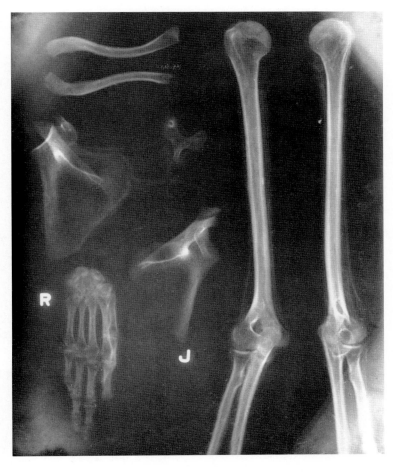

Fig. 6.29 The lower extremity girdle preserved as a whole, in anterior view.
Photo ES

>Fig. 6.30 The lower extremity girdle preserved as a whole, in posterior view.
Photo ES

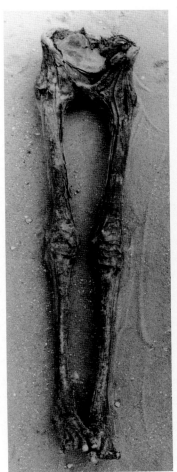 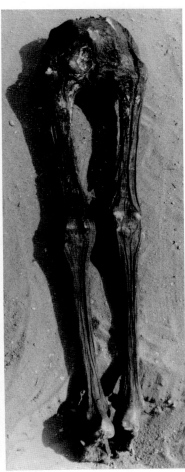

Fig. 6.31 Islets of the abdominal skin deeply depressed into the pelvis over its fillings.
Photo ES

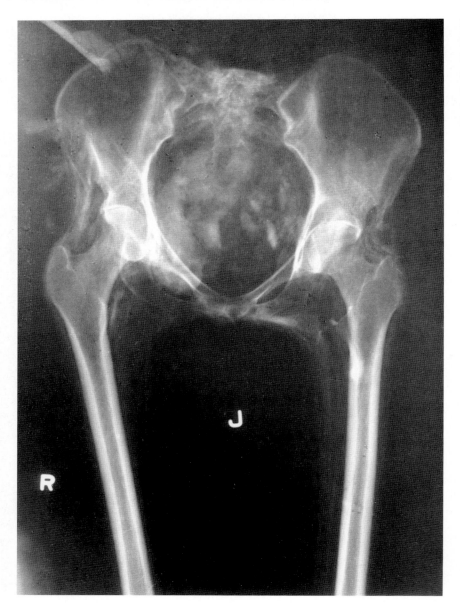

Fig. 6.32 X-rays of the pelvis and upper half of the femurs with fillings of the small pelvis. Gluteal and femoral muscles are barely visible.
Photo AMS *et al.*

Fig. 6.33 X-rays reveal the perfectly healthy state of the knee joints.
Photo AMS *et al.*

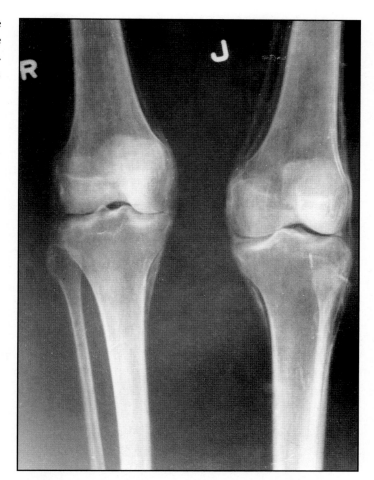

Fig. 6.34 X-rays of the lower thirds of the crural bones and feet rotated artificially to the left.
Photo AMS *et al.*

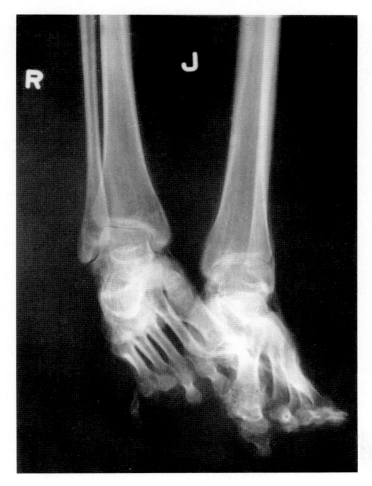

Fig. 6.35 Dorsal view of both feet which lost several phalangae of the toes.
Photo ES

Fig. 6.36 Plantar view with deeply excavated longitudinal vault and a flat transversal vault.
Photo ES

Appendix
Stone Vessels from the Cemetery of Members of the Royal Families of Abusir

Vivienne Gae Callender

A.1. Introduction and terminology

Stone vessels first appeared in Egypt during the Predynastic Period and an extensive industry was in existence during the first two-to-three dynasties of Egyptian history. The vessels that were made at this time, sometimes of rare or exotic stone, were one of the distinctive objects found in elite tombs in Abydos and Saqqara. (One might here single out the huge number of stone vessels found beneath the pyramid of Djoser, in Saqqara, most of which, unfortunately, have only been partially published.[1] Most of those appear to have been donations of vessels that had been manufactured in the Archaic Period.)

The workmanship from this period has seldom been surpassed – as collections in prestigious museums around the world (most particularly in Cairo Museum) eloquently testify. Some of the stone vessel collections discovered in J. Garstang's excavations at Raqaqnah, Mahasna and Bêt Khallâf, for example, produced some astounding works of art – such as the miniature jars in stone materials that were difficult to work – like the little diorite vases which Garstang exclaimed were as 'thin as paper'.[2] Despite the tremendous skill displayed in these examples, and the fact that stone vessels continued to be made in Egypt right up to, and including even the Roman period, the industry was in decline after the Archaic Period. After that time, coloured or patterned stones seldom made their appearance in any but royal tombs and the most common stones used by the stone-making industry were the less challenging varieties of travertine and limestone.[3]

Because so many stone vessels were found in dated tombs from the Archaic Period, the organization of a datable classification and typology of stone vessels seemed to be a relatively uncomplicated exercise to undertake but, in fact, those early scholars who attempted classification methodologies in the past proved just how difficult this task could be.[4] In his three volume study of stone vessels, A. El Khouli points to significant disappointments – sometimes due to the untimely death of the scholar concerned – within these early classification systems.[5] He notes that it was not until the time of the meticulous W. B. Emery, that an Archaic cemetery was consistently and effectively recorded. Once again, however, much of Emery's work remained unpublished before his death, a task which El Khouli himself later undertook.[6]

Similar difficulties are found within studies devoted to Old Kingdom stone vessels, too, including more recent typologies for various large burial deposits (such as those of Queen Hetepheres I's assemblage[7] and that from King Menkaure's valley temple[8] and other fields) where scholars have tried to work out a satisfactory methodology for analyzing stone vessels: the most comprehensive of these being

---

[1] Only those vessels bearing inscriptions have been fully published: see Lacau, Lauer, *Pyr. à degrés* IV, V.

[2] Garstang, *Reqaqneh*, 25: "Of the hard stones, diorite is the most frequent and is often worked down with wonderful skill until translucency is obtained"…"In the upper row are two tiny vases, thin as paper…".

[3] Khouli, *Egyptian Stone Vessels*, vii.

[4] For example, see Petrie, *Stone and Metal Vases*.

[5] Khouli, *Egyptian Stone Vessels*, p. xf. *E.g.* Petrie's system frequently lacked mention of key important features, such as the materials used, the thickness of the walls of vessels, the depth of their interiors or details of the rims of some of the vessels, while both Quibell and Firth, whose catalogues were more rigorous and systematic, died before they could finish their work.

[6] Khouli, *Egyptian Stone Vessels*, 1, xii.

[7] Reisner, Smith, *Giza Necropolis* II, Appendix II.

[8] Reisner, *Mycerinus*, 130–202.

G. Reisner's impressive work. However, the biggest problem with all these later classification systems has been their idiosyncratic nature. In his extremely detailed and exhaustive study of Archaic stone vessels, El Khouli tried to provide one system that could apply to all present and future discoveries of stone vessels. It is, however, necessary to mention that, by his provision of scores and scores of categories, El Khouli has made a system that is too cumbersome to use in the field, where most classification is initially carried out.

A.1.1. Terminology and forms (or shapes) of vessels[9]

Of more practical use seems to be B. Aston's system, where a comprehensive coverage of different vessel classification and typologies is readily apparent in her vessel typology chart (*fig. A.1*) provided in Appendix C of her excellent study, *Ancient Egyptian Stone Vessels*.

Fig. A.1 Aston's shape classification system for stone vessels.

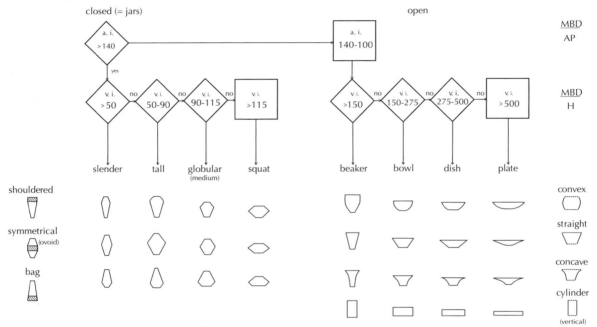

Aston has a simple 5-step methodology. Her first classification step divides all stone vessels into two groups: forms which are closed and those that are open. The initial criterion she chooses for determining which vessels are "closed" and which are "open" is the width of the mouth (sometimes referred to as the "aperture" or the "opening" of the vessel). This measurement is then compared to the width of the vessel at its widest part. The widest part of any vessel is called its Maximum Body Diameter (MBD).[10]

To paraphrase her classification rule, vessels whose apertures are the widest (or nearly widest) part of the vessel are *open* forms. These stone vessels include beakers, bowls, dishes, plates and trays. (Significantly, Aston included beakers among the open forms, where some catalogues include them with forms classed as jars.) Those vessels whose apertures are substantially smaller than their widest wall intervals are *closed* forms.[11] These forms she calls "jars", but scholars also refer to such vessels

---

[9] Aston, *Stone Vessels*, fig. 22.

[10] The system Aston uses is derived from pottery analysis which was devised by H.-Å. Nordström. (See Fascicle 2: *Ceramic Technology: Clays and Fabrics*, in: Arnold, Bourriau, *Ancient Egyptian Pottery*.)

[11] The basic formula used by B. Aston is derived from the Egyptian pottery classification system (Aston, *Stone Vessels*, 179ff.). The ratio of the vessel mouth to the widest body part is the determining factor and is calculated as the Maximum Body Diameter (MBD) divided by the diameter of the Aperture (AP) multiplied by 100. This gives an Aperture Index (AI). When a vessel has convex sides, its AI alters and becomes smaller towards the rim. Those with an AI of 141–116 feature mouths which are more restricted than at the vessels widest diameter. These vessels are called "restricted forms". Aston groups these sorts of vessels with open forms, adding the label "restricted", which seems to be a practical way of classifying such objects.

as "vases". Sometimes, a jar may have a profile which curves inward a little at the top, thus restricting the size of the vessel's diameter at the mouth. Such vessels are called "restricted forms" and can be grouped with open forms if the difference between mouth and MBD is slight (*table A.1*).

Open	Closed
trays, plates, dishes, bowls, beakers	squat, globular, tall, slender jars
convex, straight, concave, cylindrical sided	shouldered, symmetrical, bag-shaped

After this initial classification has sorted vessels into two groups (open and closed forms), the second step of Aston's methodology considers the ratio of a vessel's height in relation to its width. This results in a figure which is called the Vessel Index (VI). The basic calculation is Maximum Body Diameter divided by the Height of the vessel and multiplied by 100, MBD/H × 100. This is not a precise measurement, of course, particularly when the sides of vessels bulge outwards, curve inwards or are even conical, nevertheless, it is the system which has been utilised in both the catalogue of stone vessels and in this chapter. Vessels which are taller than they are wide are called "tall", while those which are broader than they are tall are referred to as "squat". Vessels whose VI is less than 50 (see *fig. A.1*) are labelled as "slender"; those whose height and breadth are similar to each other are called "globular".

The third step sorts out these open and closed shapes even further by looking at which area of the vessel has the maximum width. Looking at closed vessels first, we note that if the bulge of a vessel is widest near the top, it is called a "shouldered" jar. If the widest part is found in the middle of the vessel, it is called "ovoid" or "symmetrical", depending on its overall shape. When the MBD is low down on the vessel, it is called "bag-shaped".

When analysing open forms, the process is to consider the height in relation to the width of the vessel: dishes, plates and trays have heights approximately 1/3 or less than the MBD. Bowls have heights less than 2/3 of the MBD but more than 1/3 of the bowl's width. Beakers are the tallest of the open forms: they usually have heights that are greater than 1/3 and less than 2/3 of the width of the vessel. However, some beakers may actually be of the same height as the width of the vessel, or they may be of even greater height than the MBD measurement. Without exception, though, beaker heights must be at least greater than 1/3 of the width of the vessel.[12]

The fifth step is an easy visual exercise: noting the characteristics of the side walls of the vessel. The walls may be vertical (or "straight-sided"), or they could taper into a basic cone shape – either V-shaped or one like an inverted cone. The final option is for the walls to have a visible curve, being either concave or convex.[13]

This basic classification system devised by Aston works very well in practice and – as her catalogue of shapes confirms – is applicable to stone vessels right across the historic range of Egyptian stone vessel manufacture. Within each class of vessel, however, there are variations (or types) which appeared, disappeared and sometimes reappeared over the course of time. Not each example of a restricted form vase, for example, is necessarily like the next, and this is particularly evident – and expected – when one covers a range of 3000 years and more for the period of Egyptian pharaonic history. All these individual variations within the basic classification system are referred to in this chapter as "types".

The terms "class" and "type" are used frequently within the works of authors dealing with either pottery or stone vessel manufacture, but those words are not

---

[12] Aston, *Stone Vessels*, 180.
[13] *Loc. cit.* Included in this visual exercise is the noting of any lengthening of the necks of vessels, or the presence of any handles. With the vessels included in the catalogues of this book, such aspects were not present, although the extreme flaring of the *ḥȝts* vase neck and rim does merit discussion.

always interpreted by individual authors in the same way. In his valuable essay on the pottery found in the course of excavating Raneferef's pyramid temple and pyramidal burial mound, M. Bárta[14] has provided a most judicious differentiation between the terms "class" and "type", seeing the former as having a fluid temporal meaning, whilst the other, focussing on transformations of the shape within a narrow band of time, is seen as time specific. This differentiation of terminology is followed here. "Class" refers to the results of the descriptors outlined above (Aston's system) being applied to any given vessel. The "type" of vessel is the result of additional descriptors being applied to that vessel. "Class", therefore, refers to a general group; "type" refers to individual examples in time and space that form sub-groups of any given class.

Finally, it needs to be explained that, within this work, the importance of the archaeological find spot is considered as vital. The prime reasons for this is due to the fact that not only does a knowledge of the discovery point (a point involving both vertical and horizontal placement) contribute towards a comprehensive history of these tomb sites,[15] but the actual place where the vessels or their fragments were found can often provide an understanding of the function of those vessels.[16] Knowing the find spot helps us to understand the function of the vessels discovered (rather than just providing a record of the measurements and materials, which, in themselves, do not tell us much about the purposes for which a vessel was used). See also *table A.1*. The detailed list and form of these classes can be viewed in *fig. A.1*.

A.2. Materials

During the late Predynastic and Archaic periods, Egyptian stone carvers made use of a wide variety of stone, concentrating on coloured and patterned varieties[17] which, of course, were often difficult to drill and shape. Some of these stone matrixes came from individual boulders found in the desert, which were then shaped into various objects, other vessels were made from stone extracted from quarry sites. During the period of the earliest state formation, the king appropriated these sources for his own use and offered to his favoured courtiers rewards in the form of finely worked stone vessels whose stone came from these quarries or desert regions.

Quite a lot of progress has been made in understanding just how these vessels were made, thanks in part to tomb illustrations and the discovery of drill bits and

---

[14] M. Bárta, *The Pottery*, in: Verner *et al.*, *Raneferef*, 295.

[15] For the history of the Abusir necropolis, see L. Bareš, The destruction of the monuments at the necropolis of Abusir, in: *Abusir and Saqqara 2000*, 1–16. He mentions earthquake and wind erosion as being the earliest forces to effect damage on limestone structures such as these (p. 3), and the presence of hemispherical cups and fragments of Twelfth Dynasty sealings in the remains of this pyramid's temple do not seem to be associated with depredations by robbers (pp. 4f.). Initial human destruction is not clearly attested before the late Eighteenth and early Nineteenth Dynasties (pp. 7–9), by which time crude shelters had been erected and the temple stripped of its limestone casing (p. 11).

[16] Again on this topic, see Bárta, *op. cit.*, 291ff., who based his analysis on observations originally made by Reisner (*Mycerinus*, 17) and M. B. Schiffer (Archaeological and Systemic context, *AmerAnt* 37, 1972, 156–165). In all three works, the difference between original (or primary) use and secondary use of vessels *etc.*, has been emphasised (see especially Bárta, *op. cit.*, 294). The primary function of a vessel was its intended use (*e.g.* a cup is a vessel for drinking a convenient amount). The secondary function is what the vessel was used for after its original purpose was no more required (*e.g.* a chipped cup might either be used to measure or to scoop out flour).

[17] In her book on stone vessels, Aston includes a long section dealing with the varieties of stone used in different periods of Egyptian history. This includes a most interesting exploration of the sources of the stone. In passing, she also corrects a series of errors inadvertently given by those who had attempted to analyse types of stones in the past (*e.g.*, Petrie's "blue marble", the use and misuse of the terms "schist", "calcite", "alabaster" and "travertine", *etc.*). She also provides scientific explanations regarding the characteristics of the stone varieties used by ancient Egyptian craftsmen.

stones in various stages of manufacture: for example, Petrie[18] provides clear and succinct explanations of how the drilling was done, with photographic evidence to corroborate his interpretation of the process. From the very earliest days of state formation, the craftsmen knew about hand drilling in hollowing out stone vases, and both stone and copper bits were used to scoop out the vessels' interiors. There are detailed accounts of this in several works.[19] (Coincidentally, a limestone weight used in a stone-cutter's drill was discovered within the precincts of the Expanded Temple of Raneferef.[20]) Further work along ethno-archaeological lines[21] has also been undertaken by recent scholars in regard to travertine working at Sheikh Abd el-Gurna – of especial interest to this study since all but a few of the finds were of travertine – as well as other experiments with the drill,[22] and this has been very instructive in understanding the process.

We do not know which vessels were given as rewards for work done during an official's lifetime and which goods were presented during the funeral service as a mark of the king's esteem, but non-royal burials of the Third Dynasty and the Archaic period were often found to contain very fine collections of well-made stone vessels, both of full-size and miniature size in a wide variety of stone.[23] Reisner, however, has noted that the supply of more exotic sorts of stones had become confined to the royal sphere by the reign of Sneferu[24] and, elsewhere, he remarks that there was "…an average of 3.6 times more stone vessels [in the Second and Third Dynasty tombs] than in each grave of Dynasty IV."[25] This trend became more accentuated between the Fourth to Sixth Dynasties when, in Reisner's experience, no "practical vessels"[26] – by which he means full-size quality stone items of daily or cultic use – were to be found in non-royal burials any more. Instead, officials and members of the élite from the Fourth Dynasty onwards accumulated miniature vessels for their burial assemblage.

The history of these full-size royal gifts as well as those of the miniature vessels reflects trends in the general economy of the time. At first, there was a wide range of forms and types of models that were well-made in the early Old Kingdom. In the course of the following dynasties, the vessels being made show a marked reduction in the quality of the work, together with a more restricted range. This was very noticeable by the Fifth Dynasty – which with rare exceptions (see below) – produced few vessels in coloured stone and miniatures were then made either in travertine[27] or else in limestone – with the exception of a few ritual cups and vases that were made of basalt and sometimes rock crystal. Miniatures were also more numerous than full-sized vessels. Generally, the travertine examples were found among the better equipped burials, but the numbers of these travertine assemblages decreased in favour of limestone models.

Reisner considered this replacement of travertine with limestone vessels, and the amount evident within the burial, as reflecting an economic decline in the tomb owner's disposable wealth,[28] but the decrease may also reflect the more restricted

---

[18] Petrie, *Tools and Weapons*, p. 44f.

[19] *E.g.* Do. Arnold, E. Pischikova, in: *Egyptian Art in the Age of the Pyramids*, 123f.; Warren, *Minoan Stone Vases*, 161–164. For a Fifth Dynasty relief of a stone vase maker's atelier, see J. Quibell, Making of Stone Vases, in: G. Maspero (ed.), *Musée egyptien* III, Cairo 1915, 25–27 and pl. XXII.

[20] Verner *et al.*, *Raneferef*, 73, fig.1.3.7.

[21] Nester, Heizer, *Making Stone Vases*.

[22] R. S. Hartenberg, J. Schmidt. Jr., The Egyptian Drill and the Origin of the Crank, *Technology and Culture* 10, 1969, 155–165.

[23] *E.g.* Garstang, *Reqaqnah*, pl. XXII; Reisner, *Naga-ed-Dêr* III, 176.

[24] Reisner, *Mycerinus*, 174.

[25] Reisner, *Naga-ed-Dêr* III, 55.

[26] Reisner, Smith, *Giza Necropolis* II, 92.

[27] Throwing further light on the combined assemblage discovered in this minor cemetery at Abusir, Lucas notes the prevalence of travertine which, after the Predynastic period, became the most popular material used for Egyptian stone vessels. Lucas, *Materials*, 421, 427.

[28] Reisner, Smith, *Giza Necropolis* II, 102.

economic means that were then being experienced by the king. These economic indicators were measuring not only the decline in the ancient economy which contributed to the collapse of the Old Kingdom, but also the enormous numbers of officials then working for the king. In the Archaic period, these numbers had been small, so it had been possible for the king to provide exotic stone vessels for his important officials. However, by the Fourth and Fifth Dynasties, the bureaucracy had expanded noticeably,[29] putting a much greater pressure on royal revenues and it then became impossible for the king to supply the lavish stone vessels that had once been distributed to Archaic officials.

A.3. The archaeological description of the assemblage

All the archaeological finds in this book were found in the area known as the royal cemetery of Abusir, which lies around the four royal pyramid complexes of the first half of the Fifth Dynasty. The lesser monuments that make up that part of the cemetery covered by this book belong to the rather restricted region of the south-eastern area of the entire necropolis. This area is bordered on the west by Raneferef's mortuary temple, together with the structure known as The House of the Knife,[30] and on the east by the collection of tombs published as *Djedkare's Family Cemetery*.[31] The southern border is marked by the edge of the plateau on which these tombs lie: the escarpment is quite noticeable. To the north, the border is framed by the enclosure wall of Neferirkare's pyramid and its adjacent temple.

A.3.1. The situation in the Pyramid Complex of Lepsius no. 24

Lepsius no. 24, whose owner is as yet nameless, lies in the eastern half of this necropolis area, about in the centre (for the general archaeological description, see *chapter 4.2.*). The monument consists of two separate archaeological areas: the pyramid (of which the burial chamber is the central focus) and the temple to the east. Both foci are badly destroyed and had been robbed of their finest pieces of stone over the course of many centuries.

On the floor of the burial chamber, in its eastern part, in the yellow sand filling of the foundation level of the pyramid itself, a number of items were found which would have belonged to the original floor deposit of the burial chamber. These were fragments of travertine **canopic jars** (41/J/94; 51/J/94; 61/J/94) a form which at that time featured tall shouldered jars. Their original function was only to contain one of four bodily parts removed during mummification: the stomach, intestines, liver and lungs. Pieces of these jars from this pyramid were found in the debris fill near the southern wall of what remains of the burial chamber: they were lying about 1 m above the floor, thrown into the accumulated sand and destruction material. From this we conclude that the initial robbery of the chamber took place after the burial room had lain open to blown sand for some time. The damage to the jars – they were probably smashed to extract any items of value within – resulted from the robbers' activities, perhaps as early as the First Intermediate Period,[32] or possibly as late as the Nineteenth Dynasty.[33] A second deposit (92/J/94), this time a fragment of the mouth of a canopic jar, came from the floor debris at the lower edge of the descending corridor. From their combined positions, close to the burial chamber, and with no more than four jars being represented (it has been estimated[34] that the combined pieces probably made up three vessels), we are confident in assuming that these were the original vessels used for the original burial and that,

---

[29] For discussion on the expanding bureaucracy, see Callender, *Eye of Horus*, 43f.

[30] See the chapter 1.4 in: Verner *et al.*, *Raneferef*, 87–99.

[31] On which cemetery see Verner, Callender, *Djedkare's Cemetery*; the stone vessels catalogue being located on pp. 31–38.

[32] M. Verner, Newly discovered royal sarcophagi from Abusir, *Abusir and Saqqara 2000*, 567.

[33] See note 15 above.

[34] P. Vlčková, Royal canopic jars from Abusir, *ArOr* 70, 2002, 157.

after smashing the jars, the robbers had thrown away the jar fragments into the debris as being worthless for their purposes. None of these separate finds made a complete jar, unfortunately and few pieces could be put together.

Near the southern wall of the burial chamber were the fragmented remains of a slightly ovoid **food receptacle** for food of some sort – perhaps a cooked fowl or a piece of meat – made out of travertine (43/J/94). These six fragments have now been put together, but it was not possible to make a complete restoration. In the same region, three further travertine fragments (46/J/94), these belonging to the edges of a separate offering case or receptacle, were also uncovered among the debris. A further three fragments (48/J/94, joined with 60/J/94), made another receptacle, this time, very probably for a case containing a meat offering. Those fragments were found near the preceding item. 55/J/94 was a more or less rectangular (10.3 × 7.5 cm) shallow dish – most likely to have been another food offering case made from travertine: it had been broken into two parts, both of which were found in the debris near the western wall of the burial chamber, ca 75 cm above the floor. (The edges of a room, near its walls, usually have higher levels of accumulated debris, due to wind action over time.) 68/J/94 was a collection of small fragments of a vessel which were found at the lower end of the descending corridor, ca 20 cm below the level of the floor of the burial chamber. The vessel evidently had a flat interior and curved raised edge, but there were different thicknesses evident within the pieces: perhaps they made up part of a sculpted food container lid? As the pieces did not join, it is impossible to be definite about this group. Finally, the rounded bottom of one other travertine case for a food offering (59/J/94) was found that was almost complete. It came from the eastern part of the burial chamber at the same height above floor level. All these food receptacles were found in close proximity to the mummy and it is not too speculative to suggest that these were originally placed near the sarcophagus to provide food for the afterlife of the deceased.

There was also a collection of **offering table** fragments (46/J/94) found in the debris in the central part of the burial chamber, ca 1 m above the floor. These twelve unjoinable fragments had come from a flat, round travertine offering table top that had once had a central column stand (only the circular space for this stand remained). No. 81/J/94 was also an offering table of a different sort: this was a typical Old Kingdom limestone slab[35] with spaces hollowed out for offerings made in the cult. It was found in the debris of the pyramid temple, near the south-eastern corner, which is the general area where one would expect to find such an item. Item no. 78/J/94 was a large collection of miscellaneous pieces of travertine, amongst which were two pieces (o) and (p), which joined up to make a small rectangular **tray,** 9.5 × 6.5 cm; max. thickness 3 cm.

Also present among the debris in different parts of the burial chamber were 18 **model vessels** made from travertine, some complete, others in fragments (45/J/94; 50/J/94; 56/J/94; 73/J/94; 78/J/94). Although their number did not approach the usual quantity for such a prestigious burial (between 70–80 miniature pieces was the norm), all these vessels found deep down in the fill should belong to the original funerary deposit. The largest group of these miniatures was found in the 73/J/94 deposit, which lay in the western part of the burial chamber (ca 2 m from the western wall), in a layer of sand and rubble, practically at floor level. 56/J/94 was a stone beaker, made from travertine. It was discovered in the western part of the burial chamber, at the bottom of a layer of grey sand mixed with the limestone chips, ca 0.75 cm above the foundation level. Its mouth diameter was 5.7 cm, but its height only reached 2.6 cm. The size of the mouth diameter makes it unlikely that this travertine cup would be part of an Opening of the Mouth set, as it is too broad.

---

[35] For discussion on the types of offering tables like this, see Mostaffa, *Opfertafeln*, chapter IV, and V. Dobrev, J. Leclant, Les Tables d'offrandes de particuliers découvertes aux complexes funéraires des Reines près de la pyramide de Pépi Ier, in: *Critères de datation*, 143–157.

The meaning of these miniature forms – referred to as being of no practical purpose by Reisner[36] – is still the subject of debate, with some seeing them as three-dimensional forms of the canonical offering list,[37] and others considering them as "unusable" except in the symbolic sense.[38] It is also possible to consider that some at least of these little dishes and vases had once held tiny amounts of food, unguents and liquids, rather similar to the "funerary feast" that Emery discovered in Saqqara.[39]

There were only a few remnants of full size vessels in the assemblage from this tomb. One was a triangular fragment of a small **bowl** made from travertine, 10 cm in diameter and 4.1 cm high, with a VI of 322 (40/J/94). It had been found in the offering hall of the mortuary temple and appears to be of the Fifth Dynasty origin, as it lay in the debris just above the ground. Just two fragments of stone bowls made from **diorite** remained within Lepsius no. 24: 17/J/94 was a fragment of the body of a bowl which had a consistent thickness of 1 cm, while 22/J/94b had a raised rounded rim and a body that progressively thickened towards its base, where its wall measured 2.3 cm. Both vessels had polished surfaces. These pieces were found in the destroyed entrance area to the temple, in the lowest layer of dark sand mixed with ash and potsherds. Perhaps they had been dropped by a robber on his way out of the temple, during the initial plundering of the temple.

Six fragments of a large limestone vessel (90/J/94) of uncertain date were also found in the mortuary temple. (This large beaker-like vessel may even have been remodelled from some limestone block coming from the pyramid casing.) It is thick-walled and had been smoothed on the outside, but with a noticeable unevenness on the inner surface: its surfaces showed clearly that it had been cut down from some larger lump of stone. It is an open beaker form with conical sides, used for mixing or storing large quantities of dry materials.

There was a huge deposit of rubble, fragments of a red granite sarcophagus, limestone fragments, yellow drift sand and fragments of mudbricks and pottery lying in the secondarily disturbed fill in which these stone vessels lay within the burial chamber. M. Verner interprets this disorder as being largely due to the previous attempts of robbers to penetrate inside the pyramid's substructure (see *chapter 4.1.*). Due to this disorder, it was seldom possible to reconstruct the stratigraphical deposits of the burial chamber either consistently or comprehensively. However, the team was fortunate to find in pyramid Lepsius no. 24 the remains of the mummy of a female of approximately twenty-five years of age. She had evidently been thrown out of her granite sarcophagus by the robbers and lay close to floor level in this unstratified debris, together with fragments of mummy wrappings, good quality pottery, copper utensils, parts of a wooden chest and the above-mentioned stone vessels and other artefacts. Her human remains (since dated to the Old Kingdom by E. Strouhal *et al.*[40], see also *chapter 6.2.2.*) among these things offers some confirmation for the opinion that these vessels were the remains of her original burial equipment and the type of goods and the materials from which they were made (particularly the travertine canopics and the red granite sarcophagus fragments) suggest that this pyramid had held the burial of a queen.

A.3.2. The situation in the Tomb Complex of Lepsius no. 25

This double monument lies on the southern escarpment edge and is close to and parallel with Lepsius no. 24 (for its detailed archaeological description, see *chapter*

---

[36] G. Reisner, *Mycerinus,* 201, where he sees such items as being "the result of an attempt to construct for the … tomb a set of old forms which had by tradition been placed in the tombs since Dynasty I."

[37] Junker, *Gîza I*, 108.

[38] Do. Arnold, in: *Egyptian Art in the Age of the Pyramids*, 493. The remark was made in reference to some late Fifth Dynasty or early Sixth Dynasty miniature vessels from the tomb of Nyankhre, which featured models that had "only diminutive cavities" for their interiors.

[39] Emery, *Funerary Repast.*

[40] E. Strouhal, V. Černý, L. Vyhnánek, An X-ray examination of the mummy found in pyramid Lepsius No. XXIV at Abusir, in: *Abusir and Saqqara 2000*, 543–550, especially p. 544.

5.2.). As has been concluded (*chapters 4.7.* and *5.8.*), both Lepsius no. 24 and no. 25 may have been built in a similar time frame.

Lepsius no. 25/1

L25/1 consists of three separate archaeological areas: the main mastaba area of a monument sharing some of the characteristics of a pyramid, in which the burial access is via a descending passage from the north side. The burial chamber – roughly in the centre of the monument – is the central focus, and its cultic room lies to the east. All three parts of this monument are badly destroyed and both stone and grave robbers have removed large quantities of material, causing severe structural damage to the unit and the loss of most of the monument's historical heritage.

In L 25/1, **fragments of canopic jars** in limestone (63/N/2003a–b) were found in the layer of limestone rubble, just below the floor level of the eastern part of the burial chamber, in a small space above the under floor blocks; 40 cm from the southern wall and 80 cm from the western wall. These are probably fragments from two separate canopic jars.[41] They are not part of a carefully made set – indeed, other examples in Abusir and elsewhere have shown that not much attention was paid to giving the jars in these sets of canopics any uniform appearance during the Old Kingdom. Like the other sets, these jars were rather individual pieces whose workmanship varies. The two pieces found in Lepsius no. 25 have thick and uneven walls and their rims are of different sizes and are manufactured differently (see catalogue for details).

The only example of a full-sized stone vessel was a smallish, roughly worked limestone **bowl** no. 16/N/01 (diameter 12.8 cm, height 5.5 cm) with thick walls and rounded base. While it is not finished, it is really quite well shaped, with a VI of 223. Its walls are thick, but even, and the rim is simply bevelled. It was found in the upper levels of the wind-blown sand in the construction pit.

99/N/2003 is a more unusual piece: it is thought to be the lid of a stone vessel, probably a jar, made out of limestone. Only ca 60 % of the lid remains (diameter 7.1 cm, thickness 2.6 cm). It is red in colour, due to two coats of paint of some sort (see *chapter 5.4.1.*). Lids are seldom found for stone vessels, as C. Lilyquist has remarked.[42] It was found in the filling of drift sand above the floor of the burial chamber. Another lid (17/N/01), this time made of quartzite, with an overall diameter of 5.5 cm, was found near the vestibule, among the sand below the surface level. The lid still has linen material stuck to its upper surface. It was, perhaps, the lid of a kohl or similar ointment jar.

The group recorded as 65/N/2003a–j consisted of **model bowls** made of travertine. They were found in the burial apartments of this tomb, in the area of the underground anteroom, 40 cm to the west from the south-western corner. The bowls were discovered above the floor, in a layer of limestone rubble, drift sand and brown sand. Evidently, the robbers considered them of no value to themselves at all. In all cases, the workmanship of these vessels is simple: their outer walls have been smoothed and the interiors, which have also been smoothed, show marks from drilling.

In addition to the above mentioned stone vessels, copper models of instruments, fragments of wooden equipment, and pottery vessels of fine quality were also recovered from this tomb. Most significantly, two travertine fragments of a female statue were found in the chapel area of this monument. The remains are those of a standing female wearing a simple robe and a necklace. Its fine workmanship has prompted J. Krejčí to suggest that these two fragments are typical of royal statuary. Thus, in his opinion (see *chapter 5.2.*), the burial equipment clearly shows the high rank of the person interred here, since it has some similarities to the burial equipment found in the neighbouring pyramid, Lepsius no. 24. (Note, however, the absence of travertine canopics for L 25/2.)

---

[41] See Vlčková, *ArOr* 70, 2002, 150–154.
[42] Lilyquist, *Egyptian Stone Vessels*, 2.

Lepsius no. 25/2

There is no apparent chapel for this tomb, although remains of offerings (including a pair of gazelle horns) were discovered outside in the middle of the southern wall of the tomb. Whether or not these offerings were intended for the burial in L 25/2 is questionable. The tomb was more savagely destroyed than its neighbour and the archaeological remains, therefore, consist only of the denuded and destroyed walls, the pit for the burial apartments and remains of the descending corridor.

Although the interior of this tomb had been thoroughly ransacked, a small number of stone vessels and fragments were discovered in the debris of the construction pit. 83/N/03 is a large fragment of a **bowl of basalt** with an inner and an upper rim; originally, it must have been quite a large vessel, since the rim of the fragment is only slightly curved. Its VI is impossible to determine because the fragment does not include any part of the base of the vessel. The piece was found in the centre of the construction pit. A basalt bowl in a non-royal tomb is one of the more uncommon finds for this period of time (see comment in the following paragraph on the basalt cup).

A narrow fragment (13 × 6.5 cm) is all that remains of a tall travertine **jar** with the beginnings of a restricted bag-shaped body. The fragment (110/N/04) reveals that the vessel, which had only a slightly closed aperture, had had an exterior rim that measures 1.15 cm at its greatest thickness and 1.4 cm at its maximum height. Because the base and MBD were not present, its VI could not be assessed (see catalogue for further details). It had been found outside the tomb, to the south of its southern wall and may have been associated with the area where the gazelle horns were found.

Two model vessels were discovered. 27/N/02 was a travertine fragment (4.8 cm high, neck diameter 3.8 cm) of a tall, high-necked **model jar** with high, rounded shoulders and narrow base; it was possibly a vase from an Opening of the Mouth set. Its upper neck and rim had been broken off, however. 31/N/2002 was a complete, travertine miniature **bowl** with a VI of 239. It had a rolled rim and fairly thick walls. The bottom of the interior showed drill marks: these created two small hollows on the bottom of the bowl. The first item was discovered in a layer of drift sand in the area of the descending corridor of L25/2. The model bowl, however, came from the so-called "eastern niche" in the construction pit.

A miniature **cup** of basalt (33/N/2002) from an Opening of the Mouth set, was found in the layer of limestone rubble in the filling that lay just above the floor of the burial chamber. The cup, which is chipped at the bottom, has a V-shaped interior. By this time in the Fifth Dynasty, basalt and other coloured stones are really rather rare to find in burials – except in the tombs of kings – but these items from the Opening of the Mouth sets were one of the exceptions for royal and non-royal persons alike. In both central Abusir and southern Abusir, several such funerary sets have been found, though none has been complete.

99/N/2003 is a more unusual piece: it is the lid of a stone vessel, probably a canopic jar (?), but this time, made out of travertine. Lids are seldom found for stone vessels, as Lilyquist has remarked (see note 42). It was found in the filling of drift sand above the floor of the burial chamber. It is interesting to see that, whereas the king's wife might well have travertine canopics (see, for example, the remnants from the burial equipment of Queen Khentkaus II[43]), it was less usual for royal children to have them. Nakhtsare, like the occupant of L 25/1, had once had a limestone set, as was the custom for most royal offspring. A telling example demonstrating this is the case of Princess Khekeretnebty,[44] known to be the bodily daughter of a king,[45] whose canopic set was also made from limestone.

---

[43] Vlčková, *ArOr* 70, 2002, 154f.

[44] See the publication of Khekeretnebty's funerary equipment in Verner, Callender, *Djedkare's Cemetery*, 31f. Fortunately, all four of Khekeretnebty's canopic vessels, together with their lids, were recovered more or less intact from the burial chamber.

[45] As B. Schmitz (*Königssohn*, pp. 132f.) has demonstrated, not all women carrying the title of *s3t nśwt* were the daughters of kings.

A.3.3. The situation in the Mastaba of Nakhtsare[46]

The Mastaba of Nakhtsare is the westernmost monument from this collection of burials. It lies near the south-east corner of the mortuary temple of King Raneferef and is close to the House of the Knife (see *chapter 3.1.* for a discussion on the excavation).

Many of the artefacts that were discovered in this monument came from debris that covered the northern part of the monument, especially in and around the vertical shaft giving access to the burial chamber.[47] From this fact, we can see that much of the burial equipment had been removed from the burial chamber and sorted outside the tomb, close to the burial shaft, when the robbers were finished their activities inside.

The remains of **canopic jars** in white limestone were found in this tomb, too, though they appeared in widely separated places. While the first group (5/Q/94) were recovered *outside* – from the rubble mound of grey sand and fragments of limestone in the south-western part of the tomb, 0.5 m above the level of the eastern part of Raneferef's enclosure wall – twelve pieces (29/Q/94) were found *inside* the tomb, in the north-eastern corner of the burial chamber, in the layer of yellow sand and limestone debris that lay above the pavement of the burial chamber. Like the other canopic vessels found in the previous tombs dealt with in this book, the original jars had been shattered. Once again, this site yielded the fragment of a lid and the complete lid of another canopic jar in white limestone (30a–b/Q/94). The main lid had a diameter of 16.7 cm on its inner edges (*i.e.* across the canopic mouth area), while its outer edges were broken away; the outer edge probably increased the width of the lid to a diameter of almost 21 cm. The height of the lid was 3 cm at its maximum. The smaller fragment differed in profile from 30a/Q/94, having a much shorter rim and further confirming the haphazard approach people at that time took to the choice of vessels in a canopic set.

While not vessels themselves, within various parts of the stratigraphy of Nakhtsare's monument were found a high number of fragments – often quite large – of travertine **dummy food offerings**. 3/Q/94 was the best preserved: it was a stone model of a bird, most likely a representation of a goose.[48] Other pieces were excavated from different parts of this monument. Two of the models seem to have borne faint traces of polychromy.

Among the finds was the fragment of a **full-sized vessel**, a bowl in local yellow limestone (6/Q/94). It had a preserved width of 18 cm, but its diameter would have been 20 cm. It was uncovered in the debris layer of grey sand and limestone splinters below the surface of the mound, together with 5/Q/94, part of a canopic vessel, in the western part of the burial mound, shortly after excavation began.

Other finds were directly connected to the funerary cult. 19/Q/94 was the top of an **offering table** made from travertine. This was also found in the grey sand of the shaft, 2.1 m below the crown of the western wall. It is a complete circular plate, 15 cm in diameter and 1.1 cm thick. Its stand was not found.

There were a few representatives of **miniature vessels** as well. Found by the eastern wall of the shaft (near the corridor leading to the burial chamber) 80 cm below the crown of the eastern wall of the corridor in the grey sand layer, 20/Q/94 was a miniature travertine offering bowl. Also from travertine, but found in the layer of grey sand that lay within the passage between the vertical shaft and the burial chamber, both 26a and 26b/Q/94 were discovered 1.40 m to the south of

---

[46] See the preliminary reports of the respective seasons by M. Verner *ZÄS* 111, 1984, 77f.; *ZÄS* 115, 1988, 168–171; *ZÄS* 124, 1997, 71–76.

[47] See J. Krejčí in this volume, p. 39–40.

[48] Similar offerings have been found in a number of other tombs from the Old Kingdom period, *e.g.* in Ikheti's tomb, close to Djoser's pyramid, a great number of trussed geese like this, made out of travertine, were found (pp. 231–234): Et. Drioton, J.-Ph. Lauer, Un groupe de tombes à Saqqarah: Icheti, Nefer-khouou-Ptah, Sébek-em-khent et Ankhi, *ASAE* 55, 1958, 207–251.

the northern wall of the shaft. 26c–e/Q/94 lay half a meter further to the south, and 26f/Q/94 was found at the same level, but in the centre of the burial chamber, while the other examples were found to the east of the sarcophagus, in the north-east corner of the burial chamber. These were uncovered from the layer of sand and limestone debris above the pavement of the burial chamber. All of these pieces were models of shallow bowls made of polished travertine with some marks of drilling. Their ratio of width and height fluctuated, but they were similar in size, being largish, as the earlier miniature dishes tended to be. The collection of fragments making up 31/Q/94 also contained parts of miniature travertine bowls that were collected from above the damaged floor in the burial chamber. The chaos evident in the burial chamber suggests that the robbers rummaged through the fill, hunting for more usable stone items.

18/Q/94 was a 9.6 cm high miniature **vase** made of basalt. It was found in the shaft in the grey sand layer, 2 m below the masonry of the western wall, not far from the shaft. Only one vase of travertine (33/Q/94) that was 9.8 cm high (with a base diameter of 2.1 cm) was found. It lay in the southern part of the corridor leading from the shaft into the burial chamber, amidst sand and limestone fragments. It was a model vase that was part of the Opening of the Mouth set. Only a small part of the interior had been hollowed out. This model was 2 mm taller than its basalt counterpart. The basalt vase was wider across its rim than the travertine one: it measured 5.5 cm, while the travertine diameter was 5 cm. These vessels were both of greater size than the example from L25, where the height was only 6.8 cm and the rim diameter 4 cm. All three vessels, however, had only token inner hollows for the unguent.

One small, white limestone object that may have been a bowl in the process of being made (a miniature vessel?) was 36/Q/94. It was found in the area of the southern wall of the burial chamber, at the level of the torn out pavement, in the layer of the grey sand and small limestone fragments. Its rough manufacture, with unsmoothed surface, suggests that this was a remodelling made in later times. (Lepsius no. 24 also had two roughly worked limestone bowls – 54/J/94, 65/J/94 – that were unfinished.)

Finally, from either the Late Period or Ptolemaic Period came a well polished travertine vessel, with flat bottom and everted rim (11/Q/94). The interior of the vessel was made by means of drilling. It was found in the debris of the burial chamber.

A.3.4. The situation in the Mastaba of Nebtyemneferes

In Nebtyemneferes' tomb only three small fragments of **bowls** were found: one in gabbro, one in diorite and part of a miniature dish in travertine. Of particular interest is the fragment of a well-made bowl in gabbro (5/M/87). Objects in diorite or gabbro were only occasionally found in the tombs of persons other than kings in the Fifth Dynasty, so this first fragment might be an intrusive item. However, the circumstances of its find seem authentic and they may in fact indicate that the bowl may have been a rare funerary gift – perhaps from the king. It was found in the storeroom in the north-western corner of the mastaba, on the floor, in the centre of the room, below the mudbrick destruction and limestone detritus. The vessel is a rectangular dish on the exterior, but the inner cavity is oval in shape. It has a flat, rather narrow rim that widens to a triangular shape at the four corners of the vessel. (In this, it is identical in shape to 56/J/94 from Lepsius no. 24.) Its surface has been well polished.

The second item is also a fragment of a bowl (9/M/87), but it is made from diorite. It is part of a bowl with a re-curved rim whose surface has been polished. In some respects, the shape resembles the shape of some Meidum ware bowls. The fragment was found on the surface of the terrain, during the initial survey in the area of the south-western corner of the mastaba.

The final item is a fragment of a **miniature bowl** in travertine (10/M/87). Enough has been preserved to suggest that it belongs to a miniature bowl with a rounded bottom. The surface of the bowl had been polished.

A.4. Summary

In assessing the stratigraphical position of the above examples of stone vessels, it is noticeable that, with the exception of some of the canopic fragments from Nakhtsare's tomb, most of the canopic vessels and fragments were found in the burial chambers where they had originally been deposited. In each of these tombs, the canopic vessels had been reduced to fragments, suggesting that the robbers either knew or suspected that valuable items might have been included within them and that smashing the jars was the easiest way to extract the contents. In contrast to other forms of major stone vessels – few remnants of which survived – the canopic jars themselves were not seen by the robbers as having any practical secondary use. This may well be because canopic jars had a particular function which would lend to their reuse in daily life a rather abhorrent aspect.

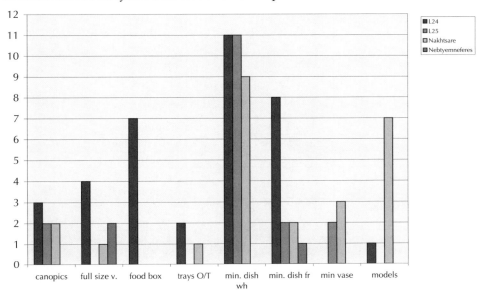

Fig. A.2 Proportion of classes of vessels in the four tombs in which stone vessels were found.

v = vessels;
wh = whole vessels;
fr = fragments of vessels recorded with register nos.

The greatest frequency of stone vessels found in all of these burials was not canopic jars but miniature stone vessels (see *fig. A.2*). Probably, the reason for this large figure is not only due to the greater numbers of these small objects within each important burial assemblage, but also due to the low reuse potential of miniatures: the ancient robbers were not interested in them. In this chart, canopics are represented by the number of (incomplete) jars found in each tomb. The proportion of fragmented miniature dishes (fr) is also shown, since the fragments in Lepsius no. 24 (J) were almost complete, as was the sample in Nakhtsare (Q). Their numbers complement the figures of the unbroken vessels.

A.4.1. Classes present in each assemblage

Taking the entire corpus of stone vessels found in this minor south-eastern cemetery at Abusir, one notices immediately the limited range present within these four burial sites. Most noticeable is the situation regarding the tomb of Nebtyemneferes, whose assemblage was only represented by a single miniature vessel and the remains of two vessels of coloured stone. All of the tombs had been robbed and the disturbed nature of the stratigraphy within these burial chambers testifies to several attacks by robbers, who took away the useful vessels – or items that could be remodelled – leaving very little behind. The remaining stone vessels were:

A.4.2. Analysis of classes
Trays

Two fragmented trays in travertine (56/58/J/94 and 78/J/94) and one circular offering plate (46/J/94), were discovered in Lepsius no. 24: the two small rectangular

	Lepsius no. 24	Lepsius no. 25	Nakhtsare	Nebtyemneferes
Class: full size vessels				
Trays (offering table, plate)	2 fr. trays (travertine), 1 circular offering plate (travertine) 1 limestone offering table		1 circular offering plate (travertine)	
Trays (food containers)	7 fr. groups (travertine)			
Dishes	2 rough (limestone)			1 fr. (gabbro) 1 fr. (diorite)
Bowls	2 fr. (diorite) 2 frgs (travertine)	1 (basalt) 1 (limestone)	1 (yellow limest.)	
Beakers	1 (limestone)			
Tall shouldered jars (incl. canopics)	3 (?) fr. (travertine)	1 fr. (travertine) 2 fr. (limestone)	2 fr. (limestone)	
Lids		1 fr. (limestone) lid 1 (quartzite) lid	2 fr. (limestone) lids	
Slender baggy jar		1 fr. (trav.)		
Class: miniatures				
Dishes	19 (travertine)	11 (travertine)	9 (travertine)	1 (travertine)
Beaker (cup)		1 (basalt)		
Slender vases w/flaring rim		1 (basalt) 1 (travertine)*	1 (basalt) 1 (travertine)	
Tall shouldered jars			model beer jar (travertine)	

trays have each been joined from fragments. All four pieces were found in the burial chamber, approximately one metre above the floor. In Nakhtsare's burial another circular table top was found (19/Q/94). It had a diameter of 15.2 cm. Although the top was present, the stand to which it had once been joined was not found. It was a typical offering table, as seen in slab stelae,[49] the lintels and the panels of false doors,[50] and probably representative of the real tables from which the individual ancient Egyptian ate. Offering tables were one of the canonical items in the offering list of the Old Kingdom.

An offering table of a different sort, 81/J/94, consisted of four pieces of limestone which could not be joined. It was a typical Old Kingdom offering slab made from limestone, with spaces hollowed out for offerings made in the cult, outside the tomb. It was found in the debris of the pyramid temple of Lepsius no. 24, near the south-east corner, which is the general area where one would expect to find such an item. See *table A.3.*

Offering tables first appeared at the end of the Predynastic period, when they were made in pottery and had a rim rising vertically from the edge.[51] This type had a long history throughout the Old Kingdom and is well represented at the Abusir sites. The earliest stone tables made their appearance during the First Dynasty[52] and, by the Second Dynasty, the classic form of a flat and rimless round table top supported by a single central leg was so common that it was nearly always represented in the slab stelae from Saqqara and Helwan. 46/J/94 formed the remnants of such a table in travertine. (For discussion on the offering tablet type, see the notes under 81/J/94 in *chapter 3.4.*)

Table A.2 Basic classes of stone vessels of the minor tombs in the Abusir Royal Necropolis.

* This vase is most likely to have been part of the Opening of the Mouth set. Unfortunately, it has lost its top, giving it a distorted VI of 70, whereas its missing (additional) height would put it into the "slender" category.

---

[49] Manuelian, *Slab Stelae*. The frontispiece has an excellent reproduction of a circular table like the one found in this tomb, but there are many other examples in the book. For examples of actual travertine tables found in tombs, see Reisner, *Naga-ed-Dêr* III, pl. 32.f, *etc.*
[50] Verner, Callender, *Djedkare's Cemetery*, 27–29.
[51] Reisner, *Mycerinus*, 132.
[52] *Loc. cit.*

Table A.3 Tray types present in the entire assemblage.

Assemblage of trays	Round table top	Rectangular tray	Offering slab
Lepsius no. 24	1	2	1
Lepsius no. 25	1	0	0
Nakhtsare	0	0	0
Nebtyemneferes	0	0	0

Also grouped as trays (although some of these may have been lids to cover them[53]), are the 7 lots of travertine fragments making up containers or receptacles for food (probably ten vessels were represented in this collection). Their pieces were scattered throughout the burial chamber of the queen's pyramid: some of these were found 20 cm under the level of the floor of the chamber, in a layer of grey sand and tiny limestone chips, but near the entrance to the descending corridor, so they were probably moved from their original place during the first rifling of the tomb. Two containers are clearly for meat dishes, the others may have been for cooked birds. Where edges are present, these are horizontal, flat incurving forms, suitable for closing a container whose body and lid had flat edges. Comparisons with other containers of a similar function[54] show that all of them have these flat edges and it has been suggested that these boxes and lids would have been tied together when the meat was inside – as was found in the tomb of Seniu[55] (early Eighteenth Dynasty) and Yuya and Thuya's burial (see note 56). Although no food had been found from the Old Kingdom containers previously, in South Abusir, a set of such vessels was discovered recently which contained both meat and birds in their respective containers. (The meat had not been mummified and the remains consisted only of the bones of the offering – see M. Bárta *et al.*, *Qar*. As a further note of interest, one observes that whereas Prince Nakhtsare had model birds and meat made from travertine in his tomb remains, no actual food cases were found.

Food containers continued to be used in the wealthier tombs of later times. They are attested in Middle Kingdom tombs, in the tomb of Kha of Deir el Medina. Those of Tutankhamun are very familiar, of course, but his great-grandparents also had food containers with dried food still in them when their tomb was found.[56]

Dishes

Only two limestone dishes remained within any site (54/J/94; 65/J/94) and these were both roughly-worked cores, rather than proper dishes. The second of these, measuring 6 cm, is almost small enough to fit in the miniature class, but is grouped here because of its similarity to the other piece. A third rough item – probably intended to be a miniature bowl in limestone (36/Q/94) – would fit definitely into the miniature class, but for the fact that it is far from finished. Presumably, the absence of travertine dishes from the archaeological record is either due to their usefulness for those who took them, or else their fragility made it easy for them to be pulverised among the rubble. Certainly, no recognisable fragments remained.

Bowls

There was evidence for only nine bowls of full size within the combined assemblage. These consisted of: two separate fragments of travertine and two small and separate basalt fragments that were found in Lepsius no. 24; one large basalt fragment and a limestone bowl from Lepsius no. 25; a yellow limestone bowl fragment from Nakhtsare's tomb, and a gabbro and diorite bowl fragments from

---

[53] 56/J/94, with its flat edges and curved, vaulted body shape is definitely such a lid.
[54] *E.g.* see the photograph in: *Mummies and Magic*, Catalogue item no. 26 a–e.
[55] S. D'Auria, in: *Mummies and Magic*, 142, Cat. No. 81.
[56] Quibell, *Yuaa and Thuiu*, Nos. 51088, 51089, 51100 are shown in pl. XXIII. These food containers were made of wood, plastered over, then coated with resin inside. They contained various meats, which were wrapped in linen cloths. Some of the foods present were: a leg of veal, a side of pigeon, a shoulder of antelope, four ribs of beef, a duck and several geese, *etc.*

the tomb of Nebtyemneferes. One of the travertine bowl fragments from Lepsius no. 24 came from the offering hall of the pyramid temple, in the layer of above ground debris. The two diorite[57] pieces from Lepsius no. 24 (22/J/94b and 17/J/94) have already been mentioned. Only one piece had a rim and profile 22/J/87 (*fig.A.3*) that was noticeably elegant. When intact, this had been a fairly deep bowl with an incurved, rounded rim and body walls that gradually thickened towards the base. There is every possibility that the vessel had had a flat bottom, since the flat base was much more popular for diorite vessels like this.[58] Such vessels could be used for unguents or fatty materials which the stone would help keep cool, but with its deeply-angled, open shape, this vessel is more likely to have held liquids, the incurved rim inhibiting spillage. Despite its chronological horizon in the tomb, it is doubtful whether this bowl could have come from the Middle Kingdom, however, for convex sided bowls with high shoulders and incurved rims like this belong to either the Fourth or Fifth Dynasty: this particular type originated with the reign of Mycerinus.[59] It may even have been an heirloom when it was placed among the queen's cult objects.

Fig. A.3 Rim and profile of vessel 22/J/87.

The second bowl meriting discussion consist of several fragments of travertine which came from Prince Nakhtsare's burial chamber. They were found in the filling consisting of sand and limestone fragments in the south-eastern corner of the burial chamber, just above the floor. The bowl was therefore likely to have been part of the original burial assemblage. It had a flat bottom, attenuated side walls and, strangely, a thickened, obliquely cut inner rim (31b/Q/94; *fig. A.4*).

Fig. A.4 A fragment of a diorite bowl 31b/Q/94.

One limestone bowl came from Lepsius no. 25 and a basalt bowl fragment came from L25/2, the smaller of the conjoined tombs. The limestone example (16/N/01) has been discussed above (for further details see *chapters 5.4.1.* and *5.4.2.*). The original basalt bowl (83/N/03), which had been quite large, had a graceful, projecting rim profile. The vessel had walls that were as narrow as 0.5 cm at the neck below the rim, but these swelled to 1.5 cm towards the base. However, it is the rim which merits most attention, because of its many angles. There had been a distinct, sloping inner rim running just below the upper edge of the bowl. The overall effect has been to give the bowl a profile like the prow of a ship. The walls of the vessel taper to a narrow neck, before rising obliquely to the inner rim. This rim marks the start of a level area that makes a broad band of stone that ends in a second, inner and clearly marked angle. At this point, the outer rim, which has a V-edge shape (see *fig. A.5*), turns nearly 90° before it meets the outer skin of the bowl. This elaborate system of rims is a work of a very skilled craftsman.

Fig. A.5 The basalt bowl (83/N/03) with a projecting rim profile.

Finally, from Nebtyemneferes' tomb came two pieces of separate bowls, one fragment of gabbro and one of diorite. The presence of two rare coloured stones among this woman's collection, together with the actual position of her tomb, endorse the idea that Nebtyemneferes had indeed been a member of the royal family – perhaps from the time of Niuserre.

Beakers

To be classed as a beaker are the six large fragments in limestone from the mortuary temple of Lepsius no. 24 (90/J/94 – *figs. A.6 a–b*) In this example, not

---

[57] Reisner, *Mycerinus*, 148, reports that diorite vessels did not appear until the time of King Khasekhemwy and had their heyday in private tombs during the Third Dynasty. By the time of the Fourth Dynasty, diorite (and other expensive stone) vessels again became the sort of find associated mainly with royal burials. After the Third Dynasty, fine pottery vessels (especially Meidum Ware) replaced the quantities of stone vessels that had been appearing in non-royal tombs up until that time. Evidently, the cost of the enormous construction works undertaken by King Sneferu contributed a great deal to the diminishing quantities of expensive stone vessels that the king could contribute to the burial equipment of his officials.

[58] Reisner, *Mycerinus*, 196.

[59] Reisner (*Mycerinus*, 186, Type Xc, example 41) dates its origins to the time of this king. He remarks, 196, that it is one of the characteristic types for this particular period.

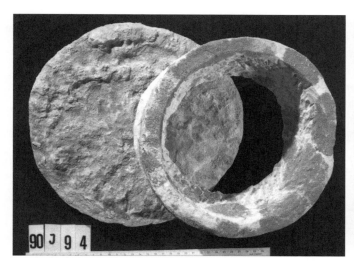

Fig. A.6 Limestone fragments from the mortuary temple of Lepsius no. 24 (90/J/94). Photo MZ

only four pieces from the side walls, but also the entire neck rim and the base of this vessel were preserved. The vessel had a mouth diameter of 26.5 cm, with a rim thickness of 1.9 cm. It was a fairly shallow vessel, however, for its preserved height was only 10 cm. This type of beaker would have been useful for storing dry goods, for its weight would make it impractical for carrying, and its material would make it useless for storing liquids. The base was 2.3 cm thick and the average thickness of its walls was 2.35 cm. (For further details, see this number in *chapter 4.5.1.*)

Slender bag-form jar

This sole example of this form is represented by a fragment (110/N/04) of travertine that was found in the wind-blown sand south of the southern wall of L25/2 at a height equal to the preserved crown of the southern wall. It was dated to the Fifth Dynasty. There is an exterior rim and the vessel has been polished. It has a carinated rim jutting out on the exterior (Aston refers to such rims as "obtuse angle rims" with a bevelled top – a form dating back to the Early Dynastic period), but this top curves downwards on the inner edge. The width of the piece is 6.5 cm, but it is difficult to gauge the original width of the vessel's mouth or, indeed, its true length, so its VI cannot be measured.

Tall shouldered jars

This group contained only the canopic jars,[60] jars which stored the four bodily organs removed from the dead during the mummification process. In the early Fourth Dynasty, those organs were wrapped and stored in a canopic recess or a canopic box (the earliest box known belonged to Queen Hetepheres I). Two generations later, the organs seem to have been covered with natron and wrapped in linen, then put into canopic vessels.

The name for these vessels derives from a legend retold by Herodotos. As is widely known, canopic jars of the Middle Kingdom, New Kingdom and Late Period frequently had heads modelled on the lids. From New Kingdom times, these were often the jackal-headed Duamutef, the baboon-headed Hapy, the human-headed Imsety, and hawk-headed Qebehsenuef, but in the Middle Kingdom and other periods, human-headed canopic jars were also made. It is probably because of this human-headed type that the legend of a Greek sailor named Canopus originated, for it was said that he was worshipped as a jar. The adjective, *canopic,* derives from this.

These canopic jars from Abusir belonging to a well-established tradition of using

---

[60] Vlčková (in the chapter on stone vessels from the complex of Raneferef) assigns canopic jars to a separate group within the class of storage jars (see Verner *et al., Raneferef,* 338). This scheme is one of the many different schemes devised for cataloguing and analysing stone vessels, but it is not followed here.

tall, shouldered jars, which were closed shapes. This vessel had had a long history and is well attested during the Archaic Period[61] and Third Dynasty.[62] Reisner[63] has remarked that this form of jar seems to have been an imitation of a pottery form, rather than a form originating in stone, and those specimens having a collar and small, flat base in the Fifth and Sixth Dynasties occur in both stone and pottery.

It is worth remarking that the height of the Abusir jars (to the extent that they can be measured, due to their fragmented state) was not uniform. In shape, however, they show a marked similarity to a set now kept in the Museum of Fine Arts in Boston[64] (MFA 20.1943a–d), but too many precise vectors are missing within this Abusir collection to be able to draw reasonable comparisons between this group and any others (see *table A.4*).

	Canopic heights	Mouth Diameter	Base diameter	Body width
Lepsius no. 24	x* + 9 cm; x + 11.5 cm; x + 18.5 cm; 21 cm; 23 cm	?	A: outer = 15 cm A: inner = 9.5 cm	x + 18.5 cm x + 16 cm; x + 21.5 cm
Lepsius no. 25	x + 11.5 cm; x + 6 cm	?	14 cm	x + 10 cm
Nakhtsare	30 cm	14 cm	13 cm	
Raneferef	35–38 cm	ca 12 cm	13 cm	ca 20 cm

Table A.4 Dimensions of the canopic jars found in the minor tombs of the Abusir Necropolis and in Raneferef's Unfinished Pyramid.

*As all the canopic vessels were fragmentary, x = the section missing.

The thickness of all of the vessels showed considerable variations, both between each other and within their own individual items. Samples of those measurements made are:

> Lepsius no. 24: body thickness 4.5 cm; max. 4.7 cm; rim 5.5 cm; rim thickness max. 5.7 cm
> Lepsius no. 25: body thickness 2 cm; max thickness 2.5 cm
> Nakhtsare: body thickness 2 cm; max. thickness not measured

Since few of the pieces could be considered comparable where measurements of each fragment were given, valid comparisons between the vessels could not be made, but the most notable observation was that the limestone canopic fragments were about half the thickness of the travertine pieces. One would assume that the relative brittleness of the travertine might cause the craftsman to make the walls of travertine vessels thicker to avoid cracking the stone, but perhaps the thicker walls were also considered a more secure protection for the organs of a queen.

Although all of the canopic vessels were of a basic pattern, there was some variation in the shape. 29/Q/94 seems to have had a smaller base (this was missing, but the angle of the vessel wall is clear to see) than 5/Q/94, despite the fact that the vessels came from the same burial set. 63/N/02 has a mouth that appears to be wider than those of the other vessels, and also has only a slight bulge at the shoulder level – the other shouldered bulges are more pronounced. Where preserved, all the canopic vessels have flat bases and a cusp collar rim, but that of the J series slopes at a steeper angle towards the opening of the vessel than the other rims do (*fig. A.7*).

Canopic jar lids
In Nakhtsare's tomb there was found the lid of a canopic jar (30a/Q/94) in white limestone, in addition to a small fragment of another lid that differs in size and shape (30b/Q/94). The first example had a diameter of 16.7 cm on its inner edges

---

[61] In Reisner, *Naga-ed-Dêr* III, pl. 32b, item 523 is a miniature version of the collared jar and is an offering jar, as are the miniatures depicted in pl. 32d and pl. 34a, *etc.*
[62] For example, see form Type Va in alabaster from Naga ed-Der, stairway tomb No. 587 (as in Reisner, *Mycerinus*, 167, Fig. 39.4), and Garstang's "Great Stone Vases" in alabaster recorded from Raqaqnah, see: Garstang, *Reqaqnah*, Pl. XI, No. 35.
[63] Reisner, *Mycerinus*, 176.
[64] See the photograph of containers which came from G 2385, from the Senedjemib Complex in Giza: *Mummies and Magic*, Catalogue item no. 26, with comments by E. Brovarski (p. 93).

(*i.e.* across the canopic mouth area). Its outer edges were broken away but, probably, the lid had had a diameter of almost 21 cm. The height of the lid was 3 cm at its maximum. The second piece features a lid that may have been a little higher than the first; its central plug was certainly closer to the actual edge of the lid.

Fig. A.7 Comparisons in preserved profiles between some of the canopic jars in the assemblage from the minor cemetery in the Abusir Royal Necropolis.

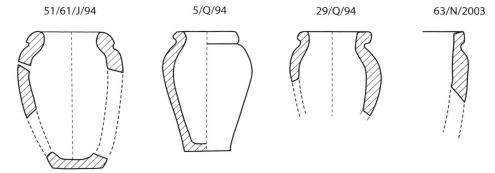

51/61/J/94   5/Q/94   29/Q/94   63/N/2003

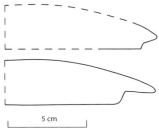

5 cm

Fig. A.8 Profile of canopic lids found in the minor tombs of the Abusir Royal Necropolis.

Fig. A.9 Diagram of a canopic jar from the tomb of Queen Meresankh III, Fourth Dynasty (Dunham, Simpson, Mersyankh, pl. XIV).

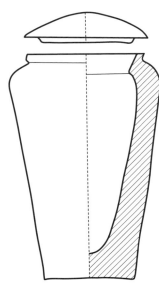

From some time around Year 15 or so of Djedkare, Khekeretnebty's tomb was erected.[65] This represents about two generations after Nakhtsare's tomb was built. Nonetheless, the canopic lids of Khekeretnebty[66] and Nakhtsare are similar in type. Khekeretnebty's examples also vary widely in diameter, but the height hovers around 3 cm, which is the same as that of Nakhtsare's lids. The canopic jars, however, are much taller in the case of Djedkare's daughter. (Reisner had already remarked on the tendency of these jars to increase in length as time progressed.)

A lid was also present for the canopic set of King Raneferef (12/I/98-4). That travertine lid is slightly convex, round and low, with an inner diameter of 14.5 cm, a measurement that fits with none of the king's canopic mouths exactly, although its best fit was with the third vessel belonging to the king.[67] A similar type of lid made from travertine (359/A/78) was found for the canopic equipment of Queen Khentkaus II in a secondary deposit in a room belonging to that queen's mortuary temple.[68] The profile of this lid[69] differs from the one found in Nakhtsare's tomb. (No profile was published for the king's lid, unfortunately.) The Khentkaus lid had an inner diameter of 11 cm and was 2 cm high.

Tall, restricted jars of large height, like the canopic forms found in all these burials, have their origins in the Early Dynastic period, when their rims were more likely to be rounded, rather than cusp in profile.[70] The oldest evidence for the use of jars like these as canopic containers comes from a few Saqqara burials and tomb M 17 (the tomb of an unknown male in Meidum dating no later than the time of Sneferu), where it is rather circumstantial. Small, truncated barrel shaped jars with both rolled and cusp rim were all used at Naga ed-Der's N Cemetery up until the Fourth Dynasty.[71] It is therefore assumed that the early Fourth Dynasty marks the beginnings of evisceration in the mummification process. Clear proof of evisceration, however, dates to the later period of Khufu, with the canopic niche and box of Queen Hetepheres I in G 7000x. The remains – presumably of the four canopic organs – are still inside the travertine canopic chest, which is divided into four compartments. At this juncture in time, jars were not used for the remains of the organs: the compartmental chest was evidently considered a suitable receptacle for these but, by the time of Khafre (once again, the evidence of a pit in the floor of the burial chamber is circumstantial), or a little later, canopic vessels become evident

[65] Verner, Callender, *Djedkare's Cemetery*, 108.
[66] *Ibid.*, 31; see figs B20 and B21.
[67] Vlčková, *ArOr* 70, 2002, 152.
[68] *Ibid.*, 154f.
[69] See fig. 4 on the same page in the above article.
[70] See Aston, *Stone Vessels,* 122, example 83.
[71] *E.g.* Reisner, *Naga-ed-Dêr* III, 42f., and fig. 10: Cemetery N, 4 N 529/1; 5 N 523/1; 10 N 542.

and are, for example, attested in the burial of Queen Meresankh III, at Giza (see *fig. A.9*),[72] whose burial should date to the time of Menkaure. It should be stressed, however, that evisceration was only evident for the most privileged upper class within Old Kingdom society during the Fourth and Fifth Dynasties.

From the time of Hetepheres I, it is evident that travertine was seen as a suitable material for the canopic receptacles of queens. This usage is confirmed at Abusir, where both Khentkaus II and the nameless (but surely queenly) occupant of Lepsius no. 24 seem to have had travertine canopic vessels. Limestone seems to have been the material designated for other people, even those of princely rank.[73]

While the evidence is very restricted, one further observation that might be interesting is that it is likely that travertine vessels were reserved for queen mothers, rather than women who only claim the title of *hmt nswt*. Among the queen mothers for whom evidence is available, Hetepheres I, probably Khentkaus I and Khentkaus II have travertine canopics. But those wives of the king who were not mothers, such as Meresankh III and Rekhetre had limestone canopics, while Iput I, who was buried as a wife and not a king's mother, had pottery canopics. Other queens had either no jars, or else they were not recorded. Unfortunately, the earlier publications for the burials of queens are seldom as careful as the published records of most kings.

Miniature forms
Slender Jars

There were four slender miniatures – known as *h3ts* jars – found in this cemetery: two of travertine and two of basalt.[74] Three of them were clearly slender vases of a new type: pieces with exaggerated flaring rims, while the fourth vessel (made of travertine) was broken part-way up its neck, although it seemed to be similar in every way to the others that were complete. In their chapter on stone vases, Do. Arnold and E. Pischikova[75] remark that it was in the Sixth Dynasty that the "mannerist" style is met for the first time after the Archaic period. In these exaggeratedly flared Abusir *h3ts* jars, however, the mannerist style may well be said to be present in the Fifth Dynasty as well! All of the vessels had been bored in only a token way, not even hollowed down into the neck. The reason for this is the symbolic nature of each vase: if oil had ever been inserted in the small cavity, it had only been a small amount. They had been tube-bored.

Judging from their similar sizes, the basalt and travertine examples from Lepsius no. 25 were part of the same set. The examples from this tomb would have been of similar size to each other if the neck and rim of the travertine example had been intact. Amongst the references cited by Aston for this form of vase, only one was found to be of travertine: the major light-coloured ones were of rock crystal.

These jars are part of the Opening of the Mouth set, a small tray with *h3ts* jars, a *pss-kf* instrument, miniature *hnt* cups and, sometimes, *ntrj* blades set into shaped hollows within the stone tray. These ritual sets are well attested in burials at Abusir,[76] but none as yet has been complete. The one from Raneferef's storeroom *CO* contained a *pss-kf* knife, finely worked in basalt, a crystal *hnt* jar and a basalt *hnt* jar

[72] Dunham, Simpson, *Mersyankh*, pl. XIV. Like Khafre's burial chamber, Meresankh's burial crypt contained a canopic recess in the floor, but one of the jars was found on the floor of this room (see *Mersyankh III*, p.21). The pit was about 70 × 70 cm square and it 48 cm deep. The jars were made of limestone.
[73] See, for example, the canopics of Princess Khekeretnebty (Verner, Callender, *Djedkare's Cemetery*, 31f.) and Prince Nakhtsare (p. 265 in this chapter).
74 Aston provides less exaggerated examples as No. 137 in her Classification Tables, *Stone Vessels*, 140.
[75] Arnold, Pischikova, *Egyptian Art in the Age of the Pyramids*, 123.
[76] E.g., they were present in the tomb of Khekeretnebty, Raneferef and Nakhtsare as well as being present in the assemblage of the unknown owner of tomb Lepsius no. 25. Remains of these sets have also been found at South Abusir by the Czech team. For a discussion on the pieces found in Khekeretnebty's burial equipment, see Verner, Callender, *Djedkare's Cemetery*, 32f.
[77] Verner *et. al.*, *Raneferef*, 61.

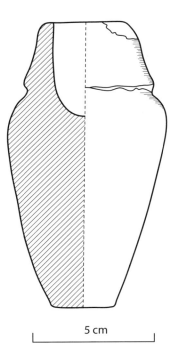

5 cm

Fig. A.10 Model beer jar 17/Q/94.

that was half the size of the crystal one.[77] This difference in size might indicate that there had originally been two different sets within Raneferef's burial equipment, but no other pieces of the sets were found. This is usually the case with sets in other cemeteries, which is why, for the exhibition, *Mummies and Magic,* the organisers had to use items from no less than three burial sets to make up the "set" photographed in that stone tray that was put on display.[78]

Tall jars

The model beer jar made of travertine (*fig. A.10*) comes under the classification of a collared jar, because of its neck cap. It is a shouldered jar representative of one of the types of jars used for storing beer or wine, a form that derives from the pointed beer and wine jars of the Early Dynastic period. Aside from its tall collar and pointed base, the jar shape is similar to some canopic forms of the later Old Kingdom.

Beakers

There were two miniature vessels in this category. A miniature beaker in travertine with the number 56/J/94 is a miniature cup from the Fifth Dynasty (5.7 cm broad and 2.6 cm high, giving it a VI of 219). It has a flat base. The cup was discovered with other objects in the western part of the burial chamber, ca 0.75 cm above the floor of the chamber. It has steep conical sides and its exterior walls are smoothed, although its interior is more roughly worked in the bottom section. It seems to be too broad to have been a *ḥnt* cup.

There was only one other beaker (33/N/2002) amongst the three major assemblages. It was a *ḥnt* cup, from an Opening of the Mouth set and measures 3.6 cm in breadth, 3.3 cm in height. It came from the complex Lepsius no. 25 and was a miniature cup of basalt (?) from an Opening of the Mouth set. It lay in the limestone rubble filling of the burial chamber, not far from a miniature basalt jar. The cup has some parity with Reisner's Xb model from G 7350. Closer in time to this beaker from Lepsius no. 25 is the cup found near the south-western corner of Khekeretnebty's sarcophagus[79] a hundred metres or so from Lepsius no. 25. Like Khekeretnebty's cup, the one from Lepsius no. 25 had an interior that had been scooped out (unlike the flared *ḥȝts* jars, which only have token cavities), but the princess's cup was better made and had a larger cavity and thinner walls than 33/N/2002. Its dimensions were 3.4 cm broad and 2.5 cm high.

Stone vessels such as this cup were modelled on metal prototypes, but a variety of materials have been recorded from later periods. The cups continued to be in use during the New Kingdom and the Late Period in Egypt: two of these truncated cone cups were present in the burial of Thuya, mother of Queen Tiye.[80] They were covered with gold foil and were empty. From the tomb of Tutankhamen, two other cups, this time made of bronze, were set down on either side of a *pss-kf* instrument, a model which is now on display in the Cairo Museum (JE 61489). Those particular cups held natron and resin.[81] A. M. Roth,[82] however, mentions that the Pyramid Texts record that such cups were used for wine and beer in the Old Kingdom. From the intact burial of the Twenty-sixth Dynasty priest and Controller of the Palace, Iufaa (who was buried at Abusir), came two, small, blue-green faience cups of similar nature, joined at the rim with a layer of plaster (exc. no. 98938); they also were empty inside.[83]

---

[78] See the excellent discussion by A. M. Roth in *Mummies and Magic,* 81, catalogue No. 11. And for the role of the enigmatic *pss-kf* knife, in the burial ritual, see her two articles: The *pss-kf* and the "Opening of the Mouth" ceremony: a ritual of birth and rebirth, *JEA* 78, 1992, 113–147, and *idem.,* Fingers, Stars, and the "Opening of the Mouth": the Nature and Function of the *nṯrj* blades, *JEA* 79, 1993, 57–79.

[79] Verner, Callender, *Djedkare's Cemetery,* 32.

[80] Quibell, *Yuaa and Thuiu,* Nos. 30177, 30178.

[81] Carter, Mace, *Tutankhamen* III, 214f., pl. 53.h.

[82] Roth, *JEA* 78, 1992, 135.

[83] See V. G. Callender, The Amulets of Iufaa of West Abusir, in L. Bareš *et al., The tomb complex of Iufaa* (in press).

Usually, there were two black *ḥnwt* cups and two white ones in the Old Kingdom Opening of the Mouth sets, but sometimes only one black cup and one white one were present. The white and black cups are named as the eyes of Horus in Spell 43 of the *Pyramid Texts* and, in the pyramid of Unas, the pictogram defining the name is the *ḥnt* cup.[84] Perhaps these cups might represent the Breast of Horus and the Breast of Eset, one set being equal to a pair of breasts, and two sets being representatives for each of the gods. As Roth[85] has remarked, the Breast of Horus contains milk, but that of Eset is empty. This could be because males do not produce milk (and therefore do need to be supplied with this), whereas females do (and therefore do not require additional milk).

Bowls

The dividing line between a shallow bowl and a dish is very small, but dishes are flatter than bowls, and most of the items in the assemblage fall more readily into the dishes class of open vessels. All of the assemblage had vessel walls that were convex, so there was no difference within the walls of the vessels.

31/N/02 from Lepsius no. 25 is the most obvious bowl because of its proportions and steeper sides (*fig. A.11*): the other bowls are so shallow that they tend towards the "dishes" class. Nonetheless, judging by the VI done for each vessel from Lepsius no. 25, three items fell into the "bowl" category; the other eight were dishes.

From Lepsius no. 24 the VI index sorted out five bowls and fourteen dishes, but two of the bowls were the result of calculations projected on possible shapes of finished forms. Three of the dishes also are the result of such calculations. These five items have been removed from the grid, but there was in most cases sufficient of the vessel remaining to estimate the overall shape.

In the deposit 26/Q/94a–h from Nakhtsare's collection, four (e–h) came into the bowl class – but only marginally, in most instances – while five of those vessels were classed as dishes. One of the bowls was a fragment and has been removed from the overall view of the assemblage. The comparison figures see at the *table A.5*.

Tomb	Total no. of vessels	Bowls (VI = 275–500)	Dishes (VI = 50–275)
Lepsius no. 24	14	3	11
Lepsius no. 25	11	3	8
Nakhtsare	8	3	5
Nebtyemneferes	1	1	0
Totals	39	10	24

Table A.5 Proportion of stone bowls to stone dishes.

Bases of the vessel assemblage

The basic differences between these open miniature vessels themselves lay in the nature of their bases and the nature of their rims. Dealing first with the bases, these were divided into the flat bottomed and the round bottomed types. It was very difficult to fix a canon for the difference between these types, since none of the vessels had a true carinated base edge. Nonetheless, some of them were stable on flat surfaces while others were not, so the flat surface areas at the bottom were all measured and these are the results of the diameter of level bases:

Nakhtsare's miniature vessels had only one vessel (a bowl, 26h/Q/94) with a small flat area of 1 cm in diameter, which is only just sufficient to keep the bowl steady on a table. The Lepsius no. 24 group had eight vessels with the following flat base diameters:

45/J	1.5 cm	73a/J	2.8 cm
56c/J	2.0 cm	73b/J	1.8 cm
59b/J	2.8 cm	73d/J	3.0 cm
59c/J	2.4 cm	73g/J	3.0 cm

---

[84] Roth, in: *Mummies and Magic*, 81.
[85] Roth, *JEA* 78, 1992, 120.

It is thus likely that these vessels might be termed "flat based". Using the same criteria, Lepsius 25 had four flat based vessels. These were:

65b/N	1.4 cm	65f/N	1.8 cm
65e/N	1.6 cm	65g/N	3.0 cm

The rest were round bottomed vessels. The bowl from Nebtyemneferes' collection was broken off before the base, so this has been excluded; one broken base has been deleted from Nakhtsare's assemblage and five base-broken fragments have been deleted from the Lepsius no. 24 collection. For the total results of the other vessels, see *table A.6.*

Table A.6 Variations within the bases of open stone vessels.

Tomb	Number of miniature dishes	Round based	Flat based
Lepsius no. 24	13	5	8
Lepsius no. 25	11	7	4
Nakhtsare	8	7	1
Totals	32	19	13

As can be seen from *table A.6*, the ratio of round to flat bases is 19 : 13, but whether this division can be called acceptable or not depends on what the observer sees as the definition of a base. Those vessels shading into the flat-based category did so because of their greater surface coverage on a level surface. Only one dish, 65c/N/03, *fig. A.12*, had anything like the sharp angle that one expects to see in a dish. Interestingly, when one looks at the numbers of flat bases found on bowls, only one (26g/N/94) could be found; it had a VI of 205, so it is approximately in the mid-range of bowl types, and this was the bowl whose flat base diameter measured just one centimeter, so it was only minimally "flat based". All the other flat bases belonged to dishes, leaving a residue of nineteen dishes that had rounded bases instead of flat ones.

Fig. A.11 Model bowl 31/N/2003.

>**Fig. A.12 Model dish 65c/N/2003.**

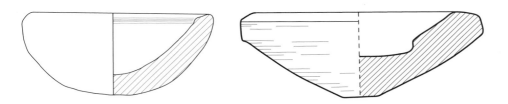

Since there is presumably more work in making a flat based miniature when one has to ensure its stability on a flat surface – even more so, when a sharp edge is produced – this may account for the different ratios and may explain the greater number of round based miniatures, whose bottom surfaces do not have to be so precise. Nonetheless, even though they are miniatures, the flat-based vessels would be more stable on a flat surface – such as a table top – whereas the rounded base types would be better balanced on the more fluid surface that something like sand would provide. It is therefore suggested that these different bases were probably designed for different purposes.

One could suppose that liquid offerings to be placed on a table (water, beer, wine, oils) would be better suited to flat based dishes, while more solid items (individual foodstuffs, such as meat, vegetables and seeds etc.), would be more stable if placed in round based dishes that were cushioned on a sandy floor of a burial chamber or similar surface. Rounded dishes would be very unsuitable for liquids. When put on a flat surface, round bottomed dishes will rock, so their contents should be dry goods. Flat bottomed dishes and bowls are stable on flat surfaces, such as tables. This is the best sort of base for liquids that will be picked up and put down frequently. 59.5 % of the dishes were round based, supporting the idea that the rounded form was used for dry goods, the remainder being suggestive of liquids, of which we normally have less variety than dry goods. It is suggested from the numbers given above, therefore, that the round type is one classic form of a dish, while the flat bottomed type is another type because they may have served different purposes.

Rim differentiation

The second variation present in these dishes was in the nature of the rims. Given that there is such a small difference between a dish and a bowl within the combined assemblage from this cemetery, it is convenient to put the two classes together to discuss the rims and the bases. For such a small vessel, there was a surprising variation within the shape of the rim, as *fig. A.13* below indicates.

Fig. A.13 Profiles of model dishes and bowls from the stone vessel assemblage from the minor tombs in the Abusir Royal Necropolis.

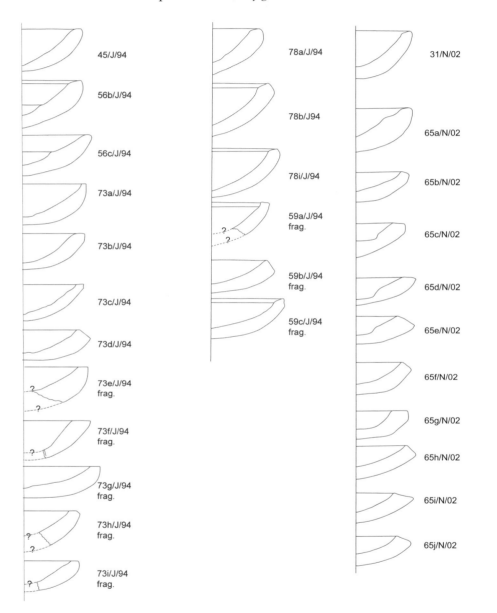
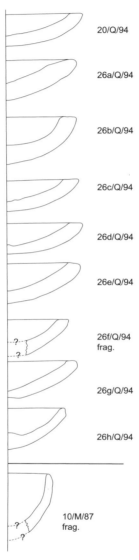

In defining these rim types, there is a variety of terms one can choose among the literature: for example, what does a "plain rim" indicate? One scholar will judge a flat surface plain, whilst others will see it as a simple curved rim formed at the top of a vessel. Some call rounded rims "rolled", while others choose "round", or even "cylindrically cant"; some prefer "oblique" to "sloping", *etc.*, while others judge rims in terms of "narrow or wide". For this reason, I have sketched an icon beside each category term I have chosen. As long as analysts explain the terms they are using, it is not so important if there are terminology differences between one work and another, see *table A.7*.

Assemblage of dishes = 9 rim types	Rounded rim	Bevelled rim	Oblique flat	Flat, incurving	Incurving rounded	Projecting rounded	Projecting V-shaped	Upper rim w/inner rim
Lepsius no. 24	1	6	2	2	1	-	7	1
Lepsius no. 25	1	0	5	-	1	1	1	2
Nakhtsare	-	2	3	1	-	2	1*	0
Nebtyemneferes	-	-	-	-	1	-	-	-

Table A.7 Variations within the rims of miniature stone dishes.

* This is very slightly incurving.

It is difficult to work out why there should be such a variation within the rims of what really is a fairly small group of vessels, but those items we do have is due to the vagaries of history. In the original state, this collection should be at least eight times larger than it is, and no doubt, if we had the entire assemblage, the tabulations would be very different from those that are here. *Mutatis mutandis*, we must work with what we have. The fact that the rims of these miniatures were of different shapes in other collections of miniature offering vessels can be verified by the collection from the tomb of Neferihi, Giza mastaba D 208, a Steindorff excavation from 1903.[86]

The incurving rims present in this collection would, undoubtedly, make a more secure storage space for liquids or unguents, as would the vessels with inner rims that provide a very convenient wipe for excess unguent. It has been suggested that rounded rims make it easier to drink the contents of a vessel – certainly, bevelled and oblique rims – especially if those rims were wide, as some of those in the collection were – would tend to make drinking more difficult, as would an incurving round rim to a bowl or dish. It is surprising that, if models were copies of real vessels, not one of these vessels has a notched rim which would make it easy to fasten on a lid with string. Also strange is the total absence of flat, incurving rims, which was one of the most popular shapes in the stone vessel repertoire during the Old Kingdom. There are also a few other popular Old Kingdom rim types for practical stone vessels – such as the cusp-form, and collared rims – none of which appear within this miniature collection. It is thus suggested that while some attempt may have been made to imitate practical stone and pottery forms, the artisans who made these little dishes were more concerned with turning out a finished product quickly – the oblique flat form and the lack of polishing would certainly suggest this – rather than rigorously imitating genuine vessel forms. The miniatures of this collection, therefore, can only be evaluated in comparison to other miniature forms and not with full-scale vessels.

A.5. Conclusion

After so much analysis of the fragmentary collection of stone vessels in the minor tombs in the Abusir Royal Cemetery, it is necessary to remind ourselves that, while we may appreciate such stone vessels for what we can discover about the ancient Egyptian society, and even as we admire the intrinsic beauty of many of these vessels, in the end, we have to realise that the purpose of these vessels has really not been explored in all its aspects. Such items were significant elements in the religious culture of the Old Kingdom that so saturates the artefacts that these ancient people made, and this dimension has barely been mentioned. As Do. Arnold so well expressed it, for the thinking Egyptian of that time, these vessels were an aspect of a "belief in the powers of rejuvenation

[86] Junker, *Gîza X*, 126–129, Abb. 15; 105–109. For drawings of the rims of these dishes from this collection see E. Martin-Pardey, *CAA* 6, No. 421, p. 3 a–x.

and rebirth",[87] and these beliefs were more important factors than the physical attributes of the stone vessels made for the royal cemeteries. We are aware that the offering lists[88] throughout the Old Kingdom called for provisions of food and drink, incense and oils and also stone vessels, and it is for this purpose that nearly all of the vessels discussed above were made. Whether those items were only empty symbolic vessels or once provided with actual token foodstuffs we can never be sure, but it seems at least probable that the unwritten prayers and incantations those people used during the funeral would have included some that would be intended to make those vessels full of food and drink in the Afterlife of the deceased. This intention, it seems very likely, was the purpose of these vessels made for the tomb.

---

[87] Arnold, Pischikova, in: *Egyptian Art in the Age of the Pyramids*, 129. See especially, the remarks about the role of the queen in particular (but also female members of the royal family) put forward by these authors.
[88] The standard work on offering lists is Barta, *Opferliste*.

Index

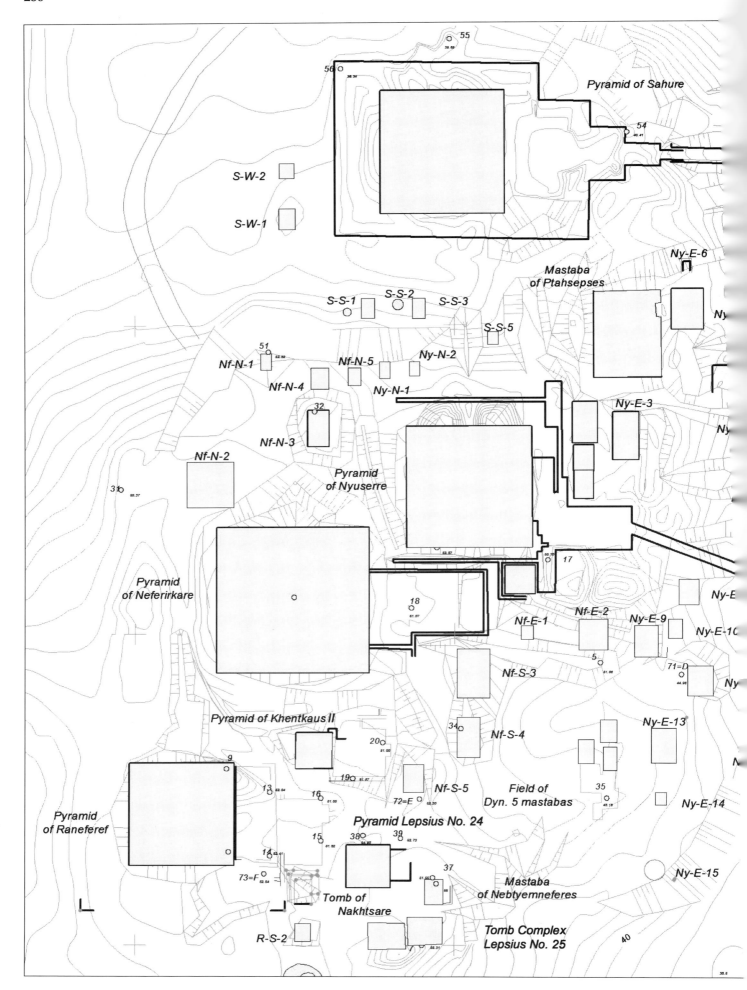

55

56

Pyramid of Sahure

54

S-W-2

S-W-1

Ny-E-6

Mastaba
of Ptahsepses

S-S-1   S-S-2   S-S-3

S-S-5

51

Nf-N-1   Nf-N-5   Ny-N-2

Nf-N-4   Ny-N-1

Ny-E-3

32

Nf-N-3

Nf-N-2

Pyramid
of Nyuserre

31

17

Pyramid
of Neferirkare

18

Ny-E

Nf-E-1   Nf-E-2   Ny-E-9   Ny-E-10

5

71=D   Ny

Nf-S-3

Ny-E-13

Pyramid of Khentkaus II   34   Nf-S-4

20

9

19   Nf-S-5   Field of   35   Ny-E-14
13   16   72=E   Dyn. 5 mastabas

Pyramid
of Raneferef   Pyramid Lepsius No. 24

15   38   39

14   37   Ny-E-15

73=F   Mastaba
of Nebtyemneferes

Tomb of
Nakhtsare

Tomb Complex
Lepsius No. 25   40

R-S-2

Schematic plan of the
Abusir Royal Necropolis

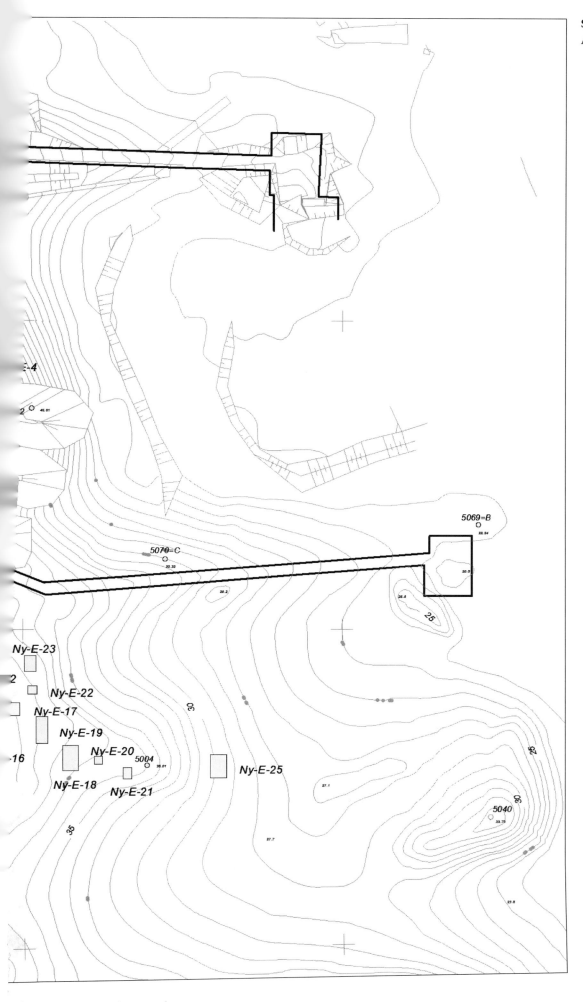

Ny-E-23

Ny-E-22

Ny-E-17

Ny-E-19

Ny-E-20   5004

Ny-E-18   Ny-E-21   Ny-E-25

5069=B

5070=C

5040

ABUSIR XII

MINOR TOMBS IN THE ROYAL NECROPOLIS I
(THE MASTABAS OF NEBTYEMNEFERES AND NAKHTSARE,
PYRAMID COMPLEX LEPSIUS no. 24
AND TOMB COMPLEX LEPSIUS no. 25)

Mgr. Jaromír Krejčí, Ph.D., Dr. Vivienne G. Callender,
prof. PhDr. Miroslav Verner, DrSc.

with contributions by Mgr. Viktor Černý, Dr., Mgr. Martina Kujanová,
prof. MUDr. PhDr. Eugen Strouhal, DrSc., PhDr. Hana Vymazalová, Ph.D.

Vydal
Český egyptologický ústav Filozofické fakulty Univerzity Karlovy v Praze,
nám. Jana Palacha 2, 110 00 Praha 1

Kniha vychází s finanční podporou MŠMT ČR, grant č. MSM-0021620826

Obálka (s použitím fotografie Kamila Voděry) a grafická úprava: Jolana Malátková
Fotografie: Archiv Českého egyptologického ústavu Filozofické fakulty Univerzity
Karlovy v Praze, Jan Brodský, Jaromír Krejčí, Martina Kujanová, A. M. Sarry,
Eugen Strouhal, Kamil Voděra, Milan Zemina
Ilustrace: Jaromír Krejčí, Jolana Malátková, Lucie Vařeková, Hana Vymazalová,
Luděk Wellner

Vydání první, Praha 2008

Sazba Český egyptologický ústav Filozofické fakulty Univerzity Karlovy v Praze,
Celetná 20, 110 00 Praha 1
Tisk Serifa s. r. o., Jinonická 80, 150 00 Praha 5

ISBN 978-80-7308-181-2